Portrait of Tolstoy
when commencing Anna Karénina. 1873.
by Kramskóy.

THE
LIFE OF TOLSTOY
FIRST FIFTY YEARS

BY

AYLMER MAUDE

'A man so various that he seemed to be
Not one, but all mankind's epitome.'
DRYDEN

FIFTH EDITION

NEW YORK
DODD, MEAD AND COMPANY
1911

First Edition	. . .	*September 1908*
Second Edition	. . .	*October 1908*
Third Edition	. . .	*September 1910*
Fourth Edition	. . .	*January 1911*
Fifth Edition	. . . .	*April 1911*

PREFACE

THE reason I have written this work is because so many among us are interested in Tolstoy and so few seem to understand him. It would seem therefore that an English Life of Tolstoy is needed, and having lived in Russia for twenty-three years, known Tolstoy well for several years, visited him frequently in Moscow, and stayed with him repeatedly at Yásnaya Polyána, I am perhaps as well qualified as any one to write it, especially as I have long made a careful study of his views. My wife and I have translated several of his works, have known people closely connected with him, and some ten years ago we took part in an unsuccessful 'Tolstoy' Colony; besides which I went to Canada at his wish to make arrangements for the Doukhobór migration, of which I subsequently wrote the history.

Moreover, I am impartial. That is to say, I have taken pains to understand Tolstoy's views, and to see the good there is in them; but being a Westerner, I see also certain things Tolstoy overlooks, and I know that these things knock big holes in some of his most cherished 'principles.'

The book has had the great advantage of being carefully revised by his wife, the Countess S. A. Tolstoy, who both verbally and in writing has rendered me most valuable assistance.

I owe sincere thanks also to my friend P. I. Birukóf, Tolstoy's Russian biographer. He modestly speaks of his own work as 'a collection of those materials for the biography of Leo Tolstoy which are accessible to me.' I have no hesitation in saying that his care and integrity in gathering and using those materials, entitle him to the gratitude of all who deal with the same subject.

There is one small matter of typography which needs a word of explanation. I have sought to tell as much of the story as possible in Tolstoy's own words, and have also had occasion to quote other writers. At times the Russian text quoted contains allusions or expressions which might perplex an English reader unless a word or two of explanation were added. To introduce paragraphs of explanation would interrupt the narrative, besides lengthening the book. To have recourse to frequent footnotes in cases where two or three words of explanation are all that is required is unsightly and unsatisfactory; so I have adopted the plan of using square brackets [   ] to enclose such explanations. The ordinary round parentheses (   ) I have kept for their common use, and for cases where, for clearness' sake, words are added that are not contained in the original.

Beyond indicating the varying value of sums of money mentioned, I have not troubled the reader with the fluctuations of the rouble, which went from over 38 pence before the Crimean war, to 19 pence after the Russo-Turkish war of 1878. If he wants a concise history of the Russian currency, he can find it in the preface to my edition of *Sevastopol.*

In that as in other matters I have tried to be accurate without being pedantic. It is Tolstoy and his views that I aim at presenting to English readers; and I have kept in the background, as far as I could, the obstacles resulting from the Tower of Babel.

AYLMER MAUDE.

GREAT BADDOW,
CHELMSFORD, 20th *August* 1910.

CONTENTS

CHAP.   PAGE

PREFACE . . . . . .   **V**

NOTE ON PRONUNCIATION OF RUSSIAN NAMES . .   xiii

I. ANCESTRY AND PARENTAGE . . .   1

II. YOUTH AND EARLY MANHOOD . . .   16

III. THE CAUCASUS . . . , .   59

IV. THE CRIMEAN WAR   93

V. PETERSBURG; LOVE AFFAIR; DROUZHÍNIN .   138

VI. TRAVELS ABROAD   166

VII. AT YÁSNAYA AGAIN; TOURGÉNEF; ARBITER;
MAGAZINE   214

VIII. THE SCHOOL   246

IX. MARRIAGE   282

X. NEARING THE CRISIS   329

XI. CONFESSION   399

XII. WORKS: 1852-1878   427

CHRONOLOGY   450

INDEX   457

LIST OF ILLUSTRATIONS

PORTRAIT OF TOLSTOY WHEN COMMENCING *Anna Karé-nina*, 1873. By Kramskóy . . *Frontispiece*

Facing page

TOLSTOY IN 1848, AFTER LEAVING THE UNIVERSITY . 48

MAP OF SEVASTOPOL 113

PROMINENT RUSSIAN WRITERS, 1856: TOURGÉNEF, SOLOGOÚB, TOLSTOY, NEKRÁSOF, GRIGORÓVITCH, AND PANÁEF 142

TOLSTOY IN 1856, THE YEAR HE LEFT THE ARMY . 152

TOLSTOY IN 1860, THE YEAR HIS BROTHER NICHOLAS DIED 200

TOLSTOY IN 1862, THE YEAR OF HIS MARRIAGE . 290

TOLSTOY'S LIBRARY, SHOWING THE WOODEN CROSSPIECE FROM WHICH HE WISHED TO HANG HIMSELF . 402

NOTE ON PRONUNCIATION OF RUSSIAN NAMES

THE spelling of Russian names in Latin letters in a work of this kind, presents great difficulties. To begin with, we have as yet (though it is much needed) no accepted method of transliteration from Russian into English; and though it is not difficult for any one to frame or select his own system of transliteration—as I have done for my translations—this does not entirely meet the case when one has to deal with the names of people, many of whom have adopted a spelling of their own.

On the one hand, a man has a right to decide how he will have his own name spelt; but on the other hand, the inclusion of a dozen different systems of transliteration in one book, is apt to create confusion.

I have had to do the best I could under the circumstances. To pronounce the names correctly, in accord with the system of transliteration I have adopted, the reader should note the following:

    I. Lay stress on the syllable marked with an accent.

    II. Vowel sounds are broad and open:

        a as in f*a*ther.

        e as *a* in f*a*te.

But *e* initial and unaccented is pronounced *ye*.

        i as *ee* in m*ee*t.

        o as in l*o*ch.

        u as *you*.

In diphthongs the broad sounds are retained:

ou as *oo* in b*oo*t.

ya as in *ya*rd.

ye as in *ye*s.

yo as in *yo*re.

ay as *eye*.

ey as in th*ey*.

oy as in b*oy*.

III. *y* with a vowel forms a diphthong; *y* at the end of a word, after a consonant, sounds something like *ie* in hyg*ie*ne.

IV. Consonants:

G is hard, as in *g*o.

Zh is like *z* in a*z*ure.

R is sounded strongly, as in *r*ough, ba*rr*en.

S is sharp, as in *s*eat, pa*ss*.

Where I know of a spelling deliberately adopted by the owner of a name, I have felt bound to follow it. For instance, the name which under my system of transliteration I should have spelt 'Suhotín,' appears in the book as Soohoteén, but in such cases, on the first occasion on which the name occurs, I have given my usual transliteration in square brackets.

I hope the day is not distant when some system will be generally agreed upon in this matter. Any system would be better than the present anarchy.

CHAPTER I

ANCESTRY AND PARENTAGE

Ancestors. Count Peter. Russian titles. Tolstoy's grandfather and father. His maternal grandfather and mother.
First recollections. Aunty Tatiána. Antecedents.

In the annals of the Russian nobility it is recorded that
a man named Idris came from 'the lands of Cæsar,'
that is to say, from the Holy Roman Empire, in
the year 1353 with two sons and 3000 followers, ¹³⁵³
and settling at Tchernígof in Little Russia was received
with favour by the reigning Grand Duke, who granted
him much land. A great-grandson of this Idris, Andrew
by name, migrated to Moscow, where he was well received
by the reigning Grand Duke Vasíly, who conferred upon
him the surname of Tolstóy.

As, however, the annals of the Russian nobility were
to a large extent concocted in the reign of Peter the
Great, it is extremely doubtful whether this story is
reliable. Be that as it may, it is certain that
Peter Tolstoy, born in 1645, was a Russian who ¹⁶⁴⁵
distinguished himself in the service of the State. During
the struggles which preceded the acquisition of power
by Peter the Great, he made the mistake of allying
himself with that autocrat's ambitious half-sister, Sophia.
The defeat of her Guards, the Streltsí, caused him quickly
to transfer his allegiance to Peter, whose favour he eventually managed to secure. When drinking with his

A

chosen companions in later days, the Tsar would often pat Tolstoy's head, saying, 'Little head, little head, had you been less wise, you would have come off your shoulders long ago.'

This Peter Tolstoy held a commission in the Guards, and fought in the Azof campaign of 1696; but later on 1697 he went abroad to study shipbuilding when Peter the Great was seeking volunteers for that purpose. He was sent in 1701 as Ambassador to the Sublime Porte, and in the years 1710-1713, when political affairs were critical, he twice suffered severe imprisonment in the Seven Towers—the stronghold wherein the Sultan occasionally confined the ambassadors of States with whose conduct he felt dissatisfied. Returning to Russia in 1714, Tolstoy obtained the favour of Prince Ménshikof and became a Minister of State. He married; but his wife does not appear to have been of sufficient importance for 1716 any one to have said anything about her. He accompanied Peter the Great to Holland and France, and rendered him an important though discreditable service. Peter the Great's son, the refractory 1717 Alexis, who disliked his father's reforms, had escaped from Russia and was living with his mistress Euphrosyne at St. Elmo, near Naples. By threats and promises, and by the aid of this woman, Tolstoy induced the unfortunate Tsarévitch to return to Russia, and when he had got him there, took a leading part in his trial and secret execution.

For this service Tolstoy received large estates and was promoted to the headship of the Secret Chancellery. 30 Aug. On the day of the coronation of Peter's second 1725 wife, Catherine, Tolstoy was made a Count. His coat of arms shows seven towers, in memory of his imprisonment by the Sultan, and is appropriately supported by two wolf-hounds rampant, looking outwards.

On the death of Peter the Great, Tolstoy actively supported Ménshikof in securing the throne for Catherine the First, and he was one of the seven members of the Upper Secret Council which practically ruled Russia. On the question of choosing a successor to Catherine, he ventured however to oppose Ménshikof. The latter was too powerful for him ; and forfeiting his title of Count and deprived of all offices rewards and estates, Tolstoy, at the age of eighty-two, was banished for life to the Solovétz Monastery, situated on an island in the White Sea. Here, two years later, he died. Ménshikof himself, one may remark in passing, finished his life that same year in Siberia, having been banished by an order signed by the boy he had placed on the throne. To be a Russian Minister of State in those days was almost as dangerous as it is in our times to be a revolutionary conspirator.

6 May 1727

1729

The title of Count was revived in the family in 1770, for the benefit of Peter Tolstoy's grandson ; whose son, Count Elias Tolstoy (he figures in *War and Peace* as the elder Count Rostóf), was the grandfather of Leo Tolstoy, whose life this book narrates.

There is one matter which it may be as well to explain at the outset, as English readers are so often puzzled by it : I refer to the nature of Russian titles of nobility. The only really Russian title is that of *Knyaz*, commonly translated 'Prince.' It is borne by descendants of Rúrik, by descendants of the Lithuanian Prince Ghedimin, and by descendants of various Tartar Khans whose dominions Russia has annexed. It has also been conferred by Imperial Decree on a dozen or more other Russian families. Though *Knyaz* is translated 'Prince,' *Velíky Knyaz*, curiously enough, is not translated 'Great Prince,' but 'Grand Duke,' and this indicates how difficult it is to find suitable equivalents for these titles. Not till the time of Peter the Great were the German titles, Count

(*Graf*) and Baron, introduced into Russia. Both of these are now common among the Russo-German landlords of the Baltic Provinces; and less so among real Russians.

It must be borne in mind that there is no law of primogeniture in Russia. Each son and daughter inherits the family title, so that there are usually several, and sometimes many, people with equal rights to use the same title. Though springing from one stock, they may be only distantly connected. There are for instance other Counts Tolstoy, contemporaries of Leo Tolstoy and distant cousins of his. One of these, the poet Count Alexis Tolstoy, was a well-known author and dramatist. Another, the reactionary Count Dmítry Tolstoy, was successively Head of the Holy Synod, Minister of Education, and Minister of the Interior.

Tolstoy's grandfather already mentioned, Count Elias Tolstoy, was an easy-going generous trustful and extravagant man, who married a wealthy Princess Gortchakóf, but ran through her money and his own, and at last to secure a means of livelihood, procured the post of Governor of Kazán. This he was able to do, thanks to his family influence. It is recorded to his credit that, contrary to the general custom of the time, he accepted no bribes (except from the Government contractor, who was considered the natural financial prop of a Provincial Governor), though his wife accepted presents without his knowledge.

Their eldest daughter married a Count Osten-Saken. She became guardian of Leo Tolstoy and of his brothers and sister, after they had lost their parents. Another daughter married V. I. Úshkof. Leo Tolstoy was under her charge when he lived in Kazán and studied at its University.

The first fact known to us about his father, Count Nicholas Tolstoy, is characteristic of the manners of his class and day. When he was only sixteen, his parents arranged a *liaison* between him and a peasant girl, such connections being considered necessary for the health of young men. A son was born, and Tolstoy records his ' strange feeling of consternation when (in after years) this brother of mine, fallen into destitution and bearing a greater resemblance to my father than any of us, used to beg help of us, and was thankful for the ten or fifteen roubles we used to give him.'

Nicholas Tolstoy was not yet seventeen when Napoleon invaded Russia; but in spite of his parents' efforts to dissuade him, he insisted on entering the army, and thanks to his mother's family influence, quickly obtained 1812 an appointment as Adjutant to Prince Andrew Gortchakóf, a General in command. He went through the campaigns of 1813 and 1814; and in the latter year he 1814 and his orderly, while on their way to rejoin the Russian army in Germany, after taking despatches to Petersburg, were captured by the French. The orderly managed to hide his master's gold coins in his boots, and for months never risked taking them off, though his feet grew sore and he suffered extreme discomfort. Thanks to this devotion, Nicholas Tolstoy, after reaching Paris, was able to live in comfort.

Having attained the rank of Lieutenant-Colonel, he left the army when the war was over, and, disillusioned with military service, returned to Kazán, where his father (completely ruined by that time) was still Governor.

In 1820 Count Elias died, leaving his estate so encumbered that his son declined to accept the inheritance. The young man had to face the task of providing 1820 for his old mother, who was accustomed to great luxury, as well as for his sister and a distant cousin, Tatiána Alexándrovna Érgolsky, who had been adopted into the family; and so a marriage was arranged for him with the wealthy but plain Princess Marie Volkónsky, who was no longer very young.

His father's life, Tolstoy tells us, was then

passed in attending to the estate, a business in which he was not very expert, but in which he exercised a virtue great for those days : he was not cruel, but perhaps even lacked firmness. During his lifetime I never heard of corporal punishment. If it ever was administered to the serfs, the cases were so rare and my father took so little part in them, that we children never heard them mentioned. It was after his death that I learnt, for the first time, that such punishment ever took place at home.

Like most men who served in the army in the early years of Alexander's reign, he [Count Nicholas Tolstoy] was not what is now called a Liberal, but out of self-respect he considered it impossible to serve during the latter [reactionary] part of Alexander's reign, or under Nicholas. During all my childhood and youth, our family had no intimate relations with any Government official. I, of course, understood nothing about this in childhood, but I understood that my father never humbled himself before any one, nor altered his brisk, merry, and often chaffing tone. This feeling of self-respect, which I witnessed in him, increased my love and admiration for him.

Leo Tolstoy's mother's family, the Volkonskys, were descended from Rúrik (the first ruler mentioned in Russian history) as well as from St. Michael the martyr, Prince of Tchernígof ; and through them, even more than on his father's side, Tolstoy is connected with many of the leading families of the Russian aristocracy. Prince Nicholas Volkónsky, his mother's father, came into conflict with the most powerful of the favourites of Catherine the Great, for Tolstoy tells us that :

Having attained the high position of Commander-in-Chief, he lost it suddenly by refusing to marry Potémkin's niece and mistress, Varvára Engelhardt. To Potémkin's suggestion that he should do so, he replied : 'What makes him think I will marry his strumpet ?'

He married instead, a Princess Catherine Troubetskóy, and after retiring from the service, settled down on his estate at Yásnaya Polyána. His wife soon died, leaving him only one surviving child, a daughter, Tolstoy's mother. Tolstoy writes of this grandfather :

He was regarded as a very exacting master, but I never heard any instance of his being cruel or inflicting the severe punishments usual in those days. I believe such cases did occur on his estate, but the enthusiastic respect for his importance and cleverness was so great among the servants and peasants whom I have often questioned about him, that though I have heard my father condemned, I have heard only praise of my grandfather's intelligence, business capacity, and interest in the welfare both of the peasants and of his enormous household.

Later, a strange chance brought Prince Volkónsky again into touch with Varvára Engelhardt, whom he had refused to marry. She married a Prince Sergius Golítsin, who consequently received promotions and decorations and rewards ; and Tolstoy tells us :

With this Sergius Golítsin and his family, my grandfather formed so close a friendship that my mother from her childhood was betrothed to one of his ten sons. . . . This alliance, however, was not destined to be consummated, for the young man died prematurely of fever.

In a portrait of Prince N. Volkónsky which has been preserved in the family there is much that corresponds to Leo Tolstoy's own appearance. 'Both,' as his brother-in-law remarks, 'have high, open foreheads and large organs of the creative faculty, and in both the organs of musical talent are exceedingly prominent and are covered by thick, overhanging eyebrows, from beneath which small, deep-set, grey eyes literally pierce the soul of the man on whom they are turned.'

Prince N. Volkónsky died in 1820, and two years later his daughter married Count Nicholas Tolstoy. Of ₁₈₂₂ her Tolstoy tells us :

I do not remember my mother. I was a year-and-a-half old

when she died. By some strange chance no portrait of her has been preserved, so that as a real physical being I cannot picture her to myself. I am in a way glad of this, for in my conception of her there is only her spiritual figure, and all that I know about her is beautiful ; and I think this has come about not merely because all who spoke to me of my mother tried to say only what was good, but because there actually was much good in her.

She was well educated, spoke five languages, played the piano well, and had a wonderful gift for improvising tales in the most delightful manner. It is said that at balls her young lady friends would leave the dance and gather in a dark room to hear her tell a story, which shyness induced her to do where she could not be seen. Tolstoy remarks that 'her most valuable quality was that though hot-tempered, she was yet self-restrained. "She would get quite red in the face and even cry," her maid told me, "but would never say a rude word."' She had one quality Tolstoy values very highly—that of never condemning any one. It was a quality shared by her eldest son, Nicholas ; and Leo Tolstoy says :

In the *Lives of the Saints* by D. Rostóvsky, there is a short story which has always touched me exceedingly, of a certain monk, who to the knowledge of all his brethren had many faults, but whom an old monk, in a dream, saw occupying a place of honour among the saints. The old man asked in astonishment, 'How could this monk, so unrestrained in many ways, deserve so great a reward ?' The answer was : 'He never condemned any one.'

Tolstoy adds : 'If such rewards did exist, I think my brother and my mother would have received them.'

Another feature Tolstoy records of his mother is 'her truthfulness and the simple tone of her correspondence.' He tells us that in his imagination his mother

appeared to me a creature so elevated, pure and spiritual,

that often in the middle period of my life, during my struggles with overwhelming temptations, I prayed to her soul begging her to aid me; and such prayer always helped me much.

Five children were born to Nicholas and Marie Tolstoy. First came four sons, of whom Leo was the youngest. His name in Russian is Lyóf Nikoláyevitch (Leo, son-of-Nicholas) Tolstóy. Leo Tolstoy is the way he signs himself when using the Latin alphabet; and when pronouncing his name it should be remembered that the accent falls on the second syllable, and that that syllable rhymes with 'boy.' The fancy spellings *Tolstoi* and *Tolstoï* are due to the fact that some of the early translators and reviewers, not being able to read Russian, relied on French versions, and did not know how Tolstoy spells or pronounces his own name. He was born on 28th August 1828 [1] at Yásnaya Polyána, with a caul—which both in 1828 Russia and in England is considered a sign of good-fortune.

A year and a half later a daughter, Marie, was born; and in giving birth to her the mother died, on 7th March 1830.

Pilgrims, monks, nuns, and various half-crazy devotees were frequent visitors at the house, and even took up their abode there. One of these was a nun, Márya Gerásimovna, who in her youth had made pilgrimages to various holy places dressed as a man. After the birth of four boys Tolstoy's mother longed for a daughter, and promised Márya Gerásimovna that she should be godmother if by prayer she enabled her to obtain her desire. The next child really was a daughter. The promise was kept, and thereafter Márya Gerásimovna, though she lived partly in the Toúla convent, was free of the Tolstoys' house and spent much of her time there.

---

[1] The dates mentioned in the text are usually old style (twelve days behind our calendar), unless the contrary is expressly stated.

Tolstoy gives us his earliest reminiscences in an auto-biographical fragment published in 1878:

These are my first recollections. I cannot arrange them in order, for I do not know which come first or last. Of some of them I do not even know whether they happened in a dream or when I was awake. I lie bound[1] and wish to stretch out my arms, but cannot. I scream and cry, and my screams are disagreeable to myself, but I cannot stop. Some one—I do not remember who—bends over me. This all happens in semi-darkness. I only know there were two people there. My cries affect them: they are agitated by my screams, but do not untie me as I want them to, and I scream still louder. To them it seems necessary that I should be bound, but I know it is unnecessary and I wish to prove this to them, and I again burst into cries which are unpleasant to myself but are yet un-restrainable. I feel the injustice and cruelty—not of people, for they pity me, but—of fate, and I pity myself. I do not know and shall never know, what it was all about: whether I was swaddled while still a baby at the breast, and struggled to free my hands; whether they swaddled me when I was more than a year old, to prevent my scratching some sore, or whether I have gathered into this one recollection (as one does in a dream) many different impressions. The one sure thing is, that this was the first and strongest impression of my life. And what remains on my memory is not my cries nor my suffering, but the complexity and contradictoriness of the im-pressions. I desire freedom, it would harm no one, but I who need strength am weak, while they are strong.

The next impression is a pleasant one. I am sitting in a tub, and am surrounded by a new and not unpleasant smell of some-thing with which they are rubbing my tiny body. Probably it was bran, put into the water of my bath; the novelty of the sensation caused by the bran aroused me, and for the first time I became aware of, and liked, my own little body with the visible ribs on my breast, and the smooth, dark, wooden tub, the bared arms of my nurse, the warm, steaming, swirling

[1] Russian babies are usually swaddled tightly with bands, making them look like fresh mummies.

water, the noise it made, and especially the smooth feel of the wet rim of the tub as I passed my hands along it.

My next recollections belong to the time when I was five or six, and there are very few of them, and not one that relates to life outside the walls of the house. Nature, up to the age of five, did not exist for me. All that I remember, happened in bed or in our rooms. Neither grass, nor leaves, nor sky, nor sun existed for me. It cannot be that no one ever gave me flowers and leaves to play with, that I never saw any grass, that they never shaded me from the sun ; but up to the time when I was five or six years old, I have no recollection of what we call Nature. Probably, to see it, one has to be separate from it, and I was Nature.

The recollection that comes next after the tub is that of Ereméyevna. 'Ereméyevna' was the name with which they used to frighten us children. Probably they had long frightened us with it, but my recollection of it is this : I am in bed and feel well and happy as usual, and I should not remember it, but that suddenly the nurse, or some one of those who made up my life, says something in a voice new to me, and then goes away ; and in addition to being happy I am also frightened. And besides me there is some one else like me. (Probably my sister Mary, whose crib stood in the same room.) And I now remember a curtain near my bed ; and both my sister and I are happy and frightened at the strange thing happening to us, and I hide in my pillow : hide, and glance at the door from behind which I expect something new and merry. We laugh, and hide, and wait. And then some one appears in a dress and cap quite unknown to me, but I recognise that it is the same person who is always with us (whether my nurse or aunt I do not remember), and this some one says something about bad children and about Ereméyevna in a gruff voice which I know. And I squeal with fear and pleasure, and really am frightened, and yet am glad to be frightened, and wish her who is frightening me not to know that I have recognised her. We become quiet, but presently begin whispering to one another again, on purpose that Ereméyevna may come back.

I have another recollection similar to this of Ereméyevna (but as it is clearer it probably belongs to a later date) which has always remained inexplicable to me. In this recollection the chief part is played by our German tutor, Theodore Ivánitch, but I am sure I was not yet in his charge; so the event must have taken place before I was five. It is my first recollection of Theodore Ivánitch, and it took place at so early an age that I can remember no one else: neither my brothers nor my father nor any one. If I have some notion of some one individual person, it is only of my sister, and this only because she, like me, was afraid of Ereméyevna. With this recollection is joined my first conception of the fact that our house had a top story. How I climbed there—whether I went by myself or whether any one carried me—I have quite forgotten, but I remember that many of us are there, and we all form a circle holding each other's hands; among us are some women I did not know (for some reason I remember that they were washer-women), and we all begin to go round and to jump; and Theodore Ivánitch jumps, lifting his legs too high and too loudly and noisily, and I at one and the same instant feel that this is bad and depraved, and notice him and (I believe) begin to cry—and all is over.

That is all I remember up to the age of five. Neither my nurses, aunts, brothers, sister, nor my father, nor the rooms, nor my toys, do I remember. My more distinct recollections begin from the time I was moved downstairs to Theodore Ivánitch and the elder boys.

When I was moved downstairs to Theodore Ivánitch and the boys, I experienced for the first time and therefore more strongly than ever since, the feeling which is called the sense of duty, the consciousness of the cross every man is called upon to bear. It was hard to leave what I was accustomed to from the beginning of things, and I was sad, poetically sad, not so much at parting from people: sister, nurse, and aunt, as at parting with my crib, the curtain and the pillow; and I feared the new life into which I was entering. I tried to see the jolly side of this new life awaiting me; I tried to believe the caressing words with which Theodore Ivánitch lured me to him. I tried not to see the contempt with which the boys received me, the youngest boy. I tried to think it was a shame for a big boy to live with girls, and that there was nothing good in the life upstairs with nurse; but my heart was terribly sad, I knew I was irreparably losing my innocence and happiness; and only a feeling of personal dignity and the consciousness of doing my duty upheld me. (Often in after-life I have experienced similar moments at the parting of cross-roads, when entering on a fresh course.) I experienced quiet grief at the irreparableness of my loss; I was unable to believe that it would really happen. Though I had been told that I should be moved to the boys' rooms, I remember that the dressing-gown with a cord sewn to its back, which they put on me, seemed to cut me off for ever from upstairs, and I then for the first time observed—not all those with whom I had lived upstairs, but—the chief person with whom I lived, and whom I did not remember before. This was my Aunty Tatiána Alexándrovna Érgolsky. I remember her short, stout, black-haired, kindly, tender, and compassionate. It was she who put the dressing-gown on me, and embracing me and kissing me, tied it round my waist; and I saw that she felt as I did, that it was sad, terribly sad, but had to be; and for the first time I felt that life is not a game but a serious matter.

'Aunty' Tatiána Alexándrovna Érgolsky, mentioned in the above reminiscences, was a very distant relative who being left an orphan, had been brought up by Tolstoy's paternal grandparents. She was very attractive and affectionate. She loved and was loved by Count Nicholas, Leo's father, but stood aside that he might marry the rich Princess Marie Volkónsky and repair the family fortunes. Six years after his wife's death Count Nicholas asked Tatiána to marry him and be a mother to his children. Not wishing (Tolstoy tells us) to spoil her pure, poetic relations with the family, she refused the first but fulfilled the second of these requests.

The joyousness of Tolstoy's boyhood was largely due to the care and affection of this excellent woman, and in the most firmly rooted of his principles—such as his detestation of corporal punishment and his approval of complete chastity—it is easy to trace her unconscious influence.

Here for instance is one episode :

We children were returning home from a walk with our tutor, when near the barn we met the fat steward, Andrew, followed by the coachman's assistant, 'Squinting Kouzmá' as he was called, whose face was sad. He was a married man and no longer young. One of us asked Andrew where he was going, and he quietly replied that he was going to the barn, where Kouzmá had to be punished. I cannot describe the dreadful feeling which these words and the sight of the good-natured crestfallen Kouzmá produced on me. In the evening I told this to my Aunt Tatiána, who hated corporal punishment and, wherever she had influence, never allowed it for us any more than for the serfs. She was greatly revolted at what I told her, and rebuking me said, 'Why did you not stop him?' Her words grieved me still more. . . . I never thought that we could interfere in such things, and yet it appeared that we could. But it was too late, and the dreadful deed had been done.

To sum up what we know of Tolstoy's antecedents : he was descended on his father's side and still more on his mother's, from aristocratic families who were more or less in passive opposition to the Government, and who shared the humanitarian sympathies current in the early years of the reign of Alexander I. A cousin of Tolstoy's mother was one of the Decembrists, and on the accession of Nicholas I in 1825 took part in their abortive attempt to establish Constitutional Government. He was exiled to Eastern Siberia for thirty years, doing hard labour in irons part of the time. His wife (another Princess Marie Volkónsky) voluntarily accompanied him, as Nekrásof has told in a well-known Russian poem. Several members of the family towards the end of their lives retired into convents or monasteries.

We find strong family love uniting the homes of Tolstoy's parents and grandparents ; and even after their death, Tolstoy's nature ripened in a congenial atmosphere of family affection; and many of his most pronounced sympathies and antipathies are not peculiar to himself, but were shared equally by other members of the family.

CHIEF AUTHORITIES FOR CHAPTER I

P. Birukof : *Lyof Nikolayevitch Tolstoy. Biografiya* : Moscow, 1906. (The Russian edition is much more readable and accurate than the English.)
        Referred to hereafter as *Birukof*.
S. A. Behrs : *Vospominaniya o Grafe L. N. Tolstom*, Smolensk, 1894, is very valuable as being the work of one who spent twelve summers at Yasnaya, and knew Tolstoy intimately.
        Referred to hereafter as *Behrs*.
    There is an English edition of this book : *Recollections of Count Leo Tolstoy*, London, 1893, but it is incomplete, and inferior to the Russian in many ways. It gives the author's name wrongly as C. A. Behrs.
Leo Tolstoy, *First Recollections*, a fragment : Tolstoy's collected works, Moscow, 1892.
Supplement to *Novy Mir*, Graf Lyof Tolstoy : St. Petersburg, 1903.
        Referred to hereafter as *Novy Mir*.

CHAPTER II

CHILDHOOD AND EARLY MANHOOD

Yásnaya Polyána.   Aunt Tatiána.   The German Tutor.
The brothers: Nicholas, Sergius and Demetrius.   Doún-
etchka.   The house-serfs.   A family scene.   Pilgrims and
saints.   Death of father and grandmother.   Flying.   Per-
sonal appearance.   Corporal punishment.   Originality.   Rid-
ing lessons.   The Countess Osten-Saken.   Aunt P. I.
Úshkof.   Books.   Abstract speculations.   Kazán University.
Imprisonment.   Diary.   Demetrius.   Books: Dickens and
Rousseau.   Yásnaya again.   Petersburg.   Consistency.
Rudolph the Musician.   Women.   Gambling.   Gipsy girls.
Money difficulties.   The liberty of Russian nobles.

YÁSNAYA POLYÁNA (Bright Glade), where Tolstoy was born, had been an ancestral estate of the Volkónskys and belonged to his mother, the Princess Marie. It is situated ten miles south of Toúla, in a pleasantly undulating country. The estate, which is enclosed by an old brick wall, is well wooded and has many avenues of lime-trees, a river and four lakes. In Tolstoy's grandfather's time, sentinels kept guard at the small, round, brick towers, which now stand neglected at the entrance of the main birch avenue leading to the house. Something of the great confidence in himself and readiness to despise others, which despite all his efforts to be humble, characterise Tolstoy, may be due to the fact that he was born and grew up on an estate where for generations his ancestors had been the only people of importance.

16

'Aunty' Tatiána Alexándrovna Érgolsky had been brought up by his grandmother on an equality with her own children. She (Tatiána) was resolute, self-sacrificing, and, says Tolstoy,

must have been very attractive with her enormous plait of crisp, black, curly hair, her jet-black eyes, and vivacious, energetic expression. When I remember her she was more than forty, and I never thought about her as pretty or not pretty. I simply loved her eyes, her smile, and her dusky broad little hand, with its energetic little cross vein.

We had two aunts and a grandmother; they all had more right to us than Tatiána Alexándrovna, whom we called Aunt only by habit (for our kinship was so distant that I could never remember what it was), but she took the first place in our upbringing by right of love to us (like Buddha in the story of the wounded swan), and we felt her right.

I had fits of passionately tender love for her.

I remember once, when I was about five, how I squeezed in behind her on the sofa in the drawing-room and she caressingly touched me with her hand. I caught it and began to kiss it, and to cry with tender love of her. . . .

Aunty Tatiána had the greatest influence on my life. From early childhood she taught me the spiritual delight of love. She taught me this joy not by words; but by her whole being she filled me with love. I saw, I felt, how she enjoyed loving, and I understood the joy of love. This was the first thing.

Secondly, she taught me the delights of an unhurried, quiet life.

Another, though a much less important, influence was that of the tutor, Theodore Rössel (who figures as Karl Ivánovitch Mauer in Tolstoy's early sketch, *Childhood*). Tolstoy owes his excellent knowledge of German and French to the fact that his father, following a custom common among well-to-do Russians, engaged foreign teachers and let his children learn languages not so much from books as by conversation, while they were still quite young. Rössel's 'honest, straightforward, and loving nature' helped to develop the boy's good qualities.

Tolstoy got on well, too, with his brothers, who were five-and-a-half, two, and one year older than himself, as well as with his little sister Marie, his junior by a year-and-a-half.

He not only loved, but deeply respected, his eldest brother Nicholas (pet name, Nikólenka), whose influence lasted until, and even after, his death in 1860. Of him Tolstoy says :

He was a wonderful boy, and later a wonderful man. Tourgénef used to say of him very truly, that he only lacked certain faults to be a great writer. He lacked the chief fault needed for authorship—vanity, and was not at all interested in what people thought of him. The qualities of a writer which he possessed were, first of all, a fine artistic sense, an extremely developed sense of proportion, a good-natured gay sense of humour, an extraordinary inexhaustible imagination, and a truthful and highly moral view of life ; and all this without the slightest conceit. His imagination was such that for hours together he could tell fairy-tales or ghost-stories, or amusing tales in the style of Mrs. Radcliffe, without a pause and with such vivid realisation of what he was narrating that one forgot it was all invention. . . . When he was not narrating or reading (he read a great deal) he used to draw. He almost invariably drew devils with horns and twisted moustaches, intertwined in the most varied attitudes and engaged in the most diverse occupations. These drawings were also full of imagination.

It was he who, when I was five and my brothers, Dmítry six and Sergéy seven, announced to us that he possessed a secret by means of which, when disclosed, all men would become happy : there would be no more disease, no trouble, no one would be angry with anybody, all would love one another, and all would become ' Ant-Brothers.' . . . We even organised a game of Ant-Brothers, which consisted in sitting under chairs, sheltering ourselves with boxes, screening ourselves with handkerchiefs, and cuddling against one another while thus crouching in the dark. . . . The Ant-Brotherhood was revealed to us, but not the chief secret : the way for all men to cease suffering any misfortune, to leave off quarrelling and being angry, and become continuously happy ; this secret he said he had written on a green stick, buried by the road at the edge of a certain ravine, at which spot (since my body must be buried somewhere) I have asked to be buried in memory of Nikólenka. Besides this little stick, there was also a certain Fanfarónof Hill, up which he said he could lead us, if only we would fulfil all the appointed conditions. These were : first, to stand in a corner and not think of a white bear. I remember how I used to get into a corner and try (but could not possibly manage) not to think of a white bear. The second condition was to walk without wavering along a crack between the boards of the floor ; and the third was, for a whole year not to see a hare, alive or dead or cooked ; and it was necessary to swear not to reveal these secrets to any one. He who fulfilled these, and other more difficult conditions which Nikólenka would communicate later, would have one wish, whatever it might be, fulfilled.

Nikólenka, as I now conjecture, had probably read or heard of the Freemasons—of their aspirations toward the happiness of mankind, and of the mysterious initiatory rites on entering their order ; he had probably also heard about the Moravian Brothers [in Russian ant is *mouravéy*].

Writing when he was over seventy, Tolstoy adds :

The ideal of ant-brothers lovingly clinging to one another, though not under two arm-chairs curtained by handkerchiefs, but of all mankind under the wide dome of heaven, has remained the same for me. As I then believed that there existed a little green stick whereon was written the message which could destroy all evil in men and give them universal welfare, so I now believe that such truth exists and will be revealed to men, and will give them all it promises.

It was, however, Tolstoy's second brother, Sergius (or

Sergéy: pet name, Seryózha), whom Tolstoy in his young days most enthusiastically admired and wished to imitate. Sergius was handsome, proud, straightforward, and singularly sincere. Of him Leo Tolstoy says:

I loved and wished to be like him. I admired his handsome appearance, his singing (he was always singing), his drawing, his gaiety and especially (strange as it may seem to say so) the spontaneity of his egotism. I myself was always aware of myself and self-conscious; I always guessed, rightly or wrongly, what other people thought or felt about me, and this spoilt my joy in life. This probably is why in others I specially liked the opposite feature—spontaneity of egotism. And for this I specially loved Seryózha. The word *loved* is not correct. I loved Nikólenka; but for Seryózha I was filled with admiration as for something quite apart from and incomprehensible to me.

Of the third brother, Demetrius (or Dmítry: pet name, Mítenka), only a year older than himself, Tolstoy tells us:

I hardly remember him as a boy. I only know by hearsay that as a child he was very capricious. He was nearest to me in age and I played with him oftenest, but did not love him as much as I loved Seryózha, nor as I loved and respected Nikólenka. He and I lived together amicably. I do not recollect that we quarrelled. Probably we did, and we may even have fought. . . . As a child I remember nothing special about Mítenka except his childish merriment.

Tolstoy says he was 'afraid of beggars, and of one of the Volkónskys, who used to pinch me; but, I think, of no one else.'

A girl, Doúnetchka Temeshóf, was adopted as a member of the family. She was a natural daughter of a wealthy bachelor friend of Tolstoy's father.

I remember how, when I had already learnt French, I was made to teach her that alphabet. At first it went all right (we were both about five years old), but later she probably became tired, and ceased to name correctly the letters I pointed out. I insisted. She began to cry. I did the same, and when our elders came, we could say nothing owing to our hopeless tears.

In his later recollections of her he says:

She was not clever, but was a good, simple girl; and, above all, so pure that we boys never had any but brotherly relations with her.

By which he means that there was no flirtation.

The relations between the family and its servants, who were serfs (and of whom there were about thirty), were, as in many a Russian family, often really affectionate. One instance of a serf's devotion has already been quoted; and such cases were not rare. In *Childhood* mention is made of the old housekeeper, Praskóvya Isáyevna, who was completely devoted to the welfare of the family, and Tolstoy says: 'All that I there wrote about her was actual truth.'

Here is another example illustrating both kindly toleration of minor offences committed by a serf, and the family affection which sweetened life:

My pleasantest recollections of my father are of his sitting with grandmother on the sofa, helping her to play Patience. My father was polite and tender with every one, but to my grandmother he was always particularly tenderly submissive. They used to sit—Grandma playing Patience, and from time to time taking pinches from a gold snuff-box. My aunts sit in armchairs, and one of them reads aloud. We children come in to say good-night, and sometimes sit there. We always take leave of Grandma and our aunts by kissing their hands. I remember once, in the middle of a game of Patience and of the reading, my father interrupts my aunt, points to a looking-glass and whispers something. We all look in the same direction. It was the footman Tíkhon, who (knowing that my father was in the drawing-room) was going into the study to take some tobacco from a big leather folding tobacco-pouch. My father sees him in the looking-glass, and notices his figure carefully stepping on tiptoe. My aunts laugh. Grandmama for a long time does not understand, but when she does, she too smiles cheerfully. I am enchanted by my father's kindness, and on taking leave of him kiss his white muscular hand with special tenderness.

An important feature of the life in which Tolstoy grew up was furnished by the half-crazy saints who swarmed in Russia in those days, and are still occasionally to be met with. Readers of *Childhood* will remember Grísha, an admirable specimen of that class, about whom Tolstoy makes the following characteristic note in his memoirs :

Grísha is an invented character. We had many of these half-crazy saints at our house, and I was taught to regard them with profound respect, for which I am deeply grateful to those who brought me up. If there were some among them who were insincere, or who experienced periods of weakness and insincerity, yet the aim of their life, though practically absurd, was so lofty that I am glad I learned in childhood unconsciously to understand the height of their achievement. They accomplished what Marcus Aurelius speaks of when he says: 'There is nothing higher than to endure contempt for one's good life.' So harmful and so unavoidable is the desire for human glory which always contaminates good deeds, that one cannot but sympathise with the effort not merely to avoid praise, but even to evoke contempt. Such a character was Márya Gerásimovna, my sister's godmother, and the semi-idiot Evdokímoushka, and some others in our house.

How deeply these early impressions were engraved on Tolstoy's mind is obvious from his earliest as well as his latest writings. Take, for instance, the lines from *Childhood* referring to Grísha's prayer overheard by the children.

Much water has flowed away since then, many recollections of the past have lost for me their meaning and become blurred fancies ; even the pilgrim Grísha himself has long since finished his last pilgrimage; but the impression he produced on me and the feeling he evoked, will never die out of my memory.

In Tolstoy's later life we shall again and again find this medieval note recurring (with whatever of truth or falsity it contains), and the assertion that it is not the usefulness or uselessness of a man's life that matters, so much as his self-abnegation and the humility of his soul.

To complete the picture of Tolstoy's early boyhood at Yásnaya Polyána, we must think of him as interested in his father's dogs and horses and hunting (in *Childhood* he tells the true story of how he hunted his first hare), and also in the games and masquerades with which the family and visitors, as well as the servants, amused themselves, especially at New Year.

In spite of his sensitive introspective nature, Tolstoy's childhood was a happy one; and to it he always looks back with pleasure. He speaks of 'that splendid, innocent, joyful, poetic period of childhood, up to fourteen,' and he tells us that the impressions of early childhood, preserved in one's memory, grow in some unfathomable depth of the soul, like seeds thrown on good ground, till after many years they thrust their bright, green shoots into God's world.

When Tolstoy was eight years old the family moved to Moscow for his elder brothers' education. The following summer they lost their father, who, having gone to Toúla on business, fell down in the street on his way 1837 to visit his friend Temeshóf, and died of apoplexy. What money he had with him was stolen, but some unnegotiable bonds were brought back to the Tolstoys in Moscow by an unknown beggar. The funeral took place at Yásnaya Polyána; and Leo, who did not attend it, long fancied that his father was not really dead. Looking at the faces of strangers in the streets of Moscow, he felt almost certain he might at any moment meet him alive again.

This event brought the problems of life and death vividly to the boy's mind, and nine months later the impression was intensified by the death of his grandmother, who never recovered from the shock of her son's death. Hers was the first death Tolstoy witnessed, and he never forgot the horror he felt when, as she lay dying of dropsy, he was admitted to kiss her swollen white hand and saw her, dressed in white, lying motionless on a high white bed. But he says:

I remember that new jackets of black material, braided with white, were made for all of us. It was dreadful to see the undertakers' men hanging about near the house, and then bringing in the coffin, with its lid covered with glazed brocade, and my grandmother's stern face, with its Roman nose, and her white cap and the white kerchief on her neck, lying high in the coffin on the table; and it was sad to see the tears of our aunts and of Páshenka; but yet the new braided jackets and the soothing attitude adopted towards us by those around, gratified us. . . . I remember how pleasant it was to me to overhear during the funeral the conversation of some gossiping female guests, who said, ' Complete orphans; their father only lately dead, and now the grandmother gone too.'

Some time after this, an event occurred that is recorded on the first page of Tolstoy's *Confession*:

I remember how, when I was about eleven, a boy Vladímir Milútin (long since dead), a Grammar School pupil, visited us one Sunday and announced as the latest novelty a discovery made at his School. The discovery was that there is no God, and all that we are taught about Him is a mere invention. I remember how interested my elder brothers were in this news. They called me to their council and we all, I remember, became animated, and accepted the news as something very interesting and fully possible.

Various stories have been preserved relating to Tolstoy's boyhood, and some of them are sufficiently characteristic to be worth repeating.

One incident which made a strong impression on the

lad, keenly sensitive as he always was to any shade of injustice, was the following :

Soon after the death of their father and grandmother, the orphan Tolstoys, then living in rather straitened circumstances (owing to the property being left in trust), were invited to a Christmas Tree at the house of an acquaintance, and the young Princes Gortchakóf, nephews of the then Minister of War, were also among the guests. All the children received presents ; but whereas the Gortchakófs had expensive ones, the Tolstoys, to their annoyance, received cheap common ones.

Another occurrence that clung to his recollection through life, was the friendly welcome they received one day when they made their way uninvited into a private garden in Moscow ; and the sad disappointment they experienced when, returning a few days later unaccompanied by a pretty and attractive girl who had been with them on the former occasion, they were coldly informed that it was private ground, not open to the public.

Other stories, told by Tolstoy himself or by the family, illustrate his impulsive, imaginative, strenuous and rather erratic nature at this period.

When he was about seven or eight years old he had an ardent desire to fly, and persuaded himself that it was possible to do so. It was only necessary to sit down tight on your heels, clasping your arms firmly round your knees, and the tighter you held them the higher you would fly. As Tolstoy was always ardent to put his beliefs into practice, it is not very surprising that one day, soon after the family had moved to Moscow, he stayed behind in the class-room when he should have come down to dinner, and climbing out on the window-sill, some six yards from the ground, threw himself out. He was picked up unconscious. The ill results of his fall were fortunately confined to a slight concussion of the brain ; and after sleeping for eighteen hours on end he woke up again quite well.

It would be a mistake to take his story, *Childhood*, as strictly autobiographical; but it contains many passages which one knows from other sources to be true of his own life, and one such is the passage in which (speaking in the character of Nikólenka) he says:

I knew very well that I was plain, and therefore every reference to my appearance was painfully offensive to me. . . . Moments of despair frequently came over me: I imagined that there could be no happiness on earth for a man with so broad a nose, such thick lips, and such small grey eyes as mine. I asked God to perform a miracle and change me into a handsome boy, and all I then had and all I could ever possess in the future, I would have given for a handsome face.

In fact, his personal appearance caused the sensitive lad much concern, but his efforts to improve it were unsuccessful. On one occasion he clipped his eyebrows, and the unsatisfactory results of that operation occasioned him great grief.

He records in his Reminiscences the following incident, which certainly intensified his lifelong antipathy to corporal punishment:

I do not remember for what, but for something quite undeserving of punishment, St. Thomas [the resident French tutor who succeeded Rössel] first locked me into a room, and secondly threatened to flog me. I thereupon experienced a dreadful feeling of anger indignation and disgust, not only towards St. Thomas himself, but towards the violence with which I was threatened.

When quite a small boy he conceived an attachment for the nine-year-old daughter of his father's friend, Islényef, and being jealous of her for daring to talk to others, he angrily pushed her off a balcony, with the result that she limped for a long time afterwards. A quarter of a century later, when he married this lady's daughter, his mother-in-law used laughingly to remind him of the incident, and say, ' Evidently you pushed me off the balcony in my child-hood that you might marry my daughter afterwards ! '

His sister relates that once when they were driving in a troika (*i.e.* three horses abreast) to Yásnaya, Leo got down during a break in the journey and went forward on foot. When the carriage started again and began to overtake him he took to running, and when the horses went faster he also increased his speed, racing as hard as he could. He was not overtaken till he had gone about two miles and was completely tired out. He was lifted back into the carriage gasping for breath, perspiring and quite exhausted. Any one not endowed with the remarkable physical vigour that, in spite of frequent attacks of ill-health, has characterised Tolstoy through life, would probably have done themselves serious injury had they taxed their vital resources as reck-lessly as he often did.

All accounts agree in representing him as an original and odd little fellow, unwilling to do things like other people. He would for instance enter a drawing-room and, carefully placing his feet together and bending his head, would make his bow backwards, saluting each of the company in turn.

Two incidents are recorded relating to the love of riding which has remained a characteristic of his through life.

When his brothers were sent to a riding-school, Leo (in spite of his father's assurances and those of the riding-master that he was too small to begin and would tumble off) also obtained permission to learn to ride. At his first lesson he duly tumbled off, but begged to be replaced in the saddle ; and he did not fall off again, but became an ex-pert horseman. In one of the short stories he wrote many years later for the use of school-children, he tells how he once wished to ride the old horse Raven after his brothers had each had a turn on it ; and how Raven being too tired to move from the stables, he beat it till he broke his switch on its sides. He then demanded a stouter switch from the serf in charge, but the man replied :

'Ah, master, you have no pity! Why do you beat him? He is twenty years old, and is tired out; he can hardly breathe. Why, for a horse, he is as old as Timoféyitch [a very old peasant living at the place]. You might as well get on Timoféyitch's back, and drive him beyond his strength like that, with a switch. Would you feel no pity for him?'

I thought of Timoféyitch, and hearkened to the man. I got off the horse's back; and when I noticed how its steaming sides were working, and how heavily it breathed through its nostrils, swishing its thin tail, I understood how hard it was for it. Till then I had thought that it was as happy as I was myself. And I felt so sorry for Raven that I began to kiss his sweaty neck and to beg his pardon for having beaten him.

Since then I have grown up, but I always have pity on horses, and always remember Raven and Timoféyitch when I see horses ill-treated.

He does not appear to have been very good at his lessons, and himself somewhere mentions the dictum of a student who used to coach his brothers and himself, and said of their aptitude for learning :

'Sergéy both wishes and can, Dmítry wishes but can't' (this was not true), 'and Leo neither wishes nor can.' (This, I think, was perfectly true.)

On the other hand, St. Thomas, the French tutor already referred to (he figures in *Childhood* as St. Jérôme), must have noticed the lad's capacity, for he used to say, ' *Ce petit a une tête : c'est un petit Molière* ' (This little one has a head : he is a little Molière).

After the father's death the family property passed under the control of the Court of Wards, and expenses had to be 1837 cut down. It was therefore decided that, though the two elder brothers had to remain in Moscow for the sake of their education, the three younger children should return to Yásnaya Polyána, where living was cheaper, in charge of their much loved Aunty Tatiána. Their legal guardian, the Countess Alexandra ('Aline') Ilýnishna Osten-Saken, remained in Moscow with the elder boys.

This lady had made what seemed a brilliant marriage with the wealthy Count Osten-Saken, whose family was among the first in the Baltic Provinces; but her married life was a terrible one. Her husband went out of his mind and tried to kill her. While he was confined in an asylum, the Countess gave birth to a still-born child. To save her from this fresh shock, a girl born of a servant, the wife of a Court cook, was substituted for the still-born baby. This girl, Páshenka, lived with the Tolstoy family, and was already grown up when Tolstoy was quite a child. Subsequently the Countess Alexandra lived first with her parents and then with her brother, Tolstoy's father. Though she was a devotee of the Orthodox Russo-Greek Church of which Tolstoy eventually became so fierce an opponent, much in her character and conduct accords with the precepts laid down in his later writings; and it is evident that certain aspects of his understanding of the Christian character, which strike most Englishmen as peculiar, far from being invented out of his own head, are derived from a deeply-rooted Russian and family tradition. He tells us:

My aunt was a truly religious woman. Her favourite occupation was reading the Lives of the Saints, conversing with pilgrims, half-crazy devotees, monks and nuns, of whom some always lived in our house, while others only visited my aunt. . . . She was not merely outwardly religious, keeping the fasts, praying much, and associating with people of saintly life, but she herself lived a truly Christian life, trying not only to avoid all luxury and acceptance of service, but herself serving others as much as possible. She never had any money, for she gave away all she had to those who asked. A servant related to me how, during their life in Moscow, my aunt used carefully on tip-toe to pass her sleeping maid, when going to Matins, and used herself to perform all the duties which it was in those days customary for a maid to perform. In food and dress she was as simple and unexacting as can possibly be imagined. Unpleasant as it is to me to mention it, I remember from childhood a specific acid smell connected with my aunt, probably due to negligence in her toilet: and this was the graceful poetic Aline with beautiful blue eyes, who used to love reading and copying French verses, who played on the harp, and always had great success at the grandest balls! I remember how affectionate and kind she always was, and this equally to the most important men and women and to the nuns and pilgrims.

Tolstoy goes on to tell how pleasantly she bore the jests and teasing that her devotion to the priests brought upon her.

I remember her dear good-natured laugh, and her face shining with pleasure. The religious feeling which filled her soul was evidently so important to her, so much higher than anything else, that she could not be angry or annoyed at anything, and could not attribute to worldly matters the importance others attach to them.

In the summer of 1839 the whole family assembled at Yásnaya Polyána. The next year, 1840, was a famine year. The crops were so poor that corn had to
1840   be bought to feed the serfs, and to raise funds for this purpose one of the Tolstoys' estates had to be sold. The supply of oats for the horses was stopped, and Tolstoy remembers how he and his brothers, pitying their ponies, secretly gathered oats for them in the peasants' fields, quite unconscious of the crime they were committing.

In the autumn of that year the whole family moved to Moscow, returning to Yásnaya for the following summer.
1841   The next autumn their guardian, the kind good Countess Alexandra Osten-Saken, died in the Convent or 'Hermitage' founded by Óptin (a robber chief of

the fourteenth century) in the Government of Kaloúga, to which she had retired.

After her death her sister, Pelagéya Ilýnishna Úshkof, became their guardian. She was the wife of a Kazán landowner. Aunty Tatiána and she were not on friendly terms; there was no open quarrel between them, but V. I. Úshkof (Pelagéya's husband) had been a suitor for Tatiána's hand in his youth, and had been refused. Pelagéya could not forgive her husband's old love for Tatiána.

The change of guardianship led to the removal of the family to Kazán, and to the children being separated from Aunty Tatiána, much to her grief.

The books which up to the age of fourteen, when he went to Kazán, had most influenced Tolstoy were, he tells us, the Story of Joseph from the Bible, the *Forty Thieves* and *Prince Kamaralzaman* from the *Arabian Nights*, various Russian folk - legends, Poúshkin's *Tales* and his poem *Napoleon*, and *The Black Hen* by Pogorélsky. The influence the story of Joseph had on him, he says, was 'immense.'

In his aptitude for abstract speculation, as in other respects, the boy was truly father to the man; and in a passage, certainly autobiographical, in *Boyhood*, he says:

It will hardly be believed what were the favourite and most common subjects of my reflections in my boyhood—so incompatible were they with my age and situation. But in my opinion incompatibility between a man's position and his moral activity is the surest sign of truth. . . .

At one time the thought occurred to me that happiness does not depend on external causes, but on our relation to them; and that a man accustomed to bear suffering cannot be unhappy. To accustom myself therefore to endurance, I would hold Tatíshef's dictionaries in my outstretched hand for five minutes at a time, though it caused me terrible pain; or I would go to the lumber room and flog myself on my bare back with a cord so severely that tears started to my eyes.

At another time suddenly remembering that death awaits me every hour and every minute, I decided (wondering why people had not understood this before) that man can only be happy by enjoying the present and not thinking of the future; and for three days, under the influence of this thought, I abandoned my lessons, and did nothing but lie on my bed and enjoy myself, reading a novel and eating honey-gingerbreads, on which I spent my last coins. . . .

But no philosophic current swayed me so much as scepticism, which at one time brought me to the verge of insanity. I imagined that except myself no one and nothing existed in the world, that objects are not objects but apparitions, appearing only when I pay attention to them and disappearing as soon as I cease to think of them. In a word, I coincided with Schelling in the conviction that what exists is not objects, but only my relation to them. There were moments in which under the influence of this fixed idea, I reached such a stage of absurdity that I glanced quickly round hoping to catch Nothingness by surprise, there where I was not.

The philosophical discoveries I made greatly flattered my vanity : I often imagined myself a great man, discovering new truths for the benefit of humanity, and I looked on other mortals with a proud consciousness of my own dignity ; yet, strange to say, when I came in contact with these mortals I grew timid before each of them. The higher I stood in my own opinion the less was I able to show any consciousness of my own dignity before others, or even to avoid being ashamed of every word or movement of my own—even the simplest.

At the time of the move to Kazán, a serf lad of about his own age was presented to each of the young Tolstoys to attend on him. Alexis, the one given to Leo Tolstoy, remained in his service all his life, and died at Yásnaya a few years ago.

For five and a half years, from the autumn of 1841 to the spring of 1847, the brothers lived at Kazán, returning each summer to Yásnaya for the vacation. They all entered Kazán University. The aunt who was their guardian, and with whom they lived the greater part of the time, was a kind but not particularly

1841

clever woman. Her house was the centre of much hospitality and gaiety.

Leo Tolstoy prepared to enter the faculty of Oriental Languages, in which a knowledge of Arabic and Turco-Tartar was required. He worked hard, and matriculated in May 1844 before he was sixteen, passing 1844 in French (for which he received the mark 5 + ; 5 being in an ordinary way the highest mark, and the + indicating exceptional distinction), German, Arabic, and Turco-Tartar very well, and in English, Logic, Mathematics and Russian Literature, well; but he did indifferently in Latin, and failed completely in History and Geography, getting the lowest mark, a 1, for each of them. Of History he says, ' I knew nothing,' and of Geography ' still less '; adding, ' I was asked to name the French seaports, but I could not name a single one.' At the end of the summer vacation he was admitted for re-examination in the subjects in which he had failed, and passed successfully.

The winter season when Tolstoy, as a student at the University and a young man of good position, entered Kazán society, was a particularly gay one. He 1844- attended many balls, given by the Governor of the 1845 Province, by the *Maréchal de la Noblesse*, and by private people, as well as many masquerades, concerts, tableaux-vivants, and private theatricals. He is still remembered by old inhabitants as having been ' present at all the balls, soirées, and aristocratic parties, a welcome guest everywhere, and always dancing, but, far from being a ladies' man, he was distinguished by a strange awkwardness and shyness.' At Carnival time in 1845 he and his brother Sergius took parts in two plays given for some charitable object. His performance was a great success.

As to the nature of Kazán society and of his surroundings there, accounts are contradictory. On the one hand, we have his own statement that (imitating his brother Sergius in this as in other matters) he became ' depraved.'

c

Birukóf, too, speaks of 'the detestable surroundings of Tolstoy's life in Kazán,' and another writer, Zagóskin, a fellow-student of Tolstoy's at the University, says that the surroundings in which the latter moved were demoralising and must have been repellent to him. On the other hand, on seeing Zagóskin's remarks, Tolstoy (in whom there is often observable a strong spirit of contradiction) replied :

I did not feel any repulsion, but was very glad to enjoy myself in Kazán society, which was then very good. I am on the contrary thankful to fate that I passed my first youth in an environment where a young man could be young without touching problems beyond his grasp, and that I lived a life which, though idle and luxurious, was yet not evil.

The explanation of these contradictions, no doubt, is that the family circle in which Tolstoy lived was an affectionate one, and that he himself not only enjoyed his life, but formed friendships and made efforts at which in later years he looked back with satisfaction. Yet there was assuredly much in his life and in the life around him which (except when others were severe on it) he recalled with grave disapproval, a disapproval he has plainly expressed in his *Confession*.

To come as near as we may to the truth, we must allow for the personal equation which, in Tolstoy's case, is violent and fluctuating.

With constant amusements going on around him, it is not surprising that at the end of his first University year he failed in his examinations. The failure does not however appear to have been entirely his fault, for he tells us :

Ivanóf, Professor of Russian History, prevented me from passing to the second course (though I had not missed a single lecture and knew Russian History quite well) because he had quarrelled with my family. The same Professor also gave me the lowest mark—a 'one'—for German, though I knew the language incomparably better than any student in our division.

Instead of remaining for a second year in the first course of Oriental Languages, Tolstoy preferred to leave that faculty, and in August 1845 he entered the faculty of Law. During the first months of this new $\quad$ 1845 course he hardly studied at all, throwing himself more than ever into the gay life of Kazán society. Before mid-winter however he began for the first time, as he tells us, ' to study seriously, and I even found a certain pleasure in so doing.' Comparative Jurisprudence and Criminal Law interested him, and his attention was especially arrested by a discussion on Capital Punishment. Meyer, Professor of Civil Law, set him a task which quite absorbed him ; it was the comparison of Montesquieu's *Esprit des Lois* with Catherine the Second's *Great Nakaz*. The conclusion to which he came was, that in Catherine's *Nakaz* one finds Montesquieu's Liberal ideas mixed with the expression of Catherine's own despotism and vanity, and that the *Nakaz* brought more fame to Catherine than good to Russia.

He passed his examinations successfully in May 1846, and was duly admitted to the second year's course of Juris-prudence. Some time previously Tolstoy and another student had disputed which of them had $\quad$ 1846 the better memory, and to test this, each of them learnt by heart the reply to one examination question in History. Tolstoy's task was to learn the life of Mazeppa, and as luck would have it that was just the question he happened to draw at his examination, so that he naturally obtained a 5, the highest mark.

From the autumn of 1846 the three brothers, Sergius Demetrius and Leo, ceased to live at their aunt's, and settled in a flat of their own, consisting of five rooms.

A fellow-student, Nazáryef, has given us his impression of Tolstoy as a student. He says :

I kept clear of the Count, who from our first meeting re-pelled me by his assumption of coldness, his bristly hair and the piercing expression of his half-closed eyes. I had never met a young man with such a strange and, to me, incomprehensible air of importance and self-satisfaction. . . .

At first I seldom met the Count, who in spite of his awkwardness and bashfulness had joined the small group of so-called 'aristocrats.' He hardly replied to my greetings, as if wishing to intimate that even here we were far from being equals, since he drove up with a fast trotter and I came on foot. . . .

It so happened that Nazáryef and Tolstoy were both late for a lecture on History one day, and were incarcerated together by order of the Inspector.

One gathers that Tolstoy was in those days particularly careful of his personal appearance, his clothes indicating his aristocratic pretensions. But though externally the Tolstoy of 1846 differed greatly from the Tolstoy of forty years later, his conversation ran on much the same lines as in later life, and was uttered with the intensity of conviction and the flashes of dry humour which have since made even the most didactic of his writings so readable.

Their conversation in their place of confinement having led to some mention of Lérmontof's poem, *The Demon*, Tolstoy took occasion to speak ironically of verse generally, and then, noticing a volume his companion had of Karamzín's *History of Russia*, he

attacked History as the dullest and almost the most useless of subjects. A collection of fables and useless details, sprinkled with a mass of unnecessary figures and proper names. . . . Who wants to know that the second marriage of John the Terrible, with Temrúk's daughter, took place on 21st August 1562; and his fourth marriage, with Anna Alexéyevna Koltórsky, in 1572? Yet they expect me to grind all this, and if I don't, the examiner gives me a 'one.'

Later on, says Nazáryef, ' the, to me, irresistible force of Tolstoy's doubts fell upon the University, and on University teaching in general. The phrase, " The Temple of Science," was constantly on his lips. Remaining perfectly serious himself, he portrayed our professors in such a comical light that, in spite of all my efforts to appear indifferent, I laughed like one possessed. . . . "Yet," said Tolstoy, "we both had a right to expect that we should leave this temple useful men, equipped with knowledge. But what shall we really carry away from the University? . . . What shall we be good for, and to whom shall we be necessary?"'

Nazáryef says that in spite of the feeling half of dislike, half of perplexity, that Tolstoy evoked in him, he well remembers that he was dimly conscious of something remarkable, exceptional, and at the same time inexplicable, about him.

From the educational articles Tolstoy wrote sixteen years later, we know that he disapproved of examinations, of the restricted groove of studies marked out for the students in each faculty, and of the system which made it necessary for the professors to deliver original lectures of their own, and obliged the students to listen to those lectures and to study them, however incompetent the professors might be.

The fact that his brother Sergius had finished his studies and was leaving, strengthened Tolstoy's dissatisfaction with the University; and finally, without waiting for the May examinations at which he might have qualified for the third year's course, we find him, soon after Easter 1847, applying to have his name removed from the University roll 'on account of ill-health and family affairs.' He really had been in hospital in March, but the plea of ill-health was a mere excuse.

His failure to take a degree was a source of great annoyance and disappointment to him, and it must not be supposed that he left Kazán with any idea of taking life easily or neglecting further study.

From the time he was a boy he had kept a diary of every little sin he had committed, and especially of any offence against the Seventh Commandment, in order that he might repent, and if possible refrain for the future, and his diary shows how full he was at this time of strenuous resolutions. During the last year of his life at Kazán he made close friends with a student named Dyákof (the Nehlúdof of *Boyhood*), and under his influence had developed

an ecstatic worship of the ideal of virtue, and the conviction that it is man's destiny continually to perfect himself. To put all mankind right and to destroy all human vices and misfortunes, appeared a matter that could well be accomplished. It seemed quite easy and simple to put oneself right, to acquire all the virtues, and to be happy.

Here are some rules he set himself at that time :

1. To fulfil what I set myself, despite all obstacles.
2. To fulfil well what I do undertake.
3. Never to refer to a book for what I have forgotten, but always to try to recall it to mind myself.
4. Always to make my mind work with its utmost power.
5. Always to read and think aloud.
6. Not to be ashamed of telling people who interrupt me, that they are hindering me : letting them first feel it, but (if they do not understand) telling them, with an apology.

Deciding to settle at Yásnaya for two years, he drew up a list of studies he intended to pursue for his own mental development, and to qualify for a University degree ; and this list was, as the reader will see, appalling in its scope.

1. To study the whole course of law necessary to get my degree.
2. To study practical medicine, and to some extent its theory also.
3. To study : French, Russian, German, English, Italian, and Latin.
4. To study agriculture, theoretically and practically.

5. To study History, Geography, and Statistics.

6. To study Mathematics (the High School course).

7. To write my [University] thesis.

8. To reach the highest perfection I can in music and painting.

9. To write down rules (for my conduct).

10. To acquire some knowledge of the natural sciences, and.

11. To write essays on all the subjects I study.

Such rules and resolutions abound in Tolstoy's Diary. After failing to act up to them, he again and again gathers his energies and maps out for himself plans of life and courses of study sufficient to tax the energies of an intellectual giant.

As to his religious opinions at this time, he tells us :

I was baptized and brought up in the Orthodox Christian faith. I was taught it in childhood and all through my boyhood and youth. But before I left the University, in my second year, at the age of eighteen, I no longer believed anything I had been taught. (*Confession.*)

His Diary nevertheless shows that he prayed frequently and earnestly ; the fact no doubt being, that though intellectually he discarded the Orthodox Russo - Greek Church, in times of trouble or distress he instinctively appealed to God for help. His opinions were wavering and immature, as he himself tells us in another passage :

The religious beliefs taught me in childhood disappeared . . . and as from the time I was fifteen I began to read philosophic works, my rejection of those beliefs very soon became a conscious one. From the age of sixteen I ceased going to Church and fasting of my own accord. I did not believe what had been taught me from childhood, but I believed in something. What it was I believed in, I could not at all have said. I believed in a God, or rather I did not deny God; but I could not have said what sort of God. Neither did I deny Christ and his teaching, but what his teaching consisted in I could also not have said.

Looking back on that time now, I see clearly that my faith— my only real faith, that which apart from my animal instincts gave impulse to my life—was a belief in perfecting oneself. But in what this perfecting consisted and what its object was, I could not have said. I tried to perfect myself mentally—I studied everything I could: anything life threw in my way; I tried to perfect my will, I drew up rules which I tried to follow; I perfected myself physically, cultivating my strength and agility by all sorts of exercises and accustoming myself to endurance and patience by all kinds of privations. And all this I considered to be perfecting myself. The beginning of it all was, of course, moral perfecting; but that was soon replaced by perfecting in general: by the desire to be better, not in one's own eyes or those of God, but in the eyes of other people. And very soon this effort again changed into a desire to be stronger than others: to be more famous, more important and richer than others. (*Confession.*)

When speaking of Tolstoy's relations with women, it should be borne in mind that incontinence for young men was then considered so natural that few of them in his position would have felt any serious qualms of conscience about such visits to houses of ill-fame as he lets us know that he began to pay at this time. His brother Dmítry however led a chaste life, and alternating with gross lapses of conduct, we find Leo noting down for his own guidance such resolutions as the following:

To regard the society of women as a necessary unpleasant-ness of social life, and to keep away from them as much as possible. From whom indeed do we get sensuality, effeminacy, frivolity in everything, and many other vices, if not from women? Whose fault is it, if not women's, that we lose our innate qualities of boldness, resolution, reasonableness, justice, etc.? Women are more receptive than men, therefore in virtuous ages women were better than we; but in the present depraved and vicious age they are worse than we are.

During his years at the University, Tolstoy saw much of his brother Dmítry, of whom he says :

I remember also at the University that when my elder brother Dmítry, suddenly in the passionate way natural to him devoted himself to religion and began to attend all the Church services, to fast, and to lead a pure and moral life, we all, and even our elders, unceasingly held him up to ridicule and called him, for some unknown reason, ' Noah.' I remember that Moúsin-Poúshkin (then Curator of Kazán University), when inviting us to a dance at his house, ironically remonstrated with my brother, who had declined the invitation, and used the argument that even David danced before the Ark. I sympathised with these jokes my elders made, and deduced from them the conclusion that though it is necessary to learn the catechism and go to church, one must not take such things too seriously. (*Confession.*)

Again we read of this brother :

His peculiarities became manifest, and are impressed on my mind from the time of our life at Kazán.   Formerly in Moscow I remember that he did not fall in love, as Seryózha and I did, and was not fond of dancing or of military pageants, but studied well and strenuously. . . . At Kazán I, who had always imitated Seryózha, began to grow depraved. . . . Not only at Kazán, but even earlier, I used to take pains about my appearance. I tried to be elegant, *comme il faut*.   There was no trace of anything of this kind in Mítenka.   I think he never suffered from the usual vices of youth ; he was always serious thoughtful pure and resolute, though hot-tempered, and whatever he did, he did to the best of his ability. . . . He wrote verses with great facility.   I remember how admirably he translated Schiller's *Der Jüngling am Bache,* but he did not devote himself to this occupation. . . . He grew up associating little with others, always—except in his moments of anger—quiet and serious.   He was tall, rather thin, and not very strong, with long, large hands and round shoulders.   I do not know how or by what he was attracted at so early an age towards a religious life, but it began in the very first year of his University career.

His religious aspirations naturally directed him to Church life, and he devoted himself to this with his usual thoroughness.

In Mítenka there must have existed that valuable characteristic which I believe my mother to have had, and which I knew in Nikólenka, but of which I was altogether devoid—complete indifference to other people's opinion about oneself. Until quite lately (in old age) I have never been able to divest myself of concern about people's opinion; but Mítenka was quite free from this. I never remember on his face that restrained smile which involuntarily appears when one is being praised. I always remember his serious quiet sad, sometimes severe, almond-shaped hazel eyes. Only in our Kazán days did we begin to pay particular attention to him, and then merely because, while Seryózha and I attached great importance to what was *comme il faut*—to externalities—he was careless and untidy, and we condemned him for this.

We others, especially Seryózha, kept up acquaintance with our aristocratic comrades and other young men. Mítenka on the contrary selected out of all the students a piteous-looking, poor, shabbily dressed youth, Poluboyárinof [which may be translated Half-noble]—whom a humorous fellow-student of ours called Polubezobédof [Half-dinnerless]—and consorted only with him, and with him prepared for the examinations. . . . We brothers, and even our aunt, looked down on Mítenka with a certain contempt for his low tastes and associates; and the same attitude was adopted by our frivolous comrades.

After their University days were over, Tolstoy saw little of his brother Demetrius; so it will be convenient here to sacrifice chronological sequence and say what more there is to tell of the latter's life and death. The material is again supplied by Tolstoy's Reminiscences.

When we divided up the family property, according to custom the estate where we lived, Yásnaya Polyána, was given to me. Seryózha, as a lover of horses and according to his wish, received Pirogóvo, where there was a stud. To Mítenka and Nikólenka were given the two other estates: to Nikólenka, Nikolsky; to Mítenka, the Kursk estate, Sherbatchóvka. I have kept a note of Mítenka's, showing how he regarded the possession of serfs. The idea that it is wrong, and that serfs ought to be liberated, was quite unknown in our circle in the 'forties. The hereditary possession of serfs seemed a necessary condition of life, and all that could be done to prevent its being an evil, was to attend not only to their material but also to their moral welfare. In this sense Mítenka wrote very seriously naïvely and sincerely. Thinking he could not do otherwise, he, a lad of twenty, when he left the University took it upon himself to direct the morality of hundreds of peasant families, and to do this (as Gógol recommended in his *Letters to a Landowner*) by threats of punishments and by punishments. . . . But, besides this duty to his serfs, there was another duty which at that time it seemed impossible not to fulfil : namely, Military or Civil service. And Mítenka decided to enter the Civil Service.

Tolstoy proceeds to tell how his brother, desiring to be useful to his country, chose legislation as his speciality, and going to Petersburg astonished the Head of the Department as well as certain aristocratic acquaintances by asking where he could find a place in which he could be *useful*. The friend to whom he went for advice, regarded the service of the State merely as a means of satisfying ambition, and ' such a question had probably never occurred to him before.' Eventually we find Demetrius returning home discouraged, and taking up some local work. All this, to some extent, helps us to understand Leo Tolstoy's sceptical attitude towards the institution of Government, and his strong belief that men in Government service are solely actuated by selfish motives.

Tolstoy continues :

After we had both left the University, I lost sight of him. I know he lived the same severe, abstemious life, knowing neither wine tobacco nor, above all, women, till he was twenty-six, which was very rare in those days. I know also that he associated with monks and pilgrims. . . . I think I was already in the Caucasus when an extraordinary change took place. He suddenly took to drinking smoking wasting money and going with women. How it happened I do not know; I did not see him at the time. I only know that his seducer was a thoroughly immoral man of very attractive appearance, the youngest son of Islényef [an uncle of the lady Leo Tolstoy subsequently married].

In this life Mítenka remained the same serious religious man he was in everything. He ransomed from the brothel a prostitute named Másha, who was the first woman he knew, and took her into his house. But this life did not last long. I believe it was less the vicious and unhealthy life he led for some months in Moscow, than his mental struggle and his qualms of conscience, that suddenly destroyed his powerful organism. He became consumptive, went to the country, was doctored in the provincial town, and took to his bed in Orél, where I saw him for the last time just after the Crimean war. He was in a dreadful state of emaciation : one could even see how his enormous hand joined on to the two bones of his lower arm; his face was all eyes, and they were still the same beautiful serious eyes, with a penetrating expression of inquiry in them. He was constantly coughing and spitting, but was loth to die, and reluctant to believe he was dying. Poor pock-marked Másha, whom he had rescued, was with him and nursed him. In my presence, at his own wish, a wonder-working icon was brought. I remember the expression of his face when he prayed to it. . . . He died a few days later !

Students of the didactic writings of Tolstoy's later years will notice how closely his injunctions to a man to keep to the first woman, whoever she be, with whom he has had intimate relations, correspond with the line actually followed by his brother Demetrius.

When Tolstoy left the University, however, these things were still unthought of. Let us, before returning to the events of his own life at that time, notice some books which he read between the ages of fourteen and twenty-one. They included :

The Sermon on the Mount from St. Matthew's Gospel,

Rousseau's *Confession* and *Émile*, and
Dickens's *David Copperfield*,

which all had an 'immense' influence on him.

In another category came works which he says had 'very great' influence. These were:

Rousseau's *Nouvelle Héloïse*,
Sterne's *Sentimental Journey*,
Poúshkin's *Eugene Onégin*,
Schiller's *The Robbers*,
Gógol's *Dead Souls*,
Tourgénef's *A Sportsman's Sketches*,
Drouzhínin's *Pólenka Sax*,
Grigoróvitch's *Antón Goremýka*, and the chapter *Tamán* from Lérmontof's *A Hero of Our Times*.

In a third category he mentions some of Gógol's Shorter Stories, and Prescott's *Conquest of Mexico*, as having had 'great' influence.

In these works one finds many ideas which have been congenial to Tolstoy throughout his life, and his adhesion to which has only become firmer with age. In illustration of this, take a couple of passages from Dickens which many readers may have passed without much attention, but which to Tolstoy represented the absolute truth of the matters they touch on. David Copperfield says of Parliament :

... I considered myself reasonably entitled to escape from the dreary debates. One joyful night, therefore, I noted down the music of the parliamentary bagpipes for the last time, and I have never heard it since ; though I still recognise the old drone in the newspapers without any substantial variation (except, perhaps, that there is more of it) all the livelong session.

To most Englishmen with memories of Pym and

Hampden, or personal knowledge of the lives of men who have devoted themselves disinterestedly to public affairs, Parliamentary or local, Dickens's sneer at Parliament seems but a paradox or a joke; but to Tolstoy, with his inherited dislike of Government, this testimony from a great English writer (who had served as a Parliamentary reporter) seemed irrefutable evidence of the futility of Parliaments.

Take, again, a passage in which Dickens hits a nail adroitly on the head :

Mr. Micawber had a relish in this formal piling up of words, which, however ludicrously displayed in his case, was, I must say, not at all peculiar to him. I have observed it, in the course of my life, in numbers of men. It seems to me to be a general rule. In the taking of legal oaths, for instance, deponents seem to enjoy themselves mightily when they come to several grand words in succession, for the expression of one idea—as, that they utterly detest, abominate, and abjure, and so forth—and the old anathemas were made relishing on the same principle. We talk about the tyranny of words, but we like to tyrannise over them too. We are fond of having a large superfluous establishment of words to wait upon us on great occasions; we think it looks important, and sounds well. As we are not particular about the meaning of our liveries on State occasions, if they be but fine and numerous enough, so the meaning or necessity of our words is a secondary consideration, if there be but a great parade of them.

No modern writer has ever more carefully eschewed the practice Dickens here attacks than Tolstoy has done throughout his career. Indeed, he is far stricter than Dickens in this respect.

But much more important than the influence of Dickens was that of Rousseau, of whom Tolstoy once remarked :

I have read the whole of Rousseau—all his twenty volumes, including his *Dictionary of Music*. I was more than enthusiastic about him, I worshipped him. At the age of fifteen I wore a medallion portrait of him next my body instead of the Orthodox cross. Many of his pages are so akin to me that it seems to me that I must have written them myself.

Another writer who influenced Tolstoy, though to a very much smaller extent, was Voltaire, of whom he says :

I also remember that I read Voltaire when I was very young, and his ridicule (of religion) not only did not shock me, but amused me very much.

Everything Tolstoy has done in his life he has done with intensity ; and that this applies to the way in which he read books in his youth, is shown by the fact that we find him as an old man, in 1898, in *What is Art?* according the highest praise to books he had read before he was twenty-one, or even before he was fourteen.

It was in the spring of 1847 that Tolstoy, who was not yet nineteen, returned to his estate of Yásnaya Polyána, to live with his dear Aunty Tatiána ; to 'perfect' himself, to study, to manage his estate, and to improve the condition of his serfs. The last part of this pro-gramme, at any rate, was not destined to have much success. Though one must never treat Tolstoy's fiction as strictly autobiographical, yet *A Squire's Morning* gives a very fair idea of his own efforts to improve the lot of his serfs, and of the difficulties and failures he encountered in the course of that attempt. In that story Prince Nehlúdof decides to leave the University and settle in the country, and writes to his aunt :

As I already wrote you, I found affairs in indescribable dis-order. Wishing to put them right, I discovered that the chief evil is the truly pitiable, wretched condition of the serfs, and this is an evil that can only be remedied by work and patience. If you could but see two of my serfs, David and Iván, and the life they and their families lead, I am sure the sight of these two poor wretches would convince you more than all I can say in explanation of my intention.

Is it not my plain and sacred duty to care for the welfare of

these seven hundred people for whom I must account to God ?
Will it not be a sin if, following plans of pleasure or ambition,
I abandon them to the caprice of coarse Elders and stewards ?
And why should I seek in any other sphere opportunities of
being useful and doing good, when I have before me such a
noble brilliant and intimate duty ?

Not only is this letter just such as Tolstoy himself
may have written, but the difficulties Nehlúdof encounters when he tries to move his peasants from the ruts
to which generations of serfdom had accustomed them, are
just those Tolstoy himself met with : the suspicion shown
by the serfs towards any fresh interference on the part of
the master, and the fact that ways to which a community
have grown accustomed are not easily changed by the
sudden effort of a well-intentioned but inexperienced
proprietor.

After spending the summer of 1847 at Yásnaya, Tolstoy
went to Petersburg, where we find him settled in autumn ;
and early next year he entered for examination at the
University of that city.

On the 13th of the following February he wrote to his
1848   brother Sergius :

I write you this letter from Petersburg, where I intend to
remain *for ever.* . . . I have decided to stay here for my
examinations and then to enter the service. . . .

In brief, I must say that Petersburg life has a great and
good influence on me : it accustoms me to activity and supplies
the place of a fixed table of occupations.   Somehow one
cannot be idle ; every one is occupied and active ; one cannot
find a man with whom one could lead an aimless life, and one
can't do it alone. . . .

I know you will not believe that I have changed, but will
say, ' It's already the twentieth time, and nothing comes of
you—the emptiest of fellows.'   No, I have now altered in
quite a new way.   I used to say to myself : ' Now I will
change,' but at last I see that I *have* changed, and I say, ' I
have changed.'

Tolstoy in 1848, after he had left the University.

Above all, I am now quite convinced that one cannot live by theorising and philosophising, but must live positively, *i.e.* must be a practical man. That is a great step in advance and a great change; it never happened to me before. If one is young and wishes to live, there is no place in Russia but Petersburg for it. . . .

On the 1st of May he wrote again to his brother, in a very different strain :

Seryózha! I think you already say I am 'the emptiest of fellows,' and it is true. God knows what I have done! I came to Petersburg without any reason, and have done nothing useful here, but have spent heaps of money and got into debt. Stupid! Insufferably stupid! You can't believe how it torments me. Above all, the *debts*, which I *must* pay *as soon as possible*, because if I don't pay them soon, besides losing the money, I shall lose my reputation. . . . I know you will cry out; but what's to be done? One commits such folly once in a lifetime. I have had to pay for my freedom (there was no one to thrash me, that was my chief misfortune) and for philosophising, and now I have paid for it. Be so kind as to arrange to get me out of this false and horrid position—penniless and in debt all round.

He goes on to mention that he had passed two examinations at the University, but that he had altered his mind, and now, instead of completing his examinations, wanted to ' enter the Horse Guards as a Junker.' (A Junker was a young man who volunteered for the army as a Cadet. Before receiving a commission, a Junker lived with the officers, while preparing to become one of them.)

God willing, I will amend and become a steady man at last, I hope much from my service as a Junker, which will train me to practical life, and *nolens-volens* I shall have to earn the rank of officer. With luck, *i.e.* if the Guards go into action, I may get a commission even before the usual two years are up. The Guards start for the front at the end of May. At present I can do nothing : first, because I have no money (of which I shall not need much, I fancy), and secondly, because my two birth-certificates are at Yásnaya.   Have them sent on as soon as possible.

Before long, Tolstoy was again writing to his brother :

In my last letter I wrote much nonsense, of which the chief item was that I intended to enter the Horse Guards; I shall act on that plan only in case I fail in my examinations, and if the war is a serious one.

The war in question was Russia's share in quelling the Hungarian rebellion of 1849.   Not a thought of the justice or otherwise of the cause seems at that time to have crossed the mind of him who in later life became so powerful an indicter of war.

This is Tolstoy's own summary, written many years later, of the period we are now dealing with :

It was very pleasant living in the country with Aunty Tatiána, but an indefinite thirst for knowledge drew me away to a distance.   This was in 1848, and I was still uncertain what to undertake.   In Petersburg two roads were open to me.   I could either enter the army, to take part in the Hungarian campaign, or I could complete my studies at the University, to enter the Civil Service.   My thirst for knowledge conquered my ambition, and I again began to study.   I even passed two examinations in Law, but then all my good resolutions broke down.   Spring came, and the charm of country life again drew me back to my estate.

Of the two examinations he passed at this time he says :

In 1848 I went to pass the examinations for my degree at Petersburg University, knowing literally nothing, and reading up during only one week.   I worked day and night; and passed with Honours in Civil and Criminal Law.

But in spite of this success he did not take the remaining examinations, and returned to Yásnaya without having

obtained a degree—finally abandoning the attempt to
do so.

In later times, when Tolstoy's reputation was world-
wide, critics often amused themselves by detecting inconsistencies in his conduct and questioning his sincerity.
But the proof of his sincerity is writ large in the story of
his life. Time after time, from the earliest pages of his
Diary, we find him vehemently resolving never more to do
certain things, but always to do other things, and again
and again confessing in the greatest tribulation, that he
had failed to carry out his intentions; yet in spite of
everything he returns, and again returns, to his earliest
ideals and gradually shapes his life into accord with them,
and eventually forms habits which, when he first extolled
them, appeared utterly beyond his reach. Not insincerity
but impetuosity, retrieved by extraordinary tenacity of
purpose, has always characterised him. It was the same
with his thirst for knowledge as with his yet deeper thirst
after righteousness. Often as he was swayed by the lures of
life, each of those two great desires found its satisfaction
at last.

The letters quoted above show some consciousness of
the fact that there is a practical side to life not to be
mastered by theorising; but the duty of learning by experience as well as by ratiocination is one Tolstoy has
very seldom dwelt on, and never, I think, realised at all
fully.

Another characteristic matter alluded to in these letters
is the difficulty he found himself in for lack of his birth-
certificates and other papers. Russia has long suffered
from a superabundance of red tape, which contrasts
strongly with the slipshod habits of its people, and pro-
motes the hatred of officialism that is there so common.
The fact that Tolstoy has on several occasions been put to
great inconvenience for lack of certificates, which it was
not in his nature methodically to keep in readiness, is a

small matter, but it has probably had its share in increasing his strong dislike of governments.

From Petersburg he brought back with him to Yásnaya a gifted but drunken German musician named Rudolph, with whom he had chanced to make acquaintance, and whose talent he had discerned. For some time Tolstoy devoted himself passionately to music, acquiring sufficient skill on the piano to become an excellent and sympathetic accompanist. He was always very susceptible to the influence of music, and in music, as in literature, he had strong sympathies and antipathies. Rudolph supplies the principal figure in Tolstoy's story *Albert*, written several years later.

Aunt Tatiána, who had played the piano excellently in youth, but had quite given it up for nearly thirty years, and who was now fifty-three years of age, resumed its practice and, Tolstoy tells us, played duets with him, and often surprised him by the accuracy and beauty of her execution.

For the next three years he lived partly at Yásnaya and partly in Moscow, and led a life alternating between the asceticism of his brother Demetrius and the self-indulgence of his brother Sergius; with dissipation, hunting, gambling, and the society of gipsy-girl singers. These were among the wildest and most wasted years of his life; but even here we find him, in the summer of 1850, resuming his Diary with penitence and self-reproach, and drawing up a time-table of how his days are in future to be spent: estate management, bathing, diary-writing, music, dinner, rest, reading, bathing, and again estate business to close the day. This curriculum was, however, neglected. Gusts of passion again swept away his good resolutions.

1849 At this time he made his first attempt to start a school for the peasant children of Yásnaya; but it was closed again two years later when he was in pecuniary difficulties; and it was not till 1862 that he discovered that he had infringed the law by opening it without official permission.

In relation to women, Tolstoy's ideal was a regular and affectionate family life. Women were for him divided into two groups : those sacred ones who could be looked on as possible wives or sisters, and those who, like the gipsy singers, could be paid for and possessed for short periods. To try to wipe out by a money payment any obligation arising from intimate relations, seems to have been his fixed rule. His animal passions were very strong, and late in life I have heard him say that neither drinking, cards, smoking, nor any other bad habit, had been nearly so hard for him to overcome as his desire for women. But he never doubted that that desire was a bad one. To judge him fairly, it must be remembered how loose was the general tone of the society in which he lived, and that the advice given him at this critical time of his life by those who were his natural guides, was not that he should live a chaste life, but that he should attach himself to a woman of good social position. In his *Confession* he tells us :

The kind aunt with whom I lived, herself the purest of beings, always told me that there was nothing she so desired for me as that I should have relations with a married woman : ' *Rien ne forme un jeune homme, comme une liaison avec une femme comme il faut* ' [Nothing so forms a young man, as an intimacy with a woman of good breeding]. Another happiness she desired for me was that I should become an aide-de-camp, and if possible aide-de-camp to the Emperor. But the greatest happiness of all would be that I should marry a very rich girl and become possessed of as many serfs as possible.

We never find Tolstoy involved in any family scandal, or called on to fight a duel about women ; but his Diary at this period contains many traces of his struggles and his falls ; as when he writes :

Men whom I consider morally lower than myself, do evil better than I. . . . I live an animal life, though not quite debauched. My occupations are almost all abandoned, and I am greatly depressed in spirit.

His pecuniary affairs became disordered, owing to his gambling and other bad habits, and towards the end of 1850 he thought of trying to earn money by taking on a contract to run the post-station at Toúla, which before railways were built was an undertaking of some importance. Varied however as Tolstoy's abilities unquestionably are, Nature never intended him to be a man of business, and this plan fortunately came to nothing.

The winter of 1850-51 he passed for the most part in Moscow, and as a foretaste of the simplification of life which was to be such a prominent feature of his later years, we find him writing to his aunt at Yásnaya : *Je dîne à la maison avec des stchi et kasha dont je me contente parfaitement* [I dine at home on cabbage soup and buckwheat porridge, with which I am quite contented]; and he goes on to say that he only awaits the preserves and home-made liqueurs (which she no doubt sent him) to have everything as he was accustomed to have it in the country.

1850-1851

We find Aunty Tatiána warning him against card-playing. Tolstoy replies in French :

* Tout ce que vous me dîtes au sujet de la perversité du jeu est très vrai et me revient souvent à l'esprit. C'est pourquoi je crois que je ne jouerai plus. . . . 'Je crois,' mais j'espère bientôt vous dire pour sûr.

In March 1851 he returned to Moscow after visiting Yásnaya, and he notes in his Diary that he went there with the treble aim of playing cards, getting married,

---

* All that you say about the perversity of play is very true, and I often think about it, and that is why I believe that I shall gamble no more. . . . 'I believe,' but I hope soon to tell you for certain.

and entering the Civil Service. Not one of these three
objects was attained. He took an aversion to cards. For
marriage he considered a conjunction of love, reason,
and fate to be necessary, and none of these was pre- 1851
sent. As to entering the service, it was again the fact that
he had not brought the necessary documents with him that
barred the way.

In March he writes to Aunty Tatiána and says he believes
it to be true that spring brings a moral renovation. It
always does him good, and he is able to maintain his good
intentions for some months. Winter is the season that
causes him to go wrong.

Next came a period of religious humility : he fasted
diligently and composed a sermon, which of course was
never preached. He also tried unsuccessfully to write a gipsy
story and an imitation of Sterne's *Sentimental Journey*.

This period of his life was brought to a close by the
return from the Caucasus, on leave of absence, of his
eldest brother Nicholas, who was by this time an artillery
officer.

Anxious to economise and pay off the debts he had contracted at cards, especially one of Rs. 4000 to Ogaryóf, a
gendarme officer, who owned a small estate not far from Yásnaya, Leo resolved to accompany his brother on the latter's
return to the Caucasus. He entrusted his estate to the care
of his brother-in-law (Mary's husband), who was to pay his
debts and allow him only Rs. 500 (then equal to about £80)
a year to live on, and he gave his word not to play cards
any more.

Tolstoy had another reason for wishing to escape from
his accustomed surroundings. His brother Sergius was very
fond of the gipsy choirs, famous in Russia for their musical
talent. These choirs used to visit Yásnaya, and Leo Tolstoy,
who shared his brother's susceptibility to the fascinations
of the gipsy girls, saw a means of safety in flight to the
Caucasus.

Before closing this chapter, let us note the extraordinary freedom enjoyed by young men of Tolstoy's class in those days of serfdom. Economically, serfdom supplied them with means, at the expense of a class deprived of almost all rights and absolutely dependent on their owners. Even if a member of the aristocracy ruined himself, family interest or a prudent marriage often retrieved the position for him. Religious restraint counted for little, for side by side with superstition, scepticism was common among the educated. The standard of morals expected of a young man was elastic and ill-defined. No irksome sense of public duty pressed on his attention. Politics, in our sense of the word, were forbidden; and though he had to enter the State service (civil or military), this was regarded either as a way of making a career for himself, or as a mere formality.

The detachment from the real business of life in which young Russians grew up, and the comparative isolation in which they lived on their country estates, explain the extremely radical conclusions often arrived at by those of them who wished to make the world better. Chain a man to the heavily laden car of social progress, and he can only advance very slowly, though any advance he does accomplish represents much effort and is of practical importance. Detach him from that car, and he may easily and pleasantly fly away on the winds of speculation to the uttermost realm of the highest heaven, without its producing any immediately perceptible result on the lives of his fellow-men. What I mean is, that the less a man is involved in practical work, the easier and pleasanter it is for him to take up extreme positions; I do not mean to deny that activity in the realm of thought and feeling exerts an unseen yet potent influence on other minds, and ultimately on practical affairs.

A knowledge of the social surroundings in which Tolstoy grew up makes it easier to understand the doctrines he subsequently taught. It was partly because he grew up in a detached and irresponsible position that the state of his own mind and soul were to him so much more important than the immediate effect of his conduct on others, and the same cause led him to remain in ignorance of lessons every intelligent man of business among us learns of necessity.

His independent position made easier the formation of that state of mind free from intellectual prejudice which enabled him later on to examine the claims of the Church, of the Bible, of the economists, of governments, and the most firmly established manners and customs of society, untrammelled by the fear of shocking or hurting other people, though all the time his feelings were so sensitive that it has never been possible for him to doubt or question the goodness of those lines of conduct which he had admired and approved when in childhood he saw them practised by those near and dear to him.

Contrasting his moral attitude with that of a young Englishman anxious to do right in our day, I should say that Tolstoy had no adequate sense of being a responsible member of a complex community with the opinions and wishes of which it is necessary to reckon. On the contrary, his tendency was to recognise with extraordinary vividness a personal duty revealed by the working of his own conscience and intellect apart from any systematic study of the social state of which he was a member.

He thus came to see things in a way we do not see them, while he remained blind to some things with which we are quite familiar. That is one reason why he is so extraordinarily interesting : he puts things in a way no Englishman would ever dream of putting them, and yet we feel how near akin we of the Western twentieth-century world are to this nineteenth-century Russian noble, who has so much in common with the medieval saint and the Oriental fatalist ; and this helps us to realise that all nations and classes of men are, indeed, of one blood.

Later on, in the sequel to this work, when we have to deal with Tolstoy's peaceful anarchism and his conviction that no external regulation of society is necessary, but that all men would naturally do right were they not hampered by man-made laws, it will be useful to bear in mind that his own strength grew through having to steer unaided through the stormy seas of passion, and from finding his own way to a haven the lights of which had first shone on him in childhood. Like the rest of mankind, he judges others by himself.

CHIEF AUTHORITIES FOR CHAPTER II

Birukof.

Behrs.

Novy Mir.

Education and Instruction, and *On the Education of the People,* in vol. iv. of Tolstoy's collected works : Moscow, 1903.

Confession. Published by the *Svobodnoe Slovo,* Christchurch, 1901.

Prof. Zagoskin, *Stoudentcheskie gody gr. Tolstogo,* in *Istoritchesky Vestnik* : January 1894.

V. N. Nazaryef, *Zhizn i ludi bylogo vremeni,* in *Istoritchesky Vestnik* : November 1900.

Tolstoy's talk with Pogodin, quoted in Mihaylovsky's *Literary Recollections* : Petersburg, 1900.

L. N. Tolstoy. By E. Solovef : Petersburg, 1897.

Light is also thrown on this period by Tolstoy's *Childhood, Boyhood,* and *Youth, The Memoirs of a Billiard Marker, Two Hussars, A Squire's Morning,* and *Albert* (which, however, are not autobiographies), as well as by stories included in Tolstoy's Readers for School-children—*The Old Horse* and *How I Learned to Ride.*

CHAPTER III

THE CAUCASUS

Journey. Russian Conquest. Letters to Aunt Tatiána. Diary.
Cossacks. He volunteers. Enters army. Hádji Mourát.
Story of a gaming debt. Sádo. Dreams for the future.
Childhood. Shooting. Boúlka. Slow promotion. *The Raid.*
The Censor. Danger. Applies for discharge. Applies to
Gortchakóf. *Memoirs of a Billiard Marker.* Receives his
commission. His retrospect.

THE brothers Nicholas and Leo left Yásnaya Polyána on
20th April 1851, and spent a couple of weeks in Moscow.
The frankness of Leo's intercourse with his Aunt
Tatiána is illustrated by the following letter which $\quad$ 1851
he wrote, telling her of a visit he paid to Sokólniki, a
pleasant outskirt of Moscow on the borders of a pine
forest, where a fête is held on May-day.

That he wrote in French is explained by the fact that
Tatiána, like many Russian ladies educated early in the
nineteenth century, knew French better than she did
Russian.

* J'ai été à la promenade de Sokólniki par un temps détes-
table, c'est pourquoi je n'ai rencontré personne des dames de la
société, que j'avais envie de voir. Comme vous prétendez que
je suis un homme à épreuves, je suis allé parmi les plébs, dans
les tentes bohémiennes. Vous pouvez aisément vous figurer le

---

* I went to the fête at Sokólniki in detestable weather, which was
why I did not meet any of the society ladies I wished to see. As you
say I am a man who tests himself, I went among the plebs in the
gipsy tents. You can easily imagine the inward struggle I there

combat intérieur qui s'engagea là-bas pour et contre.   Au reste
j'en sortis victorieux, c.à.d. n'ayant rien donné que ma béné-
diction aux joyeux descendants des illustres Pharaons.   Nicolas
trouve que je suis un compagnon de voyage très agréable, si ce
n'était ma propreté.   Il se fâche de ce que, comme il le dit, je
change de linge 12 fois par jour.   Moi je le trouve aussi compagnon très agréable, si ce n'était sa saleté.   Je ne sais lequel
de nous a raison.

On leaving Moscow, instead of travelling to the Caucasus
by the usual route *viâ* Vorónesh, Nicholas Tolstoy, who
liked to do things his own way, decided that they would
drive first to Kazán.   Here they stayed a week, visiting acquaintances, and that was long enough for Leo to fall in
love with a young lady to whom his shyness prevented his
expressing his sentiments.   He left for the Caucasus bearing
his secret with him, and we hear no more of the matter.

From Kazán they drove to Sarátof, where they hired
a boat large enough to take their travelling carriage on
board, and with a crew of three men, made their way down
the Vólga to Astrakhán, sometimes rowing, sometimes
sailing, and sometimes drifting with the stream.

The scorn of luxury and social distinctions so prominent
in Tolstoy's later philosophy, was at this period more to
the taste of his brother Nicholas.   A gentleman drove
past them in Kazán leaning on his walking-stick with
ungloved hands, and that was sufficient to cause Leo to
speak of him contemptuously, whereupon Nicholas, in his
usual tone of good-natured irony, wanted to know why a
man should be despised for not wearing gloves.

From Astrakhán they had still to drive some two hun-

---

experienced, for and against.   However, I came out victorious:
that is to say, having given nothing but my blessing to the gay
descendants of the illustrious Pharaohs.   Nicholas considers me a
very agreeable travelling companion, except for my cleanliness.   He
is cross because he says I change my linen 12 times a day.   I also
find him a very agreeable companion, except for his dirtiness.   I do
not know which of us is right.

dred and seventy miles to reach Starogládovsk, where Nicholas Tolstoy's battery was stationed. The whole journey from Moscow, including the stay in Kazán, took nearly a month.

It may be convenient here to explain why the Russians were then fighting in the Caucasus. Georgia, situated to the south of the Caucasian Mountains, had been voluntarily annexed to Russia in 1799 to escape the oppression of Persia; and it therefore became politically desirable for Russia to subdue the tribes that separated her from her newly acquired dependency. During the first half of the nineteenth century this task proceeded very slowly, but at the time we are speaking of, Prince Baryatínsky, in command of the Russian forces stationed on the left bank of the river Térek, which flows into the Caspian Sea, was undertaking a series of expeditions against the hostile native tribes. Up to that time the Russians had held hardly anything south of the Térek and north of the Caucasian Mountains, except their own forts and encampments; but in less than another decade, Baryatínsky had captured Shámyl (the famous leader who so long defied Russia) and had subdued the whole country.

Soon after the brothers Tolstoy arrived at Starogládovsk, Nicholas was ordered to the fortified camp at Goryatche-vódsk ('Hot Springs'), an advanced post recently established to protect the invalids who availed themselves of those mineral waters.

Here Leo Tolstoy first saw, and was deeply impressed by, the beauty of the magnificent mountain range which he has so well described in *The Cossacks*. In July 1851 he wrote to his Aunt Tatiána:

* Nicolas est parti dans une semaine après son arrivée, et moi je l'y suivis, de sorte que nous sommes presque depuis trois

---

* Nicholas left within a week of his arrival and I have followed him, so that we have now been almost three weeks here, lodging in a tent

semaines **ici** où nous logeons dans une tente. Mais comme le temps est beau et que je me fais un peu à ce genre de vie, je me trouve très bien. Ici il y a des coups d'œil magnifiques, à commencer par l'endroit où sont les sources. C'est une énorme montagne de pierres l'une sur l'autre, dont les unes se sont détachées et forment des espèces de grottes, les autres restent suspendues à une grande hauteur. Elles sont toutes coupées par les courants d'eau chaude, qui tombent avec bruit dans quelques endroits et couvrent surtout le matin toute la partie élevée de la montagne d'une vapeur blanche qui se détache continuellement de cette eau bouillante. L'eau est tellement chaude qu'on cuit dedans les œufs *hard* en trois minutes. Au milieu de ce ravin sur le torrent principal il y a trois moulins, l'un au-dessus de l'autre, qui sont construits d'une manière toute particulière et très pittoresque. Toute la journée les femmes tartares ne cessent de venir au-dessus et au-dessous de ces moulins pour laver leur linge. Il faut vous dire qu'elles lavent avec les pieds. C'est comme une fourmilière toujours remuante. Les femmes sont pour la plupart belles et bien faites. Les costumes des femmes orientales malgré leur pauvreté, sont gracieux. Les groupes pittoresques que forment les femmes, joint à la beauté sauvage de l'endroit fait un coup

---

But as the weather is fine and I am getting accustomed to this kind of life, I feel very well. There are magnificent views here, beginning where the springs are situated. It is an enormous mountain of rocks one upon another, some of which are detached and form, as it were, grottoes; others remain suspended at a great height. They are all intersected by torrents of hot water which fall noisily in certain parts and, especially in the morning, cover the whole upper part of the mountain with a white vapour which this boiling water continually gives off. The water is so hot that one can boil eggs hard in three minutes. In the middle of this ravine, by the chief torrent, stand three mills one above the other, built in a quite peculiar and very picturesque manner. All day long, above and below these mills, Tartar women come unceasingly to wash clothes. I should mention that they wash with their feet. It is like an ant-hill, always in motion. The women, for the most part, are beautiful and well formed. In spite of their poverty the costumes of Oriental women are graceful. The picturesque groups formed by the women, added to the savage beauty of the place, furnish a really admirable *coup d'œil.*

d'œil véritablement admirable. Je reste très souvent des heures
à admirer ce paysage. Puis le coup d'œil du haut de la montagne est encore plus beau et tout à fait dans un autre genre.
Mais je crains de vous ennuyer avec mes descriptions.

Je suis très content d'être aux eaux puisque j'en profite. Je
prends des bains ferrugineux et je ne sens plus de douleur aux
pieds.

As showing how hot these springs were, it may be
mentioned that a dog belonging to Nicholas tumbled into
the water and was scalded to death.

The officers Tolstoy met, he found to be men without
education, and he wrote: 'At first many things in this
society shocked me, but I have accustomed myself to them,
without however attaching myself to these gentlemen. I
have found a happy mean, in which there is neither pride
nor familiarity.' He was helped by the fact that Nicholas
was popular with every one; and, by adopting the plan of
having vódka, wine, and something to eat always ready for
those who dropped in to see him, he succeeded in keeping
on good terms with these men, though he did not care
to know them intimately.

The following extract from his Diary preserves the
record of the rapidly changing moods he experienced in
those days. Soon after reaching the Caucasus he noted:

STARY URT, 11*th June* 1851.

Yesterday I hardly slept all night. Having posted up my
Diary, I prayed to God. It is impossible to convey the sweetness of the feeling I experienced during my prayer. I said
the prayers I usually repeat by heart: 'Our Father,' 'To the
Virgin,' etc., and still remained in prayer. If one defines
prayer as a petition or as thanksgiving, then I did not pray.
I desired something supreme and good; but what, I cannot

I very often remain for hours admiring the view. Then again, in
quite a different way, the view from the top of the mountain is even
more beautiful. But I fear to weary you with my descriptions.

I am very glad to be at the springs, for I benefit by them. I take
ferruginous baths, and no longer have pain in my feet.

express, though I was clearly conscious of what I wanted. I wished to merge into the Universal Being. I asked Him to pardon my crimes; yet no, I did not ask that, for I felt that if He had given me this blissful moment, He had pardoned me. I asked, and at the same time felt that I had nothing to ask, and that I cannot and do not know how to ask; I thanked Him, but not with words or thoughts. I combined in one feeling both petition and gratitude. Fear quite vanished. I could not have separated any one emotion—faith, hope, or love —from the general feeling. No, this was what I experienced yesterday: it was love of God, lofty love, uniting in itself all that is good, excluding all that is bad. How dreadful it was to me to see the trivial and vicious side of life! I could not understand its having any attraction for me. How I asked God with a pure heart to accept me into His bosom! I did not feel the flesh. . . . But no, the carnal, trivial side again asserted itself, and before an hour had passed I almost consciously heard the voice of vice, vanity, and the empty side of life; I knew whence that voice came, knew it had ruined my bliss! I struggled against it, and yet yielded to it. I fell asleep thinking of fame and of women; but it was not my fault, I could not help it.

Again, on 2nd July, after writing down reflections on suffering and death, he concludes:

How strong I seem to myself to be against all that can happen; how firm in the conviction that one must expect nothing here but death; yet a moment later I am thinking with pleasure of a saddle I have ordered, on which I shall ride dressed in a Cossack cloak, and of how I shall carry on with the Cossack girls; and I fall into despair because my left moustache is higher than my right, and for two hours I straighten it out before the looking-glass.

By August he was back again at Starogládovsk, and, full of energy, risked his life as a volunteer in expeditions against the Circassians. Having met Ilyá Tolstoy, an officer and a relation, he was introduced by him to the Commander-in-Chief, General Baryatínsky. The latter had noticed Leo Tolstoy during one of the expeditions, and on making his acquaintance complimented him on his bravery and advised him to enter the army. Ilyá Tolstoy urged the same advice, and Leo accepted it. Towards the end of October he went a tiresome but beautiful seven-days' journey to Tiflis, where he had to pass the examination qualifying him to become a Junker (Cadet). From there he wrote to his Aunt Tatiána a letter containing the first intimation of the vocation that was ultimately to make him far more famous than Baryatínsky himself :

* Vous rappelez-vous, bonne tante, un conseil que vous m'avez donné jadis—celui de faire des romans ? Eh bien ! je suis votre conseil et les occupations dont je vous parle consistent à faire de la littérature. Je ne sais si ce que j'écris paraîtra jamais dans le monde, mais c'est un travail qui m'amuse et dans lequel je persévère depuis trop longtemps pour l'abandonner.

For two months he lived in the 'German' suburb of Tiflis, paying Rs. 5 a month (at that time equal to about 16s.) for his two-roomed lodging; disturbed by no one, writing *Childhood*, and trying to enter the army—the main obstacle to which was that, as usual, he found himself without his birth-certificate and other documents. He seldom enjoyed good health for many consecutive months, and during his stay in Tiflis he was confined to the house for some weeks by illness. At last, on 23rd December 1851, he was able to write to his brother, Sergius, announcing that in a few days he expected to receive his appointment as Junker in the 4th battery of artillery, and that on the day he received it he would set out for Starogládovsk, and from there go on campaign, and to the best of his ability 'assist, with the aid of a cannon,

---

* Do you remember, dear Aunt, the advice you once gave me—to write novels? Well, I am following your advice, and the occupation I mentioned to you consists in producing literature. I do not know if what I am writing will ever be published, but it is work that amuses me, and in which I have persevered too long to abandon it.

in destroying the predatory and turbulent Asiatics.' He goes on to tell of hunting. He had been out nine times, and had killed two foxes and about sixty grey hares. He had also hunted wild boar and deer, but had not killed any.

In the same letter Tolstoy mentions Hádji Mourát, the hero of a tale he wrote more than fifty years later, and that has been put aside for posthumous publication. He says: 'If you wish to show off with news from the Caucasus, you may recount that a certain Hádji Mourát (the second in importance to Shámyl himself) surrendered a few days ago to the Russian Government. He was the leading dare-devil and "brave" in all Circassia, but was led to commit a mean action.'

1852   A little later, on 6th January 1852, we find him again in Tiflis, writing to Aunt Tatiána

* Je viens de recevoir votre lettre du 24 Novembre et je vous y réponds le moment même (comme j'en ai pris l'habitude). Dernièrement je vous écrivais que votre lettre m'a fait pleurer et j'accusai ma maladie de cette faiblesse. J'ai eu tort. Toutes vos lettres me font depuis quelque temps le même effet. J'ai toujours été *Lyóva-ryóva* [Leo, Cry-baby]. Avant cette faiblesse me faisait honte, mais les larmes que je verse en pensant à vous et à votre amour pour nous, sont tellement douces que je les laisse couler, sans aucune fausse-honte. Votre lettre est trop pleine de tristesse pour qu'elle ne produise pas sur moi le même effet. C'est vous qui toujours m'avez donné des conseils et quoique malheureusement je ne

---

* I have just received your letter of 24 November, and I reply at once (as I have formed the habit of doing). I wrote you lately that your letter made me cry, and I blamed my illness for that weakness. I was wrong. For some time past all your letters have had the same effect on me. I always was Leo Cry-baby. Formerly I was ashamed of this weakness, but the tears I shed when thinking of you, and of your love for us, are so sweet that I let them flow without any false shame. Your letter is too full of sadness not to produce the same effect on me. It is you who have always given me counsel, and though unfortunately I have not always followed it, I should

les aie pas suivis quelquefois, je voudrais toute ma vie n'agir
que d'après vos avis. Permettez-moi pour le moment de vous
dire l'effet qu'a produit sur moi votre lettre et les idées qui me
sont venues en la lisant. Si je vous parle trop franchement je
sais que vous me le pardonnerez en faveur de l'amour que j'ai
pour vous. En disant que c'est votre tour de nous quitter
pour aller rejoindre ceux qui ne sont plus et que vous avez tant
aimés, en disant que vous demandez à Dieu de mettre un terme
à votre existence qui vous semble si insupportable et isolée,—
pardon, chère tante, mais il me paraît qu'en disant cela vous
offensez Dieu et moi et nous tous qui vous aimons tant. Vous
demandez à Dieu la mort, c. à dire le plus grand malheur qui
puisse m'arriver (ce n'est pas une phrase, mais Dieu m'est
témoin que les deux plus grands malheurs qui puissent m'arriver
ce serait votre mort ou celle de Nicolas—les deux personnes
que j'aime plus que moi-même). Que resterait-il pour moi si
Dieu exauçait votre prière ? Pour faire plaisir à qui, voudrais-
je devenir meilleur, avoir de bonnes qualités, avoir une bonne
réputation dans le monde ? Quand je fais des plans de bonheur
pour moi, l'idée que vous partagerez et jouirez de mon bonheur
m'est toujours présente. Quand je fais quelque chose de bon,

---

wish all my life to act only in accord with your advice. For the
moment, permit me to tell you the effect your letter has had on me,
and the thoughts that have come to me while reading it. If I speak
too freely, I know you will forgive it, on account of the love I have
for you. By saying that it is your turn to leave us, to rejoin those
who are no more and whom you have loved so much, by saying that
you ask God to set a limit to your life which seems to you so insupportable and isolated—pardon me, dear Aunt, but it seems to me that
in so saying you offend God and me and all of us who love you so
much. You ask God for death, that is to say, for the greatest misfortune that can happen to me. (This is not a phrase, for God is
my witness that the two greatest misfortunes that could come to me
would be your death and that of Nicholas—the two persons whom I
love more than myself.) What would be left to me if God granted
your prayer ? To please whom should I then wish to become better,
to have good qualities and a good reputation in the world ? When
I make plans of happiness for myself, the idea that you will share
and enjoy my happiness is always present. When I do anything
good, I am satisfied with myself because I know you will be satisfied

je suis content de moi-même, parce que je sais que vous serez contente de moi. Quand j'agis mal, ce que je crains le plus— c'est de vous faire du chagrin. Votre amour est tout pour moi, et vous demandez à Dieu qu'il nous sépare! Je ne puis vous dire le sentiment que j'ai pour vous, la parole ne suffit pas pour vous l'exprimer et je crains que vous ne pensiez que j'exagère et cependant je pleure à chaudes larmes en vous écrivant.

In the same letter he tells of one of those remarkable 'answers to prayer,' instances of thought-transference, or (if the reader pleases) simply coincidences, which have played so great a part in the history of all religious bodies.

* Aujourd'hui il m'est arrivé une de ces choses qui m'auraient fait croire en Dieu, si je n'y croyais déjà fermement depuis quelque temps.

L'été à Stáry Urt tous les officiers qui y étaient ne faisaient que jouer et assez gros jeu. Comme en vivant au camp il est impossible de ne pas se voir souvent, j'ai très souvent assisté au jeu et malgré les instances qu'on me faisait j'ai tenu bon pendant un mois; mais un beau jour en plaisantant, j'ai mis un petit enjeu, j'ai perdu, j'ai recommencé, j'ai encore perdu, la chance en était mauvaise, la passion du jeu s'est reveillée et en deux jours j'ai perdu tout ce que j'avais d'argent et celui que Nicolas m'a donné (à peu près 250 r. argent) et par dessus cela

---

with me. When I act badly, what I most fear is to cause you grief. Your love is everything to me, and you ask God to separate us! I cannot tell you what I feel for you; words do not suffice to express it. I fear lest you should think I exaggerate, and yet I shed hot tears while writing to you.

* To-day one of those things happened to me which would have made me believe in God, if I had not for some time past firmly believed in Him.

In summer, at Stáry Urt, all the officers who were there did nothing but play, and play rather high. As, living in camp, one has to meet frequently, I was very often present at play, but in spite of persuasions I kept steady for a month; but one fine day for fun I put down a small stake. I lost, staked again, and lost again. I was in bad luck; the passion for play reawoke in me, and in two days I had lost all the money I had, and what Nicholas gave me (about

encore 500 r. argent pour lequel j'ai donné une lettre de change payable au mois de Janvier 1852.

Il faut vous dire que près du camp il y a un *Aoul* qu'habitent les Tchitchéniens. Un jeune garçon (Tchitchénien) Sado venait au camp et jouait, mais comme il ne savait pas compter et inscrire il y avait des chenapans qui le trichaient. Je n'ai jamais voulu jouer pour cette raison contre Sado, et même je lui ai dit qu'il ne fallait pas qu'il jouât, parce qu'on le trompait et je me suis proposé de jouer pour lui par procuration. Il m'a été très reconnaissant pour ceci et m'a fait cadeau d'une bourse. Comme c'est l'usage de cette nation de se faire des cadeaux mutuels, je lui ai donné un misérable fusil que j'avais acheté pour 8 rb. Il faut vous dire que pour devenir *Kounák,* ce qui veut dire ami, il est d'usage de se faire des cadeaux, et puis de manger dans la maison du *Kounák.* Après cela, d'après l'ancien usage de ces peuples (qui n'existe presque plus que par tradition) on devient ami à la vie et à la mort, c.à d. que si je lui demande tout son argent, ou sa femme, ou ses armes, ou tout ce qu'il a de plus précieux, il doit me les donner, et moi aussi je ne dois rien lui refuser. Sado m'a engagé de venir chez lui

---

Rs. 250) and another Rs. 500 besides, for which I gave a note-of-hand payable in January 1852.

I should tell you that near the camp there is an Aoul [native village] inhabited by Circassians. A young fellow (a Circassian) named Sádo used to come to the camp and play; but as he could neither reckon nor write, there were scamps who cheated him. For that reason I never wished to play against Sádo, and I even told him that he ought not to play, because he was being cheated; and I offered to play for him. He was very grateful to me for this, and presented me with a purse; and as it is the custom of that nation to exchange presents, I gave him a wretched gun I had bought for Rs. 8. I should tell you that to become a *Kounák,* that is to say, a *friend*, it is customary to exchange presents, and afterwards to eat in the house of one's *Kounák.* After that, according to the ancient custom of these peoples (which hardly exists now except as a tradition) you become friends for life and death: that is to say, if I asked of him all his money, or his wife, or his weapons, or all the most precious things he has, he must give them to me, and I also must not refuse him anything. Sádo made me promise to come to his

et d'être *Kounák*. J'y suis allé. Après m'avoir régalé à leur
manière, il m'a proposé de choisir dans sa maison tout ce que je
voudrais—ses armes, son cheval . . . tout. J'ai voulu choisir
ce qu'il y avait de moins cher et j'ai pris une bride de cheval
montée en argent, mais il m'a dit que je l'offensais et m'a
obligé de prendre une *sword* qui vaut au moins 100 r. arg.

Son père est un homme assez riche, mais qui a son argent
enterré et ne donne pas le sou à son fils. Le fils pour avoir de
l'argent va voler chez l'ennemi des chevaux, des vaches; quelquefois il expose 20 fois sa vie pour voler une chose qui ne vaut
pas 10 r., mais ce n'est pas par cupidité qu'il le fait, mais par
genre. Le plus grand voleur est très estimé et on l'appelle
' *Dzhigit*,' un *Brave*. Tantôt Sado a 1000 r. arg., tantôt pas le
sou. Après une visite chez lui, je lui ai fait cadeau de la
montre d'argent de Nicolas et nous sommes devenus les plus
grands amis du monde. Plusieurs fois il m'a prouvé son
dévouement en s'exposant à des dangers pour moi, mais
ceci pour lui n'est rien—c'est devenu une habitude et un
plaisir.

Quand je suis parti de Stáry Urt et que Nicolas y est resté,
Sado venait chez lui tous les jours et disait qu'il ne savait que

---

house and become his Kounák. I went. After having regaled me
in their fashion, he asked me to choose anything in his house that I
liked: his weapons, his horse—anything. I wished to choose what
was of least value, and took a horse's bridle with silver mountings;
but he said I was offending him, and obliged me to take a sword worth
at least Rs. 100.

His father is a rather rich man, but keeps his money buried, and
does not give his son a cent. The son, to have money, goes and
steals horses and cows from the enemy. Sometimes he risks his life
20 times to steal something not worth Rs. 10, but he does it not
from greed, but because it is ' the thing.' The greatest robber is
most esteemed, and is called *Dzhigit*, ' a *Brave*.' Sometimes Sádo
has Rs. 1000, sometimes not a cent. After one visit to him, I gave
him Nicholas's silver watch, and we became the greatest friends in
the world. He has proved his devotion several times by exposing
himself to danger for my sake; but that is nothing to him—it has
become a habit and a pleasure.

When I left Stáry Urt and Nicholas remained there, Sádo used to
go to him every day, saying that he did not know how to get on

devenir sans moi et qu'il s'ennuyait terriblement. Par une
lettre je faisais connaître à Nicolas, que mon cheval étant
malade, je le priais de m'en trouver un à Stáry Urt; Sado
ayant appris cela n'eut rien de plus pressé que de venir chez
moi et de me donner son cheval, malgré tout ce que j'ai pu
faire pour refuser.

Après la bêtise que j'ai fait de jouer à Stáry Urt, je n'ai plus
repris les cartes en mains, et je faisais continuellement la
morale à Sado qui a la passion du jeu et quoiqu'il ne connaisse
pas le jeu, a toujours un bonheur étonnant. Hier soir je me suis
occupé à penser à mes affaires pécuniaires, à mes dettes; je
pensais comment je ferais pour les payer. Ayant longtemps
pensé à ces choses, j'ai vu que si je ne dépense pas trop d'argent,
toutes mes dettes ne m'embarrasseront pas et pourront petit à
petit être payées dans 2 ou 3 ans; mais les 500 rbs., que je
devais payer ce mois, me mettaient au désespoir. Il m'était
impossible de les payer et pour le moment ils m'embarrassaient
beaucoup plus que ne l'avaient fait autrefois les 4000 d'Ogaryéff.
Cette bêtise d'avoir fait les dettes que j'avais en Russie et de
venir en faire de nouvelles ici me mettait au désespoir. Le
soir en faisant ma prière, j'ai prié Dieu qu'il me tire de cette
désagréable position et avec beaucoup de ferveur. 'Mais com-

---

without me, and that he felt terribly dull. I wrote to Nicholas
saying that as my horse was ill I begged him to find me one at Stáry
Urt. Sádo having learnt this, must needs come to me and give me
his horse, in spite of all I could do to refuse it.

After the folly I committed in playing at Stáry Urt, I did not touch
a card again, and I was always lecturing Sádo, who is devoted to
gambling and, though he does not know how to play, always has
astonishing luck. Yesterday evening I was engaged in considering
my money matters and my debts, and thinking how I was to pay
them. Having long thought of these things, I saw that if I do not
spend too much, all my debts will not embarrass me, but can be paid
off little by little in 2 or 3 years; but the Rs. 500 that I had to pay
this month, threw me into despair. It was impossible for me to
pay it, and at the moment it embarrassed me much more than did
previously the 4000 of Ogaryóf. The stupidity, after having contracted
those debts in Russia, of coming here and adding fresh ones, made
me despair. In the evening while saying my prayers, I asked God—
and very fervently—to get me out of this disagreeable scrape. 'But

ment est-ce que je puis me tirer de cette affaire ?' pensai-je en
me couchant. ' Il ne peut rien arriver qui me donne la possi-
bilité d'acquitter cette dette.' Je me représentais déjà tous
les désagréments que j'avais à essuyer à cause de cela : how
when he presents the note for collection, the authorities will
demand an explanation as to why I did not pay, etc. ' Lord,
help me !' said I, and fell asleep.

Le lendemain je reçois une lettre de Nicolas à laquelle était
jointe la votre et plusieurs autres—il m'écrit :

The other day Sádo came to see me. He has won your notes-
of-hand from Knorring, and has brought them to me. He was
so pleased to have won them, and asked me so often, ' What do
you think ? Will your brother be glad that I have done this ?'
that I have grown very fond of him. That man is really
attached to you.

N'est-ce pas étonnant que de voir ses vœux aussi exaucés
le lendemain même ? C. à d., qu'il n'y a rien d'aussi étonnant
que la bonté divine pour un être qui la mérite si peu que moi.
Et n'est-ce pas que le trait de dévouement de Sado est admirable ? Il sait que j'ai un frère Serge, qui aime les chevaux et
comme je lui ai promis de le prendre en Russie quand j'y irai, il
m'a dit, que dût-il lui en coûter 100 fois la vie, il volera le
meilleur cheval qu'il y ait dans les montagnes, et qu'il le lui
amènera.

---

how can I get out of this scrape ?' thought I, as I lay down. ' Nothing can happen that will make it possible for me to meet that debt.'
I already pictured to myself all the unpleasantnesses I should have to
go through because of it. (See English sentence in the French text,
above.)

Next day I received a letter from Nicholas enclosing yours and
several others. He wrote me : (See English sentence in the French
text, above).

Is it not astonishing to see one's petitions granted like this the very
next day ? That is to say, there is nothing so wonderful as the divine
goodness to one who merits it so little as I. And is not the trait of
Sádo's devotion admirable ? He knows I have a brother Sergius, who
loves horses, and as I have promised to take him to Russia when
I go, he tells me that, if it costs him his life 100 times over, he
will steal the best horse to be found in the mountains, and will take
it to him.

Faites, je vous prie, acheter à Toúla un *6-barrelled pistol* et un *musical-box*, si cela ne coûte pas trop cher. Ce sont des choses qui lui feront beaucoup de plaisir.

In explanation of this letter one has to mention that Sádo was a 'peaceful' Circassian, that is, one friendly to Russia (though his tribe in general were hostile), and further, that the passages printed in English in the midst of the French text, are in the original written in Russian.

A few days later we find Tolstoy on his way back to Starogládovsk, stopping (probably for post-horses) at the post-station Mozdók, and again writing his aunt a long letter in which he says :

* La religion et l'expérience que j'ai de la vie (quelque petite qu'elle soit) m'ont appris que la vie est une épreuve. Dans moi elle est plus qu'une épreuve, c'est encore l'expiation de mes fautes.

J'ai dans l'idée que l'idée si frivole que j'ai eu d'aller faire un voyage au Caucase—est une idée qui m'a été inspirée d'en haut. C'est la main de Dieu qui m'a guidé—je ne cesse de l'en remercier. Je sens que je suis devenu meilleur ici (et ce n'est pas beaucoup dire puisque j'ai été très mauvais) et je suis fermement persuadé que tout ce qui peut m'arriver ici ne sera que pour mon bien, puisque c'est Dieu lui-même qui l'a voulu ainsi. Peut-être c'est une idée bien hardie, néanmoins j'ai

---

Please, have a 6-barrelled pistol bought in Toúla and sent to me, and also a musical-box, if that does not cost too much. These are things which will give him much pleasure.

* Religion and the experience I have of life (however small it may be) have taught me that life is a trial. In my case it is more than a trial, it is also an expiation of my faults.

It seems to me that the frivolous idea I had of journeying to the Caucasus was an idea with which I was inspired from above. It is the hand of God that has guided me—I do not cease to thank Him for it. I feel that I have become better here (and that is not saying much, for I was very bad) and I am firmly persuaded that all that can happen to me here can only be for my good, since it is God himself who has so willed it. Perhaps it is a very audacious notion ; never-

cette conviction. C'est pour cela que je supporte les fatigues et les privations physiques dont je parle (ce ne sont pas des privations physiques—il n'y en a pas pour un garçon de 23 ans qui se porte bien) sans les ressentir, même avec une espèce de plaisir en pensant au bonheur qui m'attend.

Voilà comment je le représente :

Après un nombre indéterminé d'années, ni jeune, ni vieux, je suis à Yásnaya ; mes affaires sont en ordre, je n'ai pas d'inquiétudes, ni de tracasseries. Vous habitez Yásnaya aussi. Vous avez un peu vieillie, mais êtes encore fraîche et bien portante. Nous menons la vie que nous avons menée,—je travaille le matin, mais nous nous voyons presque toute la journée. Nous dînons. Le soir je fais une lecture qui ne vous ennuie pas, puis nous causons—moi je vous raconte ma vie au Caucase, vous me parlez de vos souvenirs—de mon père, de ma mère, vous me contez des ' *terrible tales* ' que jadis nous écoutions les yeux effrayés et la bouche béante. Nous nous rappelons les personnes qui nous ont été chères et qui ne sont plus ; vous pleurerez, j'en ferai de même, mais ces larmes seront douces ; nous causerons des frères qui viendront nous voir de temps en temps, de la chère Marie qui passera aussi quelques mois

---

theless it is my conviction. That is why I bear the fatigues and the physical privations I have mentioned (they are not physical privations : there are none for a fellow of 23 who is in good health) without resenting them, and even with a kind of pleasure in thinking of the happiness that awaits me.

This is how I picture it :

After an indefinite number of years, neither young nor old, I am at Yásnaya ; my affairs are in order, I have no anxieties or worries. You also live at Yásnaya. You have aged a little, but you are still fresh and in good health. We lead the life we used to lead. I work in the morning, but we see one another almost all day. We have dinner. In the evening I read aloud something which does not weary you, and then we talk. I tell you of my life in the Caucasus, you tell me your recollections of my father and my mother ; and you tell me the ' terrible tales ' we used to listen to with frightened eyes and open mouths. We remind each other of those who were dear to us and who are now no more ; you will weep, I shall do the same, but those tears will be sweet ; we shall talk about my brothers, who will come to see us from time to time ; of dear Marie, who

de l'année a Yásnaya qu'elle aime tant, avec tous ses enfants. Nous n'aurons point de connaissances—personne ne viendra nous ennuyer et faire des commérages. C'est un beau rêve, mais ce n'est pas encore tout ce que je me permets de rêver.— Je suis marié—ma femme est une personne douce, bonne, aimante; elle a pour vous le même amour que moi; nous avons des enfants qui vous appellent grandmaman; vous habitez la grande maison en haut, la même chambre que jadis habitait grandmaman. Toute la maison est dans le même ordre qu'elle a été du temps de papa et nous recommençons la même vie, seulement en changéant de rôle; vous prenez le rôle de grand-maman, mais vous êtes encore meilleure; moi le rôle de papa, mais je désespère de jamais le mériter; ma femme celui de maman, les enfants le nôtre; Marie le rôle des deux tantes, leurs malheurs exceptés. . . . Mais il manquera un personnage pour prendre le rôle que vous avez joué dans notre famille; jamais il ne se trouvera une âme aussi belle, aussi aimante que la vôtre. Vous n'avez pas de successeur. Il y aura trois nouveaux personnages, qui paraîtront de temps en temps sur la scène— les frères, surtout l'un qui sera souvent avec nous : Nicolas— vieux garçon, chauve, retiré du service, toujours aussi bon, aussi noble.

---

with all her children will also spend some months of the year at Yásnaya, which she loves so much. We shall have no acquaint-ances—no one will come to weary us and carry tales. It is a beautiful dream, but it is not all that I let myself dream.—I am married. My wife is a gentle creature, kind and affectionate; she has the same love for you as I have. We have children who call you Grandmamma; you live upstairs in the big house, in what used to be Grandmamma's room. The whole house is as it was in Papa's time, and we recommence the same life, only changing our rôles. You take the rôle of Grandmamma, but you are still better; I take Papa's place, though I despair of ever deserving it; my wife, that of Mamma; the children take ours; Marie, that of the two aunts (ex-cepting their misfortunes) . . . but some one will be lacking to take the part you played in our family—never will any one be found with a soul so beautiful, so loving, as yours. You have no successor. There will be three new characters who will appear from time to time on the scene—the brothers, especially the one who will often be with us, Nicholas: an old bachelor, bald, retired from service, as

I imagine how he will, as of old, tell the children fairy tales of his own invention, and how they will kiss his greasy hands (but which are worthy of it), how he will play with them, how my wife will bustle about to get him his favourite dishes, how he and I will recall our common memories of days long past, how you will sit in your accustomed place and listen to us with pleasure; how, as of yore, you will call us, old men, 'Lyóvotchka' and 'Nikólenka,' and will scold me for eating with my fingers, and him for not having clean hands.

Si on me faisait empereur de Russie, si on me donnait le Pérou, en un mot si une fée venait avec sa baguette me demander ce que je désire—la main sur la conscience, je répondrais que je désire seulement que ce rêve puisse devenir une réalité.

He returned to Starogládovsk a Junker, and in February took part in an expedition as a non-commissioned artillery officer, and nearly received a St. George's Cross for bravery, but lost it because, once again, he had not his documents in order.

Writing to his Aunt Tatiána some months later (June 1852), he says:

* Pendant cette expédition, j'ai eu l'occasion d'être deux fois présenté à la croix de St. Georges et je n'ai pas pu la recevoir à cause du retard de quelques jours de ce maudit papier. J'ai été présenté pour la journée du 18 Février (ma fête), mais on a été obligé de refuser à cause du manque de ce

---

good and noble as ever. (See paragraph in English in the French text, above.)

If they made me Emperor of Russia, or gave me Peru: in a word, if a fairy came with her wand asking me what I wished for—my hand on my conscience, I should reply that I only wish that this dream may become a reality.

* During this expedition, I twice had the chance of being presented to receive a St. George's Cross, and I was prevented from receiving it by that confounded paper being a few days late. I was nominated to receive it on 18 February (my name's day), but it had to be refused me for want of that paper The list of nominations was

papier. La liste des présentations partit le 19, le 20 le papier
était arrivé. Je vous avoue franchement que de tous les hon-
neurs militaires c'est cette seule petite croix que j'ai eu la
vanité d'ambitionner.

On a second occasion he had the refusal of the coveted
cross, but his Colonel pointed out to him that besides
being sometimes given to Junkers favoured by their officers,
these crosses were also, and more usually, granted to old
and deserving privates, whom they entitled to a life pension; and that if Tolstoy would forego the one intended
for him, it would be given to a veteran who deserved it,
and to whom it would secure a subsistence for his old age.
Tolstoy, to his honour be it said, renounced the coveted
decoration. He had a third chance of securing it later on,
but this time, absorbed in playing chess till late at night,
he omitted to go on duty, and the Commander of the
Division noticing his absence, placed him under arrest
and cancelled the award which had been already made
in his favour. Chess, I may here mention, has always
been a favourite game of Tolstoy's. He has never
studied the game from books, but has played much and
plays ingeniously and well.

The kind of warfare in which he was now engaged, is
well described in *The Raid* and *The Wood-Felling*. A
detachment would set out to seize a Tartar village, make
a clearing in a forest, or capture cattle. It would exchange cannon- and rifle-shots with Tartar skirmishers, and
would lose perhaps half a dozen men killed or wounded
before accomplishing its object; but the more serious part
of the work came when the expedition returned to the
fortified camp from which it had started. As soon as
the retreat commenced, Tartar sharpshooters would swarm

---

sent off on the 19th, the paper came on the 20th. I frankly confess
that of all military honours, that little cross is the only one which
I have had the vanity to desire.

out, trying to cut off stragglers and inflicting as much damage as possible. Even after the Russians were beyond rifle-shot, a chance ball from a Tartar cannon might reach them within sight of their own quarters.

To see a single man one has known well, struck down by a deadly bullet, may impress an observer as vividly as the myriad corpses of a great battlefield ; and in Tolstoy's earliest war-sketches one feels the note of horror at war quite as strongly as when, later on, he described far bloodier struggles at Sevastopol.

When not on campaign, Tolstoy was generally stationed at the Cossack village of Starogládovsk, where he lived more or less the life vividly described in *The Cossacks*. The Grebénsky Cossacks located there were descended from Russian Dissenters (Old-Believers) who had fled from the persecution of former Tsars and had settled among the Mohammedan Circassians near the river Térek. They had retained the purity of their Russian speech, and re-mained nominally Christians, but had intermarried with the natives and adopted many of their manners and customs. Love of freedom, idleness, robbery, hunting, and war were their most prominent characteristics. They considered themselves altogether superior both to the semi-savage Mohammedan natives and to the tame, disciplined Russians. Drunkenness was not so much a weakness of these men as ' a tribal rite, to abandon which would have been considered as an act of apostasy.' The work was done by the women, or by hired Nogai-Tartar labourers. The women were physically better developed than the men, and were celebrated for their beauty, combining the purest type of Circassian features with the powerful build of Northern women. In their relations with men, especially before marriage, they enjoyed absolute freedom.

There was much that attracted Tolstoy in the simple life of these people : their frankness, their skill in hunting, their contempt for all that is artificial or weak, and their freedom from the moral struggles that tormented him. With one beautiful girl—Mariána—he fell deeply in love, but she remained indifferent to the attentions of a man who was inferior in the arts of war and hunting to some of the young men of her own tribe. His courtship failed (as he says of his hero in *The Cossacks*) because he could not, like a dashing young Cossack, 'steal herds, get drunk on Tchikir wine, troll songs, kill people, and when tipsy climb in at her window for a night, without thinking who he was or why he existed.'

Though one has always to be carefully on one's guard against taking Tolstoy's stories as though they were auto-biographical, there are passages in *The Cossacks* which certainly apply to himself, and give a vivid idea of some of his moods at this time, as well as of his way of life while living as a Junker at Starogládovsk.

On one occasion the hero is out hunting in the woods and asks himself:

'How must I live so as to be happy, and why was I formerly not happy?' And he remembered his previous life, and felt disgusted with himself. . . . And suddenly a new light seemed revealed to him. 'Happiness,' said he to himself, 'consists in living for others. That is clear. The demand for happiness is innate in man; therefore it is legitimate. If we seek to satisfy it selfishly: by seeking wealth, fame, comforts, or love, circumstances may render the satisfaction of these desires impossible. It follows that they are illegitimate, but not that the demand for happiness itself is illegitimate. But what desire is there that can always be satisfied in spite of external conditions? What desire? Love, self-sacrifice!' He was so glad and excited at discovering this, as it seemed to him, new truth, that he jumped up and began impatiently seeking for some one for whom he might quickly sacrifice himself: to whom he might do good, and whom he could love. 'Yes; I need nothing for myself!' he kept mentally repeating: 'Then why not live for others?'

In the same story Tolstoy tells us that his hero lived monotonously and regularly.

He had little to do with his Commander or fellow-officers. In the Caucasus the position of a Junker with means of his own was in this respect particularly favourable. He was not sent to drill nor kept at work. As a reward for going on an expedition he was recommended for a commission, and meanwhile he was left alone. The officers considered him an aristocrat, and therefore in their intercourse with him bore themselves with dignity. Card - playing and the officers' carousals with singers, of which he had had experience when on service with the detachment, seemed to him unattractive, and he avoided the officers' society.

Again he tells us that his hero

often thought seriously of abandoning all else, enrolling himself as a Cossack, buying a cottage, and marrying a Cossack girl . . . and living with Uncle Eróshka, going with him to hunt and to fish, and with the Cossacks on expeditions. 'Why don't I do this? What am I waiting for?' he asked himself. . . . But a voice told him to wait, and not to decide. He was restrained by a dim consciousness that he could not fully live the life of Eróshka and Loukáshka, because he had another happiness,—he was restrained by the thought that happiness lies in self-sacrifice. . . . He continually sought an opportunity to sacrifice himself for others, but it did not present itself.

In the same story the Cossack Loukáshka kills a Tartar 'brave' at night, and rises greatly in the popular esteem and in his own; and the hero thinks to himself:

'What nonsense and confusion! A man kills another and is as happy and satisfied as though he had done an excellent deed. Does nothing tell him there is here no cause for great rejoicing? That happiness consists not in killing others, but in sacrificing oneself?'

We have a yet safer record of Tolstoy's feelings in his

Diary, in which about this time he noted down the following reflections concerning the chief faults he was conscious of in himself:

1. The passion of gaming is a covetous passion, gradually developing into a craving for strong excitement. Against this passion one can struggle.

2. Sensuality is a physical need, a demand of the body, excited by imagination. It increases with abstinence, and therefore the struggle against it is very difficult. The best way is by labour and occupation.

3. Vanity is the passion least harmful to others and most harmful to oneself.

In another passage, indicating quite a different phase of consciousness, he writes:

For some time past repentance for the loss of the best years of life has begun to torment me, and this since I commenced to feel that I could do something good. . . . There is something in me which compels me to believe that I was not born to be like everybody else.

In May we find him going on furlough to Pyatigórsk to drink the mineral water and to be treated for rheumatism. This is his description of Pyatigórsk, written nearly twenty years later in his Reading Book for Children:

Pyatigórsk (Five Hills) is so called because it stands on Mount Besh-tau. *Besh* means in Tartar 'five,' *Tau* means 'hill.' From this mountain flows a hot sulphur stream. The water is boiling, and over the places where it springs from the mountain there is always steam, as from a samovár.

The whole place where the town stands is very gay. From the mountain flow hot springs, and at the foot of the mountain flows the river Podkoúmok. The mountain slopes are wooded, all around are fields, and afar off one sees the great Caucasian mountains. On these the snow never melts, and they are always as white as sugar. When the weather is clear, wherever one goes one sees the great mountain, Elbrus, like a sugar cone. People come to the hot springs for their health; and over the springs, arbours and awnings have been erected, and gardens and paths have been laid out all around. In the morning a band plays, and people drink the waters, or bathe, or stroll about.

Here he was joined by his sister Mary and her husband. She also came to Pyatigórsk to be cured of rheumatism. She tells how her brother Leo was at this time attracted by Spiritualism, and would sometimes even borrow a table from a *café* and have a *séance* on the boulevard. He remained in Pyatigórsk till 5th August, and then returned to Starogládovsk. From thence he wrote to his aunt, repeating what he had said before of the officers with whom he had to associate.

* Il y a une trop grande différence dans l'éducation, les sentiments et la manière de voir de ceux que je rencontre ici pour que je trouve quelque plaisir avec eux. Il n'y a que Nicolas qui a le talent, malgré l'énorme différence qu'il y a entre lui et tous ces messieurs, à s'amuser avec eux et à être aimé de tous. Je lui envie ce talent, mais je sens que je ne puis en faire autant.

He mentions that for some time past he has acquired a taste for reading history, and says that he perseveres in his literary occupations. He had already three times rewritten a work he had in hand, and intended to rewrite it again. He felt much more content with himself at this time, and adds :

† Il y a eu un temps où j'étais vain de mon esprit et de ma position dans le monde, de mon nom ; mais à présent je sais et

---

* There is too great a difference in the education, the sentiments, and the point of view of those I meet here, for me to find any pleasure in their company. Only Nicholas, in spite of the enormous difference between him and all these gentlemen, has the talent to amuse himself with them, and to be loved by all. I envy him this talent, but feel that I cannot do the same.

† There was a time when I was vain of my intelligence, of my position in the world, and of my name ; but now I know and feel that if

je sens que s'il y a en moi quelque chose de bon et que si j'ai à en rendre grâce à la Providence, c'est pour un cœur bon, sensible et capable d'amour, qu'il lui a plu de me donner et de me conserver.

On 29th June he again notes in his Diary :

He whose aim is his own happiness, is bad ; he whose aim is the good opinion of others, is weak ; he whose aim is the happiness of others, is virtuous ; he whose aim is God, is great.

On 2nd July he completed *Childhood*, and a few days later despatched the manuscript, signed only with the initials L. N. T., to the best Petersburg monthly, *The Contemporary*. On 28th August he received a reply 1852 from the editor, the poet Nekrásof, saying he would publish the story and that he thought its author had talent. Another letter followed, dated 5th September 1852, in which Nekrásof said that having re-read the story in proof, he found it ' much better than I had realised at first. I can say definitely that its author has talent.' He added that it would appear in the next number of his magazine.

Tolstoy notes in his Diary : ' Received letter from Nekrásof ; praises, but no money.'

Nekrásof's next letter is dated 30th October, and explains that it is not customary to pay authors for their first work, but that he hopes Tolstoy will send him more stories, and that in future he will pay him as much as to the very best known writers, namely Rs. 50 (nearly £7 at that time) per sheet of sixteen pages. He mentioned also that *Childhood* had been very well received by the public.

Tolstoy kept his authorship a secret, revealing it to no one except Nicholas and Aunt Tatiána. His sister Mary was by this time back at her husband's estate, situated near

---

there is anything good in me, and if I have anything to thank Providence for, it is for a good heart, sensitive and capable of love, which it has pleased it to give me and to preserve in me.

Tourgénef's village of Spássky. There Tourgénef came one day to visit her, bringing with him the last number of the *Contemporary*. Full of praise of a new story by an unknown author, he began reading it aloud, and to her great astonishment Mary recognised, one after another, various incidents from her own childhood. Her first guess was that Nicholas must have written it.

Among the writers who at once acclaimed Tolstoy's genius was Panáef, co-editor of the *Contemporary*, who, Tourgénef pretended, had to be carefully shunned by his friends on the Névsky (the chief street in Petersburg) lest he should insist on reading them extracts from the new story. Before long the work reached Dostoyévsky in Siberia, and he was so struck by it that he wrote to a friend asking him to find out who the talented L. N. T. was.

Meanwhile Tolstoy continued his military career in the Caucasus. On his return to Starogládovsk in August, he had noted in his Diary: 'Simplicity—that is the quality which above all others I desire to attain.'

He had to pass an unpleasant month in consequence of the autumn manœuvres, about which he wrote: 'It was not very pleasant to have to march about and fire off cannons; especially as it disturbed the regularity of my life'; and he rejoiced when it was over and he was again able to devote himself to 'hunting, writing, reading, and conversation with Nicholas.' He had become fond of shooting game, at which —as at all physical exercises—he was expert; and he spent two or three hours a day at it. He writes to his Aunt Tatiána:

At 100 paces from my lodging I find wild fowl, and in half an hour I kill 2, 3, or 4. Besides the pleasure, the exercise is excellent for my health, which in spite of the waters is not very good. I am not ill, but I often catch cold and suffer from sore throat or from toothache or from rheumatism, so that I have to keep to my room at least two days in the week.

One of the forms of sport he enjoyed during his stay in the Caucasus was strepet shooting : the strepet being a steppe grouse. Before they migrate in mid-August, these birds assemble in enormous flocks, and are extremely wild and difficult of approach. It is hardly possible to get within two hundred or two hundred and fifty yards of such a flock. Tolstoy had a horse that was specially trained for this particular sport. On it he used to ride at a foot-pace two or three times round a flock, carefully narrowing the circle till he got as near as possible without alarming the birds. Then he would dash forward at full gallop with his gun ready. The moment the birds rose he dropped his reins on the horse's neck, and the well-trained animal would instantly stop, allowing its master to take aim.

Tolstoy's military career was not giving him satisfaction. Having left home without any definite plans, he had neglected to bring any documents with him, and the result of this was that instead of becoming an officer within eighteen months, as he expected to do when he entered the army, he now, after serving for ten months, received notice that he would have to serve another three years before he could obtain his commission.

In this difficulty he applied to his aunt P. I. Úshkof, who by application to an influential friend eventually succeeded in hastening his promotion. Meanwhile however Tolstoy—who had made up his mind to retire from the army as soon as he received his commission—almost lost patience.

On 24th December he completed the sketch entitled *The Raid: A Volunteer's Story*, and two days later posted it to the *Contemporary*, in which magazine it appeared in March 1853. The following passage occurs in this his first story of war, and foreshadows the attitude he ultimately made definitely his own. He is describing a march through Caucasian scenery to a night attack on a Tartar *Aoul*, and he says :

Nature, beautiful and strong, breathed conciliation.

Can it be that people have not room to live in this beautiful world, under this measureless, starry heaven? Can feelings of enmity, vengeance, or lust to destroy one's fellow beings, retain their hold on man's soul amid this enchanting Nature? All that is evil in man's heart should, one would think, vanish in contact with Nature—this immediate expression of beauty and goodness.

From the very start we find Tolstoy hampered in his work by that incubus of all Russian writers, the Censor. In a letter to his brother Sergius in May he writes : ' *Childhood* was spoilt, and *The Raid* simply ruined by the Censor. All that was good in it has been struck out or mutilated.' In comparing Tolstoy's literary achievement with that of Western writers, one should make a large allowance for the continual annoyance, delay, mutilation, and suppression inflicted on him by that terrible satellite of despotism.

In January, the battery in which Leo Tolstoy served went on active service against Shámyl. The expedition assembled at Fort Grózny, where scenes of debauchery occurred.

1853

On 18th February Tolstoy's life was in great danger. A shell fired by the enemy smashed the carriage of a cannon he was pointing. Strange to say he was not even wounded. On 1st April he returned with his detachment to Starogládovsk ; and in May we find him writing to his brother Sergius that he had applied for his discharge, and hoped in six weeks' time to return home a free man. Difficult as his admission to the army had been, he found, however, that to retire was a yet harder matter, destined to take not weeks but years.

On 13th June his life was again in danger owing to an adventure which supplied him with the subject he utilised later on in *A Prisoner in the Caucasus.*

It being dangerous to travel between the Russian forts without an escort, non-combatants, as well as stores and baggage, were periodically convoyed from one post to another. On these expeditions it was forbidden for any one to detach himself from the main body ; but the intolerable slowness of the infantry march on a hot day, frequently tempted those who were mounted, to ride on, and to run the risk of being attacked by the 'Tartars' (who were generally Circassians). On one such occasion five horsemen, including Tolstoy and his friend Sádo, disobeyed the regulations and rode ahead. The two friends ascended the hillside to see whether any foes were visible, while their three companions proceeded along the valley below. Hardly had the two reached the crest of the ridge when they saw thirty mounted Tartars galloping towards them. Calculating that there was not time to rejoin their companions in the valley, Tolstoy shouted them a warning, and raced off along the ridge towards Fort Grózny, which was their destination. The three did not, at first, take his warning seriously, but wasting some precious moments before turning to rejoin the column, were overtaken by the Tartars, and two of them were very severely wounded before a rescue party from the convoy put the enemy to flight. Meanwhile Tolstoy and Sádo, pursued by seven horsemen along the hill ridge, had to ride nearly three miles to reach the fort. It so happened that Tolstoy was trying a young horse of Sádo's, while Sádo was riding Tolstoy's ambler, which could not gallop. Though Tolstoy could easily have escaped on Sádo's fiery horse, he would not desert his comrade. Sádo had a gun, unluckily not loaded, and so he could only make a pretence with it of aiming at his pursuers. It seemed almost certain that both fugitives would be killed ; but apparently the Tartars decided to capture them alive, perhaps wishing to revenge themselves on Sádo for being a pro-Russian, and therefore they did not shoot them down. At last a sentinel at Grózny having espied their plight, gave the alarm and some Cossacks galloped to their rescue. At sight of these, the Tartars made off and the fugitives escaped uninjured.

Tolstoy continued his habit of forming resolutions; and about this time he wrote: ' Be straightforward, not rough, but frank with all men ; yet not childishly frank without any need. . . . Refrain from wine and women . . . the pleasure is so small and uncertain, and the remorse so great. . . . Devote yourself completely to whatever you do. On experiencing any strong sensation, wait ; but having once considered the matter, though wrongly, act decisively.'

From the middle of July to October, Tolstoy again stayed at Pyatigórsk.

A companion he had brought with him to the Caucasus was his black bulldog, Boúlka. He intended to leave it at home, but after he had started, the dog had broken a pane of glass and escaped from the room in which it was confined, and when Tolstoy, after stopping at the first post-station, was just resuming his journey, he saw something black racing along the road after him. It was Boúlka, who rushed to his master, licked his hand, and lay down panting in the shade of a cart. The dog had galloped nearly fourteen miles in the heat of the day, and was rewarded by being taken to the Caucasus, where it was destined to meet with many adventures.

On one occasion this dog boldly attacked a wild boar, and had its stomach ripped open by the latter's tusk. While its wound was being sewn up, the dog licked its master's hand.

On another occasion, when Tolstoy was sitting at night with a friend in the village street, intending to start for Pyatigórsk at daybreak, they suddenly heard a sucking-pig squeal, and guessed that a wolf was killing it. Tolstoy ran into the house, seized a loaded gun, and returned in time to see a wolf running straight towards him from the other side of a wattle-fence. The wolf jumped on to the top of the fence and descended close to Tolstoy who, almost touching him with the muzzle of his gun, drew the trigger. The gun missed fire, and the wolf raced off, chased by Boúlka and by Tolstoy's setter, Milton. The wolf escaped, but not till it had snapped at Boúlka and inflicted a slight wound on his head. Strange to say, the wolf ventured to return a little later into the middle of the street, and again escaped unhurt.

Not long after, in Pyatigórsk, shortly before Tolstoy left the Caucasus, while drinking coffee in the garden of his lodging, he heard a tremendous noise of men and dogs, and, on inquiry, learnt that convicts had been let out of gaol to kill the dogs, of whom there were too many in the town, but that orders had been given to spare dogs wearing collars. As ill-luck would have it, Tolstoy had removed Boúlka's collar; and Boúlka, apparently recognising the convicts as his natural enemies, rushed out into the street and flew at one of them. A man had just freed the long hook he carried, from the corpse of a dog he had caught and held down while his companions beat it to death with bludgeons. He now adroitly hooked Boúlka and drew the unfortunate dog towards him, calling to his mate to kill it, which the latter prepared to do. Boúlka however bounded aside with such force that the skin of his thigh burst where the hook held it, and with tail between his legs and a red wound on his thigh, he flew back into the house and hid under Tolstoy's bed. His escape was not of much use. The wolf that had snapped at him six weeks before must have been mad, for Boúlka after showing premonitory symptoms of rabies, disappeared, and was never heard of more.

Tolstoy's state of mind during the latter part of this year is indicated by his letters. To his brother Sergius he wrote on 20th July:

I think I already wrote you that I have sent in my resignation. God knows, however, on account of the war with Turkey, whether it will be accepted, or when. This disturbs me very much, for I have now grown so accustomed to happy thoughts of soon settling down in the country, that to return to Starogládovsk and again wait unendingly—as I have to wait for everything connected with my service—will be very unpleasant.

Again, in December, he writes from Starogládovsk :

Please write about my papers quickly. This is necessary. *' When shall I come home ? '* God only knows. For nearly a year I have been thinking only of how to sheath my sword, but still cannot manage it. And as I must fight somewhere, I think it will be pleasanter to do so in Turkey than here, and I have therefore applied to Prince Serge Dmítrievitch [Gortchakóf] about it, and he writes me that he has written to his brother, but what the result will be, I do not know.

It will be remembered that Tolstoy's paternal grand-mother was a Gortchakóf. Through her he was nearly related to Prince S. D. Gortchakóf and to his brother, Prince Michael Dmítrievitch Gortchakóf, who had been a friend of his father's in the war of 1812, and was now in command of the Russian army on the Danube.

The letter continues :

At any rate by New Year I expect to change my way of life, which I confess wearies me intolerably. Stupid officers, stupid conversations, and nothing else. If there were but a single man to whom one could open one's soul ! Tourgénef is right : ' What irony there is in solitude,'—one becomes palpably stupid oneself. Although Nikólenka has gone off with the hounds—Heaven knows why (Epíshka [1] and I often call him ' a pig' for so doing)—I go out hunting alone for whole days at a time from morning to evening, with a setter. That is my only pleasure—and not a pleasure but a narcotic. One tires oneself out, gets famished, sleeps like the dead, and a day has passed. When you have an opportunity, or are yourself in Moscow, buy me Dickens' *David Copperfield* in English, and send me *Sadler's English Dictionary* which is among my books.

---

[1] The Cossack hunter Epíshka, the original of Eróshka, who figures so prominently in *The Cossacks*.

Of the entries in his Diary at this time, we may note the following :

All the prayers I have invented I replace by the one prayer, 'Our Father.' All the requests I can make to God are far more loftily expressed and more worthily of Him, in the words 'Thy Kingdom come, as in heaven so on earth.'

About this time he completed his *Memoirs of a Billiard Marker*, and sent it to the *Contemporary* with a letter expressing his own dissatisfaction with the hasty workmanship of the story ; it did not appear till more than a year later. He was also now at work on *Boyhood*.

Seventeen years after Tolstoy had left the Caucasus, an officer stationed at Starogládovsk found his memory still fresh among the Cossacks, and saw Mariána (comparatively aged by that time), as well as several elderly Cossack hunters who had shot wild fowl and wild boars with Tolstoy. In his regiment he left the reputation of being an excellent narrator, who enthralled every one by his conversation.

Not till January 1854 did the long-expected order arrive allowing him to pass the examination (a pure formality at that time) entitling him to become an officer. On the 19th he left for home, and on 1854 2nd February reached Yásnaya, where he enjoyed a three weeks' stay with his Aunt Tatiána, his brother, and a friend. On this journey he encountered a severe storm, to which we owe *The Snow Storm*, published a couple of years later, and probably also much of the storm description in *Master and Man*, written in later life.

The Russo-Turkish war had now begun in earnest, and, as a result of his application, he received orders to join the army of the Danube, which he set out accordingly to do.

Of the Caucasian period of his life, as of his University days, Tolstoy has at different times expressed himself differently. To Birukóf, in 1905, he spoke of it as one of the best times of his life, notwithstanding all his deflections from his dimly recognised ideals. Yet two years earlier, writing of the four periods of his life, he had spoken of 'the terrible twenty years of coarse dissipation, the service of ambition, vanity, and above all, of lust,' which followed after the age of fourteen.

But what it comes to is, that Tolstoy is a man of moods, and judges himself and others, sometimes by ordinary and sometimes by extraordinary standards.

CHIEF AUTHORITIES FOR CHAPTER III

Birukof.

Behrs.

U. Bitovt, *Graf L. Tolstoy v literatoure i iskousstve*: Petersburg, 1903. (Hereafter called 'Bitovt.') Though ill-arranged, this book is valuable to any one engaged on the difficult task of compiling a Bibliography of Tolstoy's works.

Nekrasof's letters to Tolstoy published in the Literary Supplement to the *Niva*, February 1898.

Much light is also thrown on this period of Tolstoy's life by the following works, which must not be considered autobiographical:

> *The Raid.*
> *The Wood-Felling.*
> *Meeting a Moscow Acquaintance.*
> *The Cossacks*, and
> *The Snow Storm,*

as well as by stories included in Tolstoy's *Readers*:

> *Boulka.*
> *Boulka and the Wild Boar.*
> *Milton and Boulka.*
> *Boulka and the Wolf.*
> *What Happened to Boulka in Pyatigorsk.*
> *Boulka's and Milton's End.*
> *A Prisoner in the Caucasus.*

CHAPTER IV

THE CRIMEAN WAR

Joins army of the Danube.   Siege of Silistria.   Sevastopol.
Projected Newspaper.   *Sevastopol in December*.   Battle of the
Tchérnaya.   Capture of the Maláhof.   Courier to Peters-
burg.   Song.   Relations with superiors and fellow-officers.
Self-depreciation.   *The Wood-Felling*.   *Sevastopol in May*.
The Censor.   On War.

AT twenty-five years of age it fell to Tolstoy's lot to take
part in a great European war and thereby to extend the
range of his experience in a way that considerably affected
his subsequent life and writings.

Tolstoy tells us that he got his first understanding of
war from Stendhal, the author of *Le Rouge et le Noir* and
La Chartreuse de Parme.   In conversation with Paul
Boyer, Tolstoy once spoke of those novels as inimitable
works of art, adding, 'I am greatly indebted to Stendhal.
He taught me to understand war.   Re-read the description of the battle of Waterloo in *La Chartreuse de Parme*.
Who ever before so described war?   Described it, that is,
as it is in reality?   Do you remember Fabrice riding
over the field of battle and understanding " nothing "?'

Tolstoy's brother Nicholas, though fond of war, also
disbelieved in the popular romantic view of it, and used to
say: 'All *that* is embellishment, and in real war there is
no embellishment.'——'A little later, in the Crimea,' added
Tolstoy in his talk with Boyer, 'I had a grand chance to
see with my own eyes that this is so.'

Of the causes that led to the war it need only be said that the rule of the Turks over Christian populations had long kept a dangerous sore open in Europe, and the consequent diplomatic difficulties were complicated by the indefiniteness of two lines in the Treaty of Kainardji, which Catherine the Great had imposed upon Turkey in 1774. There was also friction between the Eastern and Western Churches, with reference to the custody of the Places in Palestine rendered holy by their traditional connection with the Prince of Peace. Nicholas I, who had wellnigh drilled all intelligence out of those near him in his Government and in his army, was not accustomed to be thwarted. Dimly conscious of the first faint symptoms of that growth of Liberalism which a few years later, in the early 'sixties, led to sweeping reforms in Russia, he felt inclined to demonstrate the beneficence of his rule not by allowing changes to be made at home, but by arbitrarily inflicting reforms on Turkey. Failing to get his way by diplomatic pressure, he rashly proceeded to occupy the Danubian Principalities as a 'material guarantee' of Turkey's compliance with his demands.

He was opposed by Austria and Prussia as strongly as by England and France, and the pressure exerted by the four powers sufficed to compel him to withdraw his army from Turkish soil. Thereupon the war, which had as yet been waged only between Russia and Turkey, might well have ended, had not England and France undertaken a quite needless invasion of the Crimea: an enterprise in which Austria and Prussia refused to join. The end did not justify the proceedings, for in spite of success in this war, Napoleon the Third's dynasty crumbled to dust within twenty years, while within a like period after Palmerston's death Lord Salisbury frankly admitted that we had 'put our money on the wrong horse.' As to Nicholas I, his pride was destined to be bitterly mortified by the results of an enterprise which not only failed of its immediate object, but by its failure actually hastened the coming of those reforms in Russia against which he had set his face. Even Turkey did not really benefit by being allowed to oppress her subject races for a couple of generations longer.

It was the influence of Napoleon III, as Kinglake has pointed out, that led England to take part in the war. Having by treachery and murder made himself Emperor of the French, that monarch found himself for a time dangerously isolated from the support of people of good repute. In consultation with Palmerston, he decided to subordinate the traditional Eastern policy of his country to that of England if thereby he could succeed in being publicly paraded as the friend and ally of Queen Victoria. As soon as he had secured an alliance with England, with Palmerston's aid, and helped by the extraordinary war fever which seized the English nation, he quickly forced the peacefully disposed Lord Aberdeen along an inclined plane which ultimately plunged both nations into a war for which no sufficient motive justification or excuse existed.

Hostilities between Russia and Turkey had begun in October 1853, but France and England did not break off negotiations with the former power till the end of March 1854, the very month in which Tolstoy 1854 reached Bucharest on his way through Wallachia to join the army.

From there he wrote to his aunt, telling of his journey. The roads after he had passed Khersón, and especially after he had crossed the frontier, were abominable; his journey lasted nine days; and he 'arrived almost ill with fatigue.'

A few days later, on 17th March, he wrote of his first interview with Gortchakóf:

* Le prince Gortchakóf n'était pas ici. Hier il vient d'arriver et je viens de chez lui. Il m'a reçu mieux que je ne

---

* Prince Gortchakóf was not here. He arrived yesterday, and I have just come from his lodgings. He received me better than I ex-

croyais—en vrai parent. Il m'a embrassé, il m'a engagé de
venir dîner tous les jours chez lui et il veut me garder auprès
de lui, mais ce n'est pas encore décidé.

Pardon, chère tante, que je vous écris peu—je n'ai pas encore
la tête à moi,—cette grande et belle ville, toutes ces présentations, l'opéra italien, le théâtre français, les deux jeunes
Gortchakóf qui sont de très braves garçons . . . de sorte que
je ne suis pas resté deux heures chez moi, et je n'ai pas pensé
à mes occupations.

On 22nd March he adds : ' I learnt yesterday that I am
not to remain with the Prince, but am to go to Oltenitza
to join my battery.'

In May he wrote :

* Tandis que vous me croyez exposé à tous les dangers de
la guerre je n'ai pas encore senti la poudre turque, et je suis
très tranquillement à Boukarest à me promener, à faire de la
musique et à manger des glaces. En effet tout ce temps,
excepté deux semaines que j'ai passées à Oltenitza où j'ai été
attaché à une batterie, et une semaine que j'ai passée en courses
par la Moldavie, Valachie et Bessarabie par ordre du gén.
Serjpoutóvsky auprès duquel je suis à présent *by special appointment*, je suis resté à Boukarest et à vous avouer franchement,

---

pected—quite as a relation. He embraced me, and made me promise
to dine at his house every day. He wants to keep me near him, but
this is not yet decided.

Forgive me, dear Aunt, for writing but little to you—I have not
yet collected my wits ; this large and fine town, all these presenta-
tions, the Italian opera, the French theatre, the two young Gortchakófs, who are very fine lads . . . so that I have not remained two
hours at home, and have not thought of my duties.

* While you are fancying me exposed to all the dangers of war, I
have not yet smelt Turkish powder, but am very quietly at Bucharest,
strolling about, making music, and eating ices. In fact, all this time,
except for two weeks I spent at Oltenitza, where I was attached to a
battery, and one week I passed making excursions in Moldavia
Wallachia and Bessarabia by order of General Serzhpoutóvsky, on
whose staff I now am by special appointment, I have been at Bucha-

ce genre de vie un peu dissipé, tout à fait oisif et très coûteux que je mène ici me déplaît infiniment. Auparavant c'était le service qui m'y retenait, mais à présent j'y suis resté pendant près de trois semaines à cause d'une fièvre que j'ai attrapée pendant mon voyage, mais dont, Dieu merci, je suis pour le moment assez rétabli pour rejoindre dans deux ou trois jours mon général qui est au camp près de Silistrie. A propos de mon général, il a l'air d'être un très brave homme et paraît, quoique nous nous connaissons fort peu, être bien disposé à mon égard. Ce qui est encore fort agréable est que son état-major est composé pour la plupart de gens comme il faut.

We shall find Tolstoy modifying this opinion, a little later on ; but it is worth noting that at this time he was fully alive to the superiority of ' *gens comme il faut*,' and that his depreciation of them in later years may have been partly a reaction from a previous over-valuation.

By June 1854 the military and political situation was as follows. The Russians had advanced through Moldavia and Wallachia to the Danube, had crossed that river, and were besieging Silistria. Austria, supporting the other great powers, had massed a powerful army on the Turkish frontier, and a glance at the map of Europe will show that the Russian army, far removed from its base, was in imminent danger of being cut off by the Austrians, who peremptorily summoned Russia to evacuate the Principalities, and on 14th June concluded a formal alliance with the Porte. These circumstances explain the sudden

rest; and to speak frankly, the rather dissipated, quite idle and very expensive kind of life that I lead here, displeases me very much. Formerly it was the service that kept me here ; but now for three weeks I have been kept here by a fever caught during my journey, but from which, thank God, I have for the present recovered sufficiently to be able in two or three days' time to rejoin my General, who is in camp near Silistria. Apropos of my General, he appears to be a very fine fellow, and though we know each other very slightly, seems well disposed toward me. What is also agreeable is that his staff consists for the most part of gentlemen.

abandonment of the siege of Silistria mentioned in the
following letter, addressed by Leo Tolstoy to his Aunt
Tatiána and to his brother Nicholas conjointly; though
when he wrote it, the causes which produced the result he
described were a mystery to him.

* Je vais vous parler donc de mes souvenirs de Silistrie.
J'y ai vu tant de choses intéressantes, poétiques et touchantes
que le temps que j'y ai passé ne s'effacera jamais de ma mémoire.
Notre camp était disposé de l'autre côté du Danube c.à d. sur
la rive droite sur un terrain très élevé au milieu de superbes
jardins, appartenant à Mustafa Pasha—le gouverneur de Silistrie. La vue de cet endroit est non seulement magnifique,
mais pour nous tous du plus grand intérêt. Sans parler du
Danube, de ces îles et de ces rivages, les uns occupés par nous,
les autres par les Turcs, on voyait la ville, la forteresse, les petits
forts de Silistrie comme sur la main. On entendait les coups
de canons, de fusils qui ne cessaient ni jour ni nuit, et avec
une lunette d'approche on pouvait distinguer les soldats turcs.
Il est vrai que c'est un drôle de plaisir que de voir de gens
s'entretuer et cependant tous les soirs et matins je me mettais
sur ma *cart* et je restais des heures entières à regarder et ce
n'était pas moi le seul qui le faisait. Le spectacle était vraiment beau, surtout la nuit. Les nuits ordinairement mes

---

* I am going to tell you of my recollections of Silistria. I there
saw so much that was interesting, poetic and touching, that the time
I passed there will never be effaced from my memory. Our camp was
on the other side of the Danube, *i.e.* on the right bank, on very high
ground amid splendid gardens belonging to Mustafa Pasha, the
Governor of Silistria. The view from that place is not only magnificent, but of the greatest interest to us all. Not to speak of the
Danube, its islets and its banks, some occupied by us, others by the
Turks, one could see the town, the fortress and the little forts of
Silistria as on the palm of one's hand. One heard the booming of
cannon and musket-shots unceasingly day and night; and with a spy-
glass one could distinguish the Turkish soldiers. It is true it is
a queer sort of pleasure to see people killing one another, yet every
evening and every morning I got on to my cart and remained for
hours at a time, watching: nor was I the only one who did so. The
sight was really fine, especially at night. At night my soldiers usually

soldats se mettent aux travaux des tranchées, et les Turcs se
jettent sur eux pour les en empêcher, alors il fallait voir et
entendre cette fusillade.   La première nuit que j'ai passée au
camp ce bruit terrible m'a reveillé et effrayé, je croyais qu'on
est allé à l'assaut et j'ai bien vite fait seller mon cheval, mais
ceux qui avait déjà passé quelque temps au camp me dirent que
je n'avais qu'à me tenir tranquille, que cette canonnade et
fusillade était une chose ordinaire et qu'on appela en plaisantant,
'Allah'; alors je me suis recouché, mais ne pouvant m'endor-
mir je me suis amusé, une montre à la main, à compter les coups
de canon que j'entendais et j'ai compté 110 explosions dans
l'espace d'une minute.   Et cependant tout ceci n'a eu de près
l'air aussi effrayant que cela le paraît.   La nuit, quand on n'y
voyait rien, c'était à qui brûlerait le plus de poudre et avec ces
milliers de coups de canons on tuait tout au plus une trentaine
d'hommes de part et d'autre.

Ceci donc est un spectacle ordinaire que nous avions tous
les jours et dans lequel, quand on m'envoyait avec des ordres
dans les tranchées, je prenais aussi ma part; mais nous avions
aussi des spectacles extraordinaires, comme celui de la veille de
l'assaut quand on a fait sauter une mine de 240 pouds de poudre
sous un des bastions de l'ennemi.   Le matin de cette journée

---

undertake trench-work, and the Turks fling themselves upon them to
hinder them; then one should see and hear the fusillade!   The first
night I passed in camp, this dreadful noise awoke and frightened me:
I thought an assault had begun.   I very soon had my horse saddled;
but those who had been already some time in camp told me that I had
only to keep quiet: that this cannonade and fusillade was an ordinary
affair, and they jestingly called it 'Allah.'   Then I lay down again;
but not being able to sleep, I amused myself, watch in hand, counting
the cannon-shots, and I counted 110 reports in a minute.   And yet,
at close quarters, all this did not look so terrible as might be supposed.
At night, when nothing was visible, it was a case of who could burn
most powder, and with all these thousands of cannon-shots at most
some thirty men were killed on each side. . . .
This then was an ordinary performance we had every day, and one
in which I took a share when I was sent to the trenches with orders;
but we also had extraordinary performances, such as the one on the eve
of the attack, when a mine of 240 poods (8600 lbs.) of gunpowder was
exploded under one of the enemy's bastions.   On the morning of that

le prince avait été aux tranchées avec tout son état-major (comme le général auprès duquel j'étais en fait partie, j'y ai aussi été) pour faire les dispositions définies—vu pour l'assaut du lendemain. Le plan, trop long pour que je puisse l'expliquer ici, était si bien fait, tout était si bien prévu que personne ne doutait de la réussite. A propos de cela il faut que je vous dise encore que je commence à avoir de l'admiration pour le prince (au reste il faut en entendre parler parmi les officiers et les soldats, non seulemènt je n'ai jamais entendu dire du mal de lui, mais il est généralement adoré).

Je l'ai vu au feu pour la première fois pendant cette matinée. Il faut voir cette figure un peu ridicule avec sa grande taille, ses mains derrière le dos, sa casquette en arrière, ses lunettes et sa manière de parler comme un dindon. On voit qu'il était tellement occupé de la marche générale des affaires que les balles et les boulets n'existaient pas pour lui; il s'expose au danger avec tant de simplicité, qu'on dirait qu'il n'en a pas l'idée et qu'involontairement qu'on n'a plus peur de lui que pour soi-même; et puis donnant ses ordres avec tant de clarté et de précision et avec cela toujours affable avec chacun. C'est un

---

day the Prince had been to the trenches with all his staff (and as the General I was attached to belongs to it, I was there too) to make the final arrangements for next day's assault. The plan—too long for me to explain here—was so well arranged, all was so well foreseen, that no one doubted its success. Apropos of this I must tell you further that I am beginning to feel admiration for the Prince (for that matter you should hear how the officers and soldiers speak of him : not only have I never heard him spoken ill of, but he is generally adored).

That morning I saw him under fire for the first time. You should see his rather absurd tall figure, his hands behind his back, his cap on the back of his head, his spectacles, and his way of speaking like a turkey-cock. One could see that he was so preoccupied with the general trend of affairs that the balls and bullets did not exist as far as he was concerned. He exposes himself to danger so simply that one would say he was unconscious of it, and involuntarily one fears it only for oneself; [The text here is obscure, and the meaning a little doubtful] and then he gives his orders with such clearness and precision, and is at the same time always so affable with everybody.

grand, c.à d. un homme qui s'est voué toute sa vie au service de sa patrie et pas par l'ambition, mais par le devoir. Je vais vous raconter un trait de lui qui se lie à l'histoire de cet assaut que j'ai commencé à raconter. L'après-dîner du même jour on a fait sauter la mine, et près de 600 pièces d'artillerie ont fait feu sur le fort qu'on voulait prendre, et on continuait ce feu pendant toute la nuit, c'était un de ces coups d'œil et une de ces émotions qu'on n'oublie jamais. Le soir de nouveau le prince, avec tout le tremblement, est allé coucher aux tranchées pour diriger lui-même l'assaut qui devait commencer à 3 heures de la nuit même.

Nous étions tous là et comme toujours à la veille d'une bataille nous faisions tous semblant de ne pas plus penser de la journée de demain qu'à une journée ordinaire et tous, j'en suis sûr, au fond du cœur ressentaient un petit serrement de cœur et pas même un petit mais un grand, à l'idée de l'assaut. Comme tu sais que le temps qui précède une affaire est le temps le plus désagréable—c'est le seul où on a le temps d'avoir peur, et la peur est un sentiment des plus désagréables. Vers le matin, plus le moment approchait, plus le sentiment diminuait et vers 3 heures quand nous attendions tous à voir partir le bouquet de

---

He is a great man, *i.e.* a capable and honest man, as I understand the word : one who has dedicated his whole life to the service of his country, and not from ambition, but for the sake of duty. I will give you a trait of his character connected with the story I had begun to tell you of the assault. After dinner that same day, the mine was sprung, and nearly 600 guns opened fire on the fort we wished to take, and this continued the whole night. It was such a sight and such an emotion as one never forgets. That evening the Prince, amid all the commotion, went to sleep in the trenches, that he might personally direct the assault, which was to begin at 3 o'clock the same night.

We were all there, and as usual on the eve of a battle, we all made believe not to think of the morrow more than of any other day, and we all, I am sure, at bottom, felt our hearts contract a little (and not a little, but a great deal) at the thought of the assault. As you know, the time before a fight is the most disagreeable : it is only then that one has time to be afraid, and fear is a most disagreeable feeling. Towards morning, the nearer the moment came the more the feeling diminished, and towards 3 o'clock when we were all expecting to see

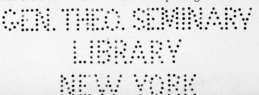

fusées qui était le signal de l'attaque—j'étais si bien disposé
que si l'on était venu me dire que l'assaut n'aurait pas lieu, cela
m'aurait fait beaucoup de peine. Et voilà que juste une heure
avant le moment de l'assaut arrive un aide de camp du maréchal avec l'ordre d'ôter le siège de Silistrie. Je puis dire sans
craindre de me tromper que cette nouvelle a été reçue par tous
—soldats, officiers et généraux—comme un vrai malheur, d'autant plus qu'on savait par les espions, qui nous venaient très
souvent de Silistrie, et avec lesquels j'avais très souvent l'occasion de causer moi-même, on savait que ce fort pris,—chose
dont personne ne doutait—Silistrie ne pouvait tenir plus de
2 ou 3 jours. N'est-ce pas que si cette nouvelle devait faire de
la peine à quelqu'un ce devait être au prince, qui pendant toute
cette campagne ayant fait toute chose pour le mieux, au beau
milieu de l'action vit venir le maréchal sur son dos pour gâter
les affaires et puis ayant la seule chance de réparer nos revers
par cet assaut, il reçoit le contre ordre du maréchal au moment
de le commencer. Eh bien, le prince n'a pas eu un moment de
mauvaise humeur, lui, qui est si impressionable, au contraire il a

---

a shower of rockets let off, which was the signal for the attack,
I was so well inclined for it that I should have been much dis-
appointed if any one had come to tell me that the attack was not to
take place. And there! Just an hour before the time for the attack,
an aide-de-camp comes from the Field-Marshal [Paskévitch, who for
a time took over the supreme command of the army of the Danube]
with orders to raise the siege of Silistria! I can say, without fear of
making a mistake, that this news was received by all, soldiers, officers,
and generals, as a real misfortune, the more so as we knew from the
spies—who very often came to us from Silistria, and with whom I very
often had occasion to speak—that once we had taken this fort (about
which none of us felt any doubt) Silistria could not have held out for
more than 2 or 3 days. Is it not true that if this news was calculated
to pain any one, it must have been the Prince, who having all through
this campaign arranged everything for the best, yet saw, in the very
middle of the action, the Field-Marshal override him and spoil the
business? Having this one chance to repair our reverses by this
assault, he received counter-orders from the Field-Marshal at the
moment of commencing! Well, the Prince was not put out of temper
for a moment. He who is so impressionable, was, on the contrary,

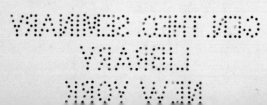

été content de pouvoir éviter cette boucherie, dont il devait porter la responsabilité et tout le temps de la retraite qu'il a dirigé lui-même, ne voulant passer qu'avec le dernier des soldats, qui s'est faite avec un ordre et une exactitude remarquables, il a été plus gai qu'il n'a jamais été. Ce qui contribuait beaucoup à sa bonne humeur, c'était l'émigration de près de 7000 familles bulgares, que nous prenons avec pour le souvenir de la férocité des Turcs—férocité à laquelle malgré mon incredulité, j'ai été obligé de croire. Dès que nous avons quitté des différents villages bulgares que nous occupions, les Turcs y sont revenus et excepté les femmes assez jeunes pour un harem, ils ont fait main basse sur tout ce qu'il y avait. Il y a un village dans lequel je suis allé du camp pour y prendre du lait et des fruits qui a été exterminé de la sorte. Alors dès que le prince avait fait savoir aux Bulgares que ceux qui voulaient pouvaient avec l'armée passer le Danube et devenir sujets russes, tout le pays se soulève et tous avec leurs femmes, enfants, chevaux, bétails arrivent au pont,—mais comme il était impossible de les prendre tous, le prince a été obligé de refuser à ceux qui sont venus les derniers et il fallait voir comme cela

---

pleased to be able to avoid that butchery, the responsibility for which he would have had to bear ; and during the whole time of the retreat —which he directed personally, not wishing to cross (the Danube) before the last of the soldiers—which took place with remarkable order and exactitude, he was gayer than he has ever been. What contributed much to his good humour, was the emigration of nearly 7000 Bulgarian families, whom we took with us as a reminder of the ferocity of the Turks : a ferocity in which, in spite of my incredulity, I was obliged to believe. As soon as we quitted the different Bulgarian villages we had occupied, the Turks returned to them, and except women young enough for a harem, they made a clean sweep of all that was in them. There was one village to which I went from the camp for milk and fruit, which had been exterminated in this way. So, as soon as the Prince let the Bulgarians know that those who wished to, could cross the Danube with our army and could become Russian subjects, the whole country rose, and with their wives, children, horses and cattle, came to the bridge : but as it was impossible to take them all, the Prince was obliged to refuse the last arrivals, and you should have seen how it grieved him to do so. He

le chagrinait. Il recevait toutes les députations qui venaient de ces pauvres gens, il causait avec chacun d'eux, tâchait de leur expliquer l'impossibilité de la chose, leur proposait de passer sans leurs chariots et leur bétail et en se chargeant de leurs moyens de subsistence jusqu'à ce qu'ils arrivassent en Russie, payant de sa propre bourse des vaisseaux particuliers pour les transporter, en un mot faisant tout son possible pour faire du bien à ces gens.

Oui, chère tante, je voudrais bien que votre prophétie se réalise. La chose que j'ambitionne le plus, est d'être l'aide de camp d'un homme comme lui que j'aime et que j'estime du plus profond de mon cœur. Adieu, chère et bonne tante; je baise vos mains.

The army retired to Bucharest, and here, at an officers' ball, Tolstoy seized an opportunity to beg Gortchakóf to have him transferred to where service would be most active.

The retreat from Silistria took place at the end of June, and on 2nd August we find Tolstoy starting for Russia. On the journey he fell ill and had to lie up in hospital. On 13th November in Kishinéf he renewed his application for an appointment in the Crimea, and was ordered to Sevastopol, which he reached on the 20th of that month.[1]

---

received all the deputations which came from these poor folk, and spoke with them all: trying to explain the impossibility of the matter, offering to let them cross without their carts and cattle, charging himself with their support till they could reach Russia, and out of his own purse paying for private ships to transport them; in a word, doing his very best for the welfare of these people.

Yes, dear Aunt, I should much like your prophecy to come true. What I desire most is to be aide-de-camp to such a man as he, whom I love and esteem from the bottom of my heart. Adieu, dear and kind Aunt. I kiss your hands.

---

[1] In this chapter the dates, when possible, are given new style (12 days later than the Russian style), in order that they may tally with English accounts of the Crimean war.

The situation there, at this time, was the following. The Allies had landed in the Crimea to the north of Sevastopol on 14th September, and had defeated the Russian army under Ménshikof on the 20th ^{1854} at Alma. Instead of marching straight into the town, which was almost undefended, they had then gone round and encamped on the south side, where they remained inactive till 17th October, by which time Todleben, an engineer of rare genius, had thrown up earthworks and mounted guns (many of them taken from the Russian ships Ménshikof sank at the entrance to the Roadstead). Ménshikof himself had practically abandoned the town, withdrawing the bulk of his army northward; but the situation was saved by the patriotism of just that section of the Russian forces which had been least exposed to the deadening influence of Nicholas the First's militarism,—namely by the officers and men of the fleet. Inspired by the example of the heroic Admiral Kornílof (who lost his life during the siege) they rallied to the defence with a courageous devotion seldom paralleled. Their example awoke enthusiasm throughout Russia and compelled Ménshikof to supply reinforcements, which enabled the town to hold out for eleven months, in spite of the great superiority of the Allies in rifles, artillery and the modern equipments of war generally.

Tolstoy reached Sevastopol when the defence was already fully organised, and when (in spite of the repulse experienced by the Russians at Inkerman) the garrison had gained confidence in their powers of resistance, and had settled down to a dogged defence.

Of the hospitals, in which the wounded saw one another's limbs amputated while waiting their own turn; of the staff officers, who managed to amuse themselves pretty well during the siege; of the commissariat officers, flourishing amid the general havoc; as well as of the line- and non-commissioned officers and privates, upon whom the greatest hardships fell, Tolstoy gives vivid glimpses in the Sketches he wrote during the siege.

A fortnight after his arrival he writes, from somewhere outside the town, to his brother Sergius, apologising for not having sent him a letter sooner, and adds :

So much have I learnt, experienced, and felt this year that I positively do not know what to begin to describe, nor how to describe it as I wish to. . . . Silistria is now ancient history, and we have Sevastopol, of which I suppose you all read with beating hearts, and where I was four days ago. Well, how can I tell you all I saw there, and where I went and what I did, and what the prisoners and wounded French and English say ; and *whether it hurts them and hurts very much*,[1] and what heroes our enemies are, especially the English ? I will tell all that later at Yásnaya or at Pirogóvo ; and you will learn much of it from me through the press. How this will happen, I will explain later ; but now let me give you an idea of the position of affairs in Sevastopol. The town is besieged from one side, the south, where we had no fortifications when the enemy approached it. Now we have on that side more than 500 heavy guns, and several lines of earthworks, positively impregnable. I spent a week in the fortress, and to the last day used to lose my way among that labyrinth of batteries, as in a wood. More than three weeks ago the enemy advanced his trenches at one place to within 200 yards, but gets no further. When he makes the smallest advance he is overwhelmed with a hailstorm of shot and shell.

The spirit of the army is beyond all description. In the times of ancient Greece there was not such heroism. Kornílof, making the round of the troops, instead of greeting them with, ' Good health to you, lads ! ' says : ' If you have to die, lads, will you die ? ' and the troops shout, ' We 'll die, Your Excellency ! Hurrah ! ' and they do not say it for effect. On every face one saw that it was not jest but earnest ; and 22,000 men have already fulfilled the promise.

---

[1] This must refer to some family joke, as it occurs in other letters home, apropos of people who were killed.

A wounded soldier, almost dying, told me they captured the 24th French Battery but were not reinforced; and he wept aloud. A Company of Marines nearly mutinied because they were to be withdrawn from batteries in which they had been exposed to shell-fire for thirty days. The soldiers extract the fuses from the shells. Women carry water to the bastions for the soldiers. Many are killed and wounded. The priests with their crosses go to the bastions and read prayers under fire. In one brigade, the 24th, more than 160 wounded men would not leave the front. It is a wonderful time! Now, however, after the 24th, we have quieted down; it has become splendid in Sevastopol. The enemy hardly fires, and all are convinced that he will not take the town; and it is really impossible. . . . I have not yet succeeded in being in action even once; but thank God that I have seen these people and live in this glorious time. The bombardment of the 5th [17 October, n.s.] remains the most brilliant and glorious feat not only in the history of Russia, but in the history of the world. More than 1500 cannon were in action for two days against the town, and not only did not cause it to capitulate, but did not silence one two-hundredth part of our batteries. Though, I suppose, this campaign is unfavourably regarded in Russia, our descendants will place it above all others; do not forget that we, with equal or even inferior forces, and armed only with bayonets, and with the worst troops in the Russian army (such as the 6th corps) are fighting a more numerous enemy aided by a fleet, armed with 3000 cannon, excellently supplied with rifles and with their best troops. I do not even mention the superiority of their Generals.

Only our army could hold its ground and conquer (we shall yet conquer, of that I am convinced) under such circumstances. You should see the French and English prisoners (especially the latter): they are each one better than the other—morally and physically fine fellows. The Cossacks say it is even a pity to cut them down, and alongside of them you should see some Chasseurs or others of ours : small, lousy, and shrivelled up.

Now I will tell you how you will get printed news from me of the deeds of these lousy and shrivelled heroes. In our artillery staff, consisting, as I think I wrote you, of very good and worthy men, a project has been started for publishing a military newspaper, in order to maintain a good spirit in the army—a cheap paper (at Rs. 3) and popularly written, so that the soldiers may read it. We have drawn up a plan and submitted it to the Prince. He likes the idea very much, and has submitted the project and a specimen sheet which we also wrote, for the Emperor's sanction. I and Stolýpin [1] are advancing the money for the publication. I have been chosen joint editor with a Mr. Konstantínof, who published *The Caucasus*, a man experienced in such work. The paper will publish descriptions of the battles (but not such dry and mendacious ones as other papers) courageous deeds, biographies, and obituaries of good men, especially the unknown ; military stories, soldiers' songs, and popular articles on engineering, artillery, etc. This plan pleases me very much : in the first place, I like the work ; and secondly, I hope the paper will be useful and not quite bad. It is as yet merely a project, until we know the Emperor's reply, about which I confess I have my fears. In the specimen sheet sent to Petersburg, we rashly inserted two articles, one by me and one by Rostóvtsef, not quite orthodox. For this business I want Rs. 1500, which I have asked Valeryán to send me.

I, thank God, am well, and live happily and pleasantly since I returned from Turkey. In general, my army service divides up into two periods : beyond the frontier—horrid : I was ill, poor, and lonely. This side of the frontier—I am well and have good friends, though I am still poor : money simply runs away.

As to writing, I do not write ; but, as Aunty teases me by saying, ' I test myself.' One thing disquiets me : this is the fourth year I live without female society ; and I may become quite coarse and unsuited for family life, which I so enjoy.

A few days later his battery was moved to Simferópol, a town lying to the north of Sevastopol, beyond the sphere of actual fighting.

---

[1] Father of the present (1908) Premier of Russia.

On 6th January (o.s.) he wrote to his Aunt: 1855

* On ne se bat plus en rase campagne, à cause de l'hiver qui est extraordinairement rigoureux, surtout à présent ; mais le siège dure toujours. . . . J'avais parlé je crois d'une occupation que j'avais en vue et qui me souriait beaucoup ; à présent que la chose est décidée, je puis le dire. J'avais l'idée de fonder un journal militaire. Ce projet auquel j'ai travaillé avec le concours de beaucoup de gens très distingués fut approuvé par le prince et envoyé à la décision de sa Majesté, mais l'empereur a refusé.

Cette déconfiture, je vous l'avoue, m'a fait une peine infinie et a beaucoup changé mes plans. Si Dieu veut que la campagne de Crimée finisse bien et si je ne reçois pas une place dont je sois content, et qu'il n'y ait pas de guerre en Russie, je quitterai l'armée pour aller à Pétersbourg à l'académie militaire. Ce plan m'est venu, 1° parce que je voudrais ne pas abandonner la littérature dont il m'est impossible de m'occuper dans cette vie de camp, et 2° parce qu'il me paraît que je commence à devenir ambitieux, pas ambitieux, mais je voudrais faire du bien et pour le faire il faut être plus qu'un Sub-Lieutenant ; 3° parce que je vous verrai tous et tous mes amis.

---

* There is no more fighting in the open country on account of the winter, which is extraordinarily rigorous, particularly just now ; but the siege still goes on. . . . I think I have mentioned an occupation I had in view, which promised very well—as I may say, now that it is settled. I had the idea of founding a military newspaper. This project, at which I worked with the co-operation of many very distinguished men, was approved by the Prince and submitted to His Majesty for his consent, but he has refused.

This disappointment has, I confess, distressed me greatly, and has much altered my plans. If God wills that the Crimean campaign should end well, and if I do not receive an appointment that satisfies me, and if there is no war in Russia, I shall leave the army and go to Petersburg to the Military Academy. I have formed this plan, (1) because I do not want to abandon literature, at which it is impossible to work amid this camp life ; (2) because it seems to me that I am becoming ambitious : not ambitious, but I want to do some good, and to do it one must be something more than a Sub-Lieutenant, and (3) because I shall see you all and all my friends.

In May he wrote again to his brother:

From Kishinéf on 1st November (o.s.), I petitioned to be sent to the Crimea, partly in order to see this war, and partly to break away from Serzhpoutóvsky's staff, which I did not like, but most of all from patriotism, of which at that time, I confess, I had a bad attack. I did not ask for any special appointment, but left it to those in authority to dispose of my fate. In the Crimea I was appointed to a battery in Sevastopol itself, where I passed a month very pleasantly amid simple, good companions, who are specially good in time of real war and danger. In December our battery was removed to Simferópol, and there I spent 6 weeks in a squire's comfortable house, riding into Simferópol to dance and play the piano with young ladies, and in hunting wild goats on the Tchatyrdag [the highest point of the chain of mountains running across the southern part of the Crimea] in company with officials. In January there was a fresh shuffling of officers, and I was removed to a battery encamped on the banks of the Belbék, 7 miles from Sevastopol. There I got into hot water: the nastiest set of officers in the battery; a Commander who, though good-hearted, was violent and coarse; no comforts, and it was cold in the earth huts. Not a single book, nor a single man with whom one could talk; and there I received the Rs. 1500 [=about £180 at that time] for the newspaper, sanction for which had already been refused; and there I lost Rs. 2500, and thereby proved to all the world that I am still an empty fellow, and though the previous circumstances may be taken into account in mitigation, the case is still a very, very bad one. In March it became warmer, and a good fellow, an excellent man, Brenévsky, joined the battery. I began to recover myself; and on 1 April, at the very time of the bombardment, the battery was moved to Sevastopol, and I quite recovered myself. There, till 15 May (o.s.) I was in serious danger, i.e. for four days at a time, at intervals of eight days, I was in charge of a battery in the 4th Bastion; but it was spring and the weather was excellent, there was abundance of impressions and of people, all the comforts of life, and we formed a capital circle of well-bred fellows; so that those six weeks will remain among my pleasantest re-

collections. On 15 May Gortchakóf, or the Commander of the
Artillery, took it into his head to entrust me with the formation
and command of a mountain platoon at Belbék, 14 miles from
Sevastopol, with which arrangement I am up to the present
extremely well satisfied in many respects.

The transfer of Tolstoy from Sevastopol to Belbék was
not, as he supposed when he wrote this letter, a whim of
Gortchakóf's or of the Commander of the Artillery, but a
result of his having written the first of his three sketches
of the siege of Sevastopol, *Sevastopol in December*. The
article, though not published in the *Contemporary* till
June, had been read in proof by the Emperor Alexander II
[Nicholas had died 2nd March, n.s.], and had caused
him to give instructions to 'take care of the life of
that young man,' with the result that Tolstoy was
removed from Sevastopol. The Dowager Empress Alexándra Fédorovna also read the story and, it is said, wept
over it.

It was, perhaps, at this time (though I am not sure of
the date) that Tolstoy found himself obliged to consent to
the sale of the large wooden house in which he had been
born, for the wretched price of 5000 'assignation' roubles
(about £170). The house was taken to pieces, and
removed to the estate of the purchaser, where it still stands,
though not now in use.

Apropos of the above letter it should be mentioned that
the Fourth Bastion was the one English writers call 'the
Flagstaff Bastion.' It formed the southernmost point of
the fortifications, as a glance at the accompanying map will
show, and it was for a long time the point exposed to the
fiercest fire.

Throughout the siege Tolstoy was accompanied by
Alexis, one of the four serfs presented to the young
Tolstoys when they entered the University. This man
(who figures in more than one of Tolstoy's works under

the name of Alyósha) brought him his rations to the bastion, a duty involving considerable danger. What the

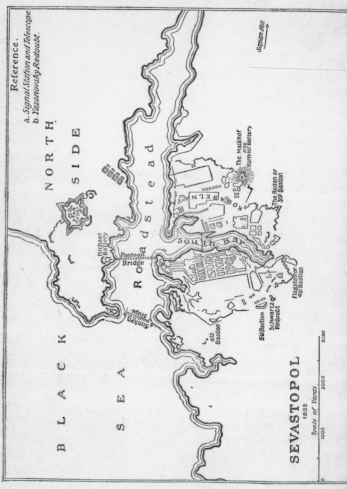

bastions were like in the first months of the siege, we learn from the following passages in the first part of *Sevastopol*:

. . . You want to get quickly to the bastions, especially to

that Fourth Bastion about which you have been told so many
and such different tales. When any one says, ' I am going to the
Fourth Bastion,' a slight agitation or a too marked indifference is
always noticeable in him; if men are joking they say, 'You
should be sent to the Fourth Bastion.' When you meet some
one carried on a stretcher, and ask, ' Where from ? ' the answer
usually is, ' From the Fourth Bastion.' . . .

. . . Beyond this barricade the houses on both sides of the
street are unoccupied : there are no signboards, the doors are
boarded up, the windows smashed ; here a corner of the walls
is knocked down, and there a roof is broken in. The buildings
look like old veterans who have borne much sorrow and priva-
tion ; they even seem to gaze proudly and somewhat contemptuously at you. On the road you stumble over cannon-balls
that lie about, and into holes full of water, made in the stony
ground by bombs. You meet and overtake detachments of
soldiers, Cossacks, officers, and occasionally a woman or a child
—only it will not be a woman wearing a bonnet, but a sailor's
wife wearing an old cloak and soldier's boots. Farther along
the same street, after you have descended a little slope, you
will notice that there are now no houses, but only ruined walls
in strange heaps of bricks, boards, clay and beams, and before
you, up a steep hill, you see a black untidy space cut up by
ditches. This space you are approaching is the Fourth Bastion.
. . Here you will meet still fewer people and no women at
all, the soldiers walk briskly by, traces of blood may be seen
in the road, and you are sure to meet four soldiers carrying a
stretcher, and on the stretcher probably a pale, yellow face and
blood-stained overcoat. . . .

The whiz of cannon-ball or bomb near by, impresses you
unpleasantly as you ascend the hill, and you at once understand the meaning of the sounds very differently from when
they reached you in the town. . . . You have hardly gone a
little way up, when bullets begin to whiz past you right and
left, and you will perhaps consider whether you had not better
walk inside the trench which runs parallel to the road ; but the
trench is full of such yellow, liquid, stinking mud, more than
knee deep, that you are sure to choose the road, especially as
everybody keeps to the road. After walking a couple of hundred

H

yards, you come to a muddy place much cut up, surrounded by gabions, cellars, platforms, and dug-outs, and on which large cast-iron cannon are mounted, and cannon-balls lie piled in orderly heaps. All seems placed without any aim, connection, or order. Here a group of sailors are sitting in the battery; here, in the middle of the open space, half sunk in mud, lies a shattered cannon; and there a foot-soldier is crossing the battery, drawing his feet with difficulty out of the sticky mud. Everywhere, on all sides and all about, you see bomb-fragments, unexploded bombs, cannon-balls, and various traces of an encampment, all sunk in the liquid, sticky mud. You think you hear the thud of a cannon-ball not far off, and you seem to hear the different sounds of bullets all around—some humming like bees, some whistling, and some rapidly flying past with a shrill screech like the string of some instrument. You hear the awful boom of a shot which sends a shock all through you, and seems most dreadful.

'So this is it, the Fourth Bastion! This is that terrible, truly dreadful spot!' So you think, experiencing a slight feeling of pride and a strong feeling of suppressed fear. But you are mistaken; this is still not the Fourth Bastion. This is only the Yazónovsky Redoubt—comparatively a very safe and not at all dreadful place. To get to the Fourth Bastion you must turn to the right, along that narrow trench, where a foot-soldier, stooping down, has just passed. In this trench you may again meet men with stretchers, and perhaps a sailor or a soldier with spades. You will see the mouths of mines, dug-outs into which only two men can crawl, and there you will see the Cossacks of the Black Sea Battalions, changing their boots, eating, smoking their pipes, and, in short, living. And you will see again the same stinking mud, the traces of camp life, and cast-iron refuse of every shape and form. When you have gone some three hundred steps more, you come out at another battery—a flat space with many holes, surrounded with gabions filled with earth, and cannons on platforms, and the whole walled in with earthworks. Here you will perhaps see four or five soldiers playing cards under shelter of the breastworks; and a naval officer, noticing that you are a stranger and inquisitive, is pleased to show you his 'household' and everything that can interest you. . . . He will tell you (but only if you ask) about the bombardment on the 5th of October; will tell you how only one gun in his battery remained usable and only eight gunners were left of the whole crew, and how, all the same, next morning, the 6th, he fired all his guns. He will tell you how a bomb dropped into one of the dug-outs and knocked over eleven sailors; he will show you from an embrasure the enemy's batteries and trenches, which are here not more than seventy-five to eighty-five yards distant. I am afraid, though, that when you lean out of the embrasure to have a look at the enemy, you will, under the influence of the whizzing bullets, not see anything; but if you do see anything, you will be much surprised to find that this whitish stone wall which is so near you, and from which puffs of white smoke keep bursting—that this white wall is the enemy: is *him*, as the soldiers and sailors say.

It is even very likely that the naval officer, from vanity, or merely for a little recreation, will wish to show you some firing. 'Call the gunner and crew to the cannon'; and fourteen sailors —clattering their hob-nailed boots on the platform, one putting his pipe in his pocket, another still chewing a rusk—quickly and cheerfully man the gun and begin loading.

Suddenly the most fearful roar strikes not only your ears but your whole being, and makes you shudder all over. It is followed by the whistle of the departing ball, and a thick cloud of powder-smoke envelops you, the platform, and the moving black figures of the sailors. You will hear various comments by the sailors concerning this shot of ours, and you will notice their animation, the evidences of a feeling which you had not perhaps expected: the feeling of animosity and thirst for vengeance which lies hidden in each man's soul. You will hear joyful exclamations: 'It's gone right into the embrasure! It's killed two, I think. . . . There, they're carrying them off!' 'And now *he's* riled, and will send one this way,' some one remarks; and really, soon after, you will see before you a flash and some smoke; the sentinel standing on the breastwork will call out 'Ca-n-non,' and then a ball will whiz past you and squash into the earth, throwing out a circle of stones and mud. The commander of the battery will be irritated by this shot, and will give orders to fire another and another cannon, the enemy will reply in like manner, and you will experience interesting sensations and see interesting sights. The sentinel will again call 'Cannon!' and you will have the same sound and shock, and the mud will be splashed round as before. Or he will call out 'Mortar!' and you will hear the regular and rather pleasant whistle—which it is difficult to connect with the thought of anything dreadful—of a bomb; you will hear this whistle coming nearer and faster towards you, then you will see a black ball, feel the shock as it strikes the ground, and will hear the ringing explosion. The bomb will fly apart into whizzing and shrieking fragments, stones will rattle into the air, and you will be bespattered with mud.

At these sounds you will experience a strange feeling of mingled pleasure and fear. At the moment you know the shot is flying towards you, you are sure to imagine that this shot will kill you, but a feeling of pride will support you and no one will know of the knife that is cutting your heart. But when the shot has flown past and has not hit you, you revive, and, though only for a moment, a glad, inexpressibly joyous feeling seizes you, so that you feel some peculiar delight in the danger—in this game of life and death—and wish that bombs and balls would fall nearer and nearer to you.

But again the sentinel, in his loud, thick voice, shouts 'Mortar!' again a whistle, a fall, an explosion; and mingled with the last you are startled by the groans of a man. You approach the wounded man just as the stretchers are brought. Covered with blood and dirt he presents a strange, not human, appearance. Part of the sailor's breast has been torn away. . . .

'That's the way with seven or eight every day,' the naval officer remarks to you, answering the look of horror on your face, and he yawns as he rolls another yellow cigarette.

As the siege progressed, things became worse, and in the last part of *Sevastopol* Tolstoy, after telling how one of the characters felt satisfied with himself, continues:

This feeling, however, was quickly shaken by a sight he came upon in the twilight while looking for the Commander of the

bastion. Four sailors stood by the breastwork holding by its
arms and legs the bloody corpse of a man without boots or coat,
swinging it before heaving it over. (It was found impossible in
some parts to clear away the corpses from the bastions, and
they were, therefore, thrown out into the ditch, so as not to
be in the way at the batteries.) Volódya felt stunned for a
moment when he saw the body bump on the top of the breastwork and then roll down into the ditch, but luckily for him
the Commander of the bastion met him just then and gave him
his orders, as well as a guide to show him the way to the
battery and to the bomb-proof assigned to his men. We will
not speak of all the dangers and disenchantments our hero
lived through that evening; how—instead of the firing he was
used to, amid conditions of perfect exactitude and order which
he had expected to meet with here also,—he found two injured
mortars, one with its mouth battered in by a ball, the other
standing on the splinters of its shattered platform; how he
could not get workmen to mend the platform till the morning;
how not a single charge was of the weight specified in the
Handbook; how two of the men under him were wounded,
and how he was twenty times within a hair's-breadth of death.
Fortunately a gigantic gunner, a seaman who had served with
the mortars since the commencement of the siege, had been
appointed to assist Volódya, and convinced him of the possibility of using the mortars. By the light of a lantern, this
gunner showed him all over the battery as he might have
shown him over his own kitchen-garden, and undertook to have
everything right by the morning. The bomb-proof to which
his guide led him was an oblong hole dug in the rocky ground,
25 cubic yards in size and covered with oak beams nearly $2\frac{1}{2}$
feet thick. He and all his soldiers installed themselves in it.

It was during one of his sojourns in the Fourth Bastion,
that Tolstoy noted down in his Diary the following
prayer :

Lord, I thank Thee for Thy continual protection. How
surely Thou leadest me to what is good. What an insignificant
creature should I be, if Thou abandoned me! Leave me not,

Lord; give me what is necessary, not for the satisfaction of my poor aspirations, but that I may attain to the eternal, vast, unknown aim of existence, which lies beyond my ken.

It was due to Tolstoy's own choice that he was exposed to the rough life of the bastion, for Prince Gortchakóf, at whose house he was a constant visitor, had offered him an appointment on his staff. This offer, which at Silistria he had so ardently desired, Tolstoy declined, having come to the conclusion, subsequently expressed in his writings, that the influence exercised by the staff on the conduct of a war is always pernicious! This opinion not only influenced his conduct, and expressed itself in his novels, but fitted into a general view of life he ultimately arrived at, a view the consequences of which must be dealt with in the sequel to this work. For the moment, let it suffice to mention that whereas he shows a keen appreciation of Admiral Kornílof's achievement in rousing the spirit of the garrison, he nowhere praises Todleben's achievement in organising the defence of the town and improvising that 'labyrinth of batteries' in which Tolstoy used constantly to lose his way. He says, for instance:

Now you have seen the defenders of Sevastopol. . . . The principal, joyous thought you have brought away is a conviction of the strength of the Russian people; and this conviction you gained, not by looking at all these traverses, breastworks, cunningly interlaced trenches, mines and cannon, one on top of another, of which you could make nothing; but from the eyes, words and actions—in short, from seeing what is called the 'spirit' of the defenders of Sevastopol.

To everything a man can do off his own bat and by his own effort, Tolstoy is keenly alive and sympathetic; but when it comes to a complex, co-ordinated plan, involving the subordination of many parts to one whole, he is suspicious or even hostile. Had he remained a subordinate officer, or even a novelist, it would not have been specially necessary to draw attention to this peculiarity; but that we may understand his later teachings, it is important to note all the roots of feeling from which they grew, and this one among the rest.

To get on however with our tale. One evening, while Tolstoy was sitting with the adjutants of Count Osten-Sáken, Commander of the Garrison, Prince S. S. Ouroúsof, a brave officer and first-rate chess player (he took part in the International Chess Tournament of 1862, in London) and a friend of Tolstoy's, entered the room and wished to speak to the General. An adjutant took him to Osten-Sáken's room, and ten minutes later Ouroúsof passed out again, looking very glum. After he had gone, the adjutant explained that Ouroúsof had come to suggest that a challenge should be sent to the English to play a game of chess for the foremost trench in front of the Fifth Bastion: a trench that had changed hands several times and had already cost some hundreds of lives. Osten-Sáken had naturally refused to issue the challenge.

On 16th August Tolstoy took part in the battle of the Tchérnaya (Black River) in which the Sardinian contingent, which had arrived in May to reinforce the Allies, much distinguished itself. This last attempt to relieve Sevastopol failed, as its forerunners had done. Three days later Tolstoy wrote to his brother saying that he had not been hurt, and that 'I did nothing, as my mountain artillery was not called on to fire.'

The end of the siege was now approaching, and on 8th September Tolstoy, having volunteered for service in Sevastopol, reached the Star Fort on the North Side of the Roadstead just in time to witness the capture of the Maláhof by the French, as he has described in *Sevastopol in August*.[1]

On the North Side of the Roadstead, at the Star Fort, near noon, two sailors stood on the 'telegraph' mound; one of

---

[1] The *8th September*, new style, was *24th August*, old style.

them, an officer, was looking at Sevastopol through the fixed telescope. Another officer, accompanied by a Cossack, had just ridden up to join him at the big Signal-post. . . . Along the whole line of fortifications, but especially on the high ground on the left side, appeared, several at a time, with lightnings that at times flashed bright even in the noonday sun, puffs of thick, dense, white smoke, that grew, taking various shapes and appearing darker against the sky. These clouds, showing now here now there, appeared on the hills, on the enemy's batteries, in the town, and high up in the sky. The reports of explosions never ceased, but rolled together and rent the air.

Towards noon the puffs appeared more and more rarely, and the air vibrated less with the booming.

'I say, the Second Bastion does not reply at all now!' said the officer on horseback; 'it is quite knocked to pieces. Terrible!'

'Yes, and the Maláhof, too, sends hardly one shot in reply to three of theirs,' said he who was looking through the telescope. 'Their silence provokes me! They are shooting straight into the Kornílof Battery, and it does not reply.'

'But look there! I told you that they always cease the bombardment about noon. It's the same to-day. Come, let's go to lunch; they'll be waiting for us already. What's the good of looking?'

'Wait a bit!' answered the one who had possession of the telescope, looking very eagerly towards Sevastopol.

'What is it? What?'

'A movement in the entrenchments, thick columns advancing.'

'Yes! They can be seen even without a glass, marching in columns. The alarm must be given,' said the seaman.

'Look! look! They've left the trenches!'

And, really, with the naked eye one could see what looked like dark spots moving down the hill from the French batteries across the valley to the bastions. In front of these spots dark stripes were already visibly approaching our line. On the bastions white cloudlets burst in succession as if chasing one another. The wind brought a sound of rapid small-arm firing, like the beating of rain against a window. The dark stripes were moving in the midst of the smoke and came nearer and nearer. The sounds of firing, growing stronger and stronger, mingled in a prolonged, rumbling peal. Puffs of smoke rose more and more often, spread rapidly along the line, and at last formed one lilac cloud (dotted here and there with little faint lights and black spots) which kept curling and uncurling; and all the sounds blent into one tremendous clatter.

'An assault!' said the naval officer, turning pale and letting the seaman look through the telescope.

Cossacks galloped along the road, some officers rode by, the Commander-in-Chief passed in a carriage with his suite. Every face showed painful excitement and expectation.

'It's impossible they can have taken it,' said the mounted officer.

'By God, a standard! . . . Look! look!' said the other, panting, and he walked away from the telescope: 'A French standard on the Maláhof!'

The point from which the officer in the story, and Tolstoy himself in reality, watched the assault through a telescope is the spot marked 'a' on the map on page 112.

The loss of the Maláhof rendered the further defence of the town impossible, and the following night the Russians blew up and destroyed such munitions of war as they could not remove from the bastions. Tolstoy was deputed to clear the Fifth and Sixth Bastions before they were abandoned to the Allies. When telling me this he added, 'The non-commissioned officers could have done the work just as well without me.' While the destruction was proceeding, the Russian forces crossed the Roadstead by a pontoon bridge which had been constructed during the siege. The town south of the Roadstead was abandoned, and the defenders established themselves on the North Side, where they remained till peace was concluded in February 1856.

After the retreat, Tolstoy was given the task of collating the twenty or more reports of the action from the Artillery

Commanders.   This experience of how war is recorded
produced in him that supreme contempt for detailed
military histories which he so often expressed in later years.
He says :

I regret that I did not keep a copy of those reports.   They
were an excellent example of that naïve, inevitable kind of
military falsehood, out of which descriptions are compiled.   I
think many of those comrades of mine who drew up those
reports, will laugh on reading these lines, remembering how,
by order of their Commander, they wrote what they could
not know.

Carrying among other despatches the report he had
himself compiled, Tolstoy was sent as Courier to Petersburg ; and this terminated his personal experience of war.
He was still only Sub-Lieutenant, his hopes of promotion
had come to nothing in consequence of a suspicion that he
was the author of some soldiers' songs which were sung
throughout the army at this time.   No translation can do
justice to these slangy, topical satires ; but that the reader
may have some idea of them, my wife has put into English
the following stanzas :

> In September, the eighth day,[1]
> From the French we ran away,
> > For our Faith and Tsar !
> > For our Faith and Tsar !
>
> Admiral Alexander,[2] he
> Sank our vessels in the sea
> > In the waters deep,
> > In the waters deep.

[1] The Battle of Alma, fought on 8th September, old style = 20th September,
new style.
[2] Prince Alexander Ménshikof, who was Commander-in-Chief in the Crimea
till replaced by Gortchakóf.   Besides being diplomatist and General, he was
also an Admiral.   In the other verses he is nicknamed ' Ménshik.'

'Luck to all I wish,' he said then.
To Baktchiseráy [1] he sped then;
     'May you all be blowed!
     'May you all be blowed!'

Saint Arnaud [2] got out of sight;
And in manner most polite,
     Came round to our back,
     Came round to our back.

And on Tuesday, I'm afraid
Had no saint come to our aid,
     He'd have bagged us all,
     He'd have bagged us all.

Our Liprandi, it is true
Captured 'trenchments not a few,
     But to no avail!
     But to no avail!

Out of Kishinéf a force
Was expected: Foot and Horse,
     And at last they came,
     And at last they came.

Dannenberg was in command:
Strictly told to understand
     Not to spare his men,
     Not to spare his men.

.   .   .   .   .

Two Grand Dukes a visit paid:
But the French, quite undismayed,
     Blazed away with shells,
     Blazed away with shells.

---

[1] After the Battle of Alma, Ménshikof retreated northward to Baktchiseráy, almost abandoning Sevastopol.
[2] Saint Arnaud, the French Commander-in-Chief.

Some ten thousand men were shot:
From the Tsar *they* never got
        Any great reward!
        Any great reward!

Then the Prince [1] in anger spoke:
'Oh! our men are wretched folk:
        'Why, they've turned their backs!
        'Why, they've turned their backs!'

And in this great battle's flare
Heroes only two there were:
        The two Royal Dukes!
        The two Royal Dukes!

George's Crosses they were given
And to Petersburg were driven
        To be fêted there!
        To be fêted there!

All the priests with heads bent down
Prayed our God the French to drown,
        And there came a storm,
        And there came a storm!

There arose a dreadful gale,
But the French just shortened sail,
        And remained afloat!
        And remained afloat!

Winter came.   Sorties we made;
Many soldiers low were laid,
        Near those bags of sand,
        Near those bags of sand.[2]

----

[1] Prince Alexander Ménshikof.
[2] Bags of sand were used as temporary protection from behind which to
fire.

For re'nforcements Ménshik prayed ;
But the Tsar sent to his aid
    Only Osten-Sáken,
    Only Osten-Sáken.[1]

Ménshik, Admiral so wise,
To the Tsar writes and replies :
    ' Oh, dear Father Tsar,
    ' Oh, dear Father Tsar.

' Sáken is not worth a grain,
And your Royal youngsters twain [2]
    They 're no good at all !
    They 're no good at all !'

Royal wrath on Ménshik fell,
And the Tsar felt quite unwell
    At the next review,
    At the next review.

Straight to heaven he did fare
(Seems they wanted him up there)
    Not a whit too soon,
    Not a whit too soon !

As on his deathbed he lay ;
To his son [3] he this did say :
    'Now just you look out,
    'Now just you look out !'

And the son to Ménshik wrote :
'My dear Admiral, please note,
    You may go to hell,
    You may go to hell !'

[1] Count Osten-Sáken was sent to advise Ménshikof and to report to the Tsar on his operations.

[2] The Grand Dukes alluded to above.

[3] Alexander II, who succeeded Nicholas I on 2nd March (n.s.) 1855.

' And in place of you I 'll name
Gortchakóf, you know, the same
    Who fought 'gainst the Turks!
    Who fought 'gainst the Turks!'

' With few troops he 'll go ahead,
And a pair of breeches red
    Shall be his reward,
    Shall be his reward!'

As a matter of fact the responsibility for these songs, which gave satirical expression to the discontent then very generally felt, was not entirely Tolstoy's. They originated with a group of officers on the staff of Kryzhanóvsky, Commander of the Artillery, and some others (including Tolstoy) who used to meet at Kryzhanóvsky's rooms almost daily. One of this company used to preside at the piano, while the others stood round and improvised couplets. In such cases some one has usually to pay the piper, and that this one should have been Tolstoy, was a natural result both of the fact that he seems to have been the chief culprit, and of the attention his literary work was attracting at this time.

Another matter which appears to have done Tolstoy no good in the eyes of his superiors, was his refusal to fall in with a reprehensible practice which by long usage had become as well established as, for instance, among ourselves, is the purchase of peerages by contributions to Party funds.

Those in command of various divisions of the army, including the Commanders of Batteries, used to pay for various things, such as shoes for the horses, medicine, office expenses, and certain extras for the soldiers, for which no official allowance was made; and the way the money for this was obtained was by overestimating the cost and quantity of stores, and of the fodder required for the horses. The difference between the actual and estimated cost supplied a revenue which different Commanders used in different ways. Some spent it all for the good of the service, though in a manner not shown in the accounts ; others did not scruple to make private profit of it. Tolstoy, during his command of a battery, refused to take a balance of cash which had accumulated, and insisted on showing it in the accounts. He thereby evoked the displeasure of less scrupulous Commanders and called down upon himself a rebuke from General Kryzhanóvsky, who did not consider that it lay with a Sub-Lieutenant in temporary command, to attempt to upset so well-established a custom.

From his letters and memoirs we get clear indications of Tolstoy's feelings towards his brother officers ; his distaste for the common run of them, and his preference for those who were gentlemanly. Here and there, in memoirs and magazine articles, one finds records of the impression he in his turn produced on his companions. One of them relates :

How Tolstoy woke us all up in those hard times of war, with his stories and his hastily composed couplets ! He was really the soul of our battery. When he was with us we did not notice how time flew, and there was no end to the general gaiety. . . . When the Count was away, when he trotted off to Simferópol, we all hung our heads. He would vanish for one, two or three days. . . . At last he would return—the very picture of a prodigal son ! sombre, worn out, and dissatisfied with himself. . . . Then he would take me aside, quite apart, and would begin his confessions. He would tell me all : how he had caroused, gambled, and where he had spent his days and nights ; and all the time, if you will believe me, he would condemn himself and suffer as though he were a real criminal. He was so distressed that it was pitiful to see him. That's the sort of man he was. In a word, a queer fellow, and, to tell the truth, one I could not quite understand. He was however a rare comrade, a most honourable fellow, and a man one can never forget !

One who entered the battery just after Tolstoy left it, says he was remembered there as an excellent rider, first-rate company, and an athlete who, lying on the floor, could let a man weighing thirteen stone be placed on his hands, and could lift him up by straightening his arms. At a tug-of-war (played not with a rope, but with a stick) no one could beat him ; and he left behind him the recollection of many witty anecdotes told in that masterly style of which he never lost the knack.

His private Diary bears witness to the constantly renewed struggle that went on within him, as well as to his profound dissatisfaction with himself. Here, for instance, is an estimate entered in his Diary at the commencement of the war, while he was still at Silistria :

I have no modesty. That is my great defect. What am I ? One of four sons of a retired lieutenant-colonel, left at seven years of age an orphan under the guardianship of women and strangers ; having neither a social nor a scholarly education, and becoming my own master at seventeen; with no large means, no social position, and, above all, without principle ; a man who has disorganised his own affairs to the last extremity, and has passed the best years of his life without aim or pleasure ; and finally who having banished himself to the Caucasus to escape his debts and more especially his bad habits —and having there availed himself of some connection that had existed between his father and the general in command—passed to the army of the Danube at twenty-six, as a Sub-Lieutenant almost without means except his pay (for what means he has he ought to employ to pay what he still owes) without influential friends, ignorant of how to live in society, ignorant of the service, lacking practical capacity, but with immense self-esteem—such is my social position. Let us see what I myself am like.

I am ugly, awkward, uncleanly, and lack society education. I am irritable, a bore to others, not modest, intolerant, and as shame-faced as a child. I am almost an ignoramus. What I do know, I have learned anyhow, by myself, in snatches, without sequence, without a plan, and it amounts to very little. I am incontinent, undecided, inconstant and stupidly vain and vehement, like all characterless people. I am not brave. I am not methodical in life, and am so lazy that idleness has become an almost unconquerable habit of mine.

I am clever, but my cleverness has as yet not been thoroughly tested on anything; I have neither practical nor social nor business ability.

I am honest, that is to say, I love goodness, and have formed a habit of loving it, and when I swerve from it I am dissatisfied with myself and return to it gladly; but there is a thing I love more than goodness, and that is fame. I am so ambitious, and so little has this feeling been gratified, that should I have to choose between fame and goodness, I fear I may often choose the former.

Yes, I am not modest, and therefore I am proud at heart, though shame-faced and shy in society.

That is a grossly unfair estimate of himself, but shows just that sort of eager injustice to any one who fails to reach the high standard he sets up, that has always characterised him. His account is inaccurate in details. For instance, he was not seven, but nearly nine when his father died. He had not wrecked his affairs to the extent he suggests. Though his studies had been desultory, he had read widely, with a quick understanding and a retentive memory. He was master of the Russian, French and German languages, besides having some knowledge of English, Latin, Arabic, and Turco-Tartar. (Later in life he added a knowledge of Italian, Greek and Hebrew.) As for not yet having tested his cleverness : he had published stories for which the editor of the best Russian magazine paid him the rate accorded to the best-known writers ; while his awkwardness in society did not depend on ignorance ; on the contrary, he had grown up among people who paid much attention to manners, and he was himself gifted with social tact, which became plainly apparent as soon as he attained self-confidence. Any defect in his manners must have been merely a result of that nervous shyness natural to highly-strung, sensitive natures, conscious of powers of a kind society recognises but scantily. Yet, when all is said, his description gets home : over-emphatic and unfair, like much of his other writing, it still leaves you in no doubt as to what he meant, and hits the real points of weakness in the victim he is flaying.

On 5th March 1855 (old style) when he was just recovering from that fit of depression at Belbék which, as already mentioned, drove him to gamble, he writes in his Diary :

A conversation about Divinity and Faith has suggested to me a great, a stupendous idea, to the realisation of which I feel myself capable of devoting my life. This idea is the founding of a new religion corresponding to the present state of mankind : the religion of Christianity, but purged of dogmas and mysticism : a practical religion, not promising future bliss, but giving bliss on earth. I understand that to accomplish this the conscious labour of generations will be needed. One generation will bequeath the idea to the next, and some day fanaticism or reason will accomplish it. *Deliberately* to promote the union of mankind by religion—that is the basic thought which, I hope, will dominate me.

In that passage one has, quite clearly stated before he was twenty-seven, the main idea which actuated Tolstoy from the age of fifty onwards. Already by the literary work he accomplished amid the bustle and excitement of the siege, he was half consciously moving in the direction that allured him. During the three months that elapsed between leaving Bucharest and reaching Sevastopol, he wrote part of *The Wood-Felling*, a sketch of an expedition such as he had taken part in in the Caucasus ; and during the siege of Sevastopol he wrote the first two parts of *Sevastopol* and began *Youth*, a sequel to *Childhood* and *Boyhood*.

It was *Sevastopol* that first brought European fame to Tolstoy. When, as already mentioned, *Sevastopol in December* appeared in the June *Contemporary*, the Emperor ordered it to be translated into ¹⁸⁵⁵ French. That same month Tolstoy completed and despatched *The Wood-Felling*; in July he sent off *Sevastopol in May*. Here once again the Censor exercised his malignant power, and Panáef wrote to Tolstoy from Petersburg:

In my letter delivered to you by Stolýpin, I wrote that your article has been passed by the Censor with unimportant alterations, and begged you not to be angry with me that I was obliged to add a few words at the end to soften. . . . 3000 copies of the article had already been printed off, when the Censor suddenly demanded it back, stopped the appearance of the number (so that our August number only appeared in Petersburg on 18 August) and submitted it to Poúshkin, President of the Committee of Censors. If you know Poúshkin, you will be able partly to guess what followed. He flew into a rage, was very angry with the Censor, and with me for submitting such an article to the Censor, and altered it with his own hand. . . . On seeing these alterations I was horror-struck, and wished not to print the article at all, but Poúshkin explained to me that I must print it in its present shape. There was no help for it, and your mutilated article will appear in the September number, but without your initials—which I could not bear to see attached to it after that. . . .

Now a word as to the impression your story produces on all to whom I have read it in its original form. Every one thinks it stronger than the first part, in its deep and delicate analysis of the emotions and feelings of people constantly face to face with death, and in the fidelity with which the types of the line-officers are caught, their encounters with the aristocrats, and the mutual relations of the two sets. In short, all is excellent, all is drawn in masterly fashion; but it is all so overspread with bitterness, is so keen, so venomous, so unsparing and so cheerless, that at the present moment when the scene of the story is almost sacred ground, it pains those who are at a distance from it; and the story may even produce a very unpleasant impression.

The Wood-Felling, with its dedication to Tourgénef, will also appear in September (Tourgénef begs me to thank you very, very much for thinking of him and paying him this attention). . . . In this story also (which passed three Censors: the Caucasian, the Military, and our Civil Censor) the types of officers have been tampered with, and unfortunately a little has been struck out.

Tolstoy's dedication of *The Wood-Felling* to Tourgénef proceeded from his admiration for that writer's *A Sportsman's Sketches,* which to the present time he continues to value very highly, considering Tourgénef's descriptions of Nature in that book not merely excellent, but inimitable by any one else.

Nekrásof wrote to Tolstoy in September, about *Sevastopol in August,* saying:

The revolting mutilation of your article quite upset me. Even now I cannot think of it without regret and rage. Your work will, of course, not be lost . . . it will always remain as proof of a strength able to utter such profound and sober truth under circumstances amid which few men would have retained it. It is just what Russian society now needs: the truth—the truth, of which, since Gógol's death, so little has remained in Russian literature. You are right to value that side of your gifts most of all. Truth—in such form as you have introduced it into our literature—is something completely new among us. I do not know another writer of to-day who so compels the reader to love him and sympathise heartily with him, as he to whom I now write; and I only fear lest time, the nastiness of life, and the deafness and dumbness that surround us, should do to you what it has done to most of us, and kill the energy without which there can be no writer—none, at least, such as Russia needs. You are young: changes are taking place which, let us hope, may end well, and perhaps a wide field lies before you. You are beginning in a way that compels the most cautious to let their expectations travel far. . . .

The Wood - Felling has passed the Censor pretty fairly, though from it also some valuable touches have disappeared. . . . In that sketch there are many astonishingly acute remarks, and it is all *new*, interesting, and to the point. Do not neglect such sketches. Of the common soldier our literature has as yet not spoken, except frivolously.

Tourgénef, writing from his estate at Spássky to Panáef, said :

Tolstoy's article about Sevastopol is wonderful ! Tears came into my eyes as I read it, and I shouted, Hurrah ! I am greatly flattered by his wish to dedicate his new tale to me. . . Here his article has produced a general furore.

By the side of these contemporary estimates one may set Kropótkin's appreciation written fifty years later :

All his powers of observation and war-psychology, all his deep comprehension of the Russian soldier, and especially of the plain un-theatrical hero who really wins the battles, and a profound understanding of that inner spirit of an army upon which depend success and failure : everything, in short, which developed into the beauty and the truthfulness of *War and Peace*, was already manifested in these sketches, which undoubtedly represented a new departure in war-literature the world over.

It is worth while to note the very different conclusions to which Kinglake, the historian of this war, and Tolstoy, its novelist, arrived. Kinglake holds the war to have been unnecessary, and attributes it chiefly to the unscrupulous ambition of Napoleon III ; yet he blames the Peace Party very severely for protesting against it, for had they not done so Nicholas, he thinks, would not have dared to act aggressively. Kinglake feels that negotiations between rulers and diplomatists are important, and that anything that prevents a Government from speaking with authority, makes for confusion and disaster.

Tolstoy, on the other hand (if I may anticipate and speak of conclusions not definitely expressed by him till much later), regards all war and preparation for war as

immoral, and wishes this conviction to become so strong
and so general that it will be impossible for any future
Napoleon to plunge five nations into war to gratify his
own ambition.

Kinglake understands things as they are, and knows
how easy it is to do harm with good intentions, but is
somewhat blind to the trend of human progress, and as
to what the aim before us should be. Tolstoy, on the
contrary, is chiefly concerned about the ultimate aim, and
about the state of mind of the individual. The actual
working of our political system and international relations
are things he ignores. The English writer sees clearly
what is, and cares little about what should be; the
Russian writer cares immensely about what should be, and
rather forgets that it can only be approached by slow and
difficult steps, to take which surefootedly, needs an
appreciation of things as they are.

Neither of them manages to say the word which would
synthesize their divergent views : namely, that no self-
respecting people should support or tolerate as rulers,
men who seek to gain national advantages by means not
strictly fair, honest and even generous. That is the real
key to the world's future peace. Kinglake's appeal to us
not to hamper the government that represents us, and
Tolstoy's appeal to us not to spend our lives in preparing
to slay our fellow men, can both be met in that way, and,
I think, in that way alone.

For an ambitious young officer actually engaged in a
war, related to the Commander-in-Chief, and favourably
noticed by the Emperor, even *partially* to express disapproval of war, was difficult; and Tolstoy has told me
that, contending with his desire to tell the truth about things
as he saw it, he was at the same time aware of another
feeling prompting him to say what was expected of him.

He, however, like the child in Andersen's story who sees
that the king has nothing on, when every one else is in
ecstasies over the magnificence of the monarch's robes, had

the gift of seeing things with his own eyes, as well as a
great gift of truthfulness. These were the qualities which
ultimately made him the greatest literary power of his
century; and in spite of his own hesitation and the
Censor's mutilations, we may still read the description he
then wrote of the truce in which the French and Russian
soldiers hobnobbed together in friendship, a description
closing with these words:

White flags are on the bastions and parallels; the flowery
valley is covered with corpses; the beautiful sun is sinking
towards the blue sea; and the undulating blue sea glitters in
the golden rays of the sun. Thousands of people crowd together, look at, speak to, and smile at one another. And these
people—Christians confessing the one great law of love and
self-sacrifice—seeing what they have done, do not at once fall
repentant on their knees before Him who has given them life
and laid in the soul of each a fear of death and a love of goodness and of beauty, and do not embrace like brothers with tears
of joy and happiness.

The white flags are lowered, again the engines of death and
suffering are sounding, again innocent blood flows, and the air
is filled with moans and curses.

In *Sevastopol*, and in Tennyson's *Charge of the Light
Brigade* (with its rhymes about 'hundred' and 'thun-
dered,' and its panegyric of those who knew it was not
their business to think, and at whom 'all the world
wondered'), we have two typical expressions of conflicting
views on war: the view of a man who knew it from the
classics and was Poet Laureate, and the view of a man who
was in the thick of it, and whose eyes were connected with
his brain.

Thirty-four years later Tolstoy wrote a Preface to a
fellow-officer's *Recollections of Sevastopol*. It could not
pass the Censor, but has been used as a Preface to his
own sketches of war in the English version of *Sevastopol*,
translated by my wife and myself, and I cannot conclude
this chapter better than by quoting a few sentences from it.

Speaking of the position of a young officer engaged in the Crimean war, he says:

To the first question that suggests itself to every one, Why did he do it? Why did he not cease, and go away?—the author does not reply. He does not say, as men said in olden times when they hated their enemies as the Jews hated the Philistines, that he hated the Allies; on the contrary, he here and there shows his sympathy for them as for brother men.

Nor does he speak of any passionate desire that the keys of the Church at Jerusalem should be in our hands, or even that our fleet should, or should not, exist. You feel as you read, that to him the life and death of men are not commensurable with questions of politics. And the reader feels that to the question: Why did the author act as he did?—there is only one answer; It was because I enlisted while still young, or before the war began, or because owing to inexperience I chanced to slip into a position from which I could not extricate myself without great effort. I was entrapped into that position, and when they obliged me to do the most unnatural actions in the world, to kill my brother men who had done me no harm, I preferred to do this rather than to suffer punishment and disgrace. . . . One feels that the author knows there is a law of God: love thy neighbour, and therefore do not kill him,—a law which cannot be repealed by any human artifice.

The merit of the book consists in that. It is a pity it is only felt, and not plainly and clearly expressed. Sufferings and deaths are described; but we are not told what caused them. Thirty-five years ago—even that was well, but now something more is needed. We should be told what it is that causes soldiers to suffer and to die,—that we may know, and understand, and destroy these causes.

'War! How terrible,' people say, 'is war, with its wounds, bloodshed, and deaths! We must organise a Red Cross Society to alleviate the wounds, sufferings and pains of death.' But, truly, what is dreadful in war is not the wounds, sufferings and deaths. The human race that has always suffered and died, should by this time be accustomed to suffering and death, and should not be aghast at them. Without war people die by famine, by inundations, and by epidemics. It is not suffering and death that are terrible, but it is that which allows people to inflict suffering and death. . . .

It is not the suffering and mutilation and death of man's body that most needs to be diminished,—but it is the mutilation and death of his soul. Not the *Red* Cross is needed, but the simple cross of Christ to destroy falsehood and deception. . . .

I was finishing this Preface when a cadet from the Military College came to see me. He told me that he was troubled by religious doubts. . . . He had read nothing of mine. I spoke cautiously to him of how to read the Gospels so as to find in them the answers to life's problems. He listened and agreed. Towards the end of our conversation I mention wine, and advised him not to drink. He replied : 'but in military service it is sometimes necessary.' I thought he meant necessary for health and strength, and I intended triumphantly to overthrow him by proofs from experience and science, but he continued : 'Why, at Geok-Tepe, for instance, when Skóbelef had to massacre the inhabitants, the soldiers did not wish to do it, but he had drink served out and then. . . .' Here are all the horrors of war—they are in this lad with his fresh young face, his little shoulder-straps (under which the ends of his hood are so neatly tucked), his well-cleaned boots, his naïve eyes, and with so perverted a conception of life.

This is the real horror of war !

What millions of Red Cross workers could heal the wounds that swarm in that remark—the result of a whole system of education !

CHIEF AUTHORITIES FOR CHAPTER IV

Birukof.
Behrs.
Bitovt.
Nekrasof's letters to Tolstoy, *Niva*, February 1898.
Also, Tolstoy's *Sevastopol*, and his
Preface to Ershof's *Recollections of Sevastopol*.
Kropotkin, *Ideals and Realities in Russian Literature* : London, 1905.

CHAPTER V

PETERSBURG ; LOVE AFFAIR ; DROUZHÍNIN

Petersburg. Tourgénef. The *Contemporary*. Death of his
brother Demetrius. Drouzhínin. The Behrs. Love affairs.
Engagement with V.V.A. Illness. Leaves the army. Engagement broken off. Correspondence with Tourgénef.
Writings. Drouzhínin's criticism of *Youth* and of Tolstoy's
style. Books that influenced him. Emancipation of serfs.
Poúshkin. Self-condemnation in his *Confession*.

A NUMBER of distinguished writers have recorded their
opinions of the talented young officer who appeared in
Petersburg before the war was quite over, and immediately entered the fraternity then supporting the
Contemporary. From their memoirs one sees what
Tolstoy was like at this, perhaps the stormiest and least
satisfactory period of his life.

The *Contemporary* was a monthly review founded by
Poúshkin and Pletnéf in 1836. It passed in 1847 to
Panáef and the poet Nekrásof, and when Tolstoy began to
write, was recognised as the leading and most progressive
Russian literary periodical. Its chief contributors formed
an intimate group, united by close personal acquaintance,
by sympathy with the Emancipation movement then
making itself felt, and also by a common agreement (not
it is true very strictly or very permanently observed) to
write exclusively for the *Contemporary*. The point to be
noticed is that the circle Tolstoy entered consisted of a
friendly, sociable group of people who considered themselves

ardent reformers; and that though Tolstoy's talent and his wish to have his works published, threw him and them together, he never appears to have had the least inclination to co-operate on that footing of mutual give-and-take toleration which is so essential in public life. Certainly he never became friendly with the more advanced men, Tchernyshévsky, Miháylof, and the ultra-democratic Dobrolúbof, who were intent on spreading democratic and socialistic ideas in Russia.

It has been suggested that this was due to the fact that he was an aristocrat and that they were democrats; but one has to go deeper than that for the explanation, which lies, to a considerable extent, in the fact that the advanced Russian Radicals were, for the most part, admirers of Governmental Jacobinism, whereas Tolstoy has from the very start tended to be a No-Government man, an Anarchist, and has objected to linking himself closely with any group, since such alliance always implies some amount of compromise, and some subordination of one's own opinions.

The poet Fet, himself a young officer, made Tolstoy's acquaintance at this time. A couple of years later he purchased an estate at no very great distance from Yásnaya Polyána, and became a friend of Tolstoy's—one in fact of the very few people, not of his own family, with whom the latter ever formed a close personal friendship.

His first acquaintance with Tolstoy was however hardly auspicious. Calling on Tourgénef in St. Petersburg at ten o'clock one morning, he saw an officer's 1855 sword hanging in the hall, and asked the man-servant whose it was. 'It's Count Tolstoy's sword,' replied the man. 'He is sleeping in the drawing-room. Iván Sergéyevitch [Tourgénef] is having breakfast in the study.' During Fet's visit of an hour's duration, he and his host had to converse in low tones for fear of waking Tolstoy. 'He is like this all the time,' said Tourgénef. 'He came back from his Sevastopol battery; put up here, and is going the pace. Sprees, gipsy-girls and cards all night long— and then he sleeps like a corpse till two in the afternoon. At first I tried to put the break on, but now I 've given it up, and let him do as he likes.'

Fet tells us that as soon as he met Tolstoy he noticed his instinctive defiance of all accepted opinions; and at Nekrásof's lodgings, the first time he saw Tolstoy and Tourgénef together, he witnessed the desperation to which the former reduced the latter by his biting retorts.

'I can't admit,' said Tolstoy, 'that what you say expresses your convictions. If I stand at the door with a dagger or a sword, and say, "While I am alive no one shall enter here," that shows conviction. But you, here, try to conceal the true inwardness of your thoughts from one another, and call *that* conviction!'

'Why do you come here?' squeaked Tourgénef, panting, his voice rising to a falsetto (as always happened when he was disputing). 'Your banner is not here! Go! Go to the salon of Princess B—— !'

'Why should I ask you, where I am to go? Besides, empty talk won't become conviction, merely because I am, or am not here,' replied Tolstoy.

Though he cared little for politics, Fet's sympathies inclined to the Conservative side, and he found himself in accord with Tolstoy rather than with Tourgénef and the other Contemporarians; but Fet's stay in Petersburg at this time was a short one, and he therefore saw little of Tolstoy. D. V. Grigoróvitch, the novelist, however, reported to him another scene which also occurred at Nekrásof's lodging.

You can't imagine what it was like! Great Heavens! said Grigoróvitch. Tourgénef squeaked and squeaked, holding his hand to his throat, and with the eyes of a dying gazelle whispered: 'I can stand no more! I have bronchitis!' and began walking to and fro through the three rooms.—'Bronchitis is an imaginary illness,' growls Tolstoy after him: 'Bronchitis is a metal!'

Of course Nekrásof's heart sank: he feared to lose either of these valuable contributors to the *Contemporary*. We were all agitated, and at our wits' end to know what to say. Tolstoy, in the middle room, lay sulking on the morocco sofa; while Tourgénef, spreading the tails of his short coat and with his hands in his pockets, strode to and fro through the three rooms. To avert a catastrophe, I went to the sofa and said, 'Tolstoy, old chap, don't get excited! You don't know how he esteems and loves you!'

'I won't allow him to do anything to spite me!' exclaimed Tolstoy with dilated nostrils. 'There! Now he keeps marching past me on purpose, wagging his democratic haunches!'

The rest of the evidence is of much the same nature. Of desire to agree, there was hardly a trace in Tolstoy, who never doubted his own sincerity and seldom credited that quality to others. The aristocratic influences that surrounded his upbringing never induced him to be lenient to men of his own class, such as Tourgénef; but they led him to judge harshly and unsympathetically new men who were pushing their way to the front by their own ability. Fet, in his *Mémoires*, speaks with regret of the fact that the educated classes ('the Intelligents') attracted by Liberal ideas which made for the Emancipation of the serfs, formed so strong a current of opinion that even the literature produced by the nobility (and he claims that the nobles supplied all the truly artistic literature) advocated changes which struck at the root of the most fundamental privileges of their class. This tendency, he tells us, revolted 'Tolstoy's fresh, unwarped instinct.'

Grigoróvitch, in his *Literary Memoirs*, tells us that, knowing how out of sympathy Tolstoy was with Petersburg, and how evident it was that everything in Petersburg irritated him, he was surprised to find that the latter took permanent lodgings there. Grigoróvitch, himself a Contemporarian, had met Tolstoy in Moscow, and coming across him again in Petersburg, and hearing that he was invited to dine with the staff of the *Contemporary*, but did not yet know any of the members intimately, agreed to accompany him.

On the way I warned him to be on his guard about certain matters, and especially to avoid attacking George Sand, whom he much disliked, but who was devoutly worshipped by many Contemporarians. The dinner passed off all right, Tolstoy being rather quiet at first, but at last he broke out. Some one praised George Sand's new novel, and he abruptly declared his hatred of her, adding that the heroines of the novels she was then writing, if they really existed, ought to be tied to the hangman's cart and driven through the streets of Petersburg. He had, adds Grigoróvitch, already then developed that peculiar view of women and of the woman-question, which he afterwards expressed so vividly in *Anna Karénina*.

With all the curious convolutions of Tolstoy's character, there is a remarkable tenacity of conviction running through his whole life, and a remark in *Resurrection*, written nearly half a century later, throws a flood of light on the fact of his so detesting George Sand's emancipated heroines while he was himself living a loose life. In that book, the hero has been attracted as well as repelled first by Mariette, the General's wife, and then by a handsome demi-mondaine he passes in the street, and this is his reflection :

The animalism of the brute nature in man is disgusting, thought he; but as long as it remains in its naked form we observe it from the height of our spiritual life and despise it; and, *whether one has fallen or resisted*, one remains what one was before. But when that same animalism hides under a cloak of poetry and esthetic feeling, and demands our worship—then we are swallowed up by it completely, and worship animalism, no longer distinguishing good from evil. Then it is awful !

PROMINENT RUSSIAN WRITERS, (1856): TOURGÉNEF, SOLOGOÚB, TOLSTOY, NEKRÁSOF, GRIGÓRYEF, PANÁEF.

Grigoróvitch in another place speaks of Tolstoy's 'readiness to contradict.' It did not matter what opinion was being expressed; and the more authoritative the speaker appeared to be, the more eager was Tolstoy to oppose him and to begin a verbal duel. 'Watching how he listened to the speaker and pierced him with his eyes, and noticing how ironically he pressed his lips together, one conjectured that he was preparing not a direct reply, but such an expression of opinion as would perplex his opponent by its unexpectedness.'

Danílevsky, the novelist, confirms this impression of Tolstoy's eagerness to oppose. They met at the house of a well-known sculptor. Tolstoy entered the drawing-room while a new work of Herzen's was being read aloud, and quietly took up a position behind the reader's chair. When the reading was over, he began, at first gently and with restraint, then hotly and boldly, to attack Herzen and the enthusiasm then current for his revolutionary and emancipatory works; and he spoke so convincingly and with such sincerity, that Danílevsky says he never afterwards saw one of Herzen's publications in that house.

Tourgénef once said : 'In Tolstoy the character which afterwards lay at the base of his whole outlook on life early made itself manifest. He never believed in people's sincerity. Every spiritual movement seemed to him false, and he used to pierce those on whom his suspicion fell with his extraordinarily penetrating eyes '; and Tourgénef went on to say that personally he had never encountered anything more disconcerting than that inquisitorial look, which, accompanied by two or three biting words, was enough to goad to fury any man who lacked strong self control.

The different sides of men's characters do not always advance simultaneously or harmoniously; and it frequently happens that those awakening to a sense of public duty remain self-indulgent in respect to wine or women, while others become abstainers or respectable husbands while

remaining oblivious of the political duties they owe to the
community. Among the reformers whose acquaintance
Tolstoy made in Petersburg, there was unfortunately a
great deal of gluttony, drinking, gambling and loose
living, and Tolstoy—though he was often remorseful and
repentant about his own excesses with wine, women, and
cards—with his innate propensity for demanding *all or
nothing*, bitterly resented this in others. He would no
doubt have considered it hypocritical had he himself
come forward as a reformer before obtaining mastery over
his own appetites, and he judged others by the same
standard.

The ill success of the Crimean war had dealt a blow to
the prestige of the Tsardom, and a series of wide-reaching
reforms were being prepared at this time—among which the
most important were the abolition of serfdom, the reform
of civil and criminal law, the introduction of trial by jury
and of oral proceedings in the law courts, the establishment of a system of Local Government somewhat resembling
our County Councils, and some relaxation of the insensate
severity of the press censorship. But though Tolstoy
reached Petersburg at a moment when Russia was entering on this hopeful and fruitful period of internal reform,
neither in his published writings nor in any private
utterance we know of, does he express much sympathy
with those reforms, or show any perception of the
advantage that accrues to a nation whose inhabitants
interest themselves in public affairs. He never realised
that even if a people make for themselves bad laws, the
very fact of being invited to think about large practical
matters, and being allowed to test their own conclusions
in practice, fosters a habit of not fearing to think and to
act in accord with one's thought; and that this habit of
applying thought to the guidance of practical affairs,
overflows into a nation's commerce and industry and
agriculture, and ultimately causes the difference between

the comparative material security of our Western world and the chronic fear of famine that oppresses many Eastern lands.

But complex problems of public policy — which are always difficult, and call for patience, tolerant co-operation, and a willingness to accept half-loaves when whole ones are unobtainable — never were to Tolstoy's taste. He hankers after simple, clear-cut solutions, such as are obtainable only subjectively, in the mind.

A few years later than the time of which we are speaking, Tolstoy commenced a novel called *The Decembrists*, which begins with a description of these reform years. The passage shows how scornfully he regarded the whole movement for the liberation of the people and the democratisation of their institutions. These are his words:

This happened not long ago, in the reign of Alexander II, in our times of civilisation, progress, *problems*, re-birth of Russia, etc. etc.; the time when the victorious Russian army returned from Sevastopol which it had surrendered to the enemy; when all Russia was celebrating the destruction of the Black Sea fleet; and white-walled Moscow greeted, and congratulated on that auspicious event, the remainder of the crews of that fleet, offering them a good old Russian goblet of vódka, and in the good old Russian way bringing them bread and salt and bowing at their feet. This was the time when Russia, in the person of her far-sighted virgin politicians, wept over the destruction of her dream of a Te Deum in the Cathedral of St. Sophia, and the deep-felt loss to the fatherland of two great men who had perished during the war (one who, carried away by impatience to hear the Te Deum referred to above, had fallen on the fields of Wallachia, not without leaving there two squadrons of Hussars; and the other an invaluable man who distributed tea, other people's money, and sheets, to the wounded without stealing any of them); in that time when from all sides, in all departments of human activity in Russia, great men sprang up like mushrooms: commanders, administrators,

K

economists, writers, orators, and simply great men without any special calling or aim; in that time when at the Jubilee of a Moscow actor, public opinion, fortified by a toast, appeared and began to punish all wrongdoers; when stern Commissioners galloped from Petersburg to the South and captured, exposed, and punished the commissariat rascals; when in all the towns dinners with toasts were given to the heroes of Sevastopol, and to those of them whose arms and legs had been torn off, coppers were given by those who met them on the bridges or highways; at that time when oratorical talents were so rapidly developed among the people that one publican everywhere and on all occasions wrote, printed, and repeated by heart at dinners, such powerful speeches that the guardians of order were obliged to undertake repressive measures to subdue his eloquence; when even in the English Club in Moscow a special room was set apart for the consideration of public affairs; when periodicals appeared under the most varied banners; journals developing European principles on a European basis but with a Russian world-conception, and journals on an exclusively Russian basis, developing Russian principles but with a European world-conception; when suddenly, so many journals appeared that it seemed as if all possible titles had been used up: ' The Messenger,' ' The Word,' ' The Discourse,' ' The Eagle,' and many others; when nevertheless fresh titles presented themselves continually; at that time when pleiades of new author-philosophers appeared, proving that Science is national and is not national and is international, and so on: and pleiades of writer-artists, who described woods and sun-rises, and thunders, and the love of a Russian maiden, and the idleness of one official, and the misconduct of many officials; at that time when from all sides appeared problems (as in the year '56 every concourse of circumstances was called of which nobody could make head or tail); the problem of the Cadet Schools, the Universities, the Censor, oral tribunals, finance, the banks, the police, the Emancipation, and many others; everybody still tried to discover new questions, and everybody tried to solve them; they wrote, and read, and talked, and drew up projects, and all wished to amend, destroy and alter, and all Russians, as one man, were in an indescribable state of enthusiasm. That was a condition which has occurred twice in Russia in the nineteenth century : the first time was in the year '12 when we thrashed Napoleon I, and the second time was in '56 when Napoleon III thrashed us. Great, unforgettable epoch of the re-birth of the Russian people! Like the Frenchman who said that he had not lived at all who had not lived during the Great French Revolution, so I make bold to say that he who did not live in Russia in '56, does not know what life is. The writer of these lines not merely lived at that time, but was one of the workers of that period. Not merely did he personally sit for some weeks in one of the casemates of Sevastopol, but he wrote a work about the Crimean War which brought him great fame, and in which he clearly and minutely described how the soldiers in the bastion fired off their muskets, how in the hospitals people were bound up with bandages, and how in the cemetery they were buried in the earth.

Having performed these exploits, the writer of these lines arrived at the heart of the Empire, at a rocket-station, where he reaped his laurels. He witnessed the enthusiasm of both capitals and of the whole people, and experienced in his own person how Russia can reward real service. The great ones of the earth sought his acquaintance, pressed his hands, offered him dinners, persistently invited him to come and see them, and in order to hear from him particulars about the war, narrated to him their own sensations. Therefore the writer of these lines knows how to appreciate that great and memorable time. But that is not what I want to tell about.

The very day he reached Petersburg from Sevastopol, in September 1855, Tolstoy called on Tourgénef, who pressed him to stay with him and introduced him to all that was most interesting in Petersburg literary and artistic circles, watching over his interests ' like an old nurse,' as Tourgénef himself once expressed it. Tourgénef fully appreciated Tolstoy's artistic genius, but was strangely blind to the specially Tolstoyan side of Tolstoy's complex nature. As we have already seen, friction soon arose between the two men, and though they again and again made friends, their friendship was very unstable and easily upset.

Early in 1856 Tolstoy's third brother, Demetrius, died in Orél. His history has been told in Chapter II. Tolstoy
1856
says : ' I was particularly horrid at that time. I went to Orél from Petersburg, where I frequented society and was filled with conceit. I felt sorry for Mítenka, but not very sorry. I paid him a hurried visit, but did not stay at Orél, and my brother died a few days after I left.' On 2nd February the news reached Leo ; but he says : ' I really believe that what hurt me most, was that it prevented my taking part in some private theatricals then being got up at Court, and to which I had been invited.'

In March the war ended, and Tolstoy obtained furlough. On 25th March he wrote to his brother Sergius :

I want to go abroad for eight months, and if they give me leave I shall do so. I wrote to Nikólenka about it, and asked him to come too. If we could all three arrange to go together it would be first-rate. If each of us took Rs. 1000, we could do the trip capitally.

Please write and tell me how you like *The Snow Storm*. I am dissatisfied with it—seriously. But I now want to write many things, only I positively have no time in this damned Petersburg. Anyway, whether they let me go abroad or not, I intend to take furlough in April and come to the country.

On 13th May he was still in Petersburg, and we find him noting in his Diary :

The powerful means to true happiness in life, is to let flow from oneself on all sides, without any laws, like a spider, a cobweb of love, and to catch in it all that comes to hand: women old or young, children, or policemen.

Among his literary acquaintances at this time the one for whom he seems to have felt most sympathy and respect was Drouzhínin, a critic, writer of stories, and translator of Shakespear. Before long we find Drouzhínin leading a revolt against the *Contemporary* and attracting some of the contributors to the *Reading Library*, a rival magazine, to which Tolstoy contributed an article in December 1856.

It was not till the end of May that he got away from Petersburg; and on his road home he stopped in Moscow and visited the family of Dr. Behrs, a Russian of German origin, who had married Miss Islényef. The first mention one gets of Tolstoy's future wife is a note in his Diary relating to this visit to the Behrs's country house near Moscow. He says: 'The children served us. What dear, merry little girls!' Little more than six years later, the second of these 'merry little girls' was Countess Tolstoy!

Three days later he writes to his brother Sergius: 'I spent ten days in Moscow . . . very pleasantly, without champagne or gipsies, but a little in love—I will tell you later on with whom.' The object of his affection at that time was of course not Dr. Behrs's twelve-year-old daughter.

From Yásnaya he made a round of visits to see his married sister and other neighbours; among them Tourgénef, at whose house a gathering of the Tolstoys took place. Special honour was paid to Leo, who comically posed as the hero of a Triumph. He was being crowned and almost covered with flowers, leaves, grass, and anything that came handy, when the approach of an unwelcome guest—a lady neighbour of Tourgénef's—was announced. Thereupon the host seized his head in despair; the triumpher, with a howl, began to turn rapid catherine-wheel somersaults through the rooms; and his sister's husband was quickly bandaged up as an invalid, to be used as an excuse and a protection from the unwelcome intruder.

The letter to Sergius, quoted above, contains an allusion to Tolstoy's first serious matrimonial project.

He had in childhood been much attached to a certain Sónitchka Kalóshina. While at the University, he had had a sentimental love affair with a certain Z. M., who seems hardly to have been aware of his devotion. Then there was the Cossack damsel who figures in *The Cossacks*, and subsequently he much admired a society lady, Madame Sch., who may also have been scarcely aware of his feelings, for Tolstoy was shy and timid in these matters—which were quite different from his affairs with gipsy girls and other hireable women.

The present affair with V. V. A. was more serious than any of its predecessors. It led to a long correspondence, and even to their engagement being announced among relations and friends. The lady was the good-looking daughter of a landowner in the neighbourhood of Yásnaya Polyána.

In August she accompanied her family to Moscow for the Coronation of Alexander II. At these festivities she enjoyed herself greatly, and described her feelings in a letter which dealt the first blow to Tolstoy's admiration. He at once assumed towards her the rôle which more than twenty-five years later he assumed towards mankind in general, and upbraided her with the insignificant and unworthy nature of her interests and enjoyments, besides indulging in scathing sarcasms about the fashionable circles with which she was so enraptured.

The young lady did not reply. Tolstoy then begged pardon—which was granted.

Meanwhile he had fallen ill; and early in September he wrote to his brother Sergius:

Only now, at nine o'clock on Monday evening, can I give you a satisfactory reply, for till now things went worse and worse. Two doctors were sent for, and administered another forty leeches, but only now have I had a good sleep and, on waking up, feel considerably better. All the same, there can be no question of my leaving home for five or six days yet. So *au revoir*; please let me know when you go (shooting) and whether it is true that your farming has been seriously neglected; and do not kill all the game without me. I will send the dogs, perhaps, to-morrow.

He recovered. The young lady returned to her family's estate at Soudakóva, and his visits being renewed, Tolstoy's intimacy with her continued and grew closer.

Yet to ' test himself,' he started for a visit to Petersburg, and as soon as he had got as far as Moscow, wrote a letter to the young lady in which he dwelt on the importance of the mutual attraction of the sexes, the serious nature of his and her relation to one another, and the necessity of testing themselves by time and distance.

While living in Petersburg, he learnt the particulars of a flirtation the young lady had carried on at the time of the Coronation with a French music-master, Mortier; and he wrote her a letter full of reproaches. Instead of posting it, however, he wrote her another—telling her of the one he had written, which he intended to show her when they met.

After once breaking off relations with Mortier, the young lady allowed them to be again renewed, and what Tolstoy learned of the matter caused him seriously to reconsider his position. For some time his feelings evidently wavered. The very day after posting his remonstrance, he wrote another letter in a conciliatory tone, and though no reply came, he assumed that all was well, and continued the correspondence by sending her a detailed plan of the life they might hope to live together : its surroundings, circle of acquaintance, and the arrangement of their time. He also tried to interest her in the most serious problems of life.

No answer reaching him for a long time, he became agitated and perplexed. Then several letters, delayed in the post, arrived all at once, and cordial intercourse was re-established between the lovers. But though the engagement and correspondence continued, and expressions of affection were interchanged, it gradually became more and more evident that there was something artificial and unsatisfactory in their relation to one another.

Meanwhile Tolstoy was having other difficulties in Petersburg. On 10th November 1856 he writes to his brother Sergius :

Forgive me, dear friend Seryózha, for only writing two words —I have no time for more. I have been most unlucky since I left home ; there is no one here I like. It seems that I have been abused in the *Fatherland Journal* for my war stories—I have not yet read the attack ; but the worst is that Konstantínof [the General under whose command was the battery to which Tolstoy was attached] informed me as soon as I got here that the Grand Duke Michael, having learnt that I am supposed to have composed the Soldiers' Song, is displeased, particularly at my having (as rumour says) taught it to the soldiers. This is abominable. I have had an explanation with the Head of the Staff. The only satisfactory thing is that my health is good, and that (Dr.) Schipoulínsky says my lungs are thoroughly sound.

On 20th November 1856 Tolstoy left the army, in which he had never secured promotion though he had private influence enough to enable him, about this time, to save from trial by Court Martial the Commander of the battery in which he had served in the Crimea.

Early in December he left Petersburg for Moscow. From there, on 5th December, he writes to Aunt Tatiána :

When I first went away and for a week after, I thought I was 'in love' as it is called ; but with an imagination such as mine that was not difficult.

Now, however, especially since I have set to work diligently, I should like—and very much like—to be able to say that I am in love, or even that I love her ; but it is not the case. The only feeling I have for her is gratitude for her love of me, and the thought that of all the girls I have known or know, she would have made me the best wife, as I understand family life. And that is what I should like to have your candid opinion about. Am I mistaken or not ? I should like to hear your advice because, in the first place, you know both her and me ; and chiefly because you love me, and those who love are never wrong. It is true that I have tested myself very badly, for from the time I left home I have led a solitary rather than a

TOLSTOY IN 1856, THE YEAR HE LEFT THE ARMY.

dissipated life, and have seen few women; but notwithstanding that, I have had many moments of vexation with myself for having become connected with her, and I have repented of it. All the same, I repeat that if I were convinced that she is of a steadfast nature, and would love me always—even though not as now, yet more than any one else—then I should not hesitate for a moment about marrying her. I am confident that then my love of her would increase more and more and that through that feeling she would become a good woman.

The young lady in question visited Petersburg for part of the winter season, but Tolstoy does not appear to have met her there, being himself away in Moscow for several weeks. The correspondence was largely didactic on his side, and was so unsatisfactory to the young lady that she finally forbade him to write again. He disobeyed the injunction, asking her pardon, telling her he was going abroad, and begging that she would write to him once more, to an address in Paris.

He wrote to Aunt Tatiána from Moscow, on 12th January 1857, a letter in which Russian and French alternate.

* CHÈRE TANTE !—J'ai reçu mon passeport pour l'étranger et je suis venu à Moscou pour y passer quelques jours avec Marie arranger mes affaires et prendre congé de vous.

But now I have reconsidered the matter, especially on Máshenka's advice, and have decided to remain with her here a week or two and then to go straight through Warsaw to Paris. You no doubt understand, *chère tante*, why I do not wish and why it is not right for me to come now to Yásnaya, or rather to Soudakóva. I, it seems, have acted very badly in relation to V., but were I to see her now, I should behave still worse. As I wrote you, I am more than indifferent to her, and feel that I can no longer deceive either her or myself. But were I to come, I might perhaps, from weakness of character, again delude myself.

---

* DEAR AUNT,—I have received my passport for abroad, and I have come to Moscow to pass some days with Mary, and to take leave of you. (See sentences in English in letter above.)

Vous rappelez-vous, chère tante, comme vous vous êtes moquée de moi, quand je vous ai dit que je partais pour Péters-bourg 'pour m'éprouver,' et cependant c'est à cette idée que je suis redevable de n'avoir pas fait le malheur de la jeune per-sonne et le mien, car ne croyez pas que ce soit de l'inconstance ou de l'infidélité ; personne ne m'a plu pendant ces deux mois, mais tout bonnement j'ai vu que je me trompais moi-même ; que non seulement jamais je n'ai eu, mais jamais je n'aurais pour V. le moindre sentiment d'amour véritable. La seule chose qui me fait beaucoup de peine c'est que j'ai fait du tort à la demoiselle et que je ne pourrai prendre congé de vous avant de partir. . . .

After reaching Paris (an event belonging properly to the next chapter) he received a last communica-tion from V. V. A. and wrote her a friendly letter in reply, speaking of his love as of something past, thanking her for her friendship, and wishing her every happiness.

His Aunt Tatiána—generally the mildest of critics where he was concerned—appears to have blamed him for his conduct ; and the friends of V. V. A., including a French governess, Mlle. Vergani, did so yet more severely. In one of his letters, which contains indi-cations of an agitation too strong to allow him to complete the construction of the opening sentence, he says :

Do you remember, dear Aunt, how you made fun of me when I told you I was going to Petersburg 'to test myself'? Yet it is that idea that has saved me from bringing misery on the young lady and on myself ; for do not suppose that it is a case of inconstancy or un-faithfulness. No one has taken my fancy during these two months, but simply I have come to see that I was deceiving myself, and that I not only never had, but never shall have, the least feeling of true love for V. V. A. The only things which give me much pain are that I have hurt the young lady, and that I cannot take leave of you before my departure. . . .

* Si Mlle. V. qui m'a écrit une lettre aussi ridicule, voulait ~~ie~~ rappeler toute ma conduite vis-à-vis de V. V. A., comment ~~ie~~ tâchais de venir le plus rarement possible, comment c'est ~~elle~~ qui m'engageait à venir plus souvent et à entrer dans des ~~relations~~ plus proches. Je comprends qu'elle soit fâchée de ~~ce~~ qu'une chose qu'elle a beaucoup désirée ne s'est pas faite ~~(j'en~~ suis fâché peut-être plus qu'elle) mais ce n'est pas une ~~raison~~ pour dire à un homme qui s'est efforcé d'agir le mieux possible, qui a fait des sacrifices de peur de faire le malheur ~~des~~ autres, de lui dire, qu'il est un *pig* [this one word is in Russian in the original] et de le faire accroire à tout le monde. Je suis sûr que Toúla [the town nearest his estate] est convaincu que je suis le plus grand des monstres.

Turning from love to literature and friendship, we have two letters of this period from Tourgénef. The first is dated Paris, 16th November 1856, and is as follows:

DEAREST TOLSTOY,—Your letter of 15 October took a whole month crawling to me—I received it only yesterday. I have thought carefully about what you write me—and I think you are wrong. It is true I cannot be quite sincere, because I can't be quite frank, with you. I think we got to know each other awkwardly and at a bad time, and when we meet again it will be much easier and smoother. I feel that I love you as a man (as an author it needs no saying); but much in you is trying to me, and ultimately I found it better to keep at a distance from you. When we meet we will again try to go hand in hand—perhaps we shall succeed better; for strange as it may sound, my heart turns to you when at a distance, as to a brother:

---

* If Mlle. Vergani, who has written me so absurd a letter, would remember my whole conduct towards V. V. A., how I tried to come as seldom as possible, and how it was she who induced me to come more frequently and to enter into closer relations. I understand her being vexed that an affair she much desired has not come off (I perhaps am more vexed about it than she) but that is no reason for her to tell a man who has tried to act as well as he could, and who has made sacrifices in order not to make others unhappy, that he is a pig, and to spread that report about. I am sure all Toúla is convinced that I am the greatest of monsters. . . .

I even feel tenderly towards you. In a word, I love you—that is certain; perchance from that, in time, all good will follow. I heard of your illness and grieved; but now, I beg you, drive the thought of it out of your head. For you too have your fancies, and are perhaps thinking of consumption—but, God knows, you have nothing of the sort. . . .

You have finished the first part of *Youth*—that is capital. How sorry I am to be unable to hear it read! If you do not go astray (which I think there is no reason to anticipate) you will go very far. I wish you good health, activity—and freedom, spiritual freedom.

As to my *Faust*, I do not think it will please you very much. My things could please you and perhaps have some influence on you, only until you became independent. Now you have no need to study me; you see only the difference of our manners, the mistakes and the omissions; what you have to do is to study man, your own heart, and the really great writers. I am a writer of a transition period—and am of use only to men in a transition state. So farewell, and be well. Write to me.

On 8th December 1856 he writes again :

DEAR TOLSTOY,—Yesterday my good genius led me past the post-office, and it occurred to me to ask if there were any letters for me at the *poste-restante* (though I think that all my friends ought long ago to have learnt my Paris address) and I found your letter, in which you speak of my *Faust*. You can well imagine how glad I was to read it. Your sympathy gladdened me truly and deeply. Yes, and from the whole letter there breathes a mild, clear and friendly peacefulness. It remains for me to hold out my hand across the 'ravine' which has long since become a hardly perceptible crack, about which we will speak no more—it is not worth it.

I fear to speak of one thing you mention : it is a delicate matter,—words may blight such things before they are ripe; but when they are ripe a hammer will not break them. God grant that all may turn out favourably and well. It may bring you that spiritual repose which you lacked when I knew you.

You have, I see, now become very intimate with Drouzhínin

—and are under his influence. That is right, only take care not to swallow too much of him. When I was your age, only men of enthusiastic natures influenced me; but you are built differently, and perhaps also the times are changed. . . . Let me know in which numbers of the *Contemporary* your *Youth* will appear; and by the way, let me know the final impression made on you by *Lear*, which you probably have read, if only for Drouzhínin's sake.

About the same time Tourgénef wrote to Drouzhínin:

I hear that you have become very intimate with Tolstoy—and he has become very pleasant and serene. I am very glad. When that new wine has finished fermenting, it will yield a drink fit for the Gods. What about his *Youth*, which was sent for your verdict?

The allusion to Drouzhínin's translation of *King Lear* is worth noticing because fully fifty years later it was this play that Tolstoy selected for hostile analysis in his famous attack on Shakespear. One gathers from a letter written by V. P. Bótkin, that Drouzhínin's rendering impressed Tolstoy favourably at the time.

Before quoting Drouzhínin's criticism of *Youth*, it will be in place to mention other works by Tolstoy, not yet enumerated, which appeared at this period. *Memoirs of a Billiard Marker*, giving a glimpse of temptations Tolstoy had experienced, was published in January 1855, while he was in Sevastopol. In January 1856 came *Sevastopol in August*. In March 1856 appeared *The Snow Storm*. In May 1856 came a rollicking tale, with flashes of humour like that of Charles Lever, entitled *Two Hussars*. It is the only story Tolstoy ever wrote in that vein; and in it are introduced gipsy singers such as those of whom repeated mention occurs in his letters. In December, before he went abroad, two more tales were published: one of these, entitled *Meeting a Moscow Acquaintance in the Detachment*, containing a scathing portrayal of the cowardice a man, who had passed muster in 'good society,' displayed when circumstances put him to the test. The other story, *A Squire's Morning*, is closely drawn from Tolstoy's own experience when on first leaving the University he settled on his estate and attempted to better the condition of his serfs. Their stolidity, their distrust, and the immense difficulty of introducing any changes, are all brought out.

In a letter to Drouzhínin, Tourgénef wrote :

I have read his *Squire's Morning,* which pleased me exceedingly by its sincerity and almost complete freedom of outlook. I say 'almost' because in the way he set himself the task, there still is hidden (without his perhaps being aware of it) a certain amount of prejudice. The chief moral impression produced by the story (leaving the artistic impression aside) is that so long as the state of serfdom exists, there is no possibility of the two sides drawing together, despite the most disinterested and honourable desire to do so; and this impression is good and true. But beside it, like a horse cantering beside a trotter, there is another: namely, that in general to try to enlighten or improve the condition of the peasants leads to nothing ; and this impression is unpleasant. But the mastery of language, the way it is told, and his character-drawing, are grand.

1857 In January 1857 appeared *Youth*, the continuation of *Childhood* and *Boyhood*.

How great Drouzhínin's influence was with Tolstoy at this time, may be judged by the tone of his letter to him, giving an opinion on *Youth*. He writes :

About *Youth* one ought to write twenty pages. I read it with anger, with yells and with oaths—not on account of its literary quality, but because of the quality of the notebooks in which it is written, and the handwritings. The mixing of two hands, a known and an unknown, diverted my attention and hindered an intelligent perusal. It was as though two voices shouted in my ear and purposely distracted my attention, and I know that this has prevented my receiving an adequate impression. All the same I will say what I can. Your task was a terrible one, and you have executed it very well. No other writer of our day could have so seized and sketched the agitated and disorderly period of youth. To those who are developed, your *Youth* will furnish an immense pleasure; and if any one tells you it is inferior to *Childhood* and *Boyhood* you may spit in his physiognomy. There is a world of poetry in it —all the first chapters are admirable; only the introduction is dry till one reaches the description of spring. . . In many chapters one scents the poetic charm of old Moscow, which no one has yet reproduced properly. Some chapters are dry and long: for instance all the stipulations with Dmítry Nehlúdof. . . . The conscription of Semyónof will not pass the Censor.

Do not fear your reflections, they are all clever and original. But you have an inclination to a super-refinement of analysis which may become a great defect. You are sometimes on the point of saying that so-and-so's thigh indicated that he wished to travel in India. You must restrain this tendency, but do not extinguish it on any account. All your work on your analyses should be of the same kind. Each of your defects has its share of strength and beauty, and almost every one of your qualities carries with it the seed of a defect.

Your style quite accords with that conclusion: you are most ungrammatical, sometimes with the lack of grammar of a reformer and powerful poet reshaping a language his own way and for ever, but sometimes with the lack of grammar of an officer sitting in a casemate and writing to his chum. One can say with assurance that all the pages you have written with love are admirable,—but as soon as you grow cold, your words become entangled, and diabolical forms of speech appear. Therefore the parts written coldly should be revised and corrected. I tried to straighten out some bits, but gave it up; it is a work which only you can and must do. Above all, avoid long sentences. Cut them up into two or three; do not be sparing of full-stops. . . . Do not stand on ceremony with the particles, and strike out by dozens the words: *which, who,* and *that.* When in difficulties, take a sentence and imagine that you want to say it to some one in a most conversational way.

As a translator I may testify that Tolstoy never fully learned the lesson Drouzhínin here set him, and that to the very last he continued occasionally to intermingle passages of extraordinary simplicity and force with sentences that defy analysis and abound in redundances.

Nearly fifty years later Tolstoy himself criticised the subject-matter of *Childhood*, *Boyhood*, and *Youth* as follows :

I have re-read them and regret that I wrote them; so ill, artificially and insincerely are they penned. It could not be otherwise : first, because what I aimed at was not to write my own history but that of the friends of my youth, and this produced an awkward mixture of the facts of their and my own childhood ; and secondly, because at the time I wrote it I was far from being independent in my way of expressing myself, being strongly influenced by two writers : Sterne (his *Sentimental Journey*) and Töpffer (his *Bibliothèque de Mon Oncle*).

I am now specially dissatisfied with the two last parts, *Boyhood* and *Youth*, in which besides an awkward mixture of truth and invention, there is also insincerity : a desire to put forward as good and important what I did not then consider good and important, namely, my democratic tendency.

Before concluding this chapter it will be in place to give a list of books Tolstoy mentions as having influenced him after he left the University and before his marriage. They were : Goethe's *Hermann und Dorothea* ; Hugo's *Notre Dame de Paris* ; Plato's *Phaedo* and *Symposium* (in Cousin's French translation) ; and the *Iliad* and *Odyssey* in Russian versions. All these, he says, had a 'very great' influence on him, while the poems of his compatriots, Tútchef, Kóltsof, and his friend Fet, had 'great' influence.

He tells us that artistic talent in literature influenced him more than any political or social tendency ; and this is quite in accord both with his highly artistic nature and with his general apathy towards public affairs. There was a Slavophil theory (built to justify things as they were) which proclaimed it natural for a Slavonic people to leave the task of governing to its rulers, while retaining its intellectual freedom to disapprove of what was done amiss; and though Tolstoy never joined the Slavophils, this has been very much his own attitude on the matter.

Even in early childhood he had appreciated some of Poúshkin's poems, such as *To the Sea* and *To Napoleon*, and had learned them by heart and recited them with feeling; but curiously enough it was the perusal of Mérimée's French prose translation of Poúshkin's *Gipsies* that, after he was grown up, aroused Tolstoy's keen admiration of Poúshkin's mastery of clear, simple, direct language. Later in life Tolstoy used to say that Poúshkin's prose stories, such as *The Captain's Daughter*, are his best works; but he never lost his appreciation of Poúshkin's power of expression in verse. In his Diary (4th January 1857) he wrote:

I dined at Bótkin's with Panáef alone; he read me Poúshkin; I went into Bótkin's study and wrote a letter to Tourgénef, and then I sat down on the sofa and wept causeless but blissful tears. I am positively happy all this time, intoxicated with the rapidity of my moral progress.

Despite his headstrong outbursts and many vacillations, he seems to have been always a welcome guest in almost any society he cared to frequent, and none of his critics has spoken as harshly of him as he speaks of himself when describing these

terrible twenty years of coarse dissipation, the service of ambition, vanity, and above all of lust. . . . It is true that not all my life was so terribly bad as this twenty-year period from fourteen to thirty-four; and it is true that even that period of my life was not the continuous evil that during a recent illness it appeared to me to be. Even during those years, strivings towards goodness awoke in me, though they did not last long, and were soon choked by passions nothing could restrain.

L

In his *Confession*, written more than twenty years later, when speaking of his religious beliefs at this time, Tolstoy tells us:

With all my soul I wished to be good; but I was young, passionate, and alone, completely alone when I sought goodness. Every time I tried to express my most sincere desire, namely, to be morally good, I met with contempt and ridicule; but as soon as I yielded to nasty passions I was praised and encouraged.

Ambition, love of power, covetousness, lasciviousness, pride, anger and revenge—were all respected. . . . I cannot think of those years without horror, loathing and heartache. I killed men in war, and challenged men to duels in order to kill them; I lost at cards, consumed the labour of the peasants, sentenced them to punishments, lived loosely and deceived people. Lying, robbery, adultery of all kinds, drunkenness, violence, murder— there was no crime I did not commit, and people approved of my conduct, and my contemporaries considered and consider me to be a comparatively moral man.

So I lived for ten years.

During that time I began to write from vanity, covetousness and pride. In my writings I did the same as in my life. To get fame and money, for the sake of which I wrote, it was necessary to hide the good and to show the evil. And I did so. How often in my writings did I contrive to hide under the guise of indifference or even of banter, those strivings of mine towards goodness, which gave meaning to my life! And I succeeded in this, and was praised.

At twenty-six years of age [1] I returned to Petersburg after the war, and met the writers. They received me as one of themselves and flattered me. And before I had time to look round I had adopted the class views on life of the authors I had come among, and these views completely obliterated all my former strivings to improve. Those views furnished a theory which justified the dissoluteness of my life. The view of life of these people, my comrades in authorship, consisted in this: that life in general goes on developing, and in this

[1] Tolstoy makes a slip here: he was over twenty-seven.

development we—men of thought—have the chief part; and among men of thought it is we—artists and poets—who have the chief influence. Our vocation is to teach mankind. And lest the simple question should suggest itself: What do I know, and what can I teach? it is explained in this theory that this need not be known, and that the artist and poet teach unconsciously. I was considered an admirable artist and poet, and therefore it was very natural for me to adopt this theory. I, artist and poet, wrote and taught, without myself knowing what. For this I was paid money; I had excellent food, lodging, women and society; and I had fame, which showed that what I taught was very good.

This faith in the meaning of poetry and in the development of life, was a religion, and I was one of its priests. To be its priest was very pleasant and profitable. And I lived a considerable time in this faith without doubting its validity. But in the second, and especially in the third year of this life, I began to doubt the infallibility of this religion and to examine it. My first cause of doubt was that I began to notice that the priests of this religion were not all in accord among themselves. Some said: We are the best and most useful teachers; we teach what is wanted, but the others teach wrongly. Others said: No! we are the real teachers, and you teach wrongly. And they disputed, quarrelled, abused one another, cheated, and tricked one another. There were also many among them who did not care who was right and who was wrong, but were simply bent on attaining their covetous aims by means of this activity of ours. All this obliged me to doubt the validity of our creed.

Moreover, having begun to doubt the truth of the authors' creed itself, I also began to observe its priests more attentively, and I became convinced that almost all the priests of that religion, the writers, were immoral, and for the most part men of bad, worthless character, much inferior to those whom I had met in my former dissipated and military life; but they were self-confident and self-assured as only those can be who are quite holy or who do not know what holiness is. These people revolted me, and I became revolting to myself, and I realised that that faith is a fraud.

But strange to say, though I understood this fraud and renounced it, yet I did not renounce the rank these people gave me: the rank of artist, poet, and teacher. I naïvely imagined that I was a poet and artist and could teach everybody without myself knowing what I was teaching, and I acted on that assumption.

From my intimacy with these men I acquired a new vice: abnormally developed pride, and an insane assurance that it was my vocation to teach men, without knowing what.

To remember that time, and my own state of mind and that of those men (though there are thousands like them to-day) is sad and terrible and ludicrous, and arouses exactly the feeling one experiences in a lunatic asylum.

We were all then convinced that it was necessary for us to speak, write, and print as quickly as possible and as much as possible, and that it was all wanted for the good of humanity. And thousands of us, contradicting and abusing one another, all printed and wrote—teaching others. And without remarking that we knew nothing, and that to the simplest of life's questions: What is good and what is evil? we did not know how to reply, we all, not listening to one another, talked at the same time, sometimes backing and praising one another in order to be backed and praised in turn, sometimes getting angry with one another—just as in a lunatic asylum.

Thousands of workmen laboured to the extreme limit of their strength day and night setting the type and printing millions of words which the post carried all over Russia, and we still went on teaching and could nohow find time to teach enough, and were always angry that sufficient attention was not paid to us.

It was terribly strange, but is now quite comprehensible. Our real innermost consideration was, that we wanted to get as much money and praise as possible. To gain this end we could do nothing except write books and papers. So we did that. But in order to do such useless work and feel assured that we were very important people, we required a theory justifying our activity. And so among us this theory was devised: 'All that exists develops. And it all develops by means of Culture. And Culture is measured by the circulation of books and newspapers. And we are paid money and are respected because we write books and newspapers, and therefore we are the most useful and the best of men.' This theory would have been all very well if we had been unanimous, but as every thought expressed by one of us was always met by a diametrically opposed thought expressed by some one else, we ought to have been driven to reflection. But we ignored this ; people paid us money, and those on our side praised us ; so each one of us considered himself justified.

CHIEF AUTHORITIES FOR CHAPTER V

Birukof.

Behrs.

A. Fet (Shenshin): *Moi Vospominaniya*, Moscow, 1890. These *Recollections* contain much authentic information about Tolstoy, as well as a large number of his letters to Fet, which I have quoted in subsequent chapters.

Bitovt.

Golovatcheva-Panaeva, *Rousskie Pisateli i Artisty*: Petersburg, 1890.

D. V. Grigorovitch, *Literatourniya Vospominaniya*: vol. xii. p. 326.

G. P. Danilevsky, *Istoritcheskii Vestnik*: March 1886.

P. A. Sergeyenko, *Tourgenef i Tolstoy: Niva*, No. 6, 1906.

Tolstoy's *Confession*.

See also, in Tolstoy's works, *The Decembrists*, chap. i.

CHAPTER VI

TRAVELS ABROAD

Paris. Relations with Tourgénef. *Albert.* An execution.
Switzerland. *Lucerne.* Yásnaya again. The *Iliad* and the
Gospels. Moscow: gymnastics. *Three Deaths.* Musical
Society. Aunty Tatiána. 'Ufanizing.' Emancipation.
Bear-hunting. Moscow Society of Lovers of Russian Litera-
ture. Attitude towards Art in 1859. Tourgénef. Farming.
Fet. Drouzhínin. Nicholas's illness. Goes abroad again.
Germany. Educational studies. Auerbach. Nicholas dies.
Life at Hyères: children. Italy. Marseilles. Paris. Paul
de Kock. London. Herzen. Proudhon. *Polikoúshka.*
Auerbach again. Returns home.

Since he took part in the Turkish war in 1854, Tolstoy
has only twice been out of Russia. The first time was at
the period we have now reached. On 10th Feb-
1857 ruary 1857 (new style) he left Moscow by post-
chaise for Warsaw, from whence a railway already ran
westward. He reached Paris on 21st February. There
he met Tourgénef and Nekrásof, with the former of whom
he was still unable to get on smoothly. Tourgénef writes:
'With Tolstoy I still cannot become quite intimate; we
see things too differently'; and in some moment of anger
Tolstoy even challenged his fellow-writer to a duel.[1]
Nekrásof appears to have patched matters up, and in
March Tolstoy and Tourgénef went to Dijon together,
and spent some days there. During this trip Tolstoy
commenced his story *Albert*, founded on his experience

[1] See Golovátcheva-Panáeva's *Rousskie Pisateli i Artisty.*
166

with the talented but drunken musician Rudolf, already mentioned in Chapter III. After he had returned to Paris, he was present at an execution, and made the following jotting in his Diary :

I rose at seven o'clock and drove to see an execution. A stout, white, healthy neck and breast : he kissed the Gospels, and then—Death. How senseless. . . . I have not received this strong impression for naught. I am not a man of politics. Morals and art I know, love, and can (deal with). The guillotine long prevented my sleeping and obliged me to reflect.

Tolstoy has a gift of telling the essential truth in few words, and never did he sum himself up better than in the sentences, 'I am not a man of politics. Morals and art I know, love, and can.' There is hardly any possible room for doubt about the second sentence, and there is certainly none about the first, as his whole life shows.

Many years later, he wrote of this event in his *Confession* :

When I saw the head separate from the body, and how they both thumped into the box at the same moment, I understood, not with my mind but with my whole being, that no theory of the reasonableness of our present progress can justify this deed ; and that though everybody from the creation of the world, on whatever theory, had held it to be necessary, I know it to be unnecessary and bad ; and therefore the arbiter of what is good and evil is not what people say and do, and is not progress, but is my heart and I.

It was probably during this visit to Paris that Tolstoy witnessed and admired Chevet's popularisation of music by an easy system of instruction, of which he says :

I have seen hundreds of horny-handed working men sitting on benches (under which lay the tool-bags they brought from their work) singing at sight, and understanding and being interested in the laws of music.

This experience he utilised later on in his school at Yásnaya.

In spring he went to Switzerland, and from Geneva he wrote to his Aunt Tatiána:

* J'ai passé un mois et demi à Paris, et si agréablement que tous les jours je me suis dit, que j'ai bien fait de venir à l'étranger. Je suis très peu allé ni dans la société, ni dans le monde littéraire, ni dans le monde des cafés et des bals publics, mais malgré cela j'ai trouvé ici tant de choses nouvelles et intéressantes pour moi, que tous les jours, en me couchant, je me dis, quel dommage que la journée est passée si vite; je n'ai même pas eu le temps de travailler, ce que je me proposais de faire.

Le pauvre Turgenef est très malade physiquement et encore plus moralement. Sa malheureuse liaison avec Madame Viardot, et sa fille, le retiennent ici dans un climat qui lui est pernicieux et il fait pitié de voir. Je n'aurais jamais cru qu'il put aimer ainsi.

Tolstoy's friends Drouzhínin and V. P. Bótkin visited Geneva at this time, and they all three went on a walking tour into Piedmont together. After that he settled at Clarens on the lake of Geneva, from whence he again wrote to Aunt Tatiána:

18 Mai 1857.

† Je viens de recevoir votre lettre, chère tante, qui m'a trouvée

---

* I spent a month-and-a-half in Paris, and so agreeably that every day I said to myself that I had done well to come abroad. I went very little either into society or into the literary world, or into the world of *cafés* and public balls; but in spite of that I found so many things that were new and interesting to me, that every day on going to bed I said to myself, ' What a pity the day has passed so quickly.' I have not even had time to work, which I intended to do.

Poor Tourgénef is very ill physically, and still more so morally. His daughter, and especially his unfortunate *liaison* with Madame Viardot, keep him here in a climate which is bad for him, and it makes one sad to see him. I should never have believed that he could be so in love.

† I have just received your letter, dear Aunt, which found me, as you

comme vous devez le savoir d'après ma dernière lettre, aux environs de Genève à Clarens dans ce même village, où a demeuré la Julia de Rousseau. . . . Je n'essaierai pas de vous depeindre la beauté de ce pays, surtout à présent, quand tout est en feuilles et en fleurs; je vous dirai seulement, qu'à la lettre il est impossible de se détacher de ce lac et de ces rivages et que je passe la plus grande partie de mon temps à regarder et à admirer en me promenant, ou bien en me mettant seulement à la fenêtre de ma chambre.

Je ne cesse de me féliciter de l'idée que j'ai eu de quitter Paris et de venir passer le printemps ici, quoique cela m'ait mérité de votre part le reproche d'inconstance. Vraiment, je suis heureux, and begin to feel the advantage of having been born with a caul.

Il y a ici société charmante de russes : les Poúshkins, the Karamzíns and the Mestchérskys; and they have all, Heaven knows why, taken to liking me; I feel it, and the month I have spent here I have been so nice and good and cosy, that I am sad at the thought of leaving.

From Clarens he took steamer to Montreux, and from there went on foot, taking with him as companion a ten-year-old lad named Sásha, the son of some Russians whose acquaintance he had made at Clarens. They crossed the Pass of Jamon and, after changing their minds as to the

---

must know from my last letter, at Clarens, in the neighbourhood of Geneva, in the same village where Rousseau's Julie lived. . . . I will not try to depict the beauty of this country, especially at present when all is in leaf and flower; I will only say that it is literally impossible to detach oneself from this lake and from these banks, and that I spend most of my time gazing and admiring while I walk, or simply sit at the window of my room.

I do not cease congratulating myself on the thought which made me leave Paris and come to pass the spring here, though I have thereby deserved your reproach for inconstancy. Truly I am happy, and begin to feel the advantage of having been born with a caul.

There is some charming Russian society here . . . (see English in letter above).

direction they would take, finally made for Château d'Oex, from whence they proceeded by *diligence* to Thun. From that town Tolstoy went on to Lucerne, which he reached in July 1857.

Again and again in his Diary and letters Tolstoy's vivid delight in Nature shows itself in descriptions of the scenery: 'It is wonderful,' he writes, 'but I was at Clarens for two months, and every time—when in the morning, and especially after dinner towards evening—I opened the shutters on which the shadows were already falling, and glanced at the lake and the distant blue of the mountains reflected in it, the beauty blinded me and acted on me with the force of a surprise.' But together with this keen appreciation, comes now and then a sort of protest that this grandiose Swiss mountain scenery is, after all, not the Nature that most appeals to him—a yearning for the vast steppes and forests of his native land. After ascending the Pass of Jamon and describing the magnificent scenery and the pleasure of the climb, he adds:

It was something beautiful, even unusually beautiful, but I do not love what are called magnificent and remarkable views: they are, as it were, cold. . . . I love Nature when, though it surrounds me on all sides and extends unendingly, I am part of it. I love it, when on all sides I am surrounded by hot air, and that same air rolls away to unending distance, and those same sappy leaves of grass which I crush as I sit on them, form the green of the boundless meadows; when those same leaves which, fluttering in the wind, run their shadows across my face, form also the dark blue of the distant forests; while the same air one breathes makes the deep, light blue of the immeasurable sky; when you do not exult and rejoice alone in Nature, but when around you myriads of insects buzz and whirl, and beetles, clinging together, creep about, and all around you birds overflow with song.

But this is bare, cold, desolate, grey plateau; and somewhere afar there is something beautiful veiled with mist. But that something is so distant that I do not feel the chief delight of

Nature—do not feel myself a part of that endless and beautiful distance: it is foreign to me.

From Lucerne he writes :

* Je suis de nouveau tout seul, et je vous avouerai que très souvent la solitude m'est pénible, car les connaissances qu'on fait dans les hôtels et en chemin de fer ne sont pas des ressources; mais cet isolement a du moins le bon côté de me pousser au travail. Je travaille un peu, mais cela va mal, comme d'ordinaire en été.

It was here that the incident occurred described in *Lucerne*, a sketch published in the September number of the *Contemporary* that same year, and one which in its fierce castigation of the rich is a precursor of much that he wrote thirty years later. Especially the conduct of the wealthy English tourists roused his ire. The particular incident the story deals with is this :

On 7 July 1857, in Lucerne, in front of the Schweizerhof Hotel, where the richest people stay, an itinerant mendicant-singer sang songs and played his guitar for half-an-hour. About a hundred people listened to him. Three times the singer asked them to give him something, but not one of them did so, and many laughed at him.

This is not fiction, but a positive fact, which any one who cares may verify by asking the permanent inhabitants of the Schweizerhof, and by looking up the newspaper lists of foreign visitors at the Schweizerhof on 7 July.

It is an event which the historians of our times should inscribe in indelible letters of fire.

In the story, Prince Nehlúdof, indignant at such treatment of a man who was a real artist and whose songs all

---

* I am again all alone, and I confess that very often the solitude is painful to me, for the acquaintanceships one makes in hotels and on the railways are not a resource. But there is at least this much good in this loneliness—it prompts me to work. I am working a little, but it goes badly, as usual in summer.

had enjoyed, brought the singer into the hotel and treated him to a bottle of wine. He goes on to ask himself:

Which is more a man, and which more a barbarian : the lord who, on seeing the singer's worn-out clothes, angrily left the table, and for his service did not give him a millionth part of his property, and who now sits satiated, in a well-lit, comfortable room, calmly discussing the affairs of China and approving the murders that are being committed there—or the little singer who with a franc in his pocket, risking imprisonment, has tramped over hill and dale for twenty years, harming no one but cheering many by his songs, and whom they insulted to-day and all but turned out, leaving him—weary, hungry and humiliated—to make his bed somewhere on rotting straw?

After passing a few weeks at Lucerne, Tolstoy returned to Russia *viâ* Stuttgart, Berlin, and Stettin, from which port he took steamer to Petersburg, and after staying a week there to see Nekrásof and meet his colleagues of the *Contemporary*, he went through Moscow to Yásnaya, where he arrived in August. In his Diary we find this note:

This is how, on my journey, I planned my future occupations : first, literary work; next, family duties; then, estate management. But the estate I must leave as far as possible to the steward, softening him and making improvements, and spending only Rs. 2000 a year [then equal to about £270], and using the rest for the serfs. Above all, my stumbling-block is Liberal vanity. To live for oneself and do a good deed a day, is sufficient.

Further on he says : ' Self-sacrifice does not lie in saying " Take what you like from me," but in labouring and thinking, and contriving how to give oneself.'

At this time he read (in translation) the *Iliad* and the Gospels, which both impressed him greatly. ' I have finished reading the indescribably beautiful end of the *Iliad*,' he notes, and expresses his regret that there is no connection between those two wonderful works.

In October he first accompanied his brother Nicholas and his sister Mary to Moscow, and then spent a few days in Petersburg, where he found that he had been forgotten by a world absorbed in the great measures of public reform then in course of preparation. Here is a sentence from his Diary :

Petersburg at first mortified me and then put me right. My reputation has fallen and hardly gives a squeak, and I felt much hurt; but now I am tranquil. I know I have something to say and strength to say it strongly; and the public may then say what it will. But I must work conscientiously, exerting all my powers; then . . . let them spit upon the altar.

By the end of October (old style) he was back in Moscow, established in furnished apartments in the Pyátnitsky Street, with his sister and his brother Nicholas. His friend Fet was also in Moscow at this time, and in his *Recollections* makes frequent mention of the Tolstoys. He tells us that the Countess Mary (who was an exceedingly accomplished pianist) used to come to his house for music in the evenings, accompanied sometimes by both her brothers and sometimes by Nicholas alone, who would say :

' Lyóvotchka has again donned his evening clothes and white necktie, and gone to a ball.'

Tolstoy's elegance in dress was very noticeable at this period. We read of the grey beaver collar of his overcoat, of a fashionable cane he carried, and of the glossy hat he wore placed on one side, as well as of his curly, dark-brown hair.

Gymnastics were fashionable in Moscow in those days, and any one wishing to find Tolstoy between one and two o'clock in the afternoon, could do so at the Gymnasium on the Great Dmítrovka Street, where, dressed in gymnastic attire, he might be seen intent on springing over the vaulting-horse without upsetting a cone placed on its back. He always was expert at physical exercises : a first-rate horseman, quick at all games and sports, a swimmer, and an excellent skater.

Among the visitors Fet met at Tolstoy's house we note the name of Saltykóf, who under the pseudonym of Stchedrín is known as one of the keenest and most powerful of Russia's satirists, and who during the last seven years of the reign of Nicholas I had lived in banishment in the far-off town of Vyátka. Another guest was B.N.Tchitchérin, philosopher and jurist, and author of works on *Science and Religion, Property and the State,* and other subjects Tolstoy dealt with three or four decades later. Katkóf, editor of the *Moscow Gazette* and monthly *Russian Messenger,* was another acquaintance ; and in his magazine some of Tolstoy's chief works appeared.

In January 1858 Tolstoy's aunt, who had been a friend of his boyhood, the Countess Alexandra A. Tolstoy, Maid of Honour to the Grand Duchess Márya Niko- láyevna, came to Moscow. Through this aunt (who lived to a great age, and died only a few years ago) Tolstoy used to receive information of what went on at Court, and was sometimes able indirectly to exert influence ' in the highest circles.' When she returned to Petersburg Tolstoy accompanied her as far as the town of Klin, on the Nicholas railway, and took the opportunity to visit the Princess Volkónsky (a cousin of his mother's), who had a small estate in those parts. He remained some weeks with this affectionate old lady, who told him much about his mother and her family, and he greatly enjoyed his quiet stay with her. At her house he wrote *Three Deaths,* which appeared the following January in *The Reading Library.* It is an admirably written study of the deaths of a rich lady, a poor post-horse driver, and a tree.

In February he returned to Yásnaya Polyána; then again visited Moscow, and in March spent a fortnight in Petersburg. His love of music reasserted itself strongly at this period ; and in conjunction with V. P. Bótkin,

Perfílief, Mortier (his late rival in love) and others, he founded the Moscow Musical Society, which ultimately resulted in the formation of the Moscow Conservatoire of which Nicholas Rubinstein became Director.

One of Tolstoy's most intimate acquaintances at this period was S. T. Aksákof, author of stories and memoirs, lover of hunting and fishing, and father of two famous sons, both prominent Slavophil leaders.

The invigorating influence of spring shows itself in a letter Tolstoy wrote about this time to his aunt, the Countess A. A. Tolstoy (whom he calls ' Grandma ') :

GRANDMA !—Spring !
For good people it is excellent to live in the world ; and even for such men as me, it is sometimes good. In Nature, in the air, in everything, is hope, future—an attractive future. . . . Sometimes one deceives oneself and thinks that happiness and a future await not only Nature but oneself also, and then one feels happy. I am now in such a state, and with characteristic egotism hasten to write to you of things that interest only me. When I review things sanely, I know very well that I am an old, frozen little potato, and one already boiled with sauce ; but spring so acts on me that I sometimes catch myself in the full blaze of imagining myself a plant which with others has only now blossomed, and which will peacefully, simply and joyfully grow in God's world. The result is that at this time of year, such an internal clearing-out goes on in me, such a cleansing and ordering, as only those who have experienced this feeling can imagine. All the old—away ! All worldly conventions, all idleness, all egotism, all vices, all confused indefinite attachments, all regrets, even repentances—away with you all ! . . . Make room for the wonderful little flowers whose buds are swelling and growing with the spring ! . . .

After much more he concludes :

Farewell, dear Grandma, do not be angry with me for this nonsense, but answer with a word of wisdom, imbued with kindness, Christian kindness ! I have long wished to say that for

you it is pleasanter to write French, and I understand feminine
thoughts better in French.

In April he was again at Yásnaya where, in spite of
repeated visits to Moscow, he spent most of the summer.
There was at this time no railway from Moscow southward
to Toúla; and the serfs' belief concerning the new telegraph posts which stood by the side of the highroad, was
that when the wire had been completed, 'Freedom' would
be sent along it from Petersburg. Even Tatiána Alexándrovna Érgolsky did not understand these new-fangled
things, and, when driving along the road one day, asked
Tolstoy to explain how letters were written by telegraph.
He told her as simply as he could how the telegraphic
apparatus works, and received the reply : *'Oui, oui, je comprends, mon cher !'* How much she had really understood
was however shown half an hour later when, after keeping
her eye on the wire all that time, she inquired : 'But how
is it, *mon cher Léon*, that during a whole half-hour I have
not seen a single letter go along the telegraph ?'

Fet and his wife used to stay a day or two at Yásnaya
when journeying to and from Moscow, and Fet's account
of Aunt Tatiána accords with Tolstoy's own affectionate
recollections of that lady. Fet says that he and his wife
'made the acquaintance of Tolstoy's charming old aunt,
Tatiána Alexándrovna Érgolsky, who received us with that
old-world affability which puts one at once at one's ease
on entering a new house. She did not devote herself to
memories of times long past, but lived fully in the present.'

Speaking of them all by their pet names, she mentioned
that 'Seryózhenka Tolstoy had gone to his home at Pirogóvo, but Nikólenka would probably stay a bit longer in
Moscow with Máshenka, but Lyóvotchka's friend Dyákof
had recently visited them,' and so on.

Many years later, Tolstoy jotted down his memories of
the long autumn and winter evenings spent with Aunt

Tatiána to which, he says, he owed his best thoughts and impulses. He would sit in his arm-chair reading, thinking, and occasionally listening to her kindly and gentle conversation with two of the servants : Natálya Petróvna (an old woman who lived there not because she was of much use, but because she had nowhere else to live) and a maid Doúnetchka.

The chief charm of that life lay in the absence of any material care ; in good relations with those nearest—relations no one could spoil ; and in the leisureliness and the unconsciousness of flying time. . . .

When, after living badly at a neighbour's in Toúla, with cards, gipsies, hunting, and stupid vanity, I used to return home and come to her, by old habit we would kiss each other's hand, I her dear energetic hand, and she my dirty, vicious hand ; and also by old habit, we greeted one another in French, and I would joke with Natálya Petróvna, and would sit down in the comfortable arm-chair. She knew well all I had been doing and regretted it, but never reproached me, retaining always the same gentleness and love. . . . I was once telling her how some one's wife had gone away with another man, and I said the husband ought to be glad to be rid of her. And suddenly my aunt lifted her eyebrows and said, as a thing long decided in her mind, that that would be wrong of the husband, because it would completely ruin the wife. After that she told me of a drama that had occurred among the serfs. Then she re-read a letter from my sister Máshenka, whom she loved if not more, at least as much as she loved me, and she spoke of Másha's husband (her own nephew) not to condemn him, but with grief for the sorrow he inflicted on Máshenka. . . . The chief characteristic of her life, which involuntarily infected me, was her wonderful, general kindliness to every one without exception. I try to recall a single instance of her being angry, or speaking a sharp word, or condemning any one, and I cannot recall one such instance in the course of thirty years. She spoke well of our real aunt, who had bitterly hurt her by taking us away from her. . . . As to her kindly treatment of the servants—

M

that goes without saying. She had grown up in the idea that there are masters and servants, but she utilised her authority only to serve them. . . . She never blamed me directly for my evil life, though she suffered on my account. My brother Sergéy, too, whom also she loved warmly, she did not reproach even when he took a gipsy girl to live with him. The only shade of disquietude she showed on our account was that, when he was very late in returning home, she would say: 'What has become of our Sergius?' Only *Sergius* instead of *Seryózha*. . . . She never told us in words how to live, never preached to us. All her moral work was done internally; externally one only saw her deeds—and not even deeds: there were no deeds; but all her life, peaceful, sweet, submissive and loving, not troubled or self-satisfied, but a life of quiet, unobtrusive love. . . . Her affectionateness and tranquillity made her society noticeably attractive and gave a special charm to intimacy with her. I know of no case where she offended any one, and of no one who did not love her. She never spoke of herself, never of religion or of what we ought to believe, or of how she believed or prayed. She believed everything, except that she rejected one dogma—that of eternal torment. '*Dieu, qui est la bonté même, ne peut pas vouloir nos souffrances.*'[1] . . . She often called me by my father's name (Nicholas) and this pleased me very much, because it showed that her conceptions of me and of my father mingled in her love of us both.

It was not her love for me alone that was joyous. What was joyous was the atmosphere of love to all who were present or absent, alive or dead, and even to animals. . . .

After telling of her goodness and her affection Tolstoy says in his Memoirs that, though he appreciated his happiness with her, he did not at the time nearly realise its full value; and he adds:

She was fond of keeping sweets: figs, gingerbreads and dates, in various jars in her room. I cannot forget, nor remember without a cruel pang of remorse, that I repeatedly refused her money she wanted for such things and how she, sighing sadly,

[1] God, who is goodness itself, cannot desire our pain.

remained silent. It is true I was in need of money, but I cannot now remember without horror that I refused her.

Again in another place, after mentioning her self-devotion, he says :

And it was to her, to her, that I refused the small pleasure of having figs and chocolate (and not so much for herself as to treat me) and of being able to give a trifle to those who begged of her. . . . Dear, dear Aunty, forgive me ! *Si jeunesse savait, si vieillesse pouvait* [if youth but knew, if age but could], I mean not in the sense of the good lost for oneself in youth, but in the sense of the good not given and the evil done to those who are no more.

Of Leo's life at Yásnaya at this time, his brother Nicholas gave Fet the following humorous account :

Lyóvotchka is zealously trying to become acquainted with peasant life and with farming, of both of which, like the rest of us, he has till now had but a superficial knowledge. But I am not sure what sort of acquaintance will result from his efforts : Lyóvotchka wants to get hold of everything at once, without omitting anything—even his gymnastics. So he has rigged up a bar under his study window. And of course, apart from prejudice, with which he wages such fierce war, he is right : gymnastics do not interfere with farming ; but the steward sees things differently and says, 'One comes to the master for orders, and he hangs head downward in a red jacket, holding on by one knee to a perch, and swings himself. His hair hangs down and blows about, the blood comes to his face, and one does not know whether to listen to his orders or to be astonished at him !'

Lyóvotchka is delighted with the way the serf Ufán sticks out his arms when ploughing ; and so Ufán has become for him an emblem of village strength, like the legendary Michael ; and he himself, sticking his elbows out wide, takes to the plough and ' Ufanizes.'

In May 1858 Tolstoy wrote to Fet :

DEAREST LITTLE UNCLE [as we might say, Dear old Boy] !— I write two words merely to say that I embrace you with all my might, have received your letter, kiss the hand of Márya Pet-róvna [Fet's wife] and make obeisance to you all. Aunty thanks you very much for your message and bows to you, so also does my sister. What a wonderful spring it has been and is! I, in solitude, have tasted it admirably. Brother Nicholas must be at Nikólsk. Catch him and do not let him go. I want to come to see you this month. Tourgénef has gone to Winzig till August to cure his bladder.

Devil take him. I am tired of loving him. He deserts us, and won't cure his bladder.

Now good-bye, dear friend. If you have no poem ready for me by the time I come, I shall proceed to squeeze one out of you.—Your COUNT L. TOLSTOY.

Another letter to Fet runs:

Ay, old fellow, ahoy! First, you give no sign, though it is spring and you know we are all thinking of you, and that I, like Prometheus, am bound to a rock, yet thirst for sight or sound of you. You should either come, or at least send us a proper invitation. Secondly, you have retained my brother, and a very good brother, surnamed 'Firdusi' [an allusion to Nicholas's Oriental wisdom]. The chief culprit in this matter, I suspect, is Márya Petróvna, to whom I humbly bow, request-ing her to return us our own brother. Jesting apart, he bids me let you know that he will be here next week. Drouzhínin will also come, so mind you come too, old fellow.

The first record of any participation by Tolstoy in political affairs relates to the preparations for the Emanci-pation of the serfs. Immediately after the conclusion of the Crimean war Alexander II, addressing the Marshals of the Nobility, in Moscow, had said: 'The existing manner of possessing serfs cannot remain unchanged. It is better to abolish serfdom from above than to await the time when it will begin to abolish itself from below. I request you, gentlemen, to consider how this can be done, and to submit my words to the Nobility for their con-sideration.' Some time passed without any definite response to this appeal, and meanwhile the Polish nobility of the Lithuanian Provinces, dissatisfied with certain regulations enacted in the previous reign, incautiously asked to have them revised. The Government grasped the opportunity, and treating this as the expression of a wish for Emancipation, replied that 'the abolition of serfdom must be effected not suddenly, but gradually,' and authorised the Nobility to form Committees for the preparation of definite projects to that end. Four days later the Minister of the Interior, acting on secret orders from the Emperor, sent a circular to all the Governors and Marshals of the Nobility in Russia proper, stating that the Lithuanian nobles 'had recognised the necessity of liberating the peasants,' and that 'this noble intention' had afforded peculiar satisfaction to His Majesty, and explaining the principles to be observed in case the nobles of other Provinces should express a similar desire. A few weeks later the Emperor publicly expressed a hope that, with the co-operation of his nobles, the work of Emancipation would be successfully accomplished. It therefore became quite evident that, whether the nobles liked it or not, Emancipation was at hand; since the Emperor had, at last, definitely ranged himself on the side of the Emancipationists. By accepting the invitation to co-operate in the preparation of the scheme, there appeared to be a chance that the nobles might so shape the measure that their interests would not suffer; and consequently, during 1858, a Committee was chosen in almost every Province of Central Russia. Among the rest a Meeting of the Nobility of the Government of Toúla was fixed for the first of September, to elect Deputies to the Committee for the Improvement of the Condition of the Peasants. Tolstoy attended this meeting, and together with one hundred and four fellow-nobles signed a document stating that 'with the object of improving the condition of the peasants, preserving the property of the landowners, and securing the safety of both the one and the other, we consider it necessary that the peasants should be liberated not otherwise than with an allotment of a certain amount of land in hereditary possession, and that the landowners should receive for the land they give up, full, equitable, pecuniary recompense by means of such financial measures as will not entail any obligatory relations between peasants and proprietors,—relations which the Nobility consider it necessary to terminate.'

There is no indication that Tolstoy took any prominent part in this meeting; and the resolution just quoted, while approving of Emancipation, seems to attach at least equal importance to securing full compensation for the landowners. Explain it how one may, the fact remains that while the *Contemporary*, and all that was progressive in Russian literature, was preoccupied with the effort to help to shape the reforms so that they might really attain the ends aimed at, Tolstoy almost retired from the scene, and hardly appeared aware of the movement going on around him. The battle for freedom was fought in the press by Tchernyshévsky, Kosheléf, and N. Samárin, by Herzen, and by many others, including Nekrásof and Saltykóf; and Tolstoy's indifference helps to explain the fact, already alluded to, that during these years the critics ignored him, though his artistic power continued to increase. His friend Fet also took no part in the Emancipation movement; being in fact rather opposed to it.

On 24th October 1858 Tolstoy writes to Fet:

To write stories is stupid and shameful. To write verses—well, write them; but to love a good man is very pleasant. Yet perhaps, against my will and intention, not I, but an unripe story inside me, compels me to love you. It sometimes seems like that. Do what one will amid the manure and the mange, one somehow begins to compose. Thank heaven, I have not yet allowed myself to write, and will not do so. . . . Thank you exceedingly for your trouble about a veterinary. I have found one in Toúla and have begun the cure, but I do not know what will come of it.—And, may the devil take them all,—Drouzhínin is appealing to me as a matter of friendship to write a story. I really want to. I will spin such a yarn that there will be no head or tail to it. . . . But joking apart, how is your Hafiz getting on? [Fet was translating some poems by Hafiz.] Turn it which way you will, the height of wisdom and fortitude for me is to enjoy the poetry of others, and not to let my own in ugly garb loose among men, but to consume it myself with my daily bread. But at times one suddenly wishes to be a great man, and it is so annoying that this has not yet come about! One even hurries to get up quicker or to finish dinner in order to begin. . . . Send me a poem, the healthiest of those you have translated from Hafiz, *me faire venir l'eau à la bouche*,[1] and I will send you a sample of wheat. Hunting has bored me to death. The weather is excellent, but I do not hunt alone.

In company, Tolstoy was however a keen sportsman, and in December 1858 nearly lost his life while out bear-shooting. He has told the story, with some embellishments, in one of the tales for children contained in the volume, *Twenty-three Tales*.[2] The real facts were these :

Tolstoy and his brother Nicholas had made the acquaintance of S. S. Gromeka, a well-known publicist who shared their fondness for hunting—a sport very different in Russia from what it is in England, as readers of Tolstoy's descriptions well know.

Gromeka having heard that a she-bear with two young ones had her lair in the forest near the railway at Volotchók, half-way between Petersburg and Moscow, arranged matters with the peasants of that locality, and invited the Tolstoys and other guests to a hunt. The invitation was accepted, and on 21st December Leo Tolstoy shot a bear. On 22nd the members of the party, each armed with two guns, were placed at the ends of cuttings running through

---

[1] To make my mouth water.
[2] Included in the *World's Classics*.

the forest in which the big she-bear had been surrounded.
These paths or cuttings divided the wood like the lines
of a chess-board. Peasants employed as beaters were
stationed to prevent the animal escaping except by
approaching one or other of the sportsmen. Ostáshkof, a
famous professional huntsman, supervised the proceedings.
The guests were advised to stamp down the snow around
them, so as to give themselves room to move freely; but
Tolstoy (with his usual objection to routine methods)
argued that as they were out to shoot the bear and not
to box with her, it was useless to tread down the snow.
He therefore stood with his two-barrelled gun in his hand,
surrounded by snow almost up to his waist.

The bear, roused by the shouts of Ostáshkof, rushed
down a cutting directly towards one of the other sportsmen; but, perceiving him, she suddenly swerved from her
course and took a cross path which brought her out on to
the cutting leading straight to Tolstoy. He, not expecting her visit, did not fire until the beast was within
six yards, and his first shot missed. The bear was only
two yards from him when his second shot hit her in the
mouth. It failed to stop her rush, and she knocked
Tolstoy over on to his back in the snow. Carried past
him at first by her own impetus, the bear soon returned;
and the next thing Tolstoy knew was that he was
being weighed down by something heavy and warm, and
he then felt that his face was being drawn into the
beast's mouth. He could only offer a passive resistance,
by drawing down his head as much as possible between
his shoulders and trying to present his cap instead of his
face to the bear's teeth. This state of things lasted only
a few seconds, yet long enough for the bear, after one
or two misses, to get her teeth into the flesh above
and below his left eye. At this moment Ostáshkof,
armed with a small switch, came running up, shouting:
' Where are you getting to? Where are you getting

to ?' At which the beast promptly took fright, and
rushed off. Next day she was followed up and killed.
Owing to the amount of blood and torn flesh, Tolstoy's
wound at first appeared serious ; but when it had been
washed with snow, and he had been taken to the nearest
town and had had it sewn up, it turned out to be superficial. He long retained a very noticeable scar however as
a memento of the encounter ; and the bear's skin may still
be seen at Yásnaya.

Family Happiness, written partly in 1858, was published
early in 1859. It grew out of the unsuccessful love affair
mentioned in the last chapter, and is Tolstoy's imaginative
description of what might have been.

The first months of 1859 he spent in Moscow, and here
on the occasion of joining the Moscow Society of Lovers
of Russian Literature, on 4th February, he for the
first time made a public speech : a task for which, 1859
he once told me, he had no aptitude, and which he much
disliked. He wrote it out, and it was to have appeared in
the Proceedings of the Society, but for some reason never
got printed. Its subject was 'The Supremacy of the
Artistic Element in Literature,' and in it he maintained
a position almost the opposite of the one he advocated so
ardently and with such full conviction in *What is Art?*
forty years later.

He was answered by the Slavophil A. S. Homyakóf,
who presided at the meeting, and who in the course of
his remarks said :

Allow me to remark that the justice of the opinion you have
so skilfully stated is far from destroying the legitimacy of the
temporary and exceptional side of literature. That which is
always right, that which is always beautiful, that which is as
unalterable as the most fundamental laws of the soul, undoubtedly holds, and should hold, the first place in the thoughts,
the impulses, and therefore in the speech of man. It, and it
alone, will be handed on by generation to generation and by

nation to nation as a precious inheritance. But on the other hand, in the nature of man and of society there is continual need for self-indictment. There are moments, moments important in history, when that self-indictment acquires a special and indefeasible right, and manifests itself in literature with great definiteness and keenness. . . .

The rights of literature the servant of eternal beauty, do not destroy the rights of the literature of indictment, which always accompanies social deficiencies and sometimes appears as the healer of social evils. . . .

Of course, Art is perfectly free: it finds its justification and its aim in itself. But the freedom of Art in the abstract, has nothing to do with the inner life of the artist. An artist is not a theory—a sphere of thought and mental activity—but a man, and always a man of his own times, usually its best representative, completely imbued with its spirit and its defined or nascent aspirations. By the very impressionability of his nature, without which he could not be an artist, he, even more than others, receives all the painful as well as joyous sensations of the society to which he is born. . . .

So the writer, a servant of pure art, sometimes becomes an accuser even unconsciously, and despite his own will. I allow myself, Count, to cite you as an example. You consciously follow a definite road faithfully and undeviatingly; but are you really completely alien to the literature of indictment? Were it but in the picture of a consumptive post-boy, dying on top of a stove amid a crowd of comrades apparently indifferent to his sufferings [this refers to *Three Deaths*] have you not indicated some social disease, some evil? When describing that death, is it possible that you did not suffer from the horny indifference of good but unawakened human souls? Yes, you too have been and will be an involuntary indicter!

This question of the true position of literary art and its relation to the rest of life, was one which occupied Tolstoy for many years, and on which before the century closed he expressed himself in a book which must be reckoned with by all who may hereafter deal with the subject. The attitude he maintained at the time he entered

the Society of Lovers of Russian Literature, was in striking
contrast with that of the Slavophils, such as Homyakóf,
and of the great majority of the leading Russian writers
of that day, who were fired with the hope of Emancipation,
just as in America at the same time, Lowell, Emerson,
Whittier, Thoreau, Walt Whitman, Longfellow, Channing,
Lloyd Garrison, and others, were stirred by the Anti-
Slavery movement.

In April Tolstoy went to Petersburg and spent ten
days very pleasantly with his aunt the Countess A. A.
Tolstoy. By the end of the month he was back at Yásnaya.
In July, Tourgénef, from France, wrote Fet a long letter in
blank verse, a few lines of which indicate the relation between
Leo Tolstoy and himself at this time :

> ' Kiss Nicholas Tolstoy on my behalf
> And to his brother Leo make my bow,
> —As to his sister also.
> He rightly says in his postscriptum :
> " There is no cause " for me to write to him,
> Indeed, I know he bears me little love
> And I love him as little. Too differently
> Are mixed those elements of which we 're formed.'

During this winter Tolstoy devoted much time to an
attempt to organise schools on and near his estate. The
education of its peasant children was one of the 1859-
things Russia most needed, and most terribly 1860
neglected. Tolstoy recognised this, and set himself strenuously and eagerly to show how the great need could be met.
The work he did at this time was, however, only preliminary to what he undertook after his next visit to Western
Europe, and he was far from being mentally at peace. At
the commencement of the New Year he noted in his Diary :
' The burden of the estate, the burden of bachelor life, and
all sorts of doubts and pessimistic feelings agitate my
mind.'

One mention of the serfs (who were now nearing freedom) occurs in a letter Tolstoy wrote to Fet on 23rd February 1860, in reply to a note in which the latter had expressed a wish to buy an estate, settle down in the country, and devote himself to farming. Tolstoy replies that there is an estate for sale adjoining his own, containing :

Four hundred desyatíns of good land with, unfortunately, seventy souls of bad serfs. But that does not matter; they will gladly pay quit-rent [in lieu of personal service] as mine do, at the rate of Rs. 30 a *tyaglo* [man and wife with an allotment of land] or Rs. 660 for the twenty-two *tyaglos,* and you will get not less than that, if not more, at the Emancipation, and will have sufficient unexhausted land and meadow left to yield about Rs. 2000 a year, or over Rs. 2600 in all. The price asked for the estate is Rs. 24,000, besides a mortgage of about Rs. 5000. . . . At any rate it would be a good bargain to buy it for Rs. 20,000. . . . The seller is an old man who is ruined, and wants to sell it quickly in order to get rid of his son-in-law. He has twice sent to offer it me. The above calculation shows what the estate should yield in a couple of years' time if about Rs. 5000 be spent on improving it; but even in its present condition one can answer for a return of Rs. 1500, which is more than 7 per cent. on the cost.

In Russia to buy serfs was not then considered more discreditable than it is in England to-day to buy shares in a china or match factory; and in the same letter Tolstoy goes on to discuss literature :

I have read Tourgénef's *On the Eve.* This is my opinion : to write novels is undesirable, especially for people who are depressed and do not well know what they want from life. However, *On the Eve* is much better than *A Nest of Gentlefolk,* and there are in it excellent negative characters : the artist and the father. The rest are not types; even their conception, their position, is not typical, or they are quite insignificant. That however is always Tourgénef's mistake. The girl is hopelessly bad : ' Ah, how I love thee . . . her eyelashes were long.'

In general it always surprises me that Tourgénef, with his mental powers and poetic sensibility, should even in his methods not be able to refrain from banality. This banality shows itself most of all in his negative methods, which recall Gógol. There is no humanity or sympathy for the characters, but the author exhibits monsters whom he scolds and does not pity. This jars painfully with the tone and intention of Liberalism in everything else. It was all very well in the days of Tsar Goroh [a character in a fairy story] or of Gógol (though if one does not pity even the most insignificant of one's characters, one should scold them so that the heavens grow hot, or laugh at them so that one's sides split, and not as our splenetic and dyspeptic Tourgénef does). On the whole, however, there is now no one else who could write such a novel, though it will not meet with success.

Ostróvsky's *The Storm* is, in my opinion, a wretched work, but will be successful. Not Ostróvsky and Tourgénef are to blame, but the times. . . . Something else is now needed: not that we should learn and criticise, but that we should teach Jack and Jill at least a little of what we know.

This letter to Fet, who was in Moscow, ends with requests to procure some books, including a veterinary handbook, a veterinary instrument, and a lancet for use on human beings; to see about procuring six ploughs of a special make, and to find out the price of clover and timothy-grass, of which Tolstoy had some to sell.

At this time Tolstoy worked at his story *The Cossacks*, the plan of which he had sketched out in 1852, but which he did not complete till 1862.

1860

One comes across notes in his Diary which indicate his state of mind at this period with regard to religion. After reading a book on Materialism he notes:

I thought of prayer. To what can one pray? What is God, imagined so clearly that one can ask him to communicate with us? If I imagine such an one, he loses all grandeur for me. A God whom one can beseech and whom one can serve—is the expression of mental weakness. He is God, because I cannot grasp his being. Indeed, he is not a Being, but a Law and a Force.

He was a great puzzle to his friends and acquaintances —always ready to take his own line strenuously, yet sometimes far from sure what that line was. Tourgénef wrote to Fet :

Leo Tolstoy continues his eccentricities. Evidently it was so decreed at his birth. When will he turn his last somersault and stand on his feet ?

The fact that Tolstoy, like his friend Fet, was neglecting literature did not fail to call forth many remonstrances, one of the most urgent of which came to him from Drouzhínin, who wrote :

Every writer has his moments of doubt and self-dissatisfaction, and however strong and legitimate this feeling may be, no one on that account has yet ceased his connection with literature ; every one goes on writing to the end. But all tendencies, good or bad, cling to you with peculiar obstinacy ; so that you, more than others, need to think of this and to consider the whole matter amicably.

First of all, remember that after poetry and mental labour all other work seems worthless. *Qui a bu, boira* ; and at the age of thirty to tear oneself away from authorship means losing half the interest of life. But that is only half the matter ; there is something still more important.

On all of us lies a responsibility rooted in the immense importance of literature to Russian society. An Englishman or an American may laugh at the fact that in Russia not merely men of thirty, but grey-haired owners of 2000 serfs sweat over stories of a hundred pages, which appear in the magazines, are devoured by everybody, and arouse discussion in society for a whole day. However much artistic quality may have to do with this result, you cannot explain it merely by Art. What in other lands is a matter of idle talk and careless dilettantism, with us is quite another affair. Among us things have taken such shape that a story—the most frivolous and insignificant form of literature—becomes one of two things: either it is rubbish, or else it is the voice of a leader sounding throughout the Empire. For instance, we all know Tourgénef's weakness, but a whole ocean divides the most insignificant of his stories from the very best of Mrs. Eugene Tour's, with her half-talent. By some strange instinct the Russian public has chosen from among the crowd of writers four or five bell-men whom it values as leaders, refusing to listen to any qualifications or deductions. You—partly by talent, partly by the practical qualities of your soul, and partly owing simply to a concurrence of fortunate circumstances—have stepped into this favourable relation with the public. On that account you must not go away and hide, but must work, even to the exhaustion of your strength and powers. That is one side of the matter; but here is another. You are a member of a literary circle that is honourable (as far as may be), independent, and influential; and which for ten years, amid persecutions and misfortunes, and notwithstanding its members' vices, has firmly upheld the banner of all that is Liberal and enlightened, and has borne all this weight of abuse without committing one mean action. In spite of the world's coldness and ignorance and its contempt for literature, this circle is rewarded with honour and moral influence. Of course, there are in it insignificant and even stupid homunculi; but even they play a part in the general union, and have not been useless. In that circle you again, though you arrived but recently, have a place and a voice such as Ostróvsky for instance does not possess, though he has immense talent and his moral tendency is as worthy as your own. Why this has happened it would take too long to analyse, nor is it to the point. If you tear yourself off from the circle of writers and become inactive, you will be dull, and will deprive yourself of an important rôle in society. . . .

At this time the state of health of his brother Nicholas —who (like Demetrius) had consumptive tendencies—began to disturb Leo Tolstoy. It was arranged that Nicholas should go to Germany for a cure. The following letter written by Leo Tolstoy to Fet, after Nicholas had started, refers to this and other matters :

. . . You are a writer and remain a writer, and God speed you. But that, besides this, you wish to find a spot where you can dig like an ant, is an idea which has come to you and which you must carry out, and carry out better than I have done. You must do it because you are both a good man and one who looks at life healthily. . . . However, it is not for me now to deal out to you approval or disapproval with an air of authority. I am greatly at sixes and sevens with myself. Farming on the scale on which it is carried out on my estate, crushes me. To 'Ufanize'[1] is a thing I only see afar off. Family affairs, Nicholas's illness (of which we have as yet no news from abroad) and my sister's departure (she leaves me in three days' time) also crush and occupy me. Bachelor life, *i.e.* not having a wife, and the thought that it is getting too late, torments me from a third side. In general, everything is now out of tune with me. On account of my sister's helplessness and my wish to see Nicholas, I shall at any rate procure a foreign passport to-morrow, and perhaps I shall accompany my sister abroad ; especially if we do not receive news, or receive bad news, from Nicholas. How much I would give to see you before leaving, how much I want to tell you and to hear from you ; but it is now hardly possible. Yet if this letter reaches you quickly, remember that we leave Yásnaya on Thursday or more probably on Friday.

Now as to farming : The price they ask of you is not exorbitant, and if the place pleases you, you should buy it. Only why do you want so much land ? I have learned by three years' experience that with all imaginable diligence it is impossible to grow cereals profitably or pleasantly on more than 60 or 70 desyatíns [160 to 190 acres] that is, on about 15 desyatíns in each of four fields. Only in that way can one escape trembling for every omission (for then one ploughs not twice but three or four times) and for every hour a peasant misses, and for every extra rouble-a-month one pays him ; for one can bring 15 desy-

---

[1] To work like a peasant. The origin of this word is given on p. 179.

atíns to the point of yielding 30 to 40 per cent. on the
fixed and working capital; but with 80 or 100 desyatíns under
plough one cannot do so. Please do not let this advice slip
past your ears; it is not idle talk, but a result of experience I
have had to pay for. Any one who tells you differently is either
lying or ignorant. More than that, even with 15 desyatíns an
all-absorbing industry is necessary. But then one can gain
a reward—one of the pleasantest life gives; whereas with 90
desyatíns one has to labour like a post-horse, with no possibility
of success. I cannot find sufficient words to scold myself for
not having written to you sooner—in which case you would
surely have come to see us. Now farewell.

Things meanwhile were not going very well with
Nicholas, who wrote from Soden in Hesse-Nassau:

In Soden we joined Tourgénef, who is alive and well—so
well that he himself confesses that he is 'quite' well. He has
found some German girl and goes into ecstasies about her. We
(this relates to our dearest Tourgénef) play chess together, but
somehow it does not go as it should: he is thinking of his
German girl, and I of my cure. . . . I shall probably stay in
Soden for at least six weeks. I do not describe my journey
because I was ill all the time.

Eventually Leo Tolstoy made up his mind to accompany
his sister and her children abroad, and on 3rd July (old
style) they took steamer from Petersburg for Stettin *en
route* for Berlin. Besides anxiety on his brother's account,
Tolstoy had another reason for going abroad: he wished
to study the European systems of education, in order to
know what had been accomplished in the line to which he
now intended to devote himself.

On reaching Berlin he suffered from toothache for four
days, and decided to remain there while his sister proceeded to join Nicholas at Soden. He consulted a doctor,
as he was suffering also from headache and hemorrhoidal
attacks, and he was ordered to take a cure at Kissingen.

He only stayed a few days in Berlin after getting rid of his toothache, and left on 14th July (old style), having however found time to attend lectures on History by Droysen, and on Physics and Physiology by Du Bois-Reymond, and having also visited some evening classes for artisans at the *Handwerksverein*, where he was greatly interested in the popular lectures, and particularly in the system of ' question-boxes.' The method of arousing the interest of the audience by allowing them to propound questions for the lecturer to reply to, was new to him, and he was struck by the life it brought into the classes, and by the freedom of mental contact between scholars and teacher. He noticed the same thing when he was in London a few months later, for he told me that nothing he saw there interested him more than a lecture he attended in South Kensington, at which questions were put by working men, and answered by a speaker who was master of his subject and knew how to popularise it.

In Berlin he visited the Moabit Prison, in which solitary confinement was practised. Tolstoy strongly disapproved of this mechanical attempt to achieve moral reformation. From Berlin he went to Leipzig, where he spent a day inspecting schools; but he derived little satisfaction from the Saxon schools he visited, as is indicated by a remark he jotted down in his Diary, ' Have been in school—terrible. Prayers for the King, blows, everything by rote, frightened, paralysed children. . . .' He then proceeded to Dresden, where he called on the novelist Auerbach, whose story, *Ein Neues Leben* (*A New Life*), had much influenced him. The chief character in that story is Count Fulkenberg, who after being an officer in the army, gets into trouble, escapes from prison, buys the passport of a schoolmaster, Eugene Baumann, and under that name devotes himself to the task of educating peasant children. When Auerbach entered the room in which his visitor was waiting, the latter introduced himself with the words : ' I am Eugene

Baumann,' in such solemn tones and with so morose an
appearance, that the German writer was taken aback and
feared that he was about to be threatened with an action
for libel. Tolstoy however hastened to add : ' —not in
name, but in character—' and went on to explain how
good an effect Auerbach's *Schwarzwälder Dorfgeschichten*
(*Village Tales of the Black Forest*) had had on him.

After three days in Dresden, he went on to Kissingen,
which was in those days about five hours' journey from
Soden, where Nicholas was staying. Still intent on his
educational inquiries, he read *en route* a history of
pedagogics.

From Kissingen he wrote his Aunt Tatiána that he
thought the cure was doing him good, and added :

Tell the steward to write me most minutely about the
farming, the harvest, the horses and their illness. Tell the
schoolmaster to write about the school : how many pupils come,
and whether they learn well. I shall certainly return in
autumn and intend to occupy myself more than ever with the
school, so I do not wish its reputation to be lost while I am
away, and I want as many pupils as possible from different
parts.

While in Kissingen he read Bacon and Luther and
Riehl, and made the acquaintance of Julius Froebel, author
of *The System of Social Politics* and nephew of Froebel,
the founder of the Kindergarten system. Julius Froebel
was himself much interested in educational matters, and
was a particularly suitable person to explain his uncle's
ideas to Tolstoy.

The latter astonished his new acquaintance, with whom
he used to go for walks, by the uncompromising rigidity
of his views, which showed a considerable tinge of Slavophilism. Progress in Russia, declared Tolstoy, must be
based on popular education, which would give better
results in Russia than in Germany, because the Russian
people were still unperverted, whereas the Germans were

like children who had for years been subjected to a bad education.   Popular education should not be compulsory. If it is a blessing, the demand for it should come naturally, as the demand for food comes from hunger.

Tolstoy visited the country round Kissingen, and travelling northward through a part of Germany rich both in scenery and in historic interest, reached Eisenach and visited the Wartburg, where Luther was confined after the Diet of Worms. The personality of the great Protestant reformer interested Tolstoy greatly, and after seeing the room in which Luther commenced his translation of the Bible, he noted in his Diary : ' Luther was great ' ! Twenty years later Tolstoy himself attempted to free the minds of men from the yoke of an established Church, and he too shaped his chief weapon against the Church by translating, not, it is true, like Luther, the whole Bible, but the Gospels.

Meanwhile Nicholas Tolstoy's health had been growing worse rather than better. Sergius, having been unlucky at roulette, decided to return to Russia, and visiting Leo at Kissingen *en route*, told him of his fears for Nicholas.   On 9th August Sergius left Kissingen and Nicholas himself arrived there to visit Leo, but soon returned to Soden. Leo then spent a fortnight in the Harz Mountain district, enjoying nature and reading a great deal. On 26th August he rejoined Nicholas, his sister and her children, at Soden. The doctors had decided that Nicholas must winter in a warmer climate, and the place decided on was Hyères near Toulon, on the shores of the Mediterranean.

The first stage of the journey undertaken by the family party was to Frankfurt-on-Main, where their aunt, the Countess A. A. Tolstoy, was staying. She tells the following story of Leo's visit to her on this occasion :

One day Prince Alexander of Hesse and his wife were calling on me, when suddenly the door of the drawing-room opened and Leo appeared in the strangest garb, suggestive of a picture of a Spanish bandit. I gasped with astonishment. Leo apparently was not pleased with my visitors, and soon took his departure.

* ' Qui est donc ce singulier personnage ? ' inquired my visitors in astonishment.

' Mais c'est Léon Tolstoy.'

' Ah, mon Dieu, pourquoi ne l'avez vous pas nommé ? Après avoir lu ses admirables écrits, nous mourions d'envie de le voir,' said they, reproachfully.

From Frankfurt the party proceeded to Hyères, where Nicholas, growing rapidly worse and worse, died on 20th September (new style).

Few men have been so admired and loved as he was by all who knew him. The only thing recorded against him is the fact that when serving in the Caucasus he, like many of his fellow-officers, gave way to some extent to intemperance; but after returning home he recovered his self-control. I have already told of his influence over Leo in the early days of the Ant-Brotherhood, and of the green stick, buried where Tolstoy himself wishes his body to lie. Such influence he retained all through life, and men and women of most different temperaments make equally enthusiastic mention of his charm and goodness. That Leo's judgment of what is good and bad has remained strongly influenced by his love for and memory of Nicholas, is plain enough to all who have the facts before them and read his works attentively.

Tourgénef once said :

The humility which Leo Tolstoy developed theoretically, his brother actually practised in life. He always lived in the most impossible lodgings, almost hovels, somewhere in the out-of-the-

---

* Who is that singular person ?

Why, it is Leo Tolstoy !

Ah, good heavens ! Why did you not tell us who it was ? After reading his admirable writings, we were dying to see him.

way quarters of Moscow, and he willingly shared all he had
with the poorest outcast.   He was a delightful companion and
narrator, but writing was to him almost a physical impossibility,
the actual process of writing being as difficult for him as for a
labourer whose stiff hands will not hold a pen.

Nicholas did, however, as a matter of fact, contribute
some *Memoirs of a Sportsman* to the *Contemporary*.

Never was any one's death more sincerely regretted.
This is the letter Leo wrote to Aunt Tatiána, the night the
event occurred.

CHÈRE TANTE !—The black seal will have told you all.   What
I have been expecting from hour to hour for two weeks occurred
at nine o'clock this evening.   Only since yesterday did he let me
help him undress, and to-day for the first time he definitely took
to his bed and asked for a nurse.   He was conscious all the time,
and a quarter-of-an-hour before he died he drank some milk and
told me he was comfortable.   Even to-day he still joked and
showed interest in my educational projects.   Only a few
minutes before he died he whispered several times : ' My God,
my God ! '   It seems to me that he felt his position, but
deceived himself and us.   Máshenka, only to-day, some four
hours before, had gone three miles out of Hyères to where she
is living.   She did not at all expect it to come so soon.   I have
just closed his eyes.   I shall now soon be back with you and
will tell you all personally.   I do not intend to transport the
body.   The funeral will be arranged by the Princess Golítsin,
who has taken it all on herself.

Farewell, *chère tante*.   I cannot console you.   It is God's
will—that is all.   I am not writing to Seryózha now.   He is
probably away hunting, you know where.   So let him know, or
send him this letter.

On the day after the funeral he wrote to Sergius :

I think you have had news of the death of Nicholas.   I am
sorry for you that you were not here.   Hard as it is, I am glad
it all took place in my presence, and that it acted on me in the
right way—not like Mítenka's [his third brother, Demetrius]

death, of which I heard when I was not thinking at all about
him. However, this is quite different. With Mítenka only
memories of childhood and family feeling were bound up; but
this was a real man both to you and to me, whom we loved and
respected positively more than any one else on earth. You know
the selfish feeling which came latterly, that the sooner it was
over the better; it is dreadful now to write it and to remember
that one thought it. Till the last day, with his extraordinary
strength of character and power of concentration, he did everything to avoid becoming a burden to me. On the day of his
death he dressed and washed himself, and in the morning I
found him dressed on his bed. Only about nine hours before
he died did he give way to his illness and ask to be undressed.
It first happened in the closet. I went downstairs, and heard
his door open. I returned and did not find him. At first I
feared to go to him—he used not to like it; but this time he
himself said, ' Help me ! '

And he submitted and became different that day, mild and
gentle. He did not groan, did not blame any one, praised
everybody, and said to me: ' Thank you, *my friend.*' You
understand what that meant between us. I told him I had
heard how he coughed in the morning, but did not come to
him from *fausse honte* [false shame]. ' Needlessly,' said he—
' it would have consoled me.' Suffering ? He suffered; but it
was not until a couple of days before his death that he once said :
' How terrible these nights without sleep are ! Towards morning
the cough chokes one, unendingly ! And it hurts—God knows
how ! A couple more such nights—it 's terrible ! ' Not once
did he say plainly that he felt the approach of death. But he
only did not *say* it. On the day of his death he ordered a
dressing-gown, and yet when I remarked that if he did not
get better, Máshenka and I would not go to Switzerland, he
replied : ' Do you really think I shall be better ? ' in such a
tone that it was evident what he felt but for my sake did not
say, and what I for his sake did not show; all the same, from
the morning I knew what was coming, and was with him all
the time. He died quite without suffering—externally, at all
events. He breathed more and more slowly—and it was all
over. The next day I went to him and feared to uncover his

face. I thought it would show yet more suffering and be more terrible than during his illness; but you cannot imagine what a beautiful face it was, with his best, merry, calm expression.

Yesterday he was buried here. At one time I thought of transporting him, and of telegraphing for you; but I reconsidered it. It is no use chafing the wound. I am sorry for you that the news will have reached you out hunting, amid distractions, and will not grip you as it does us. It is good for one. I now feel what I have often been told, that when one loses some one who was what he was to us, it becomes much easier to think of one's own death.

On 13th October 1860 he notes in his Diary:

It is nearly a month since Nicholas died. That event has torn me terribly from life. Again the question: Why? Already the departure draws near. Whither? Nowhere. I try to write, I force myself, but do not get on, because I cannot attach enough importance to the work to supply the necessary strength and patience. At the very time of the funeral the thought occurred to me to write a Materialist Gospel, a Life of Christ as a Materialist.

One sees how bit by bit the seeds of the work Tolstoy was to do in later years planted themselves in his mind. In early childhood came the enthusiasm for the Ant-Brotherhood and the influence of his brother, of Aunt Tatiána, and of the pilgrims; then an acquaintance with the writings of Voltaire and other sceptics, undermining belief in the miraculous; then, in Sevastopol, the idea of 'founding a new religion: Christianity purged of dogmas and mysticism'; then a study of Luther's Reformation, and now the idea of a rationalist Life of Christ.

On 17th October Tolstoy writes to Fet:

I think you already know what has happened. On 20 September he died, literally in my arms. Nothing in my life has so impressed me. It is true, as he said, that nothing is worse than death. And when one reflects well that yet *that* is the end of all, then there is nothing worse than life. Why

Tolstoy in 1860, the year his brother
Nicholas died.

strive or try, since of what was Nicholas Tolstoy nothing remains his? He did not say that he felt the approach of death, but I know he watched each step of its approach and knew with certainty how much remained. Some moments before his death he drowsed off, but awoke suddenly and whispered with horror: 'What is that?' That was when he saw it—the absorption of himself into Nothingness. And if he found nothing to cling to, what can I find? Still less! And assuredly neither I nor any one will fight it to the last moment, as he did. Two days before, I said to him: 'We ought to put a commode in your room.'

'No,' said he, 'I am weak, but not yet so weak as that; I will struggle on yet awhile.'

To the last he did not yield, but did everything for himself, and always tried to be occupied. He wrote, questioned me about my writings, and advised me. But it seemed to me that he did all this not from any inner impulse, but on principle. One thing—his love of Nature—remained to the last. The day before, he went into his bedroom and from weakness fell on his bed by the open window. I came to him, and he said with tears in his eyes, 'How I have enjoyed this whole hour.'

From earth we come, and to the earth we go. One thing is left—a dim hope that there, in Nature, of which we become part in the earth, something will remain and will be found.

All who knew and saw his last moments, say: 'How wonderfully calmly, peacefully he died'; but I know with what terrible pain, for not one feeling of his escaped me.

A thousand times I say to myself: 'Let the dead bury their dead.' One must make some use of the strength which remains to one, but one cannot persuade a stone to fall upwards instead of downwards whither it is drawn. One cannot laugh at a joke one is weary of. One cannot eat when one does not want to. And what is life all for, when to-morrow the torments of death will begin, with all the abomination of falsehood and self-deception, and will end in annihilation for oneself? An amusing thing! Be useful, be beneficent, be happy while life lasts,—say people to one another; but you, and happiness, and virtue, and utility, consist of truth. And the truth I have learned in thirty-two years is, that the position in which we are placed is terrible. 'Take life as it is; you have put yourselves in that position.' How! I take life as it is. As soon as man reaches the highest degree of development, he sees clearly that it is all nonsense and deception, and that the truth—which he still loves better than all else—is terrible. That when you look at it well and clearly, you wake with a start and say with terror, as my brother did: 'What is that?'

Of course, so long as the desire to know and speak the truth lasts, one tries to know and speak. That alone remains to me of the moral world; higher than that I cannot place myself. That alone I will do, but not in the form of your art. Art is a lie, and I can no longer love a beautiful lie.

I shall remain here for the winter because I am here, and it is all the same where one lives. Please write to me. I love you as my brother loved you, and he remembered you to his last moment.

A month later we find him writing in a different state of mind:

A boy of thirteen has died in torment from consumption. What for? The only explanation is given by faith in the compensation of a future life. If that does not exist, there is no justice, and justice is vain, and the demand for justice—a superstition.

Justice forms the most essential demand of man to man. And man looks for the same in his relation to the universe. Without a future life it is lacking. Expediency is the sole, the unalterable law of Nature, say the naturalists. But in the best manifestations of man's soul: love and poetry—it is absent. This has all existed and has died—often without expressing itself. Nature, if her one law be expediency, far o'erstepped her aim when she gave man the need of poetry and love.

Nearly twenty years later, in his *Confession*, Tolstoy referred to his brother's death in the words:

Another event which showed me that the superstitious belief in progress is insufficient as a guide to life, was my brother's death. Wise, good, serious, he fell ill while still a young man, suffered for more than a year and died painfully, not understanding why he had lived, and still less why he had to die. No theories could give me, or him, any reply to these questions during his slow and painful dying.

Any one who has read the works Tolstoy wrote during the quarter of a century which succeeded his brother's death, will be aware how long he remained in doubt on this matter of a future life, and how he expressed now one, and now another view.

At Hyères he continued to study the question of education, and for that purpose made many visits to Marseilles. He also wrote: continuing *The Cossacks* and commencing an article on Popular Education. We get a glimpse of him at this period from his sister, who tells us that they had been invited to an At Home at Prince Doundoukóf - Korsákof's; but Tolstoy, who was to have been the lion of the occasion, failed to put in an appearance. The company, which included all the 'best' people, were getting dull, despite everything the hostess could devise for their amusement, when at last, very late, Count Tolstoy was announced. The hostess and her guests immediately brightened up; but what was their astonishment to see him appear in tourist garb and wearing wooden *sabots* ! He had been for a long walk, and returning late, had come to the party without calling at his lodgings; and no sooner was he in the room than he began assuring everybody that wooden *sabots* were the very best and most comfortable of foot-gear, and advising every one to adopt them. Even in those days he was a man to whom all things were allowed, and the evening, instead of being spoilt, became all the gayer from his eccentricity. There was a great deal of singing, and it fell to Tolstoy's lot to accompany the singers.

At Hyères, after his brother's death, Tolstoy lived with his sister and her three children in a *pension* where the only other lodgers were a Madame Pláksin and her delicate nine-year-old son Sergéy, whose lungs were thought to be affected, but who lived to become a poet and to publish his recollections of Tolstoy. Pláksin describes him as having been at that time a strongly built, broad-shouldered man, with a good-natured smile on his face, which was fringed by a thick, dark-brown beard. Under a large forehead, still bearing a deep scar from the wound inflicted by the bear two years before, wise, kind eyes shone out of very deep sockets. 'Tolstoy,' says Pláksin, 'was the soul of our little society, and I never saw him dull; on the contrary, he liked to amuse us with his stories, which were sometimes extremely fantastic.' Tolstoy rose early, and while he was at work the children were not allowed to disturb him beyond running in for a moment to say 'good-morning.' Being himself an indefatigable walker, Tolstoy used to plan out excursions for the company, constantly discovering new places to visit: the salterns on the peninsula of Porquerolle; the holy hill where the chapel with the wonder-working image of the Madonna stands; or the ruins of the castle called *Trou des Fées*. They used to have with them on these excursions, a small ass carrying provisions, fruit and wine.

On the way Tolstoy used to tell us various tales; I remember one about a golden horse and a giant tree, from the top of which all the seas and all towns were visible. Knowing that my lungs were delicate, he often took me on his shoulder and continued his tale as he walked along. Need I say that we would have laid down our lives for him?

At dinner-time Tolstoy used to tell the French pro-prietors of the *pension* the strangest stories about Russia, which they never knew whether or not to believe until the Countess or Madame Pláksin came to their rescue by separating the truth from the fiction.

After dinner, either on the terrace or indoors, a per-

formance commenced, opera or ballet, to the sound of the
piano : the children ' mercilessly tormenting the ears of the
audience' (which consisted of the two ladies, Tolstoy, and
Pláksin's nurse). Next came gymnastic exercises, in which
Tolstoy acted as professor. ' He would lie at full length
on the floor, making us do the same, and we had then to
get up without using our hands.' He also contrived an
apparatus out of rope, which he fixed up in the doorway ;
and on this he performed somersaults, to the great delight
of his juvenile audience.

When the latter became too turbulent and the ladies
begged Tolstoy to subdue the noise, he would set the children round the table, and tell them to bring pens and ink.

The following is an example of the sort of occupation he
provided :

'Listen,' said he one day ; 'I am going to give you a lesson.'
'What on?' demanded bright-eyed Lisa.
Disregarding his niece's question, he continued :
'Write . . .'
'But what are we to write, uncle?' persisted Lisa.
'Listen ; I will give you a theme . . . !'
'What will you give us?'
'A theme !' firmly replied Tolstoy. 'In what respect does
Russia differ from other countries? Write it here, in my
presence, and don't copy from one another ! Do you hear?'
added he, impressively.

In half an hour the ' compositions ' were ready. Pláksin had to read his own, as his lines were so irregular that
no one else could decipher them. In his opinion Russia
differed from other countries in that, at carnival time,
Russians eat pancakes and slide down ice-hills, and at
Easter they colour eggs.

'Bravo !' said Tolstoy, and proceeded to make out
Kólya's MS., in which Russia was distinguished by its
snow, and Lisa's, in which ' troikas ' (three-horse convey-
ances) played the chief part.

In reward for these evening exercises, Tolstoy brought water-colour paints from Marseilles and taught the children drawing.

He often spent nearly the whole day with the children, teaching them, taking part in their games, and intervening in their disputes, which he analysed, proving to them who was in the right and who in the wrong.

There was at this time some mutual attraction between Tolstoy and a young Russian lady, Miss Yákovlef, who was staying at Hyères; but, like many other similar affairs, it came to nothing.

On leaving Hyères, Tolstoy, his sister, and her children, went to Geneva, and from thence he proceeded alone to Nice, Leghorn, Florence, Rome, and Naples. In Italy he says he experienced his first lively impression of antiquity; but very little record remains of this journey, and it is nowhere reflected in his writings.

He returned to Paris *viâ* Marseilles, the schools and other institutions of which he observed closely, trying to discover how man's intelligence is really best developed.

He was very unfavourably impressed by the popular schools of Marseilles. The studies, he says, consisted in learning by heart the Catechism, sacred and general History, the four rules of Arithmetic, French spelling and Book-keeping—the latter without sufficient comprehension of the use of arithmetic to enable the children to deal sensibly with the simplest practical problems requiring addition and subtraction, though they could do long multiplication sums quickly and well when only abstract figures were given. Similarly, they answered well by rote questions in French History, but, when asked at hazard, they would give such answers as that Henry IV was killed by Julius Cæsar.

He observed the instruction given by the Churches, and visited the adult schools of the town, as well as its *Salles d'Asile*, in which, he says:

I saw four-year-old children perform like soldiers, evolutions round benches to orders given by whistle, and raise and cross their arms to the word of command, and with strange trembling voices sing hymns of praise to God and their benefactors ; and I became convinced that the educational establishments of Marseilles were extremely bad.

Any one seeing them would naturally conclude that the French people must be ignorant, coarse, hypocritical, full of superstition and almost savage.

Yet one need only come in contact with and chat with any of the common people, to convince oneself that on the contrary the French people are almost what they consider themselves to be : intelligent, clever, sociable, freethinking, and really civilised. Take a workman of, say, thirty years of age : he will write a letter without such mistakes as at school, sometimes even quite correctly ; he has some idea of politics, and therefore of recent history and geography ; he knows some history from novels, knows something of natural history, and he very often draws, and is able to apply mathematical formulae to his trade. Where did he get all this ?

I recently discovered the answer in Marseilles, by wandering about the streets, drink-shops, *cafés chantants*, museums, workshops, wharves and book-stalls. The very boy who told me that Henry IV was killed by Julius Cæsar, knew the history of *The Three Musketeers* and of *Monte Cristo* very well.

In Marseilles Tolstoy found that everybody had read Dumas' works, of which there were twenty-eight cheap editions. He estimated that each week, in the *cafés chantants*, at least one-fifth of the population received oral education, as the Greeks and Romans used to do. Comedies and sketches were performed, verses declaimed, and the influence for good or evil of this unconscious education far outweighed that of the compulsory education given in schools.

In January he reached Paris, where he spent a large part of his time in omnibuses, amusing himself by observing the people. He declares he never met a 1861 passenger who was not represented in one or other of Paul de Kock's stories. Of that writer, as of Dumas *père*, he thinks highly. 'Don't talk nonsense to me,' he once said, 'about Paul de Kock's immorality. He is, according to English ideas, somewhat improper. He is more or less what the French call *leste* and *gaulois*, but never immoral. In everything he says, and despite his rather free jests, his tendency is quite moral. He is a French Dickens. . . . As to Dumas, every novelist should know him by heart. His plots are admirable, not to mention the workmanship. I can read and re-read him, though he aims chiefly at plots and intrigue.'

In Paris he again met Tourgénef; and from France he went on to London, where he remained six weeks, not enjoying his visit much as he suffered severely from toothache nearly all the time. It is characteristic of Tolstoy that though he has often been a victim to toothache and has also been much tried by digestive troubles, he never appears to have had his teeth properly attended to by a dentist. A dentist's establishment seems to him so unnatural and artificial that it must be wrong. Moreover, dentists do not always do their work well; and toothache —if one endures it long enough—cures itself, and in the past the majority of mankind have got along without dentists. So he has been inclined to put up with toothache as one of the ills it is best to bear patiently.

During his stay he, and Tourgénef who had also come to London, saw a great deal of Alexander Herzen, who was editing *Kólokol* (*The Bell*)—the most influential paper ever published by a Russian exile.

I have already remarked on the fact that the Reform movements of that time left Tolstoy curiously cold; and here again it may be noted that though Tourgénef contributed to Herzen's prohibited paper, Tolstoy never wrote anything for it.

Herzen's little daughter, who had read and greatly enjoyed *Childhood*, *Boyhood*, and *Youth*, hearing that the author was coming to see her father, obtained permission to be present when he called. She ensconced herself in an arm-chair in a corner of the study at the appointed time, and when Count Tolstoy was announced, awaited his appearance with beating heart; but she was profoundly disillusioned by the entrance of a man of society manners, fashionably dressed in the latest style of English tailoring, who began at once to tell with gusto of the cock-fights and boxing-matches he had already managed to witness in London. Not a single word with which she could sympathise did she hear from Tolstoy throughout that one and only occasion on which she was privileged to listen to his conversation; and in this she was particularly unlucky, for Tolstoy saw Herzen very frequently during his stay in London, and the two discussed all sorts of important questions together.

One of Herzen's closest friends and co-workers during his long exile from Russia, was the poet N. P. Ogaryóf, who had been his fellow-student at the Moscow University. Ogaryóf, besides being a man of ability, possessed a very amiable character that greatly endeared him to his friends; but in an essay entitled *The First Step*[1] written in 1892, we get a glimpse of what alienated Tolstoy's sympathy from the progressive movement these men represented. He there says:

I have just been reading the letters of one of our highly educated and advanced men of the 'forties, the exile Ogaryóf, to another yet more highly educated and gifted man, Herzen. In these letters Ogaryóf gives expression to his sincere thoughts and highest aspirations, and one cannot fail to see that—as was natural to a young man—he rather shows off before his friend. He talks of self-perfecting, of sacred friendship, love, the service of science, of humanity, and the like. And at the same time he calmly writes that he often irritates the companion of his life by, as he expresses it, 'return-

---

[1] In the volume *Essays and Letters*, included in the *World's Classics*.

ing home in an unsober state, or disappearing for many hours with a fallen, but dear creature.' . . .

Evidently it never even occurred to this remarkably kind-hearted, talented, and well-educated man that there was anything at all objectionable in the fact that he, a married man, awaiting the confinement of his wife (in his next letter he writes that his wife has given birth to a child) returned home intoxicated, and disappeared with dissolute women. It did not enter his head that until he had commenced the struggle, and had at least to some extent conquered his inclination to drunkenness and fornication, he could not think of friendship and love, and still less of serving any one or any thing. But he not only did not struggle against these vices—he evidently thought there was something very nice in them, and that they did not in the least hinder the struggle for perfection; and therefore instead of hiding them from the friend in whose eyes he wishes to appear in a good light, he exhibits them.

Thus it was half a century ago. I was contemporary with such men. I knew Ogaryóf and Herzen themselves and others of that stamp, and men educated in the same traditions. There was a remarkable absence of consistency in the lives of all these men. Together with a sincere and ardent wish for good, there was an utter looseness of personal desire, which, they thought, could not hinder the living of a good life, nor the performance of good and even great deeds. They put unkneaded loaves into a cold oven, and believed that bread would be baked. And then, when with advancing years they began to remark that the bread did not bake—*i.e.* that no good came of their lives—they saw in this something peculiarly tragic.

This was written twenty years later; but it was latent in his mind at the time, and furnishes a clue to the fact that he never really made friends with these men.

Of Herzen as a writer Tolstoy ultimately came to have a very high opinion, and admitted that he exerted a very considerable influence on the mind of educated Russia.

In England, as elsewhere, Tolstoy saw as much as he could of the educational methods in vogue. He also visited the House of Commons and heard Palmerston speak for three hours ; but he told me he could form no opinion of the oration, for ' at that time I knew English with my eyes but not with my ears.'

While in London, he received news that he had been nominated Arbiter of the Peace for his own district, near Toúla. The duties of the office were to settle disputes between the serfs and their former proprietors. Except a short service on the Zémstvo in 1874, this was the only official position in which Tolstoy ever took much active part after leaving the army.

On 3rd March (new style), the day of Alexander II's famous Manifesto emancipating the serfs, Tolstoy left London for Russia *viâ* Brussels. In that city he made the acquaintance of Proudhon (the author of *Qu'est-ce que la Propriété ?* and a *Système des Contradictions Économiques*) to whom Herzen had given him a letter of introduction. Proudhon impressed Tolstoy as a strong man who had the courage of his opinions ; and though Proudhon's theories had no immediate effect on Tolstoy's life, the social political and economic views expounded by the latter a quarter of a century later, are deeply dyed with Proudhonism. Both writers consider that property is robbery ; interest immoral ; peaceful anarchy the desirable culmination of social progress, and that every man should be a law unto himself, restrained solely by reason, conscience and moral suasion. Another writer whose acquaintance Tolstoy made in Brussels was the Polish patriot Lelewel, who had taken a prominent part in the rebellion of 1830, and had written on Polish history and on many other subjects. He was at this time a decrepit old man living in great poverty. While in Brussels Tolstoy wrote *Polikoúshka*, almost the only story of his (besides *A Squire's Morning*) that implies a condemnation of serfdom.

Passing through Germany, Tolstoy stopped at Weimar, where he stayed with the Russian Ambassador, Von Maltitz, and was introduced to the Grand Duke Carl Alexander. Tolstoy (who had been reading Goethe's *Reineke Fuchs* not long before) visited the house in which Goethe had lived, but was more interested in a Kindergarten conducted by Minna Schelholm, who had been trained by Froebel. From another school he visited, we hear of his collecting and carrying off the essays the pupils had written, explaining to the master that he was much concerned with the problem, ' How to make thought flow more freely.'

At Jena he made acquaintance with a young mathematician named Keller, whom he persuaded to accompany him to Yásnaya to help him in his educational activities. He also stopped at Dresden, where he again visited Auerbach, concerning whom he jots down in his Diary :

21 *April, Dresden* : Auerbach is a most charming man. Has given me a light. . . . He spoke of Christianity as the spirit of humanity, than which there is nothing higher. He reads verse enchantingly. Of Music as *Pflichtloser Genuss* (dutyless pleasure). . . . He is 49 years old. Straightforward, youthful, believing, not troubled by negation.

On another occasion Tolstoy expressed surprise at never having seen Auerbach's *Village Tales of the Black Forest* in any German peasant's house, and declared that Russian peasants would have wept over such stories.

From Dresden he wrote to his Aunt Tatiána :

* Je me porte bien et brûle d'envie de retourner en Russie. Mais une fois en Europe et ne sachant quand j'y retournerai, vous comprenez que j'ai voulu profiter, autant que possible, de mon voyage. Et je crois l'avoir fait. Je rapporte une si grande quantité d'impressions, de connaissances, que je devrai tra-

---

* I am in good health and burn with desire to return to Russia. But once in Europe and not knowing when I shall return, you understand that I wanted to benefit as much as possible by my travels. And I think I have done so. I am bringing back such a

vailler longtemps, avant de pouvoir mettre tout cela en ordre dans ma tête.

I am bringing with me a German from the University, to be a teacher and clerk, a very nice, well-educated man, but still very young and unpractical.

He adds that he intends to return to Yásnaya *viâ* St. Petersburg, as he wants to obtain permission to publish an educational magazine he is projecting.

On 22nd April he was already in Berlin, where he made the acquaintance of the head of the Teachers' Seminary, the son of the celebrated pedagogue Diesterweg, whom, to his disappointment, he found to be ' a cold, soulless pedant, who thinks he can develop and guide the souls of children by rules and regulations.'

On 23rd April (old style) he re-entered Russia, after a stay abroad of nearly ten months.

He brought with him complete editions of the works of several of the greatest European writers. They were kept at the Custom House to be submitted to the Censor, and, as Tolstoy plaintively remarked nearly half a century later, ' he is still reading them ! '

CHIEF AUTHORITIES FOR CHAPTER VI

Birukof.
Bitovt.
Fet, *Moi Vospominaniya* : Moscow, 1890.
Tolstoy's *Confession.*
Golovatcheva-Panaeva, *Rousskie Pisateli i Artisty.*
Tourgenef, *Letters.*
S. Plaksin, *Graf L. Tolstoy sredi detey.*
Tolstoy's works, vol. iv. : Moscow, 1903.
R. Löwenfeld, *Leo N. Tolstoj.*
R. Löwenfeld, *Gespräche über und mit Tolstoy.*

great quantity of impressions and facts, that I must work a long time before I can get it all in order in my head.

CHAPTER VII

AT YÁSNAYA AGAIN; TOURGÉNEF; ARBITER; MAGAZINE

Quarrel with Tourgénef. Attitude towards Reforms. Arbiter of the Peace. Educational Magazine.

AFTER the winter's snow has so far thawed that sleighing is impracticable, there comes a time during which there is still too much snow left, and the roads have become too soft to allow of travelling on wheels, and when transit is practically impossible. Tolstoy reached Moscow at this transition period, but had not to wait long before the roads were dry enough for carriage traffic. He made the journey southward to Toúla in company with Mrs. Fet, wife of his friend the poet. Mrs. Fet was travelling in her own carriage, accompanied by her maid, to the estate Fet had purchased at some distance from Yásnaya. Tolstoy had his own conveyance, but for company's sake changed places with the maid and travelled with Mrs. Fet. In the cool of the evening he borrowed and wrapped himself in a cloak of Fet's, declaring that this would be sure to result in his producing a lyric poem.

Soon after reaching Yásnaya he wrote (in the third week of May) to congratulate Fet on having become a landed proprietor:

1861

How long it is since we met, and how much has happened to both of us meanwhile! I do not know how to rejoice sufficiently when I hear or think of your activity as a farmer, and I am rather proud to have had at least some hand in the matter. . . . It is good to have a friend ; but he may die or go away, or one may not be able to keep pace with him ; but Nature, to which one is wedded by a Notarial Deed, or to which one has been born by inheritance, is still better.   It is one's own bit of Nature.   She is cold, obdurate, disdainful and exacting, but then she is a friend one does not lose till death, and even then one will be absorbed into her.   I am however at present less devoted to this friend : I have other affairs that attract me ; yet but for the consciousness that she is there, and that if I stumble she is at hand to hold on to—life would be but a sad business.

A few days later, having received an invitation from Tourgénef, Tolstoy paid him a visit the first hours of which passed off to their mutual satisfaction.   Tourgénef had just finished his favourite novel, *Fathers and Sons*, and it was arranged that after dinner Tolstoy was to read it and give his opinion on it.   To do this the more comfortably, Tolstoy, left in the drawing-room by himself, lay down on a large sofa.   He began to read ; but the story seemed to him so artificially constructed and so unimportant in its subject-matter, that he fell fast asleep.

' I awoke,' he narrates, ' with a strange sensation, and when I opened my eyes I saw Tourgénef's back just disappearing.'

In spite of this occurrence and the unpleasant feeling it occasioned, the two novelists set out next morning to visit Fet, who was not expecting them that day.

While the visitors rested for a couple of hours, recovering from the fatigue of their journey, Mrs. Fet saw to it that the dinner assumed ' a more substantial and inviting appearance.'   During the meal the whole party began an animated conversation, and Tourgénef, always fond of good eating, fully appreciated the efforts Fet's excellent man-cook had made.   Champagne flowed, as was usual at such reunions.   After dinner the three friends strolled to a wood a couple of hundred yards from the house, and lying down in the high grass at its outskirts, continued their talk with yet more freedom and animation.

Next morning at the usual breakfast time, about eight o'clock, the visitors entered the room where Mrs. Fet presided at the samovár. Fet sat at the opposite end of the table, Tourgénef at the hostess's right hand, and Tolstoy at her left. Knowing the importance Tourgénef attached to the education of his natural daughter, who was being brought up in France, Mrs. Fet inquired whether he was satisfied with her English governess. Tourgénef praised the latter highly, and mentioned that, with English exactitude, she had requested him to fix the sum his daughter might give away in charity. 'And now,' added Tourgénef, 'she requires my daughter to take in hand and mend the tattered clothes of the poor.'

To Tolstoy, the foreign education Tourgénef was giving his daughter, who was quite forgetting her own language, was very distasteful; and his feeling no doubt showed itself in his question:

'And you consider that good?'

'Certainly: it places the doer of charity in touch with everyday needs.'

'And I consider that a well-dressed girl with dirty, ill-smelling rags on her lap, is acting an insincere, theatrical farce.'

'I beg you not to say that!' exclaimed Tourgénef, with dilated nostrils.

'Why should I not say what I am convinced is true?' replied Tolstoy.

'Then you consider that I educate my daughter badly?'

Tolstoy replied that his thought corresponded to his speech.

Before Fet could interpose, Tourgénef, white with rage, exclaimed: 'If you speak in that way I will punch your head!' and, jumping up from the table and seizing his head in his hands, he rushed into the next room. A second later he returned and, addressing Mrs. Fet, said:

'For heaven's sake excuse my improper conduct, which I deeply regret!' and again left the room.

Fet, realising the impossibility of keeping his visitors together after what had happened, was perplexed what to do, for they had both arrived in Tourgénef's vehicle, and, newly established in the country, Fet, though he had horses, had none accustomed to be driven in the only conveyance he possessed. To get Tourgénef off was easy; but it was not without some difficulty and even danger from the restive horses, that Tolstoy was conveyed to the nearest post-station at which a hired conveyance could be procured.

From Novosélok, the first country house Tolstoy reached, he wrote Tourgénef a letter demanding an apology; and asked for an answer to be sent to the next post-house at Bogousláf. Tourgénef, not noticing this request, sent his reply to Fet's house, in consequence of which it was several hours late in reaching Tolstoy—who was so enraged at this (as it seemed to him) fresh act of discourtesy, that from Bogousláf he sent a messenger to procure pistols, and wrote a second letter containing a challenge to Tourgénef, and stating that he did not wish to fight in a merely formal manner, like literary men who finish up with champagne, but that he was in earnest, and hoped Tourgénef would meet him with pistols at the outskirt of the Bogousláf woods.

That night was a sleepless one for Tolstoy. The morning brought Tourgénef's reply to his first letter. It commenced in the usual formal manner of polite communications:

GRACIOUS SIR, LEO NIKOLÁYEVITCH!—In reply to your letter, I can only repeat, what I myself considered it my duty to announce to you at Fet's: namely, that carried away by a feeling of involuntary enmity, the causes of which need not here be considered, I insulted you without any definite provocation; and I asked your pardon. What happened this morning proved clearly that attempts at intimacy between such opposite natures as yours and mine can lead to no good result;

and I the more readily fulfil my duty to you, because the present letter probably terminates our relations with one another. I heartily hope it may satisfy you, and I consent in advance to your making what use you please of it.

With perfect respect, I have the honour to remain, Gracious Sir, your most humble servant,   Iv. TOURGÉNEF.

SPÁSSKY, 27 *May* 1861.

P.S. 10.30 P.M.:

Iván Petróvitch has just brought back my letter, which my servant stupidly sent to Novosélok instead of to Bogousláf. I humbly beg you to excuse this accidental and regrettable mistake, and I hope my messenger will still find you at Bogousláf.

Tolstoy thereupon wrote to Fet:

I could not resist opening another letter from Mr. Tourgénef in reply to mine. I wish you well of your relations with that man, but I despise him. I have written to him, and therewith have terminated all relations, except that I hold myself ready to give him any satisfaction he may desire. Notwithstanding all my apparent tranquillity, I was disturbed in spirit and felt I must demand a more explicit apology from Mr. Tourgénef; I did this in my letter from Novosélok. Here is his answer, which I accept as satisfactory, merely informing him that my reason for excusing him is not our opposite natures, but one he may himself surmise.

In consequence of the delay which occurred, I sent besides this, another letter, harsh enough and containing a challenge, to which I have not received any reply; but should I receive one I shall return it unopened. So there is an end of that sad story, which, if it goes beyond your house, should do so with this addendum.

Tourgénef's reply to the challenge came to hand later, and ran as follows:

Your servant says you desire a reply to your letter; but I do not see what I can add to what I have already written; unless it be that I admit your right to demand satisfaction, weapons in hand. You have preferred to accept my spoken and repeated apology. That was as you pleased. I will say

without phrases, that I would willingly stand your fire in order
to efface my truly insane words. That I should have uttered
them is so unlike the habits of my whole life, that I can only
attribute my action to irritability evoked by the extreme and
constant antagonism of our views. This is not an apology—I
mean to say, not a justification—but an explanation. And
therefore, at parting from you for ever—for such occurrences
are indelible and irrevocable—I consider it my duty to repeat
once again that in this affair you were in the right and I in the
wrong. I add that what is here in question is not the courage I
wish, or do not wish, to show, but an acknowledgment of your
right to call me out to fight, in the accepted manner of course
(with seconds), as well as your right to pardon me. You have
chosen as you pleased, and I have only to submit to your decision.
I renew my assurance of my entire respect, IV. TOURGÉNEF.

The quarrel was not, however, destined to die out so
quickly. Even good-natured Fet got into trouble by
trying to reconcile the irascible novelists. Here is one
of the notes he received from Tolstoy :

I request you not to write to me again, as I shall return
your letters, as well as Tourgénef's, unopened.

Fet remarks : 'So all my attempts to put the matter
right ended in a formal rupture of my relations with
Tolstoy, and I cannot now even remember how friendly
intercourse between us was renewed.'

Before four months had passed, Tolstoy repented him
of his quarrel. Like Prince Nehlúdof in *Resurrection*, he
used from time to time to repent of all his sins and all
his quarrels, and undertook a sort of spring- or autumn-
cleaning of his soul. It was at such a moment that, on
25th September, he wrote to Tourgénef expressing regret
that their relations to one another were hostile, and he
added : 'If I have insulted you, forgive me ; I find it
unendurably hard to think I have an enemy.' Not knowing
Tourgénef's address in France, he sent this letter to a
bookseller in Petersburg (with whom he knew Tourgénef

corresponded) to be forwarded. The letter took more than three months to reach its destination, nor was this the only thing that went wrong, as is shown by the following portion of a letter, dated 8th November, from Tourgénef to Fet :

Apropos, 'one more last remark' about the unfortunate affair with Tolstoy. Passing through Petersburg I learned from certain 'reliable people' (Oh, those reliable people!) that copies of Tolstoy's last letter to me (the letter in which he 'despises' me) are circulating in Moscow, and are said to have been distributed by Tolstoy himself. That enraged me, and I sent him a challenge to fight when I return to Russia. Tolstoy has answered that the circulation of the copies is pure invention, and he encloses another letter in which, recapitulating that, and how, I insulted him, he asks my forgiveness and declines my challenge. Of course the matter must end there, and I will only ask you to tell him (for he writes that he will consider any fresh communication from me to him as an insult) that I myself repudiate any duel, etc., and hope the whole matter is buried for ever. His letter (apologising) I have destroyed. Another letter, which he says he sent me through the bookseller Davídof, I never received. And now as to the whole matter—*de profundis.*

Tolstoy noted in his Diary one day in October :

Yesterday I received a letter from Tourgénef in which he accuses me of saying he is a coward and of circulating copies of my letter. I have written him that it is nonsense, and I have also sent him a letter : 'You call my action dishonourable and you formerly wished to punch my head ; but I consider myself guilty, ask pardon, and refuse the challenge.'

Even then the matter was not at an end, for on 1862 7th January [new style ?] Tourgénef writes to Fet :

And now a plain question : Have you seen Tolstoy ? I have only to-day received the letter he sent me in September through Davídof's bookshop (how accurate are our Russian merchants!). In this letter he speaks of his intention to insult me, and apologises, etc. And almost at that very time, in con-

sequence of some gossip about which I think I wrote you,
I sent him a challenge. From all this one must conclude that
our constellations move through space in definitely hostile conjunction, and that therefore we had better, as he himself says,
avoid meeting. But you may write or tell him (if you see him)
that I (without phrase or joke) *from afar* love him very much,
respect him and watch his fate with sympathetic interest; but
that in proximity all takes a different turn. What's to be done?
We must live as though we inhabited different planets or
different centuries.

Tolstoy evidently took umbrage at Tourgénef's message,
and visited his wrath on Fet's innocent head. To be profoundly humble and forgiving at his own command, was
always, it seems, easier for Tolstoy than to let his opponent
have an opinion of his own. Tolstoy likes things to be
quite clear-cut and definite, and it complicates matters to
have to reckon with any one else's views. At any rate
Tourgénef writes:

PARIS, 14 *Jan.* [o.s.?] 1862.

DEAREST AFANÁSY AFANÁSYEVITCH! [Fet's Christian name
and patronymic].—First of all I must ask your pardon for the
quite unexpected tile (*tuile*, as the French say) that tumbled
on your head as a result of my letter. The one thing which
somewhat consoles me is that I could not possibly have
expected such a freak on Tolstoy's part, and thought I was
arranging all for the best. It seems it is a wound of a kind
better not touched at all.

To judge the relations between these two great writers
fairly, one must remember that Tourgénef was ten years
the elder and, until *War and Peace* appeared, ranked
higher in popular esteem; yet Tolstoy showed him no
deference, but on the contrary often attacked him and
his views with mordant irony. Tourgénef was neither ill-
natured nor quarrelsome. If Tolstoy had treated him with
consideration or had been willing to let him alone, there
would have been no question either of insult or of challenge.
But the younger man sought the elder's company, and then

made himself disagreeable; and this, not of malice pre-
pense, but because it is his nature to demand perfection
from great men, and vehemently to attack those who fail
to reach the standard he sets up.   This conduct was no
doubt all the more trying for Tourgénef, because Tolstoy
neither co-operated with the Liberal movement then current,
nor lived more abstemiously with regard to food, wine,
women, and cards than others of his set whom he scolded;
or if he did so, he did it so spasmodically and with such
serious lapses, as to be little entitled to condemn others
with the fervour he frequently displayed.   On the occasion
of the great quarrel Tourgénef was certainly the aggressor,
and his prompt apology was not addressed to Tolstoy,
whom he had chiefly offended, but to Mrs. Fet.   It is,
however, plain that he acted, as he said, on the irritable
impulse of the moment.   Tolstoy aggravated matters by
sending a challenge before receiving a reply to his first
letter, and also by suggesting that he despised Tourgénef
and pardoned him for reasons ' he may himself surmise.'
Again, in relation to Fet, who merely wished to pour oil on
the troubled waters, Tolstoy showed a strange irritability.
No one however can read the *Recollections* Fet wrote
thirty years later, without seeing that that poet—who not
only witnessed this affair, but had been the confidant of
both writers for years—respected Tolstoy far more than he
respected Tourgénef.

In this whole story, one may detect traces of the qualities which have made Tolstoy so interesting and so per-
plexing a personality.   He cares intensely about everything
with which he is occupied.   Tourgénef, and Tourgénef's
opinions and conduct, were of tremendous importance to
him.   So were his own views of how young ladies should
be brought up.   So was the question whether he ought to
challenge his enemy; and, later on, the question whether he
ought to forgive him, and whether Fet should be allowed to
act as mediator.   It is this fact—that he cares about things

a hundred times more than other people care about them
—that makes Tolstoy a genius and a great writer. What
was admirable in his conduct was not that he acted well
(as a matter of fact he acted very badly) but that he *wished*
to act well.

The same spirit which made him so intolerant with
Tourgénef: his strong feeling that 'To whom much is
given, of him much shall be required'—had something
to do, later in life, with his fierce attacks on Governments, on Shakespear, on Wagner, and on other great
institutions and men. At the same time, the incident
throws light on that side of Tolstoy's character which has
brought it about that, despite the very real charm he
possesses, and despite the fact that many men and women
have been immensely attracted by his writings, he has had
very few intimate friends, and has constantly been misunderstood.

V. P. Bótkin, who was in touch both with Tolstoy and
Tourgénef, wrote to Fet after hearing of the quarrel:

The scene between him [Tourgénef] and Tolstoy at your
house, produced on me a sad impression. But do you know,
I believe that in reality Tolstoy has a passionately loving soul;
only he wants to love Tourgénef ardently, and unfortunately
his impulsive feeling encounters merely mild, good-natured indifference. That is what he cannot reconcile himself to. And
then (again unfortunately) his mind is in a chaos, *i.e.* I wish to
say it has not yet reached any definite outlook on life and the
world's affairs. That is why his conviction changes so often, and
why he is so apt to run to extremes. His soul burns with unquenchable thirst; I say 'unquenchable,' because what satisfied it
yesterday, is to-day broken up by his analysis. But that analysis
has no durable and firm reagents, and consequently its results
evaporate *ins blaue hinein*. Without some firm ground under
one's feet it is impossible to write. And that is why at present
he *cannot* write, and this will continue to be the case till his
soul finds something on which it can rest.

To any one acquainted with the history of Russia at that period, but not acquainted with Tolstoy's idiosyncrasies, it must indeed seem strange that the story of his life can be told with so little reference to the Emancipation or the Reform movements of the years 1860-1864, to which allusion has already been made. Two passages written by him in 1904 state his relation to those movements with the sincerity which is so prominent and valuable a feature of his character:

As to my attitude at that time to the excited condition of our whole society, I must say (and this is a good and bad trait always characteristic of me) that I always involuntarily opposed any external, epidemic pressure; and that if I was excited and happy at that time, this proceeded from my own personal, inner motives: those which drew me to my school work and into touch with the peasants.

I recognise in myself now the same feeling of resistance to the excitement at present prevailing; which resembles that which, in a more timid form, was then current.

When the Emancipation came, the peasants received freedom, and an allotment of land, subject to a special land-tax for sixty years; while their masters retained the rest of the land and received State Bonds for the capitalised value of the peasants' land-tax. An expedient resorted to by many a proprietor was, to allot land to the peasants in such a way that the latter were left without any pasture, and (being surrounded by the owner's estate) found themselves obliged to hire pasture land of him on his own terms. There were, till the Emancipation, two ways of holding serfs: (1) the primitive way of obliging them to work so many days a week for their master, before they could, on the other days, provide for their own wants; and (2) another way, which left the serf free to work for himself, provided that he paid *obrók*, *i.e.* a certain yearly tribute to his owner. These explanations will render intelligible the second passage referred to above and quoted below:

Some three or four years before the Emancipation, I let my serfs go on *obrók*. When complying with the Emancipation Decree I arranged, as the law required, to leave the peasants in possession of the land they were cultivating on their own behalf, which amounted to rather less than eight acres per head, and (to my shame be it said) I added nothing thereto. The only thing I did—or the one evil I refrained from doing—was that I abstained from obliging the peasants to exchange land (as I was advised to do) and left them in possession of the pasture they needed. In general, however, I did not show any disinterested feeling in the affair.

In the first edition of *Tolstoy and his Problems* I erroneously stated that Tolstoy, before the Decree of Emancipation, voluntarily freed his serfs; and though this was corrected in the second edition, it is necessary to repeat the correction here, as the same mistake occurs in the article on Tolstoy in the *Encyclopædia Britannica*. I therefore quote the following passage from a letter he wrote me on the subject:

I have received your book and read it with pleasure. The short biography is excellent, except the place where you, quoting the words of Sophia Andréyevna, say that 'he liberated his peasants before the Emancipation.' That is wrong: I placed them on *obrók* instead of keeping them on *bárstchina* [*i.e.* the state in which the peasants rendered labour dues]. It would not have been possible to emancipate them. . . .

Tolstoy's curious tendency to underrate the influence of the Liberal reformers of that time, may be illustrated by an incident that occurred at a dinner in Toúla. The local elections had taken place, and a public 1861 banquet was given in honour of those Arbiters of the Peace who were visiting the town. Tolstoy was at this dinner, and when the toast to the health of Alexander II, the 'Tsar-Liberator,' was proposed, Tolstoy remarked to his neighbour: 'I drink this toast with particular pleasure.

P

No others are needed, for in reality we owe the Emancipation to the Emperor alone.'

A yet more curious instance of the same tendency occurs in an article on *Progress, and the Definition of Education,* which he published a year later, and in which, arguing that printing has been of little use to the people, he says that:

Even taking as an example the abolition of serfdom, I do not see that printing helped the solution of the problem in a progressive sense. Had the Government not said its decisive word in that affair, the press would, beyond a doubt, have explained matters in quite a different way to what it did. We saw that most of the periodicals would have demanded the emancipation of the peasants without any land, and would have produced arguments apparently just as reasonable, witty and sarcastic [as they actually produced in favour of the more Liberal solution ultimately adopted]. . . .

If, however, Tolstoy did not stand in the ranks of the Reformers, he was much less of a partisan of his own class than many of his fellow-nobles desired; and we find the Marshal of the Nobility of Toúla writing to Valoúef, Minister of Home Affairs, complaining of Tolstoy's appointment as Arbiter of the Peace on the ground that he was disliked by the neighbouring landowners. In consequence of this complaint Valoúef made inquiries, and received a 'confidential' reply from the Governor of the Province, stating that:

Knowing Count Tolstoy personally, as an educated man warmly sympathising with the matter in hand, and in view of a wish expressed to me by some of the proprietors of the district that he should be appointed Arbiter, I cannot replace him by some one I do not know.

Tolstoy tried his best to act fairly between peasants and landowners; but from the start his unsuitability for duties involving methodical care was obvious.

The very first 'charter,' regulating the relations between a landlord and his newly-liberated peasants, that he sent up to the Government Board for Peasant Affairs, was signed as follows : ' At the request of such-and-such peasants, because of their illiteracy, the house-serf so-and-so has signed this charter for them.' Not a single name did the charter contain ! As Tolstoy had dictated the words, so his servant had written them down, and the charter had been sealed and sent off without being read over.

He could at times be wonderfully patient in dealing with the peasants, though they were exasperatingly pertinacious in demanding more than it was possible to grant. An eye-witness tells how Tolstoy visited a neighbouring estate on which differences had arisen between the peasants and their former master, as to the land which should be allotted to them. Tolstoy received a deputation, consisting of three of the leading peasants of the village, and asked them :

' Well, lads, what do you want ? '

They explained what land they wished to have, and Tolstoy replied, ' I am very sorry I can't do what you wish. Were I to do so I should cause your landlord a great loss ' ; and he proceeded to explain to them how the matter stood.

' But you 'll manage it for us somehow, *bátushka* ' [literally, ' little-father '], said the peasants.

' No, I can't do anything of the kind,' repeated Tolstoy.

The peasants glanced at one another, scratched their heads, and reiterated their ' But somehow, *bátushka* ! ' and one of them added, ' If only you want to, *bátushka*, you 'll know how to find a way to do it ! ' at which the other peasants nodded their heads approvingly.

Tolstoy crossed himself, as orthodox Russians are wont to do, and said : ' As God is holy, I swear that I can be of no use at all to you.' But still the peasants repeated : ' You 'll take pity on us, and do it somehow, *bátushka* ! '

Tolstoy at last turned vehemently to the steward, who was present, and said: 'One can sooner, like Amphion, move the hills and woods, than convince peasants of anything!'

The whole conversation, says the steward, lasted more than an hour, and up to the last minute the Count retained his patient and friendly manner towards the peasants. Their obstinacy did not provoke him to utter a single harsh word.

With the landowners Tolstoy had even more trouble than with the peasants. He received many threatening letters, plans were formed to have him beaten, he was to have been challenged to a duel; and denunciations against him were sent to those in authority.

After some three months of the work, in July 1861, he jotted down in his Diary: 'Arbitration has given me but little material [for literary work], has brought me into conflict with all the landed-proprietors, and has upset my health.'

Here is a sample of the cases he had to deal with. A Mrs. Artukóf complained that a certain Mark Grigóref (who had been a house-serf, and was therefore not entitled to land) had left her, considering himself to be 'perfectly free.'

Tolstoy, in his reply to the lady, said:

Mark, by my order, is at liberty to go immediately, with his wife, where he likes; and I beg you (1) to compensate him for the three-and-a-half months he has been illegally kept at work by you since the Decree was published, and (2) for the blows still more illegally inflicted on his wife. If my decision displeases you, you have a right of appeal to the Magistrates' Sessions and to the Government Sessions. I shall not enter into further explanations on this subject.—With entire respect I have the honour to remain, your humble servant,

C⁀ L. Tolstoy.

The lady appealed to the Magistrates' Sessions, and

Tolstoy's decision was annulled; but on the case being carried to the Government Sessions, his view of the case prevailed.

Before he had been a year in office we find him writing to the Government of the Toúla Board of Peasant Affairs as follows :

As the complaints [here follows a list of several cases] lodged against my decisions have no legal justification, but yet in these and many other cases my decisions have been and are being repealed, so that almost every decision I give is subsequently reversed; and as under such conditions—destructive both of the peasants' and the landowners' confidence in the Arbiter—the latter's activity becomes not merely useless but impossible, I humbly request the Government Board to authorise one of its members to hasten the examination of the above-mentioned appeals, and I have to inform the Government Board that until such investigations are completed I do not consider it proper that I should exercise the duties of my office, which I have, therefore, handed over to the senior Candidate.

The following month he resumed official work, but six weeks later, on 30th April 1862, on the score of ill-health, he handed the duties over to a substitute ; and on 26th May—about a year after he had first assumed the office— the Senate informed the Governor of Toúla that it 'had decided to discharge the Lieutenant of Artillery, Count Leo Tolstoy, on the ground of ill-health' from the post of Arbiter of the Peace.

His unsatisfactory experience of administrative work no doubt helps to account for the anti-Governmental bias shown in his later works. Even at this time, he quite shared the dislike of civil and criminal law expressed by Rousseau when he wrote in his *Confession*:

The justice and the inutility of my appeals left in my mind a germ of indignation against our stupid civil institutions, in which the true welfare of the public, and veritable justice, are always sacrificed to I know not what apparent order, really destructive of all order, and which merely adds the sanction of public authority to the oppression of the weak and the iniquity of the strong.

We may at any rate be sure that tiresome, petty administrative work, never quite satisfactory, but at best consisting of compromises and of decisions based on necessity rather than on such principles of abstract justice as are dear to Tolstoy's soul, could never be an occupation satisfactory to him. He has not the plodding patience and studious moderation that such work demands; nor could his impulsive genius find scope in it. It has never been easy for him to be checked by others, or to have to reckon with their opinions and wishes. Like Rousseau, it suits him better to reform the world on paper, or even to alter his own personal habits of life, than to concern himself with the slow social progress, the bit-by-bit amelioration, which alone is possible to those harnessed to the car that carries a whole society of men.

Tolstoy used at this time to find recreation in hunting, and often went out for days together with his friend and relation Prince D. D. Obolénsky, who describes him as having been a bold and active hunter, leaping all sorts of obstacles, and a wonderful man to talk to.

Concurrently with his duties as Arbiter, Tolstoy had been carrying on an enterprise in which he had to deal with people younger and more easy to mould than the peasants and proprietors whose quarrels he found it so hard to adjust; and during the winter of 1861-1862 he devoted himself with especial fervour to the task of educating the peasant children of Yásnaya and the surrounding district.

As we have already seen, a chief aim of his travels abroad had been to study the theory and practice of education; and not only did he now personally devote himself to the school at Yásnaya, but in the surrounding neighbourhood eleven similar schools were soon started, all more or less inspired by his ideals and encouraged by his co-operation. The monthly magazine, *Yásnaya Polyána* (now a bibliographical rarity) which he produced and edited during 1862, aimed at propagating his theories of education and making known the results attained in his school, and it also contained an account of sums voluntarily contributed for its support. From articles published in it (and republished in his collected writings) we get a vivid description of the work carried on in November and December 1861.[1] Like many Russian magazines, *Yásnaya Polyána* always appeared late, and, to begin with, the January number was several weeks behind time.

In this educational work, Tolstoy showed the qualities and limitations which in later years marked all his propagandist activity. There was the same characteristic selection of a task of great importance; the same readiness to sweep aside and condemn nearly all that civilised humanity had accomplished up to then; the same assurance that he could untie the Gordian knot; and the same power of devoted genius enabling him really to achieve much more than one would have supposed possible, though not a tithe of what he set himself to do.

In later life Tolstoy laid no particular emphasis on what he wrote in these educational articles: in fact, we shall find him sometimes speaking very scornfully of them; but they throw so much light on his then state of mind, and often come so near to the views he strongly advocated twenty or thirty years later, that it will be worth devoting a good deal of attention to them.

Tolstoy, then, defines Education as: *a human activity*,

[1] In one edition after another of Tolstoy's works, the article referred to above is called 'Yásno-Polyána School in Nov. and Dec. 1862,' though the article itself appeared in the first number of *Yásnaya Polyána*, in February of that year. In small matters of detail of this kind, Tolstoy has always been careless.

having for its basis a desire for equality, and the constant tendency to advance in knowledge. This he illustrates by saying that the aim of a teacher of arithmetic should be to enable his pupil to grasp all the laws of mathematical reasoning he himself is master of; the aim of a teacher of French, or chemistry, or philosophy, should be similar; and as soon as that aim is attained, the activity will naturally cease. Everywhere and always, teaching which makes the pupil the master's equal, has been considered good. The more nearly and rapidly this is accomplished, the better; the less nearly and more slowly it is accomplished, the worse. Similarly in literature (an indirect method of teaching) those books are written best, in which the author succeeds in transmitting his whole message most easily to the reader.

By 'the constant tendency to advance in knowledge,' Tolstoy meant that the equality aimed at in education can only be obtained on the higher, and not on the lower, level: that is to say, not by the teacher forgetting what he knows, but by the pupil acquiring the teacher's knowledge. Much tuition however is based not on the desire to equalise knowledge, but on quite false foundations.

These are: (1) First and commonest, the child learns in order not to be punished; (2) the child learns in order to earn a reward; (3) the child learns in order to be better than others; (4) the child, or young man, learns in order to obtain an advantageous position in the world. . . .

With reference to the practice of sending boys to school, not for their natural development, but that they may be moulded into a set form, Tolstoy declares that 'Education, as a deliberate moulding of people into certain forms, is *sterile, illegitimate, and impossible.'*

Of examinations he strongly disapproves, as tending to arbitrariness on the side of the examiners, and deception on the side of the pupils.

Under what circumstances, asks Tolstoy, can a pupil acquire knowledge most rapidly? 'A child or a man is receptive only when he is aroused; and therefore to regard a merry spirit in school as an enemy or a hindrance, is the crudest of blunders.

The pupil's state of mind is the most important condition of successful education; and to secure good results, freedom is indispensable. No child should be forced to learn what it does not want to, or when it does not wish to.

One need only glance at one and the same child at home or in the street, and at school.   Here you see a vivacious, inquisitive being, with a smile in his eye and on his mouth, seeking information everywhere as a pleasure, and clearly, and often forcibly, expressing his thoughts in his own way; while there you see a weary, shrinking creature repeating, merely with his lips, some one else's thoughts in some one else's words, with an air of fatigue, fear and listlessness: a creature whose soul has retreated like a snail into its shell.   One need but glance at these two conditions to see which of them is the more conducive to the child's development.   That strange physiological condition which I call the 'School state of mind,' and which unfortunately we all know so well, consists in all the higher capacities: imagination, creative power and reflection, yielding place to a semi-animal capacity to pronounce words without imagination or reflection.

When the pupils have been reduced to this 'School state of mind' we encounter those 'not accidental, but often-repeated cases,' of the stupidest boy being at the top of the class, and the cleverest boy at the bottom.

In short, a child's mental capacities are really active only when that child is free; and the teacher's chief task lies 'in studying the free child' and discovering how to supply him with knowledge.   Therefore 'the only method of education is experiment, and its only criterion is *freedom.*'

The attempts to enforce obedience and quiet in school-rooms, converts schools into places of torture which have a stupefying effect, well called by the Germans *Verdummen.*

In Germany nine-tenths of those who pass through the primary schools leave them possessed of an ability to read and write mechanically, but imbued with so strong a loathing for the experience they have had of the paths of knowledge, that they subsequently never take a book in their hands. Let those who doubt what I say, point out to me what books are read by the labourers. . . . No one who will seriously consider the education of the people, not only in Russia but also in the rest of Europe, can help coming to the conclusion that the people get their mental development quite independently of a knowledge of reading and writing, and that usually, except in a few cases of exceptional ability, these rudiments remain a quite unapplied art—which is even harmful, since nothing in life can remain indifferent. . . .

.　　　.　　　.　　　.　　　.　　　.

Schools are not so arranged as to make it convenient for children to learn, but so as to make it convenient for teachers to teach. The voices, movements and mirth of the children, which form a necessary condition of their studying successfully, incommode the teachers, and therefore in the prison-like schools of to-day, questions, conversation, and movement are forbidden.

Schools based on compulsion, supply ' not a shepherd for the flock, but a flock for the shepherd.'

.　　　.　　　.　　　.　　　.　　　.

To deal successfully with any object, it is necessary to study it, and in education the object is a free child; yet the peda-gogues wish to teach in their own way—the way that seems good in their own eyes; and when this does not act, they want not to alter their way of teaching but the nature of the child. . . . Not till experiment becomes the basis of the School, and every school is, so to say, a pedagogic laboratory, will schools cease to lag behind the general level of the world's progress.

For boarding-schools Tolstoy had scant respect:

At home all the comforts of life—water, fires, good food, a well-cooked dinner, the cleanliness and comfort of the rooms —all depended on the work and care of the mother and of the whole family. The more work and care, the greater the comfort; the less work and care, the less comfort. A simple matter this no doubt, but more educational I think, than the French language or a knowledge of Alexander the Great. In a boarding-school, this constant vital reward for labour is so put out of sight, that not only is the dinner no better or worse, the napkins no cleaner or dirtier, and the floors no brighter or duller, because of the girl's exertion or non-exertion, but she has not even a cell or corner of her own to keep straight or leave untidy at her pleasure, and she has no chance of making a costume for herself out of scraps and ribbons.

His general charge against day-schools, boarding-schools and universities alike is that:

At the base of them all lies one and the same principle: the right of one man, or of a small group of men, to shape other people as they like.

He adds that:

It is not enough for School to tear children away from real life for six hours a day during the best years of their life: it wishes to tear three-year-old children from their mother's influence. Institutions have been contrived (*Kleinkinderbewahranstallen*, infant schools, *salles d'asile*) about which we shall have to speak more in detail later on. It only remains to invent a steam-engine which will replace the nursing mother! All agree that schools are imperfect; I, personally, am convinced that they are noxious.

He argues that no man or set of men has any right to force any particular kind of education on any one else. The teacher has no right to do more than offer such knowledge as he possesses, and he should respect the child's right to reject it as indigestible, or as badly served up :

On what grounds does the School of to-day teach this and not that, and in this and not that way?

Where, in our day, can we get such faith in the indubitability of our knowledge as would give us a right to educate people compulsorily? Take any medieval school, before or after Luther, take the whole scholastic literature of the Middle Ages, what a strength of belief and what a firm, indubitable knowledge of what was true and what was false, we see in them! It was easy for them to know that a knowledge of Greek was the one essential condition of education; for Aristotle's works were in Greek, and no one doubted the truth of his propositions till centuries later. How could the monks help demanding the study of the Holy Scriptures, which stood on an immovable foundation? It was well for Luther to demand the compulsory study of Hebrew, being sure, as he was, that in that language God himself has revealed the truth to man. Evidently, as long as man's critical sense was not aroused, the school had to be dogmatic; and it was natural for pupils to learn by heart the truths revealed by God, as well as Aristotle's science and the poetic beauties of Virgil and Cicero. For centuries after, no one could imagine any truer truth, or more beautiful beauty. But what is the position of the schools of our time, which retain these same dogmatic principles, while in the room next the class where the immortality of the soul is taught, it is suggested to the pupils that the nerves common to man and to the frog are what was formerly called 'the soul'; and where after hearing the story of Joshua the son of Nun read to him without explanations, the pupil learns that the sun never did go round the earth; and when after the beauties of Virgil have been explained to him, he finds the beauties of Alexandre Dumas (whose novels he can buy for sixpence) much greater; when the only belief held by the teacher is that nothing is true, but that whatever exists is reasonable; and that progress is good and backwardness bad, though nobody knows in what this progress, that is so generally believed in, consists?

In another article he says :

Luther insists on teaching the Holy Scriptures from the originals, and not from the commentaries of the Fathers of the Church. Bacon enjoins the study of Nature from Nature, and not from the books of Aristotle. Rousseau wants to teach life from life itself as he understands it, and not from previous experiments. Each step forward in the philosophy of pedagogics merely consists in freeing the schools from the idea of teaching the younger generations what the elder generations believed to be science, and in substituting studies that accord with the needs of the younger generations.

Again, he says

It is very usual to read and hear it said that the home conditions, the coarseness of parents, field labour, village games and so forth, are the chief hindrances to school-work. Possibly they really interfere with the kind of school-work aimed at by the pedagogues; but it is time we understood that those conditions are the chief bases of all education, and far from being inimical to, or hindrances of the School, are its first and chief motive power. . . . The wish to know anything whatever, and the very questions to which it is the School's business to reply, arise entirely from these home conditions. All instruction should be simply a reply to questions put by life. But School, far from evoking questions, fails even to answer those which life suggests. . . . To such questions the child receives no reply ; more especially as the police regulations of the School do not allow him to open his mouth, even when he wants to be let out for a minute, but obliges him to make signs in order not to break the silence or disturb the teacher.

The great questions, Tolstoy says, are : (1) What must I teach ? and (2) How must I teach it ? He remarks that a couple of centuries ago, neither in Russia nor in Western Europe could these questions have arisen. Education was then bound up with religion, and to become a scholar meant to learn the Scriptures. In Mohammedan countries this union of religion with education still exists in full force. To learn, means to learn the Koran, and therefore to learn Arabic. But as soon as the criterion of what to learn ceased to be religion, and the School became independent of the Church, the question of what to teach was bound to arise. That it did not arise suddenly, was due to the fact that the emancipation of the School from the Church took place gradually. But the day has at last come when the question must be faced; and no clear guidance is given us either by philosophy or by any definite consensus of opinion among those concerned with education. In the higher schools some advocate a classical, others a scientific, education; while in the primary schools, if the education is controlled by the priests it is carried on in one way, and if it is controlled by the anti-clericals it is carried on in another. Under these circumstances the only possible criterion must be the wish of the pupils or of their parents. Tolstoy then goes on to maintain that the demand of the mass of the Russian people is for tuition in the Russian and Ecclesiastico-Slavonic languages, and for mathematics.

As to *how* to teach, he contends that this resolves itself into the question, How to establish the best possible relations between those who want to learn and those who want to teach, and he says:

No one, probably, will deny that the best relation between a teacher and his pupils is a natural one, and that the opposite to a natural one is a compulsory one. If that be so, then the measure of all scholastic methods consists in the greater or lesser naturalness, and consequently in the less or more compulsion employed. The less the children are compelled, the better is the method; the more they are compelled, the worse is the method. I am glad that it is not necessary for me to prove this obvious truth. All are agreed that it cannot be good for health to employ foods, medicines, or exercises which create disgust or pain; and so also in learning, there can be no need to compel children to grind at anything dull or repugnant to them; and if it seems necessary to use compulsion, that fact can merely prove the imperfection of the methods employed. All who have taught children have probably noticed that the worse the teacher knows the subject he is dealing with and the less he likes it, the more he has to be stern and the more compulsion he has to use; while on the contrary, the better the teacher knows and loves his subject, the more free and natural will be his tuition.

If history be closely examined, it will be found that every advance in pedagogics has consisted merely in a diminution of compulsion, a facilitation of study, and a greater and greater approach to naturalness in the relations between teacher and pupil.

People have asked, How can we find the degree of freedom to be allowed in school? To which I reply that the limit of that freedom is naturally defined by the teacher, by his knowledge, and by his capacity to manage the school. Such freedom cannot be dictated; its measure is merely the result of the greater or lesser knowledge and talent possessed by the master. Freedom is not a rule, but it serves as a gauge when comparing one school with another, or when judging of new methods. The school in which there is less compulsion, is better than the one in which there is more. That method is good which, when introduced into a school, does not necessitate any increase of discipline; while that is certainly bad which necessitates greater severity.

From his main subject of Education, Tolstoy digresses in these articles into a discussion of other problems, in a way which reminds one of those wonderful essays he began to pour forth a quarter of a century later.

That he had been somewhat influenced by the Slavophils is indicated by his readiness to assume that Russia may advance along a line of her own, entirely different to that the Western nations have travelled. 'Progress,' in which like almost all his contemporaries he had believed, he now questions; and he indulges in a sharp attack on Macaulay for the third chapter of his *History*, which he says contains no proof that any real progress has been

achieved.   Buckle, similarly, is roughly handled for the
assumption of progress that underlies his *History of
Civilisation*; but most scathing of all is his onslaught
upon Hegel, who (till Darwin appeared) was the rock on
which many of the intellectual Liberals took their stand.

From the time of Hegel and his famous aphorism : 'What
is historic is reasonable,' a very queer mental hocus-pocus has prevailed in literary and in verbal disputes, especially among us,
under the name of 'the historic view.'   You say, for instance, that
man has a right to freedom, or to be tried on the basis of laws of
which he himself approves ; but the historic view replies that
history evolves a certain historic moment conditioning a certain
historic legislation and a people's historic relation thereto.
You say you believe in a God ; and the historic view replies
that history evolves certain historic views and humanity's
relation to those views.   You say the *Iliad* is the greatest of
epic works ; and the historic view replies that the *Iliad* is
merely the expression of the historic consciousness of a people
at a certain historic moment.   On this basis, the historic view
does not dispute with you as to whether man needs freedom,
or whether there is or is not a God, or whether the *Iliad* is good
or bad : it does nothing to establish the freedom you desire ;
to persuade or dissuade you of the existence of a God or of the
beauty of the *Iliad* ; it merely points out to you the place your
inner need or your love of truth or beauty, occupy in history.
It merely recognises—and recognises not by direct cognition,
but by historic ratiocination.

Say that you love or believe anything, and the historic view
tells you : 'Love and believe, and your love and faith will find
their place in our historic view.   Ages will pass and we shall
find the place you are to occupy in history.   Know however in
advance, that what you love is not absolutely beautiful, and what
you believe in is not absolutely true ; yet amuse yourselves, children : your love and faith will find their place and application.'

It is only necessary to add the word 'historic' to any conception you like, and that conception loses its real vital
meaning, in an artificially-formed historic world-conception.

Of the introduction of telegraphs and railways he remarks that people attribute great importance to these inventions, and boast of the progress that is being made, declaring that :

' Man is mastering the forces of Nature. Thought, with the rapidity of lightning, flies from one end of the world to the other. Time is vanquished.'

This, says Tolstoy, is excellent and touching.

But let us see who gains by it. We are speaking of the progress of the electric telegraph. Evidently the advantage and use of the telegraph is reserved for the upper, so-called ' educated ' class ; while the people, nine-tenths of the whole, only hear the droning of the wires and are hampered by the strict laws made for the protection of the telegraph.

Along the wires flies the thought that the demand for such-and-such an article has increased, and that the price must therefore be raised ; or the thought that I, a Russian landed proprietress, living in Florence, have, thank God, recovered from my nervous prostration, and that I embrace my adored husband and beg him to send me 40,000 francs as quickly as possible.

Without going into exact statistics of the messages sent, one may be quite sure that they all belong to the kind of correspondence of which the above are samples. No peasant of Yásnaya Polyána in the Government of Toúla, or any other Russian peasant (and let it not be forgotten that the peasants form the mass of the people whose welfare ' progress ' is supposed to secure) ever has sent or received, or for a long time to come will either send or receive, a single telegram. All the messages that fly above his head add no jot to his welfare, because all he needs he gets from his own fields and his own woods, and he is equally indifferent to the cheapness or dearness of sugar or cotton, to the dethronement of King Otho, the speeches of Palmerston and Napoleon III, or the feelings of the lady in Florence. All those thoughts that fly with the rapidity of lightning round the world, do not increase the fertility of his fields nor diminish the strictness of the keepers in the squire's or the Crown's forests, nor do they add to his or his family's working power, or supply him with an extra labourer. All these great thoughts may impair his welfare, but cannot secure or further it, and can have but a negative interest for him. To the True-Believers in progress, however, the telegraph wires have brought and are bringing immense advantages. I do not deny those advantages: I only wish to prove that one must not think, or persuade others, that what is advantageous for me, is a great blessing to all the world. . . .

In the opinion of the Russian people what increases their welfare is an increase of the fertility of the soil, an increase in the herds of cattle, an increase of the quantity of grain and its consequently becoming cheaper, an increase of working power, an increase in woods and pastures, and the absence of town temptations. (I beg the reader to observe that no peasant ever complains of the cheapness of bread; it is only the political economists of Western Europe who soothe him with the prospect that bread will become dearer and render it more possible for him to purchase manufactured articles, in which he is not interested.)

Which of these benefits does the railway bring to the peasant? It increases the temptations; it destroys the woods; it draws away labourers; it raises the price of grain. . . .

The real people, that is to say those who themselves work and live productively—nine-tenths of the whole nation—without whom no progress is conceivable, are always hostile to the railway. And so what it comes to is this: that the believers in 'progress,' a small part of society, say that railways increase the welfare of the people; while the larger part of the nation say that the railways decrease it.

Interesting, stimulating and suggestive as Tolstoy's articles were, and valuable as was the experience gained in his school, his magazine had very few subscribers and only existed for one year: the twelfth number was the last.

In an article written thirteen years later, he says of his attempts in 1861-2:

At that time I met with no sympathy in the educational journals, nor even with any contradiction, but only with the

completest indifference to the question I was raising. There
were, it is true, some attacks on a few insignificant details, but
the question itself evidently interested no one. I was young
at that time, and this indifference galled me. I did not understand that I with my question: How do you know what and
how to teach? was like a man who, in an assembly of Turkish
Pachas discussing how to collect more taxes from the people,
should say to them: Gentlemen, before discussing how much
to take from each man, we must first consider what right we
have to collect taxes at all? Obviously, the Pachas would
continue to discuss the methods of collecting, and would ignore
the irrelevant question.

Before passing on to tell of the actual working of the
Yásnaya Polyána school, there is one matter to be noted,
small indeed in itself, but characteristic, and helpful for the
understanding of Tolstoy's later development.

Tolstoy's personal honour has never been questioned,
and the reader will remember that at Sevastopol he flatly
refused to touch money which, according to the long-stand-
ing regimental custom, was at his disposal. Well, in his
magazine he printed a story written by one of the boys
in the school, and appraised it with enthusiasm. The hero
of the story, who had been wretchedly poor, returns from
the army with money to spare, and explains the matter
to his wife by saying: 'I was a non-commissioned officer
and had Crown money to pay out to the soldiers, and
some remaining over, I kept it.'

Commenting on this, Tolstoy says:

It is revealed that the soldier has become rich, and has done
so in the simplest and most natural manner, just as almost
everybody does who becomes rich—that is, by other people's,
the Crown's, or somebody's, money remaining in his hands owing
to a fortunate accident. Some readers have remarked that this
incident is immoral, and that the people's conception of the
Crown as a milch cow should be eradicated and not confirmed.
But not to speak of its artistic truth, I particularly value that
trait in the story. Does not the Crown money always stop

somewhere? And why should it not, once in a way, stop with a homeless soldier like Gordéy?

In the views of honesty held by the peasants and the upper class, a complete contrast is often noticeable. The peasants' demands are specially serious and strict with regard to honesty in the nearest relations of life; for instance, in respect to one's family, one's village, or one's commune. In respect to outsiders: the public, the Crown, or foreigners, or the Treasury especially, the applicability of the rules of honesty seems to them obscure. A peasant who would never tell a lie to his brother peasant, and who would bear all possible hardships for the sake of his family, and not take a farthing from a fellow-villager or neighbour without having fully earned it—will be ready to squeeze a foreigner or a townsman like an orange, and at every second word will lie to a gentleman or an official. If he is a soldier, he will without the slightest twinge of conscience stab a French prisoner, and should Crown money come his way, he would consider it a crime to his family not to take it. In the upper class, on the contrary, it is quite the reverse. . . . I do not say which is better, I only say what I believe to be the case. . . .

To return to the story. The mention of the Crown money, which at first seems immoral, in our opinion has a most sweet and touching character. How often a writer of our circle, when wishing to show his hero as an ideal of honesty, naïvely displays to us the dirty and depraved nature of his own imagination! Here, on the contrary, the author has to make his hero happy. His return to his family would suffice for that, but it was also necessary to remove the poverty which for so many years had weighed on the family. Where was he to take money from? From the impersonal Crown! If the author is to give him wealth, it has to be taken from some one, and it could not have been found in a more legitimate or reasonable way.

No doubt Tolstoy's statement of peasant morality is true enough; but Tolstoy's attitude towards the matter is remarkable. He has always had a keen sense of personal morality, but when public morality was in question, his decisions seem to me often to have been at fault.

Passing from the moral to the economic aspect of the question, to Western ears it sounds strange to hear the medieval or Oriental conception so boldly announced, that property 'has to be taken from some one' before it can be obtained. In our world, wealth has, during the last five generations, been increased enormously by inventions, by organisation, by division of labour, by the skilful utilisation of the forces of Nature, as well as by co-operation and the bringing together into one place of industries and individuals mutually helpful; and it has become impossible for us to believe that the *only* way to obtain wealth is by depriving some one else of wealth they already possess.

AUTHORITIES FOR CHAPTER VII

Birukof.
Fet.
Tolstoy's letter to A. Maude.
Tolstoy's Educational Articles.
Löwenfeld's *Leo N. Tolstoj*.
P. A. Sergeyenko in *Niva*, No. 7, 1906.

CHAPTER VIII

THE SCHOOL

Yásno-Polyána School. Freedom in class. Natural laws.
A fight. Theft and punishment. A walk and talk on art.
Peasants' opinion of the school. Gymnastics. Reading.
The Bible. Penmanship. Grammar. History. Geography.
Drawing. Singing. Composition. A literary genius. Art:
exclusive or universal? Reading useless for lack of what to
read. The value of freedom in education. A contrast.

As already mentioned, Tolstoy's magazine, besides its
theoretical articles, contained others describing the work
done at the Yásno-Polyána school, and from these we
learn in his own words, how Tolstoy and his pupils, and
the masters (including the young German, Keller, whom
he had brought back with him from abroad) were occupied in November and December 1861. The following
passages are part of his description of the school :

No one brings anything with him, neither books nor copy-
books. No homework is set them. Not only do they carry
nothing in their hands, they have nothing to carry even in
their heads. They are not obliged to remember any lesson,
nor any of yesterday's work. They are not tormented by the
thought of the impending lesson. They bring only themselves,
their receptive nature, and an assurance that it will be as jolly
in school to-day as it was yesterday. They do not think of
their classes till they have begun. No one is ever scolded for
being late, and they never are late, except perhaps some of the
older boys whose fathers occasionally keep them at home to do
some work. In such cases the boy comes to school running

fast and panting. Until the teacher arrives, some gather at the porch, pushing one another off the steps or sliding on the ice-covered path, and some go into the rooms. When it is cold, while waiting for the master, they read, write, or play about. The girls do not mix with the boys. When the boys take any notice of the girls, they never address any one of them in particular, but always speak to them collectively: 'Hey, girls, why don't you come and slide?' or, 'Look how frozen the girls are,' or, 'Now girls, all of you against me!'

Suppose that by the time-table the lesson for the youngest class is elementary reading; for the second, advanced reading; and for the third, mathematics. The teacher enters the room, on the floor of which the boys are lying in a heap, shouting, 'The heap is too small!' or, 'Boys, you're choking me!' or, 'Don't pull my hair!' etc.

'Peter Miháylovitch!' cries a voice from the bottom of the heap, to the teacher as he enters: 'Tell them to stop!'—'Good morning, Peter Miháylovitch!' cry others, continuing their scrimmage. The teacher takes the books and gives them to those who have followed him to the cupboard, while from the heap of boys on the floor, those on top, still sprawling, demand books. The heap gradually diminishes. As soon as most of the boys have taken books, the rest run to the cupboard crying, 'Me too! Me too!'—'Give me yesterday's book!'—'Give me Kóltsof!' and so forth. If a couple of boys excited by their struggle still remain on the floor, those who have taken books and settled down, shout at them, 'What are you up to? We can't hear anything! Stop it!' The excited ones submit, and, panting, take to their books; and only just at first swing their legs with unspent excitement as they sit reading. The spirit of war flies away and the spirit of reading reigns in the room. With the same ardour with which he pulled Mítka's hair, he now reads Kóltsof's works: with almost clenched teeth, with sparkling eyes, and oblivious of all around him but his book. To tear him from his reading now would need as much effort as formerly to tear him from his wrestling.

They sit where they like: on the benches, tables, window-sills, floor, or in the arm-chair. The girls always sit together.

Friends from the same village, especially the little ones (among whom there is most comradeship) always sit together. As soon as one of them decides that he will sit in a certain corner, all his chums, pushing and diving under the forms, get there too, and sit together looking about them with faces that express as much happiness and satisfaction as though, having settled in that place, they would certainly be happy for the rest of their lives. The large arm-chair (which somehow found its way into the room) is an object coveted by the more independent personalities. . . . As soon as one of them decides to sit in it, another discerns his intention from his looks, and they collide and squeeze in. One dislodges the other, and curling up, sprawls with his head far below the back, but reads like the rest, quite absorbed in his work. During lessons I have never seen them whispering, pinching, giggling, laughing behind their hands, or complaining of one another to the teacher.

The two lower classes sort themselves in one room, the upper class in another. The teacher appears, and in the first class all surround him at the blackboard, or lie on the forms, or sit on the table, near him or near one of the boys who reads. If it is a writing lesson, they place themselves in a more orderly way, but keep getting up to look at one another's exercise books, and to show their own to the teacher. According to the time-table there should be four lessons before dinner; but sometimes in practice these become three or two, and may be on quite other subjects. The teacher may begin with arithmetic and pass on to geometry; or may begin with Sacred History and end up with grammar. Sometimes teacher and pupils are so carried away, that a lesson lasts three hours instead of one. Sometimes the pupils themselves cry: 'Go on, go on!' and shout contemptuously to any who are tired: 'If you're tired, go to the little ones!'

In my opinion this external disorder is useful and necessary, however strange and inconvenient it may seem to the teacher. Of its advantages I shall have frequent occasion to speak; but of its apparent disadvantages I will say:

First, this disorder, or free order, only frightens us because we ourselves were educated in, and are accustomed to, something quite different. Secondly, in this as in many similar cases, coercion is used only from hastiness or from lack of respect for human nature. We think the disorder is growing greater and greater, and that it has no limit. We think there is no way of stopping it except by force; but one need only wait a little, and the disorder (or animation) calms down of itself, and calms down into a far better and more durable order than any we could devise.

In another place he says:

Our school evolved freely from the principles brought into it by the teachers and pupils. In spite of the predominant influence of the teacher, the pupil always had the right not to go to school; and even when in school, not to listen to the teacher. The teacher had the right not to admit a pupil. . . .

Submitting naturally only to laws derived from their own nature, children revolt and rebel when subjected to your premature interference. They do not believe in the validity of your bells and time-tables and rules. How often have I seen children fighting. The teacher rushes to separate them, and the separated enemies look at one another askance, and even in the stern teacher's presence cannot refrain from giving one another a parting blow, yet more painful than its predecessors. How often, any day, do I see some Kirúshka, clenching his teeth, fly at Taráska, seize his hair, and throw him to the ground, apparently—though it costs him his life—determined to maim his foe; yet not a minute passes before Taráska is already laughing under Kirúshka. One, and then the other, moderates his blows, and before five minutes have passed they have made friends, and off they go to sit together.

The other day, between lessons, two boys were struggling in a corner. The one, a remarkable mathematician about ten years old, is in the second class; the other, a close-cropped lad, the son of a servant, is a clever but vindictive, tiny, black-eyed lad, nicknamed Pussy. Pussy seized the mathematician's long hair and jammed his head against the wall; the mathematician vainly clutched at Pussy's close-cropped bristles. Pussy's black eyes gleamed triumphantly. The mathematician, hardly refraining from tears, kept saying: 'Well, well, what of it?'

But though he tried to keep up appearances, it was plain he was faring badly. This went on for some time, and I was in doubt what to do. 'A fight, a fight!' shouted the boys, and crowded towards the corner. The little ones laughed; but the bigger ones, though they did not interfere, exchanged serious glances, and their silence and these glances did not escape Pussy's observation. He understood that he was doing something wrong, and began to smile shamefacedly, and by degrees let go of the mathematician's hair. The mathematician shook himself free, and giving Pussy a push that banged the back of the latter's head against the wall, went off satisfied. Pussy began to cry, and rushed after his enemy, hitting him as hard as he could on his sheepskin coat, but without hurting him. The mathematician wished to pay him back, but at that moment several disapproving voices were raised. 'There now; he's fighting a little fellow!' cried the onlookers, 'get away, Pussy!'—and therewith the affair ended as though it had never occurred, except, I think, that both combatants retained a dim consciousness that fighting is unpleasant, because both get hurt.

In this case I seemed to detect a feeling of fairness influencing the crowd; but how often such affairs are settled so that one does not know what law has decided them, and yet both sides are satisfied! How arbitrary and unjust by comparison are all School methods of dealing with such cases. 'You are both to blame: kneel down!' says the teacher; and the teacher is wrong, because one boy is in the wrong, and that one triumphs while on his knees, and chews the cud of his unexpended anger, while the innocent one is doubly punished. . . .

I am convinced that the School should not interfere with that part of education which belongs to the family. The School should not, and has no right to, reward or punish; and the best police and administration of a School consist in giving full freedom to the pupils to learn and get on among themselves as they like. I am convinced of this; and yet the customary School habits are still so strong in us that in the Yásno-Polyána school we frequently break this rule. . . .

During last summer, while the school-house was being repaired, a Leyden jar disappeared from the physical cabinet;

pencils disappeared repeatedly, as well as books—and this at a time when neither the carpenters nor the painters were at work. We questioned the boys. The best pupils, those who had been with us longest, old friends of ours, blushed and were so uneasy that any Public Prosecutor would have thought their confusion a sure proof of their guilt. But I knew them, and could answer for them as for myself. I understood that the very idea of being suspected offended them deeply and painfully. A gifted and tender-hearted boy, whom I will call Theodore, turned quite pale, trembled and wept. They promised to tell me, if they found out; but they declined to undertake a search. A few days later the thief was discovered. He was the son of a servant from a distant village. He had led astray, and made an accomplice of, a peasant boy from the same village; and together they had hidden the stolen articles in a box. This discovery produced a strange feeling in the other pupils: a kind of relief and even joy, accompanied by contempt and pity for the thief. We proposed that they should allot the punishment themselves. Some demanded that the thief should be flogged, but stipulated that they should do the flogging; others said: 'Sew a card on him, with the word *thief.*' This latter punishment, to our shame be it said, had been used by us before, and it was the very boy who a year ago had himself been labelled *liar,* who now most insistently demanded a card for the thief. We consented, and when one of the girls was sewing the card on, all the pupils watched and teased the punished boys with malicious joy. They wanted the punishment increased: ' Let them be led through the village; and let them wear cards till the holidays,' said they. The victims cried. The peasant boy who had been led astray by his comrade, a gifted narrator and jester, a plump, white, chubby little chap, wept without restraint and with all his childish might. The other, the chief offender, a hump-nosed boy with a thin-featured, clever face, became pale, his lips quivered, his eyes looked wildly and angrily at his joyous comrades, and occasionally his face was unnaturally distorted by a sob. His cap, with a torn peak, was stuck on the very back of his head; his hair was ruffled, his clothes soiled with chalk. All this now struck me and everybody else as though we saw it for the first time. The unkindly attention of all was directed to him, and he felt it painfully. When, with bent head and without looking round, he started homeward with (as it seemed to me) a peculiar, criminal gait, and when the boys ran after him in a crowd, teasing him in an unnatural and strangely cruel way as though, against their will, they were moved by some evil spirit, something told me that we were not doing right. But things took their course, and the thief wore the card that whole day. From this time he began, as it seemed to me, to learn worse, and one did not see him playing and talking with his fellows out of class.

One day I came to a lesson, and the pupils informed me, with a kind of horror, that the boy had again stolen. He had taken twenty copecks (seven pence) in coppers from the teacher's room, and had been caught hiding them under the stairs. We again hung a card on him; and again the same revolting scene recommenced. I began to admonish him, as all masters admonish; and a big boy, fond of talking, who was present, also admonished him—probably repeating words he had heard his father, an innkeeper, use: 'You steal once, and you do it again,' said he distinctly, glibly, and with dignity; 'it becomes a habit, and leads to no good.' I began to get vexed. I glanced at the face of the punished boy, which had become yet paler, more suffering and harder than before; and somehow I thought of convicts, and suddenly I felt so ashamed and disgusted that I tore the stupid card off him, told him to go where he liked, and became convinced—and convinced not by reason, but by my whole nature — that I had no right to torment that unfortunate boy, and that it was not in my power to make of him what I and the innkeeper's son wanted to make of him. I became convinced that there are secrets of the soul, hidden from us, on which life may act, but which precepts and punishments do not reach.

It may be said that any department of life could be treated in this way : we have merely to invert an established order founded on the experience of men, and a topsy-turvy millennium is born. It may also be said that in the foregoing pages Tolstoy appears as the evangelist of an educational system founded on the free play of youthful instincts which, speaking merely the language of natural animal life, call for sympathetic discipline. But in his *Confession* Tolstoy has treated his educational writings with such scant respect that criticism is disarmed; more especially as the actual working of his school was extremely interesting and much more successful than might have been expected.

N. V. Ouspénsky, the writer, narrates that he visited Yásnaya Polyána in 1862, and Tolstoy, having to leave him alone for awhile, asked him to glance at some of the compositions the boys had written in school. Taking up one of these, Ouspénsky read :

One day, Lyóf Nikoláyevitch (Tolstoy) called Savóskin up to the blackboard and ordered him to solve a problem in arithmetic. 'If I give you five rolls, and you eat one of them, how many rolls will you have left?' . . . Savóskin could nohow solve this problem, and the Count pulled his hair for it. . . .

When Tolstoy returned Ouspénsky pointed out to him this essay, and Tolstoy, sighing heavily, crossed his hands before him and merely said : ' Life in this world is a hard task.'

Ouspénsky considered that he had unearthed an extraordinary contradiction between theory and practice; but no one who realises the difficulty and novelty of Tolstoy's attempt, and how far he is from claiming perfection for himself or for his achievements, should agree with Ouspénsky. On the contrary, the essay proves a freedom of relation between teacher and pupil, which would certainly not have existed had the hair-pulling been other than impulsive and exceptional.

The school was closed, or nearly so, during the summer, as most of the pupils then helped their parents with field work; obtaining, Tolstoy considers, more mental development that way than they could have done in any school. To make up for this, the hours of study in winter were long.

The classes generally finish about eight or nine o'clock (unless carpentering keeps the elder boys somewhat later), and the whole band run shouting into the yard, and there, calling to one another, begin to separate, making for different parts of the village. Occasionally they arrange to coast down-hill to the village in a large sledge that stands outside the gate. They tie up the shafts, throw themselves into it, and squealing, disappear from sight in a cloud of snow, leaving here and there on their path black patches of children who have tumbled out. In the open air, out of school (for all its freedom) new relations are formed between pupil and teacher: freer, simpler and more trustful—those very relations which seem to us the ideal which School should aim at.

Not long ago we read Gógol's story *Viy* [an Earth-Spirit] in the highest class. The final scenes affected them strongly, and excited their imagination. Some of them played the witch, and kept alluding to the last chapters. . . .

Out of doors it was a moonless, winter night, with clouds in the sky, not cold. We stopped at the crossroads. The elder boys, in their third year, stopped near me, asking me to accompany them further. The younger ones looked at us, and rushed off down-hill. They had begun to learn with a new master, and between them and me there is not the same confidence as between the older boys and myself.

'Well, let us go to the wood' (a small wood about 120 yards from the house), said one of them. The most insistent was Fédka, a boy of ten, with a tender, receptive, poetic yet daring nature. Danger seems to form the chief condition of pleasure for him. In summer it always frightened me to see how he, with two other boys, would swim out into the very middle of the pond, which is nearly 120 yards wide, and would now and then disappear in the hot reflection of the summer sun, and swim under water; and how he would then turn on his back, causing fountains of water to rise, and calling with his high-pitched voice to his comrades on the bank to see what a fine fellow he was.

He now knew there were wolves in the wood, and so he wanted to go there. All agreed; and the four of us went to the wood. Another boy, a lad of twelve, physically and morally

strong, whom I will call Syómka, went on in front and kept
calling and 'ah-ou-ing' with his ringing voice, to some one at
a distance.   Prónka, a sickly, mild and very gifted lad, from a
poor family (sickly probably chiefly from lack of food), walked
by my side.   Fédka walked between me and Syómka, talking
all the time in a particularly gentle voice: now relating how
he had herded horses in summer, now saying there was nothing
to be afraid of, and now asking, 'Suppose one should jump
out?' and insisting on my giving some reply.   We did not go
into the wood: that would have been too dreadful; but even
where we were, near the wood, it was darker, and the road was
scarcely visible, and the lights of the village were hidden from
view.   Syómka stopped and listened: 'Stop, lads! What is
that?' said he suddenly.

We were silent, and though we heard nothing, things seemed
to grow more gruesome.

'What shall we do if it leaps out . . . and comes at us?'
asked Fédka.

We began to talk about Caucasian robbers.   They remembered a Caucasian tale I had told them long ago, and I again
told them of 'braves,' of Cossacks, and of Hádji Mourát.[1]
Syómka went on in front, treading boldly in his big boots, his
broad back swaying regularly.   Prónka tried to walk by my side,
but Fédka pushed him off the path, and Prónka—who, probably
on account of his poverty, always submitted—only ran up alongside at the most interesting passages, sinking in the snow up to
his knees.

Every one who knows anything of Russian peasant children
knows that they are not accustomed to, and cannot bear, any
caresses, affectionate words, kisses, hand touchings, and so
forth.   I have seen a lady in a peasant school, wishing to pet a
boy, say: 'Come, I will give you a kiss, dear!' and actually
kiss him; and the boy was ashamed and offended, and could
not understand why he had been so treated.   Boys of five are
already above such caresses—they are no longer babies.   I was
therefore particularly struck when Fédka, walking beside me,
at the most terrible part of the story suddenly touched me

[1] The daring Caucasian leader mentioned by Tolstoy in a letter quoted in
Chapter III.

lightly with his sleeve, and then clasped two of my fingers in his hand, and kept hold of them. As soon as I stopped speaking, Fédka demanded that I should go on, and did this in such a beseeching and agitated voice that it was impossible not to comply with his wish.

'Now then, don't get in the way!' said he once angrily to Prónka, who had run in front of us. He was so carried away as even to be cruel; so agitated yet happy was he, holding on to my fingers, that he could let no one dare to interrupt his pleasure.

'Some more! Some more! It is fine!' said he.

We had passed the wood and were approaching the village from the other end.

'Let's go on,' said all the boys when the lights became visible. 'Let us take another turn!'

We went on in silence, sinking here and there in the rotten snow, not hardened by much traffic. A white darkness seemed to sway before our eyes; the clouds hung low, as though something had heaped them upon us. There was no end to that whiteness, amid which we alone crunched along the snow. The wind sounded through the bare tops of the aspens, but where we were, behind the woods, it was calm.

I finished my story by telling how a 'brave,' surrounded by his enemies, sang his death-song and threw himself on his dagger. All were silent.

'Why did he sing a song when he was surrounded?' asked Syómka.

'Weren't you told?—He was preparing for death!' replied Fédka, aggrieved.

'I think he sang a prayer,' added Prónka.

All agreed. Fédka suddenly stopped.

'How was it, you told us, your Aunt had her throat cut?' asked he. (He had not yet had enough horrors.) 'Tell us! Tell us!'

I again told them that terrible story of the murder of the Countess Tolstoy,[1] and they stood silently about me, watching my face.

[1] Some details of this crime are given in 'Why do Men Stupefy Themselves?' in *Essays and Letters*, published in the *World's Classics*.

'The fellow got caught!' said Syómka.

'He was afraid to go away in the night, while she was lying with her throat cut!' said Fédka; 'I should have run away!' and he gathered my two fingers yet more closely in his hand.

We stopped in the thicket, beyond the threshing-floor at the very end of the village. Syómka picked up a dry stick from the snow and began striking it against the frosty trunk of a lime tree. Hoar frost fell from the branches on to one's cap, and the noise of the blows resounded in the stillness of the wood.

'Lyóf Nikoláyevitch,' said Fédka to me (I thought he was going again to speak about the Countess), 'why does one learn singing? I often think, why, really, does one?'

What made him jump from the terror of the murder to this question, heaven only knows; yet by the tone of his voice, the seriousness with which he demanded an answer, and the attentive silence of the other two, one felt that there was some vital and legitimate connection between this question and our preceding talk. Whether the connection lay in some response to my suggestion that crime might be explained by lack of education (I had spoken of that) or whether he was testing himself—transferring himself into the mind of the murderer and remembering his own favourite occupation (he has a wonderful voice and immense musical talent) or whether the connection lay in the fact that he felt that now was the time for sincere conversation, and all the problems demanding solution rose in his mind—at any rate his question surprised none of us.

'And what is drawing for? And why write well?' said I, not knowing at all how to explain to him what art is for.

'What is drawing for?' repeated he thoughtfully. He really was asking, What is Art for? And I neither dared nor could explain.

'What is drawing for?' said Syómka. 'Why, you draw anything, and can then make it from the drawing.'

'No, that is designing,' said Fédka. 'But why draw figures?' Syómka's matter-of-fact mind was not perplexed.

'What is a stick for, and what is a lime tree for?' said he, still striking the tree.

'Yes, what is a lime tree for?' said I.

'To make rafters of,' replied Syómka.

'But what is it for in summer, when not yet cut down?'

'Then, it's no use.'

'No, really,' insisted Fédka; 'why does a lime tree grow?'

And we began to speak of the fact that not everything exists for use, but that there is also beauty, and that Art is beauty; and we understood one another, and Fédka quite understood why the lime tree grows and what singing is for.

Prónka agreed with us, but he thought rather of moral beauty: goodness.

Syómka understood with his big brain, but did not acknowledge beauty apart from usefulness. He was in doubt (as often happens to men with great reasoning power): feeling Art to be a force, but not feeling in his soul the need of that force. He, like them, wished to get at Art by his reason, and tried to kindle that fire in himself.

'We'll sing *Who hath* to-morrow. I remember my part,' said he. (He has a correct ear, but no taste or refinement in singing.) Fédka, however, fully understood that the lime tree is good when in leaf: good to look at in summer; and that that is enough.

Prónka understood that it is a pity to cut it down, because it, too, has life:

'Why, when we take the sap of a lime, it's like taking blood.'

Syómka, though he did not say so, evidently thought that there was little use in a lime when it was sappy.

It feels strange to repeat what we then said, but it seems to me that we said all that can be said about utility, and plastic and moral beauty.

We went on to the village. Fédka still clung to my hand; now, it seemed to me, from gratitude. We all were nearer one another that night than we had been for a long time. Prónka walked beside us along the broad village street.

'See, there is still a light in Mazánof's house,' said he. 'As I was going to school this morning, Gavrúka was coming from the pub, as dru-u-nk as could be! His horse all in a lather and he beating it! I am always sorry for such things. Really, why should it be beaten?'

'And the other day, coming from Toúla, my daddy gave his horse the reins,' said Syómka; 'and it took him into a snow-drift, and there he slept—quite drunk.'

'And Gavrúka kept on beating his horse over the eyes, and I felt so sorry,' repeated Prónka again. 'Why should he beat it? He got down and just flogged it.'

Syómka suddenly stopped.

'Our folk are already asleep,' said he, looking in at the window of his crooked, dirty hut. 'Won't you walk a little longer?'

'No.'

'Go-o-od-bye, Lyóf Nikoláyevitch!' shouted he suddenly, and tearing himself away from us, as it were with an effort, he ran to the house, lifted the latch and disappeared.

'So you will take each of us home? First one and then the other?' said Fédka.

We went on. There was a light in Prónka's hut, and we looked in at the window. His mother, a tall and handsome but toil-worn woman, with black eyebrows and eyes, sat at the table, peeling potatoes. In the middle of the hut hung a cradle. Prónka's brother, the mathematician from our second class, was standing at the table, eating potatoes with salt. It was a black, tiny, and dirty hut.

'What a plague you are!' shouted the mother at Prónka. 'Where have you been?'

Prónka glanced at the window with a meek, sickly smile. His mother guessed that he ·had not come alone, and her face immediately assumed a feigned expression that was not nice.

Only Fédka was left.

'The travelling tailors are at our house, that is why there's a light there,' said he in the softened voice that had come to him that evening. 'Good-bye, Lyóf Nikoláyevitch!' added he, softly and tenderly, and he began to knock with the ring attached to the closed door. 'Let me in!' his high-pitched voice rang out amid the winter stillness of the village. It was long before they opened the door for him. I looked in at the window. The hut was a large one. The father was playing cards with a tailor, and some copper coins lay on the table. The wife, Fédka's stepmother, was sitting near the torch-stand, looking eagerly at the money. The young tailor, a cunning drunkard, was holding his cards on the table, bending them, and looking triumphantly at his opponent. Fédka's father, the collar of his shirt unbuttoned, his brow wrinkled with mental exertion and vexation, changed one card for another, and waved his horny hand in perplexity above them.

'Let me in!'

The woman rose and went to the door.

'Good-bye!' repeated Fédka, once again.   'Let us always have such walks!'

Thus Tolstoy for the second time found himself faced by the question : What is Art ? which had arisen when he spoke to the Society of Lovers of Russian Literature. This time it was put to him by a ten-year-old peasant boy, and it seemed to him that : 'We said all that can be said about utility, and plastic and moral beauty.'   Twenty years later, after achieving the highest fame as a literary artist, he returned to the subject and tried to write an essay on the connection between life and Art, thinking that he would be able to accomplish it at a single effort. It proved, however, as he tells us, 'that my views on the matter were so far from clear, that I could not arrange them in a way that satisfied me.   From that time I did not cease to think of the subject, and I recommenced writing on it six or seven times ; but each time, after writing a considerable part of it, I found myself unable to bring the work to a satisfactory conclusion, and had to put it aside.'   Only after another fifteen years' study and reflection did he succeed, in 1898, in producing *What is Art ?* which raised such a storm in the esthetic dovecots, and induced the editor of *Literature* to declare that 'There was never any reason for inferring that Count Tolstoy's opinions on the philosophy of art would be worth the paper on which they were written'; while A. B. Walkley was asserting that 'this calmly and cogently reasoned effort to put art on a new basis is a literary event of the first importance.'

We have, however, as yet only reached the year 1862, and must not anticipate.

At first the peasants were rather afraid of the school, but before long they gained confidence and the report became current among them that: 'At Yásno-Polyána school they learn everything, including all the sciences, and there are such clever masters that it is dreadful; it is said that they even imitate thunder and lightning. Anyway, the lads understand well, and have begun to read and write.' Another very general opinion was that: 'They teach the boys everything (like gentlemen's sons) much of it is no use, but still, as they quickly learn to read, it is worth sending the children there.'

Naturally Tolstoy, himself in those days an ardent gymnast, had parallel and horizontal bars put up, and gave the children physical training. To the effects of this on the stomach, the village mothers did not fail to attribute any digestive troubles that befell their children from time to time; especially when the long Lenten fast was succeeded by a return to more appetising food, or when, after such luxuries had long been lacking, fresh vegetables again came into use in summer.

In his account of the Yásno-Polyána school, Tolstoy tells us there were about forty pupils enrolled, but more than thirty were rarely present at a time; among them were four or five girls, and sometimes three or four male adults who came either for a month or for a whole winter. Most of the boys were from seven to ten years old. (Tolstoy says that children learn to read most rapidly, easily and well, between the ages of six and eight.)

There were four teachers, and generally from five to seven lessons a day. The teachers kept diaries of their work, and discussed matters together on Sundays, when they drew up plans for the coming week. These plans were, however, not strictly adhered to, but were constantly modified to meet the demands of the pupils.

Tolstoy's sister told me of another Sunday occupation at Yásnaya Polyána in those days. Tolstoy used to invite all the boys from the neighbouring schools within reach, and used to play games with them ; the favourite game being *Barre*, which I assume to be a form of 'Storm the Castle.'

Tolstoy came to the conclusion that teachers involuntarily strive to find a method of teaching convenient for themselves, and that the more convenient a method is for the teacher, the less convenient it is for the pupil; and only *that* method is good which satisfies the pupils.

His theory of freedom as the basis of success in instruction, was put to a rude test by the fact that for a considerable time his pupils made little or no headway in learning to read. He says :

The simple thought that the time had not yet come for good reading and that there was at present no need of it, but that the pupils would themselves find the best method when the need arose, only recently entered my head.

After telling how the boys first met the difficulty of mastering the mechanical process of reading, Tolstoy goes on to tell how in the upper class progress was suddenly made owing to what seemed an accident.

In the class of advanced reading some one book is used, each boy reading in turn, and then all telling its contents together. They had been joined that autumn by an extremely talented lad, T., who had studied for two years with a sacristan, and was therefore ahead of them all in reading. He reads as we do, and so the pupils only understand anything of the advanced reading (and then not very much of it) when he reads; and yet each of them wishes to read. But as soon as a bad reader begins, the others express dissatisfaction, especially when the story is interesting. They laugh, and get cross, and the bad reader feels ashamed, and endless disputes arise. Last month one of the boys announced that at any cost he would manage, within a week, to read as well as T. ; others made the same announcement, and suddenly mechanical reading became their favourite occupation. For an hour or an hour-and-a-half at a time, they would sit without tearing themselves away from the books, which they did not understand; and they began taking books home with them; and really, within three weeks, they made such progress as could not have been expected.

In their case the reverse had happened of what usually occurs with those who learn the rudiments. Generally a man learns to read, and finds nothing he cares to read or understand. In this case the pupils were convinced that there *is* something worth reading and understanding, but felt that they lacked the capacity; and so they set to work to become proficient readers.

A difficulty of enormous importance was the absence of books really suitable for simple folk to read.

The insoluble problem was that for the education of the people an ability and a desire to read good books is essential. Good books are, however, written in a literary language the people don't understand. In order to learn to understand it, one would have to read a great deal; and people won't read willingly unless they understand what they read.

Connected with this difficulty of finding books suited to the understanding of peasants and of peasant children, was the parallel difficulty of finding literary subjects that interested them. This was first met by reading the Old Testament stories to them:

A knowledge of Sacred History was demanded both by the pupils themselves and by their parents. Of all the oral subjects I tried during three years, nothing so suited the understanding and mental condition of the boys as the Old Testament. The same was the case in all the schools that came under my observation. I tried the New Testament, I tried Russian History and Geography, I tried explanations of natural phenomena (so much advocated to-day), but it was all listened to unwillingly and quickly forgotten. But the Old Testament was remembered and narrated eagerly both in class and at home, and so well remembered that after two months the children wrote Scripture tales from memory with very slight omissions.

It seems to me that the book of the childhood of the race will always be the best book for the childhood of each man. It seems to me impossible to replace that book. To alter or to abbreviate the Bible, as is done in Sonntag's and other school primers, appears to me bad. All—every word—in it is right, both as revelation and as art. Read about the creation of the world in the Bible, and then read it in an abbreviated Sacred History, and the alteration of the Bible into the Sacred History will appear to you quite unintelligible. The latter can only be learnt by heart; while the Bible presents the child with a vivid and majestic picture he will never forget. The omissions made in the Sacred History are quite unintelligible, and only impair the character and beauty of the Scriptures. Why, for instance, is the statement omitted in all the Sacred Histories, that when there was nothing, the Spirit of God moved upon the face of the waters, and that after having created, God looked at His creation and saw that it was good, and that then it was the morning and evening of such and such a day? Why do they omit that God breathed into Adam's nostrils the breath of life, and that having taken one of his ribs He with the flesh closed up the place thereof, and so forth? One must read the Bible to unperverted children, to understand how necessary and true it all is. Perhaps one ought not to give the Bible to perverted young ladies; but when reading it to peasant children I did not alter or omit a single word. None of them giggled behind another's back; but all listened eagerly and with natural reverence. The story of Lot and his daughters, and the story of Judah's son, evoked horror but not laughter. . . .

How intelligible and clear it all is, especially for a child, and yet how stern and serious! I cannot imagine what instruction would be possible, without that book. Yet when one has learnt these stories only in childhood, and has afterwards partly forgotten them, one thinks: What good do they do us? Would it not be all the same if one did not know them at all? So it seems till, on beginning to teach, you test on other children the elements that helped to develop you. It seems as if one could teach children to write and read and calculate, and could give them an idea of history, geography, and natural phenomena, without the Bible, and before the Bible; yet nowhere is this done : everywhere the child first of all gets to know the Bible, its stories, or extracts from it. The first relations of the learner to the teacher are founded on that book. Such a general fact is not an accident. My very free relations with my pupils at the commencement of the Yásno-Polyána school helped me to find the explanation of this phenomenon.

A child or a man on entering school (I make no distinction between a ten-, thirty-, or seventy-year-old man) brings with him the special view of things he has deduced from life and to which he is attached. In order that a man of any age should begin to learn, it is necessary that he should love learning. That he should love learning, he must recognise the falseness and insufficiency of his own view of things, and must scent afar off that new view of life which learning is to reveal to him. No man or boy would have the strength to learn, if the result of learning presented itself to him merely as a capacity to write, to read, and to reckon. No master could teach if he did not command an outlook on life higher than his pupils possess. That a pupil may surrender himself whole-heartedly to his teacher, one corner must be lifted of the veil which hides from him all the delight of that world of thought, knowledge, and poetry to which learning will admit him. Only by being constantly under the spell of that bright light shining ahead of him, will the pupil be able to use his powers in the way we require of him.

What means have we of lifting this corner of the veil ? . . . As I have said, I thought as many think, that being myself in the world to which I had to introduce my pupils, it would be easy for me to do this; and I taught the rudiments, explained natural phenomena, and told them, as the primers do, that the fruits of learning are sweet; but the scholars did not believe me, and kept aloof. Then I tried reading the Bible to them, and quite took possession of them. The corner of the veil was lifted, and they yielded themselves to me completely. They fell in love with the book, and with learning, and with me. It only remained for me to guide them on. . . .

To reveal to the pupil a new world, and to make him, without possessing knowledge, love knowledge, there is no book but the Bible. I speak even for those who do not regard the Bible as a revelation. There are no other works—at least I know none—which in so compressed and poetic a form contain all those sides of human thought which the Bible unites in itself. All the questions raised by natural phenomena are there dealt with. Of all the primitive relations of men with one another: the family, the State, and religion, we first become conscious through that book. The generalisations of thought and wisdom, with the charm given by their childlike simplicity of form, seize the pupil's mind for the first time. Not only does the lyricism of David's psalms act on the minds of the elder pupils; but more than that, from this book every one becomes conscious for the first time of the whole beauty of the epos in its incomparable simplicity and strength. Who has not wept over the story of Joseph and his meeting with his brethren? Who has not, with bated breath, told the story of the bound and shorn Samson, revenging himself on his enemies and perishing under the ruins of the palace he destroys, or received a hundred other impressions on which we were reared as on our mothers' milk?

Let those who deny the educative value of the Bible and say it is out of date, invent a book and stories explaining the phenomena of Nature, either from general history or from the imagination, which will be accepted as the Bible stories are; and then we will admit that the Bible is obsolete. . . .

Drawn though it may be from a one-sided experience, I repeat my conviction. The development of a child or a man in our society without the Bible, is as inconceivable as that of an ancient Greek would have been without Homer. The Bible is the only book to begin with, for a child's reading. The Bible, both in its form and in its contents, should serve as a model for all children's primers and all reading books. A translation of the Bible into the language of the common folk, would be the best book for the people.

When pupils came from other schools where they had had to learn Scripture by heart, or had been inoculated with the abbreviated school-primer versions, Tolstoy found

that the Bible had nothing like as strong an effect as
it had on boys who came fresh to it.

Such pupils do not experience what is felt by fresh pupils,
who listen to the Bible with beating heart, seizing every word,
thinking that now, now at last, all the wisdom of the world is
about to be revealed to them.

In reading the above passages, it should be borne in
mind that in Russian usage 'The Bible' means the Old
Testament only.

Besides the Bible, the only books the people understand
and like, says Tolstoy, are those written not for the people
but by the people; such as folk-tales and collections of
songs, legends, proverbs, verses, and riddles. There was
much in his experience which fits in with what Mr. Cecil
Sharp and Miss Neal of the Espérance Club, have lately
been demonstrating by their revivals of English Folk Songs
and Dances: namely, that there is an excellent literature
and art which children and common folk appreciate and
assimilate as eagerly and excellently as any one, and which
it is the height of folly for cultured people to despise;
and his keen perception of the gap that separates the art
and literature accessible to the people from the art that
by its artificiality is beyond their reach, led him subsequently to undertake, first a series of school primers, and
then the re-telling of a number of folk-tales and legends,
which have reached more readers, and perhaps benefited
the world more, than anything else he has written.

With penmanship it happened at Yásno-Polyána school,
as with reading:

The pupils wrote very badly, and a new master introduced
writing from copies (another exercise very sedate and easy for
the master). The pupils became dull, and we were obliged to
abandon calligraphy, and did not know how to devise any way
of improving their handwriting. The eldest class discovered
the way for itself. Having finished writing the Bible stories,

the elder pupils began to ask for their exercise-books to take home [probably to read to their parents]. These were dirty, crumpled, and badly written. The precise mathematician P. asked for some paper, and set to work to rewrite his stories. This idea pleased the others. 'Give me, too, some paper!'— 'Give me an exercise-book!' and a fashion for calligraphy set in, which still prevails in the upper class. They took an exercise-book, put before them a written alphabet copy from which they imitated each letter, boasting to one another of their performance, and in two weeks' time they had made great progress.

Grammar turned out to be an unsatisfactory subject, and to have hardly any connection with correct writing or speaking.

In our youngest—the third—class, they write what they like. Besides that, the youngest write out in the evening, one at a time, sentences they have composed all together. One writes, and the others whisper among themselves, noting his mistakes, and only waiting till he has finished, in order to denounce his misplaced *e* or his wrongly detached prefix, or sometimes to perpetrate a blunder of their own. To write correctly and to correct mistakes made by others, gives them great pleasure. The elder boys seize every letter they can get hold of, exercising themselves in the correction of mistakes, and trying with all their might to write correctly; but they cannot bear grammar or the analysis of sentences, and in spite of a bias we had for analysis, they only tolerate it to a very limited extent, falling asleep or evading the classes.

History on the whole went badly, except such bits of Russian history as, when told poetically, aroused patriotic feelings. On one memorable occasion the whole class went wild with excitement and eager interest. That was when Tolstoy, with a poet's licence, told of the defeat of Napoleon's invasion of Russia in 1812.

Except in this legendary way, the teaching of history to

children is, in Tolstoy's opinion, useless. The historic sense develops later than the artistic sense :

In my experience and practice the first germ of interest in history arises out of contemporary events, sometimes as a result of participation in them, through political interest, political opinions, debates, and the reading of newspapers. Consequently the idea of beginning the teaching of history from present times should suggest itself to every intelligent teacher.

Of geography as a subject for the education of children, Tolstoy has an even lower opinion :

In Von Vizin's comedy *The Minor,* when Mitrofánoushka was being persuaded to learn geography, his mother said : ' Why teach him all the countries ? The coachman will drive him where he may have to go to.' Nothing more to the point has ever been said against geography, and all the learned men in the world put together cannot rebut such an irrefragable argument. I am speaking quite seriously. What need was there for me to know where the river and town of Barcelona are situated, when for thirty-three years I have not once had occasion to use the knowledge? Not even the most picturesque description of Barcelona and its inhabitants could, I imagine, conduce to the development of my mental faculties.

In fact, the sweeping conclusion at which Tolstoy arrives is that :

I not only see no use, but I see great harm, in teaching history or geography before the University is reached.

And he leaves it an open question whether even the University should concern itself with such subjects.

Drawing was a favourite lesson with the boys ; but I must confine myself to a single extract on that subject :

We drew figures from the blackboard in the following way : I first drew a horizontal or a vertical line, dividing it into parts by dots, and the pupils copied this line. Then I drew another or several perpendicular or sloping lines, standing in a certain relation to the first, and similarly divided up. Then we joined the dots of these different lines by others (straight or curved), and formed some symmetrical figure which, as it was gradually evolved, was copied by the boys. It seemed to me that this was a good plan : first, because the boy clearly saw the whole process of the formation of the figure, and secondly, because his perception of the co-relation of lines was developed by this drawing from the board, much better than by copying drawings or designs. . . .

It is nearly always useless to hang up a large complete picture or figure, because a beginner is quite at a loss before it, as he would be before an object from nature. But the growth of the figure before his eyes has an important meaning. In this case the pupil sees the backbone and skeleton of the drawing on which the body is subsequently formed. The pupils were always called on to criticise the lines and their relation, as I drew them. I often purposely drew them wrong, to find out in how far their judgment of the co-relation and incorrectness of the lines had been developed. Then again, when I was drawing my figure I asked the boys where they thought the next line should be added; and I even made one or other of them invent the shape of the figure himself.

In this way I not only aroused a more lively interest, but got the boys to participate freely in the formation and development of the figures; and this prevented the question, Why? which boys so naturally put when they are set to draw from copies.

The ease or difficulty with which it was understood, and the more or less interest evoked, chiefly influenced the choice of the method of instruction ; and I often quite abandoned what I had prepared for the lesson, merely because it was dull or foreign to the boys.

In the singing class, Tolstoy very soon found that notes written on the staff were not easily grasped by the pupils, and after using the staff for some ten lessons, he once showed the boys the use of numbers instead, and from that day forward they always asked him to use numbers, and they themselves always used numbers in writing music. This method is much more convenient, Tolstoy considers, for explaining both the intervals and the changes of key. The pupils who were not musical soon dropped out of the class, and the lessons with those who were, sometimes went on for three or four hours at a stretch. He tried to teach them musical time in the usual manner, but succeeded so badly that he had to take that and melody separately. First he took the sounds without reference to time, and then beat the time without considering the sounds, and finally joined the two processes together. After several lessons he found that the method he had drifted into, combined the chief features (though not some of the minor peculiarities) of Chevet's method, which, as already mentioned, he had seen in successful operation in Paris. After a very few lessons, two of the boys used to write down the melodies of the songs they knew, and were almost able to read music at sight.

From the limited experience he had in teaching music, Tolstoy——to quote his own words almost textually——became convinced that : (1) To write sounds by means of figures is the most profitable method ; (2) To teach time separately from sound is the most profitable method ; (3) For the teaching of music to be willingly and fruitfully received, one must from the start teach the *art* and not aim merely at dexterity in singing or playing. Spoilt young ladies may be taught to play Burgmüller's exercises ; but it is better not to teach the children of the people at all, than to teach them mechanically ; (4) Nothing so harms musical instruction as what looks like a knowledge of music : namely the performance of choirs, and performances at examinations, speech-days, or in church ; and (5) In teaching music to the people, the thing to be aimed at is to impart our knowledge of the general laws of music, but not the false taste we have developed among us.

In one of the most remarkable of his articles, Tolstoy tells how he discovered that Fédka and Syómka possessed literary ability of the highest order. Composition lessons had not gone well, until one day Tolstoy proposed that the children should write a story of peasant life to illustrate a popular proverb. Most of them felt this to be beyond their powers, and went on with their other occupations. One of them, however, bade Tolstoy write it himself in competition with them, and he set to work to do so, till Fédka, climbing on the back of his chair, interrupted him by reading over his shoulder. Tolstoy then began reading out what he had composed, and explaining how he thought of continuing the story. Several of the boys became interested, not approving of Tolstoy's work, but criticising and amending it, offering suggestions and supplying details. Syómka and Fédka particularly distinguished themselves, and showed extraordinary imagination, and such judgment, sense of proportion, restraint, and power of clothing their thoughts in words, that Tolstoy was carried away by the interest of the work and wrote as hard as he could to their dictation, having constantly to ask them to wait and not forget the details they had suggested. Fédka—of whom Tolstoy says that 'The chief quality in every art, the sense of proportion, was in him extraordinarily developed : he writhed at every superfluous detail suggested by any of the other boys,'—gradually took control of the work, and ruled so despotically and with such evident right, that the others dropped off and went home, except Syómka, who along his own more matter-of-fact line continued to co-operate.

We worked from seven in the evening till eleven. They felt neither hunger nor weariness and were even angry with me when I stopped writing ; and they set to work to do it themselves turn and turn about, but did not get on well and soon gave it up. . . .

I left the lesson because I was too excited.

'What is the matter with you? Why are you so pale: are you ill?' asked my colleague. Indeed, only two or three times in my life have I experienced such strong emotion as during that evening. . . .

Next day Tolstoy could hardly believe the experience of the night before. It seemed incredible that a peasant boy, hardly able to read, should suddenly display such marvellous command of artistic creative power.

It seemed to me strange and offensive that I, the author of *Childhood*, who had achieved a certain success and was recognised by the educated Russian public as possessing artistic talent, should in artistic matters not merely be unable to instruct or help eleven-year-old Syómka and Fédka, but should hardly be able, except at a happy moment of excitement, to keep up with them and understand them.

Next day we set to work to continue the story. When I asked Fédka if he had thought of a continuation, he only waved his hand and remarked: 'I know, I know! . . . Who will do the writing?' . . . We resumed the work, and again the boys showed the same enthusiasm, and the same sense of artistic truth and proportion.

Half-way through the lesson I had to leave them. They wrote two pages without me, as just in feeling and as true to life as the preceding ones. These two pages were rather poorer in detail, some of the details were not quite happily placed, and there were also a couple of repetitions. All this had evidently occurred because the actual writing was a difficulty for them. On the third day we had similar success. . . . There could no longer be any doubt or thought of its being a mere accident. We had obviously succeeded in finding a more natural and inspiring method than any we had previously tried.

This unfinished story was accidentally destroyed. Tolstoy was greatly annoyed, and Fédka and Syómka, though they did not understand his vexation, offered to stay the night at his house and reproduce it. After eight o'clock, when school was over, they came, and (to Tolstoy's great pleasure) locked themselves into his study, where at first they were heard laughing but then became very quiet. On listening at the door Tolstoy heard their subdued voices discussing the story, and heard also the scratching of a pen. At midnight he knocked and was admitted. Syómka was standing at the large table, writing busily; his lines running crookedly across the paper and his pen constantly seeking the inkstand. Fédka told Tolstoy to ' wait a bit,' and insisted on Syómka's adding something more, to his dictation. At last Tolstoy took the exercise-book; and the lads, after enjoying a merry supper of potatoes and *kvás*, divested themselves of their sheepskin coats and lay down to sleep under the writing table; their ' charming, healthy, childish, peasant laughter ' still ringing through the room.

The story just mentioned, and other stories written by the children, were published in the magazine; and Tolstoy declares them to be, in their way, superior to anything else in Russian literature. It was largely on the model of these peasant children's stories that, years later, he wrote his own famous stories for the people.

The rules for encouraging composition which he deduces from his experience are these :

(1) To offer as large and varied a choice of themes as possible; not inventing them specially for the children, but offering such as most interest the teacher and seem to him most important.

(2) To give children stories written by children to read, and to offer only children's compositions as models; because these are juster, finer and more moral than those written by adults.

(3) (Specially important.) Never, when looking through the compositions, make any remarks to the children about the neatness of the exercise-books, the handwriting, or the spelling; nor, above all, about the construction of the sentences, or about logic.

(4) Since the difficulty of composition lies not in size nor in subject, nor in correctness of language, but in the mechanism of the work, which consists : (*a*) in choosing one out of the large number of thoughts and images that offer themselves; (*b*) in choosing words wherewith to clothe it; (*c*) in remembering it and finding a fitting place for it; (*d*) in remembering what has already been written, so as not to repeat anything or omit anything, and in finding a way of joining up what has preceded to what succeeds; (*e*) and finally in so managing that while thinking and writing at one and the same time, the one operation shall not hamper the other,—I, having these things in view, proceeded as follows.

At first I took upon myself some of these sides of the work, transferring them gradually to the pupils. At first, out of the thoughts and images suggested, I chose for them those which seemed to me best, and I kept these in mind and indicated suitable places to insert them, and I looked over what had been written to avoid repetitions, and I did the writing myself, letting them merely clothe the thoughts and images in words. Afterwards I let them select, and then let them look over what had been written, and finally they took on themselves the actual writing. . . .

One of the profoundest convictions impressed on Tolstoy's mind by his educational experiments was that the peasants and their children have a large share of artistic capacity, and that art is immensely important because of its humanising effect on them, and because it arouses and trains their faculties. Unfortunately the works : literary, poetic, dramatic, pictorial and plastic, now produced, are being produced expressly for people possessed of leisure, wealth, and a special, artificial training, and are therefore useless to the people. This deflection of art from the service of the masses of whom there are millions, to the delectation of the classes of whom there are but thousands, appears to him to be a very great evil.

He says with reference to two realms of art which he had loved passionately, and with which he was specially familiar :

music and poetry, that he noticed that the demands of the
masses were more legitimate than the demands of the classes.

Terrible to say, I came to the conviction that all that we
have done in those two departments has been done along
a false and exceptional path, which lacks importance, has no
future, and is insignificant in comparison with the demands
upon, and even with the samples of, those same arts which we
find put forward by the people. I became convinced that such
lyrical compositions as, for example, Poúshkin's 'I remember
the marvellous moment,' and such musical productions as Beethoven's Last Symphony, are not so absolutely and universally
good as the song of 'Willy the Steward' or the melody of 'Float-
ing down the river, Mother Vólga'; and that Poúshkin and
Beethoven please us, not because they are absolutely beautiful, but because we are as spoiled as they, and because they
flatter our abnormal irritability and weakness. How common
it is to hear the empty and stale paradox, that to understand
the beautiful, a preparation is necessary! Who said so? Why?
What proves it? It is only a shift, a loophole, to escape from
the hopeless position to which the false direction of our art,
produced for one class alone, has led us. Why are the beauty of
the sun and of the human face, and the beauty of the sounds of
a folk-song, and of deeds of love and self-sacrifice, accessible to
every one, and why do *they* demand no preparation?

For years I vainly strove to make my pupils feel the poetic
beauties of Poúshkin and of our whole literature, and a similar
attempt is being made by innumerable teachers not in Russia
alone; and if these teachers notice the results of their efforts,
and will be frank about the matter, they will admit that the chief
result of this attempt to develop poetic feeling, is to kill it; and
that it is just those pupils whose natures are most poetic who
show most aversion to such commentaries. . . .

I will try to sum up all that I have said above. In reply to
the question: Do people need the *beaux arts*? pedagogues
usually grow timid and confused (only Plato decided the matter
boldly in the negative). They say: 'Art is needed, but with
certain limitations; and to make it possible for all to become
artists would be bad for the social structure. Certain arts and

certain degrees of art can only exist in a certain class of society. The arts must have their special servants, entirely devoted to them.' They say : 'It should be possible for those who are greatly gifted to escape from among the people and devote themselves completely to the service of art.' That is the greatest concession pedagogy makes to the right of each individual to become what he likes.

But I consider that to be all wrong. I think that a need to enjoy art and to serve art, is inherent in every human being, to whatever race or class he may belong ; and that this need has its right and should be satisfied. Taking that position as an axiom, I say that if the enjoyment and production of art by every one, presents inconveniences and inconsistencies, the reason lies in the character and direction art has taken : about which we must be on our guard, lest we foist anything false on the rising generation, and lest we prevent it from producing something new, both as to form and as to matter.

Tolstoy goes so far as to doubt whether, so long as no suitable literature is produced for the people, it is even worth their while to learn to read.

Looking closer at the results of the rudiments in the form in which they are supplied to the masses, I think most people will decide that the rudiments do more harm than good, taking into account the prolonged compulsion, the disproportionate development of memory, the false conception of the completeness of science, the aversion to further education, the false vanity, and the habit of meaningless reading acquired in these schools. . . .

'Let us print good books for the people !' . . . How simple and easy that seems—like all great thoughts ! There is only one obstacle, namely that there exist no good books for the people, either here or in Europe. To print such books, they must first be produced ; and none of our philanthropists think of undertaking *that* work !

Before closing this rapid summary of Tolstoy's educational writings, let me quote a few more sentences which sum up his essential position :

In my articles on Education I have given my theoretic reasons for considering that only freedom on the part of the pupils to select what they will learn and how they will learn it, can furnish a sound basis for any instruction. In practice I constantly applied those rules to the schools under my guidance . . . and the results were always very good both for the teachers and the pupils, as well as for the evolution of new methods; and this I assert boldly, for hundreds of visitors came to the Yásno-Polyána school and know how it worked.

For the masters, the result of such relations with the pupils was that they did not consider any methods they happened to know, to be the best, but they tried to discover new methods and made acquaintance with other teachers whose ways they could learn. They tested fresh methods, and above all, they themselves were always learning. A master never allowed himself, in cases of failure, to think that it was the pupils' fault: their laziness, naughtiness, stupidity, deafness or stuttering; but he was convinced that the fault was his own, and for every defect on the side of the pupil or pupils, he tried to discover a remedy.

For the pupils the results were that they learnt eagerly, always begged to have additional lessons on winter evenings, and were quite free in class—which, in my conviction and experience, is the chief condition of successful teaching. Between the teachers and the pupils friendly and natural relations always arose, without which it is not possible for a teacher to know his pupils fully. . . .

With reference to the methods of instruction, the results were that no method was adopted or rejected because it pleased or did not please the teacher, but only because the pupil, without compulsion, accepted or did not accept it. But besides the good results which unfailingly followed the adoption of my method both by myself and by all—more than twenty—other teachers (I say 'unfailingly' because we never had a single pupil who did not master the rudiments)—besides these results, the adoption of the principles of which I have spoken produced this effect, that during fifteen years all the different modifications to which my method has been subjected, have not only not removed it from the demands of the people, but have brought it closer and closer to them. . . . In my school . . . every teacher, while bringing his pupils forward, himself feels the need of learning; and this was constantly the case with all the teachers I had.

Moreover, the very methods of instruction themselves—since they are not fixed once for all but aim at finding the easiest and simplest paths—change and improve according to what the teacher learns from the pupils' relation to his teaching.

The children had not to pay anything for attending the school, and the relations between them and Tolstoy are illustrated by the account a visitor has given of seeing Tolstoy rush through a gate followed by a crowd of merry youngsters who were snow-balling him. Tolstoy was intent on making his escape, but on seeing the visitor he changed his mind, acknowledged his defeat, and surrendered to his triumphant pursuers.

Tolstoy does not stand before the world to-day primarily as a school-master, and even were I competent to deal with the subject, it would exceed the limits of this biography to attempt a detailed criticism of his precepts and practice; but he evidently possessed, as he claims in one of his articles, 'a certain pedagogic tact'; and he is clearly right in his belief that the rigid discipline of schools, the lack of freedom and initiative, the continual demand for silence and obedience, and the refusal to allow pupils to criticise the lessons they receive, have a constantly stupefying effect.

All that he allowed at Yásnaya Polyána was denied to us when I was at Christ's Hospital, in 1868-1874; and I look back on those six years of mental stultification as the most wretched of my life. At the preparatory school in Hertford, so stupefied were the little boys by terror and discipline, that when the head-master (traditionally an incarnation of all the virtues) became grossly harsh and unfair, they could not see what was happening until his insanity was so pronounced that the doctors had to take him in hand : an event that occurred soon after I had left for the upper school in London.

There, one of the masters (who evidently did not believe that ' history is experience teaching by example ') in intervals between whacking the boys on their backs or hands with a long cane, used, I remember, emphatically to announce that ' dates and names are the most important parts of history.' A Latin master, a barrister, who was usually busy at some sort of law work when he should have been teaching us, used to set us to learn by rote rules and illustrations which we did not in the least understand. On one occasion the example given in the grammar was :

Opes irritamenta malorum effodiuntur.
Riches the incentives of crime are dug out of the earth.

The top boy had learnt the rule and illustration by heart (which I never could do); but, departing from his usual routine, the master unexpectedly asked which Latin word corresponded to which English. Each of the first twenty-four boys in the class in turn got caned and sent to the bottom ; so that by the time I, who had been last, had come to the top, and it was my turn to reply, only one possible combination remained untried, and I was able to announce that *effodiuntur* meant ' are dug out of the earth.' Unluckily there was another rule that day, and over this I, in turn, came to grief, and was caned and sent to the bottom.

In the drawing class I remember doing the outline of a cube to the master's satisfaction, and being promoted to the shading class. I had no idea how to shade, and the attempt I made was certainly a very bad one ; but instead of receiving advice or assistance, my ears were boxed so violently that I should be tempted to attribute to that assault the slight deafness from which I have since suffered, were it not that such treatment was so common at Christ's Hospital, that none of the victims whose hearing may have been impaired, could be sure to which of the masters they owed that part of their preparation for the battle of life.

I feel sure the stultifying effects of such cruel and sense-less treatment would have been even more serious, had not the school authorities, by some strange oversight, allowed *one* really readable and interesting periodical to find a place among the Sunday magazines and other sterilised literature obtainable in the School Library. This one publication, which I read ardently during my school years, was *Chambers's Journal.* It contained novels by James Payn, and other matter suited to my powers of mental digestion. From smuggled copies of Captain Marryat's novels I also got a good deal of culture : far more, I am sure, than from any of the lessons we endured.

CHIEF AUTHORITIES FOR CHAPTER VIII

Tolstoy's Educational articles, and
N. V. Ouspensky, *Iz Proshlago.*

CHAPTER IX

MARRIAGE

The Behrs visit Yásnaya. Proposal by thought-reading. The Diary. Marriage. Ministers on magazine. The school closed and the magazine stopped. Family happiness. Health. Fet's visit. Sergius born. Children. *The Cossacks* and *Polikoúshka.* Bees. Plays. *Confession.* Saving the hay. *Decembrists.* Samára. Preparations for *War and Peace.* Collected edition. Translations. Dislocates arm. Tatiána born. Fears of famine. Sergius (brother) and Tánya Behrs. Nikólsky. Visits Borodinó. Tolstoy at home and with the children. Relations with servants. Masquerade. Moscow. Drawing school. Sculpture. Ilyá born. Pleads at court-martial. Dr. Zahárin. *Smoke.* Fet's Literary Evening. *War and Peace.* Schopenhauer. Pénza. Death of V. P. Bótkin. The Countess and the children's education. English nurse. Tolstoy's habits. Visitors. Fet. Tolstoy's ardour. Property. Untidiness. Respect for sleep. Newspapers. Characteristics. Studies the drama.

To one who admires Tolstoy's educational work, it is somewhat disconcerting to see how scornfully he spoke of it sixteen years later in his *Confession.* But that is always his way : the old is useless and worthless and bad ; only the new, the unachieved, the fresh ideal, is admirable. For it, he decries all that the past has produced—including himself and his former work. He makes his points broadly and powerfully, but to understand, we must discriminate, and allow for an artistic temperament tempting him to exaggerate. Let him however speak for himself, that the reader may judge :

On returning from abroad I settled in the country, and happened to occupy myself with peasant schools. This work was particularly to my taste, because in it I had not to face the falsity which had become obvious to me and stared me in the face when I tried to teach people by literary means. Here, also, I acted in the name of Progress, but I already regarded Progress itself critically. I said to myself: 'In some of its developments Progress has proceeded wrongly; and with primitive peasant children one must deal in a spirit of perfect freedom, letting them choose what path of Progress they please.' In reality I was ever revolving round one and the same insoluble problem, which was: How to teach without knowing what? In the higher spheres of literary activity I had realised that one could not teach without knowing what; for I saw that people all taught differently, and by quarrelling among themselves succeeded only in hiding their ignorance from one another. But here, with peasant children, I thought to evade this difficulty by letting them learn what they liked. It amuses me now, when I remember how I shuffled in trying to fulfil my desire to teach, while in the depth of my soul I knew very well that I could not teach anything needful, for I did not know what was needful.

After spending a year at school work, I went abroad a second time, to discover how to teach others while myself knowing nothing.

And it seemed to me that I had learnt this abroad, and in the year of the peasants' Emancipation I returned to Russia armed with all this wisdom; and having become an Arbiter, I began to teach both the uneducated peasants in schools, and the educated classes through a magazine I published. Things appeared to be going well, but I felt I was not quite sound mentally, and that matters could not long continue in that way. And I should perhaps then have come to the state of despair at which I arrived fifteen years later, had there not been one side of life still unexplored by me, and which promised me happiness: that was marriage.

For a year I busied myself with Arbitration work, the schools, and the magazine; and I became so worn-out—as a result especially of my mental confusion—and so hard was my struggle as Arbiter, so obscure the results of my activity in the schools, so repulsive my shuffling in the magazine (which always amounted to one and the same thing: a desire to teach everybody, and to hide the fact that I did not know what to teach) that I fell ill, mentally rather than physically, and threw up everything, and went away to the Bashkírs in the steppes, to breathe fresh air, drink *koumýs,* and live an animal life.

Tired of and dissatisfied with his work, and thinking he detected in himself signs of the malady that had carried off two of his brothers, he set off in May 1862 (accompanied by his servant Alexis and two of his pupils) to undergo a koumýs (soured and fermented mares' milk) cure in the Samára steppes east of the Vólga.

1862

He went first to Moscow, and his friend Raévsky has told how Tolstoy came up to him in the Club there, and mentioned with great indignation and vexation that his brother was playing cards and had lost Rs. 7000 in a few hours. ' How can men do such things ? ' said Tolstoy. Half-an-hour later Raévsky saw Leo Tolstoy himself playing Chinese billiards (a game something like bagatelle, played on a board with wire impediments) and learnt that he had lost Rs. 1000 to the stranger with whom he was playing ! This was, I believe, the last occasion on which Tolstoy played any game for stakes he found it difficult to pay. The occurrence led to the premature publication of his novel *The Cossacks,* which he had had in hand for several years, but to which he still intended to add a second part. Not having Rs. 1000 (then about £150) available, he let Katkóf, the well-known publicist, editor of the *Moscow Gazette* and of the monthly *Russian Messenger,* have the story for that sum paid in advance. This ' Tale of the Year 1852,' as the sub-title runs, is based on Tolstoy's Caucasian experiences. The circumstances which led to its premature publication made the work repugnant to him, and he never completed it.

Among those to whom he mentioned the occurrence were the Behrs, of whom Miss Sophie was already so interested in him that she wept at the news. At their home he was always a welcome and intimate guest, and as time went on he saw more and more of that family.

From Moscow he proceeded to Tvér by rail, and thence by steamer down the Vólga to Samára.

At Kazán he stopped to visit his relation V. I. Úshkof: and from Samára he wrote to Aunt Tatiána:

27 *May* 1862.

To-day I shall start to drive ninety miles from Samára to Karalýk. . . .

I have had a beautiful journey; the country pleases me very much; my health is better, *i.e.* I cough less. Alexis and the boys are alive and well, as you may tell their relations. Please write me about Sergéy, or let him do so. Greet all my dear comrades [probably the masters in the schools] for me, and request them to write me of what goes on, and of how they are getting on. . . .

In another letter, dated 28th June 1862, he wrote:

It is now a month since I had any news of you or from home; please write me about everybody: first, our family; secondly, the (University) students [who acted as masters in the schools] etc. Alexis and I have grown fatter, he especially, but we still cough a little, and again he especially. We are living in a Tartar tent; the weather is beautiful. I have found my friend Stolýpin—now Atamán in Ourálsk—and have driven over to see him; and have brought back from there a secretary; but I dictate and write little. Idleness overcomes one when drinking koumýs. In two weeks' time I intend to leave here, and I expect to be home by St. Elijah's day [20 July, old style]. I am tormented in this out-of-the-way place by not knowing what is going on, and also by the thought that I am horribly behindhand with the publication of the magazine. I kiss your hand. . . .

Just when Tolstoy was leaving Karalýk a most unexpected event was occurring at Yásnaya, where his sister Mary was staying with Aunt Tatiána. Owing to the denunciation of a police spy who, among other lies, pretended to have discovered a secret door in Tolstoy's house, the police authorities decided to search his estate; and one morning—to the immense astonishment of the neighbouring peasants—police, watchmen, officials, and gendarmes, under the command of a Colonel, appeared upon the scene! In the school-house a photographic apparatus was found: a thing sufficiently rare in a Russian village in those days to evoke the suspicious inquiries of the gendarme officer, to whom one of the student-teachers chaffingly volunteered the information that it was kept to photograph Herzen (the celebrated exile, then living in London); but nowhere were any secret doors found.

The floors of the stables were broken up with crowbars to see if anything was hidden there. The pond was dragged, but nothing more incriminating than crayfish and carp was found. All the cupboards, drawers, boxes and desks in the house were opened and searched, and the ladies were frightened almost to death. A police-officer from Toúla would not even allow Tolstoy's sister to leave the library till he had finished reading aloud in her presence and in that of two gendarmes, Tolstoy's Diary and letters, which contained the most intimate secrets of his life and which he had kept private since he was sixteen years old.

Finding nothing incriminating at Yásnaya, the representatives of law and order next betook themselves to the other schools working in conjunction with Tolstoy, and there also they turned tables and cupboards upside down, seized exercise-books and primers, arrested the teachers, and spread the wildest suspicions abroad among the peasants, to whom school education was still a novelty held somewhat in suspicion.

On receiving news of this event Tolstoy at once wrote to his aunt, the Countess A. A. Tolstoy, asking her to speak to those who knew him well and had influence, and on whose aid he could rely. Said he:

I cannot and will not let this affair pass. All the activity in which I found solace and happiness, has been spoilt. Aunty is so ill from fright that she will probably not recover. The peasants no longer regard me as an honest man—an opinion I had earned in the course of years—but as a criminal, an incendiary, or a coiner, whose cunning alone has enabled him to escape punishment.

'Eh, man, you've been found out! Don't talk to us any more about honesty and justice—you've hardly escaped handcuffs yourself!'

From the landed proprietors I need not say what a cry of rapture went up. Please write to me as soon as possible, after consulting Peróvsky [Count V. A. P.] and Alexéy Tolstoy [Count A. T., the dramatist and poet] and any one else you like, as to how I am to write to the Emperor and how best to present my letter. It is too late to prevent the injury the thing has done, or to extricate myself, and there is no way out except by receiving satisfaction as public as the insult has been; and this I have firmly resolved on. I shall not join Herzen; he has his way, I have mine. Neither will I hide. . . . But I will loudly announce that I am selling my estate and mean to leave Russia, where one cannot know from moment to moment what awaits one. . . .

At the end of an eight-page letter he mentions that the Colonel of gendarmes, on leaving, threatened to renew his search till he discovered 'if anything is hidden'; and Tolstoy adds, 'I have loaded pistols in my room, and am waiting to see how this matter will end.'

He also remarked : 'I often say to myself, How exceedingly fortunate it was that I was not at home at the time ! Had I been there, I should certainly now be awaiting my trial for murder !'

Soon after this, Alexander II spent some time at Petróvsky Park, near Moscow. There Tolstoy presented a letter claiming reparation, which an aide-de-camp undertook to give to the Emperor ; and some weeks later the Governor of Toúla transmitted to Tolstoy the Emperor's expression of regret for what had occurred.

It is easy to imagine the effect such an outrage as this police-search would have on a man of Tolstoy's acute self-esteem, and how it would intensify his hatred of Government.

After his return from Samára, he saw more of the Behrs than ever. Fet, whom he introduced to them, thus records his impressions of the family:

I found the doctor to be an amiable old gentleman of polite manners, and his wife a handsome, majestic brunette who evidently ruled the house. I refrain from describing the three young ladies, of whom the youngest had an admirable contralto voice. They all, notwithstanding the watchful supervision of their mother and their irreproachable modesty, possessed that attractive quality which the French designate by the words *du chien* [lively, full of go]. The service and the dinner were admirable.

Madame Behrs was on very friendly terms with Tolstoy's sister, the Countess Mary; and before he went abroad Tolstoy had frequently, at the house of the latter, played with the children of both families. In 1862 he often visited the Behrs at Pokróvskoe-Glébovo, where they lived in a *dátcha* (country house) they occupied every summer. He nearly always walked the eight miles from Moscow, and often took long rambles with the family besides. The girls had been educated at home, but Sophia Andréyevna, the second daughter, had passed a University examination entitling her to the diploma qualifying to teach both in private and in State schools.

We may judge of Tolstoy's state of mind at this time by an entry in his Diary, dated 23rd August: 'I am afraid of myself. What if this be only a *desire* for love and not real love? I try to notice only her weak points, but yet I love.' And again, 'I rose in good health, with a particularly clear head, and wrote easily, though the matter was feeble. Then I felt more sad than I have done for a long time. I have no friends at all. I am alone. I had friends when I served Mammon, but have none when I serve truth.'

On 26th August he notes that Sónya (Miss Sophia Behrs) gave him a story to read, written by herself, and her description of the hero as a man of 'unusually unattractive appearance, and changeable convictions' hit him hard; but he was relieved to find that it was not meant for him.

On his thirty-fourth birthday, 28th August 1862 (old style) he jotted down in his Diary the words: 'Ugly mug! Do not think of marriage; your calling is of another kind.'

About this time the Behrs paid a two weeks' visit to Madame Behrs' father's estate of Ívitsa, some thirty miles from Yásnaya, and *en route* they stopped a couple of days at Yásnaya to visit the Countess Mary. The day after their arrival a picnic party was arranged with some neighbours. It was haymaking time, and there was much haystack climbing by the picknickers. The general impression was that Tolstoy was in love with Lisa, the eldest Miss Behrs: this opinion being fostered by the idea, then common in Russia, that an elder daughter should be disposed of before a younger daughter may be courted.

A few days later Tolstoy followed the Behrs to Ívitsa; and here the scene occurred which he has utilised in *Anna Karénina* when describing Lévin's proposal to Kitty—a scene in which something approaching thought-reading takes place.

Sitting at a card-table with Miss Sophia Behrs, Tolstoy wrote the initial letters of the sentence:

'In your family a false opinion exists about me and your sister Lisa; you and Tánitchka should destroy it.'

Miss Sophia read the letters, understood what words they stood for, and nodded her head.

Tolstoy then wrote the initial letters of another sentence:

'Your youth and need of happiness, to-day remind me too strongly of my age and the impossibility of happiness.'

The nature of the Russian language (with its inflections instead of particles, and the absence of articles) somewhat diminishes the miracle; but the test was a very severe one, and again the girl guessed the words aright. The two understood one another, and their fate was practically sealed.

T

The Behrs returned to Pokróvskoe-Glébovo in September. Tolstoy accompanied them on the carriage-journey back to Moscow and visited them every day, bringing music for the young ladies, playing the piano for them, and accompanying the youngest—whom he nick-named 'Madame Viardot' after the famous singer.

On the 17th of that month (the name's day of Sophia) Tolstoy handed his future wife a letter containing a proposal of marriage, which she gladly accepted. Her father, displeased that the second daughter should be preferred to the eldest, at first refused his assent. But Tolstoy was strenuously insistent—I have even heard that he threatened to shoot himself—and the doctor soon yielded to the united persuasion of daughter and suitor.

The bridegroom's sense of honour led him to hand his future wife the Diary, in which, mingled with hopes, prayers, self-castigations and self-denunciations, the sins and excesses of his bachelorhood were recorded. To the girl, who had looked upon him as a personification of the virtues, this revelation came as a great shock; but after a sleepless night passed in weeping bitterly over it, she returned the Diary and forgave the past.

To get married it was necessary first to confess and receive the eucharist. Tolstoy's own experiences in this matter are narrated in Chapter I of Part V of *Anna Karénina*, where they are attributed to Lévin.

The marriage took place within a week of the proposal, namely on 23rd September 1862, in the Court church of the Krémlin, the bridegroom being thirty-four and the bride eighteen years of age. When the ceremony was over the couple left Moscow in a *dormeuse* (sleeping carriage), and drove to Yásnaya Polyána, where Tolstoy's brother Sergéy and Aunt Tatiána were awaiting them.

Fet records the letter in which Tolstoy informed him of his marriage :

FÉTOUSHKA [an endearing diminutive of Fet] UNCLE, or simply

TOLSTOY IN 1862, THE YEAR OF HIS MARRIAGE.

DEAR FRIEND AFANÁSY AFANÁSYEVITCH!—I have been married two weeks and am happy, and am a new, quite a new man. I want to visit you, but cannot manage it. When shall I see you? Having come to myself, I feel that I value you very, very much. We have so many unforgettable things in common : Nikólenka, and much besides. Do drive over and make my acquaintance. I kiss Márya Petróvna's hand. Farewell, dear friend. I embrace you with all my heart.

In another letter belonging to the same period he writes:

I am writing from the country, and while I write, from upstairs where she is talking to my brother, I hear the voice of my wife, whom I love more than the whole world. I have lived to the age of thirty-four without knowing that it was possible to love, and to be so happy. When I am more tranquil I will write you a long letter. I should not say 'more tranquil,' for I am now more tranquil and clear than I have ever been, but I should say, ' when I am accustomed to it.' At present I have a constant feeling of having stolen an undeserved, illicit, and not-for-me-intended happiness. There . . . she is coming! I hear her, and it is so good! . . . And why do such good people as you, and, most wonderful of all, such a being as my wife, love me?

It did not much disturb his happiness, when, before Tolstoy had been married a fortnight, an event occurred which might easily have led to very disagreeable consequences. On 3rd October the Minister of the Interior called the attention of the Minister of Education to the harmful nature of the *Yásnaya Polyána* magazine. This is what he wrote:

A careful perusal of the educational magazine, *Yásnaya Polyána,* edited by Count Tolstoy, leads to the conviction that that magazine . . . frequently propagates ideas which apart from their incorrectness are by their very tendency harmful. . . . I consider it necessary to direct your Excellency's attention to the general tendency and spirit of that magazine, which often infringes the fundamental rules of religion and morality. . . . I have the honour to inform you, Sir, of this, in the expectation that you may be inclined to consider it desirable to direct the special attention of the Censor to this publication.

Fortunately the decision of the matter did not lie with the Minister of the Interior, but with the Minister of Education, who on receiving this communication had the magazine in question carefully examined, and, on 24th October, replied that he found nothing harmful or contrary to religion in its tendency. It contained extreme opinions on educational matters, no doubt, but these, he said, should be criticised in educational periodicals rather than prohibited by the Censor. 'In general,' added the Minister:

I must say that Count Tolstoy's educational activity deserves full respect, and the Ministry of Education is bound to assist and co-operate with him, though it cannot share all his views, some of which after full consideration he will himself probably reject.

Other things besides the suspicion in which he was held by the Minister of the Interior, tended to discourage Tolstoy. His magazine had few subscribers and attracted but little attention. The year's issue was causing him a loss of something like Rs. 3000 (say about £450)—a larger sum than he could well afford to throw away. So he decided to discontinue it after the twelfth number. The month after his marriage he also closed the school, which was too great a tax on his time and attention.

It has often been said that the obstacles placed in his way by the Government turned him aside from educational work, but in speaking to me about it Tolstoy remarked that really the main factor was his marriage, and his preoccupation with family life.

Both he and his wife were absorbed by their personal happiness, though from time to time small quarrels and misunderstandings arose between them. So impulsive and strenuous a nature as Tolstoy's was sure to have its fluctuations of feeling, but on the whole the ties binding the couple together grew stronger and closer as the months passed into years.

The Countess's parents used to say : 'We could not have

wished for greater happiness for our daughter.' The Countess not only loved Tolstoy dearly as a husband, but had the deepest admiration for him as a writer. He on his side often said that he found in family life the completest happiness, and in Sophia Andréyevna not only a loving wife and an excellent mother for his children, but an admirable assistant in his literary work, in which, owing to his careless and unmethodical habits, an intelligent and devoted amanuensis was invaluable. The Countess acquired remarkable skill in deciphering his often extremely illegible handwriting, and was sometimes able to guess in a quite extraordinary way the meaning of his hasty jottings and incomplete sentences.

One drawback to their almost complete happiness lay in the fact that though active and possessed of great physical strength, Tolstoy seldom enjoyed any long periods of uninterrupted good health. In his correspondence we find frequent references to indisposition. In early manhood, he seems to have distended his stomach, and, especially after the hardships he endured during the war of 1854-5, he was subject to digestive troubles for the rest of his days.

Town life did not attract him. He had never felt at ease in what is called high society; nor were his means large enough to enable him to support a wife and family in a good position in town. Still, towards the close of the year of his marriage, he and the Countess spent some weeks in Moscow.

They were however soon back at Yásnaya. In February Fet visited them there, and found them overflowing with life and happiness. ₁₈₆₃ 1863

On 15th May, after the Tolstoys and Fet had by some chance just missed meeting at the house of a neighbouring proprietor, Tolstoy wrote to his friend:

We just missed seeing you, and how sorry I am that we did! How much I want to talk over with you. Not a day passes without our mentioning you several times. My wife is not at all 'playing with dolls.' Don't you insult her. She is my

serious helpmate, though now bearing a burden from which she
hopes to be free early in July.   What won't she do afterwards?
We are *ufanizing*[1] little by little.   I have made an important
discovery, which I hasten to impart to you.   Clerks and over-
seers are only a hindrance to the management of an estate.
Try the experiment of dismissing them all; then sleep ten hours
a day, and be assured that everything will get along *not worse*.
I have made the experiment and am quite satisfied with its
success.

How, oh how, are we to see one another?   If you go to
Moscow with Márya Petróvna and do not come to visit us, it
will be dreadful offensive.   (My wife, who was reading this
letter, prompted that sentence.)   I wanted to write much, but
time lacks.   I embrace you with all my heart; my wife bows
profoundly to you, and I to your wife.

Business: When you are in Orél, buy me 20 poods [720 lbs.]
of various kinds of twine, reins, and shaft-traces, if they cost
less than Rs. 2.30 per pood including carriage, and send them
me by a carter.   The money shall be paid at once.

Fet soon availed himself of the invitation, and after driving past the low towers which mark the entrance to the
birch alley leading to the house, he came upon Tolstoy
eagerly directing the dragging of a lake and taking all
possible care that the carp should not escape.   The Countess,
in a white dress, came running down the alley, with a huge
bundle of barn-door keys hanging at her waist.   After
cordially greeting the visitor, she, notwithstanding her
'exceedingly interesting condition,' leapt over the low rail-
ing between the alley and the pond.   It will however be
better to quote Fet's own account of his visit:

'Sónya, tell Nestérka to fetch a sack from the barn, and let
us go back to the house,' said Tolstoy—who had already
greeted me warmly, without losing sight of the carp-capturing
operations the while.

The Countess immediately detached a huge key from her

---

[1] This word, when first invented by Nicholas Tolstoy, meant ploughing,
but it had by now come to mean farming in general.

belt and gave it to a boy, who started at a run to fulfil the order.

'There,' remarked the Count, 'you have an example of our method. We keep the keys ourselves; and all the estate business is carried on by boys.'

At the animated dinner table, the carp we had seen captured made their appearance. We all seemed equally at ease and happy. . . .

That evening was one truly 'filled with hope.' It was a sight to see with what pride and bright hope Tatiána Alexándrovna, the kindest of aunts, regarded the young people she so loved; and how, turning to me, she said frankly, 'You see, with *mon cher Léon* of course things could not be otherwise.'

As to the Countess, life to one who in her condition leapt over fences, could not but be lit up with the brightest of hopes. The Count himself, who had passed his whole life in an ardent search for novelties, evidently at this period entered a world till then unknown, in the mighty future of which he believed with all the enthusiasm of a young artist. I myself, during that evening, was carried away by the general tone of careless happiness, and did not feel the stone of Sisyphus oppressing me.

Soon after this visit, on 28th June 1863, a son, Sergius, was born. During the first eleven years of marriage, the Countess bore her husband eight children, and another five during the next fifteen years: making in all, thirteen children in twenty-six years.

But we must turn back a few months to mention the stories by Tolstoy which appeared during this year.

In the January number of the *Russian Messenger*, Katkóf had published *The Cossacks*, which Tolstoy had kept back to revise, and had only delivered in December.

In the February number of the same magazine appeared *Polikoúshka*, the story of a serf who, having lost some money belonging to his mistress, hangs himself.

These stories are referred to in the following letter from Tolstoy to Fet, undated, but written in 1863:

Both your letters were equally important, significant, and

agreeable to me, dear Afanásy Afanásyevitch. I am living in a world so remote from literature and its critics, that on receiving such a letter as yours, my first feeling is one of astonishment. Whoever was it wrote *The Cossacks* and *Polikoúshka*? And what's the use of talking about them? Paper endures anything, and editors pay for and print anything. But that is merely a first impression; afterwards one enters into the meaning of what you say, rummages about in one's head, and finds in some corner of it, among old, forgotten rubbish, something indefinite, labelled *Art*; and pondering on what you say, agrees that you are right, and even finds it pleasant to rummage about in that old rubbish, amid the smell one once loved. One even feels a desire to write. Of course, you are right. But then there are few readers of your sort. *Polikoúshka* is the chatter of a man who 'wields a pen,' on the first theme that comes to hand; but *The Cossacks* has some matter in it, though poor. I am now writing the story of a pied gelding, which I expect to print in autumn. [It did not appear till 1888!] But how can one write now? Invisible efforts—and even visible ones—are now going on; and, moreover, I am again up to my ears in farming. So is Sónya. We have no steward; we have assistants for field-work and building; but she, single-handed, attends to the office and the cash. I have the bees, the sheep, a new orchard, and the distillery. It all progresses, little by little, though of course badly compared with our ideal.

What do you think of the Polish business? [the insurrection of 1863, then breaking out]. It looks bad! Shall we—you and I and Borísof—not have to take our swords down from their rusty nails? . . .

The bees, which Tolstoy here places first among his outdoor duties, occupied much of his time, and he often spent hours studying the habits of these interesting creatures.

Tourgénef, writing to Fet, commented on *The Cossacks* as follows:

I read *The Cossacks* and went into ecstasies over it; so did Bótkin. Only the personality of Olénin spoils the generally splendid impression. To contrast civilisation with fresh, primeval Nature, there was no need again to produce that dull, unhealthy fellow always preoccupied with himself. Why does Tolstoy not get rid of that nightmare ?

Several months later he wrote :

After you left, I read Tolstoy's *Polikoúshka* and marvelled at the strength of his huge talent. But he has used up too much material, and it is a pity he drowned the son. It makes it too terrible. But there are pages that are truly wonderful ! It made a cold shudder run down even my back, though you know my back has become thick and coarse. He is a master, a master !

Tolstoy was now fairly launched on the life he was destined to lead for sixteen years : a quiet, country life, occupied with family joys and cares. These years followed one another with so little change that the story of a decade and a half can almost be compressed into a sentence. Children came in quick succession, two great novels and an *ABC* Book were produced, a large orchard was planted with apple-trees, the Yásnaya Polyána property was improved, and new estates were purchased east of the Vólga.

During the year 1863 Tolstoy wrote two plays, which have never been published. One, a farcical comedy called *The Nihilist*, was privately performed at home with great success. The second, also a comedy, written on a topic of the day, was called *The Infected Family*. Hoping to have it staged, Tolstoy took it to Moscow early in 1864 ; but the theatrical season, which in Russia ends at the commencement of Lent, was already too far advanced ; and he never subsequently appears to have troubled himself to have it either published or acted.

The Countess Tolstoy's brother, S. A. Behrs (who from 1866 when he was a boy of eleven, till 1878, spent every summer with the Tolstoys) in his book, *Recollections of Count Tolstoy*, gives much interesting information about the life at Yásnaya. He mentions that it was a proverb about the hard fate of penniless noblemen, that prompted Tolstoy to take all possible care to provide for the future of his children ; and the passage in the letter quoted above, about the bees, sheep, new orchard and distillery with which he was occupied, shows how this care was applied.

In his *Confession*, Tolstoy says of the years now under review :

Returning from abroad I married. The new conditions of happy family life completely diverted me from all search for the general meaning of life. My whole life was centred at that time in my family, wife and children, and in care to increase our means of livelihood. My striving after self-perfection and progress, was now again replaced by the effort simply to secure the best possible conditions for myself and my family.

So another fifteen years passed.

In spite of the fact that I regarded authorship as of no importance, I yet, during those fifteen years, continued to write. I had already tasted the temptation of authorship : the temptation of immense monetary rewards and applause for my insignificant work ; and I devoted myself to it as a means of improving my material position, and of stifling in my soul all questions as to the meaning of my own life, or of life in general.

Again, writing in 1903 of this middle period of his life, Tolstoy says :

Then came a third, an eighteen-year period which may be the least interesting of all (from my marriage to my spiritual re-birth) and which from a worldly point of view may be called moral : that is to say, that during those eighteen years I lived a correct, honest, family life, not indulging myself in any vices condemned by public opinion, but with interests wholly limited to selfish cares for my family, for the increase of our property, the acquisition of literary success, and all kinds of pleasure.

(In the one place he speaks of ' fifteen years,' and in the other of ' eighteen years ' ; but that is his way, and chronological exactitude is not the important matter here.)

After the Emancipation, in many parts of Russia the landlords had more or less serious difficulty with the peasants, among whom stories were rife to the effect that the Tsar intended to give them all the land, but had been deceived by the officials into only giving half; and, for a time, riots were not infrequent. There was no serious trouble of this sort on Tolstoy's estate; but his sister (whom I met at Yásnaya in 1902, long after her husband's death and when she, a nun, had been allowed out of her convent to visit her brother, after his very serious illness) told me that on one occasion the peasants refused to make the hay; and to save it from being lost, Tolstoy, his wife, the members of the family, and the masters from eleven neighbouring schools, all set to work with a will, and by their own strenuous exertions saved the crop before the weather changed.

On settling down to married life, Tolstoy formed the plan of writing a great novel, and the epoch he at first intended to deal with was that of the Constitutional conspiracy which came to a head on the accession of Nicholas I to the throne in December 1825. That quite premature military plot was quickly snuffed out. So little were things ripe for it, that many even of the soldiers who shouted for a 'Constitution' (*Konstitútsia*) thought they were demanding allegiance to Nicholas's elder brother Constantine, who having married a Polish lady of the Roman Catholic faith had renounced his right to the throne. While considering the plan of his work, Tolstoy found himself carried back to the scenes amid which his characters had grown up: to the time of the Napoleonic wars and the invasion of Russia by the French in 1812. Here was a splendid background for a novel, and putting aside *The Decembrists* he commenced *War and Peace*, a work conceived on a gigantic scale, and that resulted in a splendid success.

His attention, as we have already seen, was however not wholly absorbed by literature, but was divided between that and the management of his property. He had during his

stay among the Kirghiz in the Province of Samára, noticed
how extremely cheap and how fertile was the land in those
parts. He therefore wished to purchase an estate there,
and visited the district in the autumn of 1864, probably
with that end in view. How long he stayed there I do not
know, but from a letter he wrote to Fet on 7th October,
saying, 'We start for home to-day and do not know how

1864   we shall make our way to happy Yásnaya,' we
know when he returned. In November he again
wrote to Fet, and mentioned the laborious preparations
he was at that time making for *War and Peace* :

I am in the dumps and am writing nothing, but work painfully. You cannot imagine how hard I find the preliminary
work of ploughing deep the field in which I must sow. To
consider and reconsider all that may happen to all the future
characters in the very large work I am preparing, and to weigh
millions of possible combinations in order to select from among
them a millionth part, is terribly difficult. And that is what I
am doing. . . .

Late in that month he wrote again to Fet :

This autumn I have written a good deal of my novel. *Ars
longa, vita brevis* comes to my mind every day. If one could but
make time to accomplish a hundredth part of what one understands—but only a thousandth part gets done ! Nevertheless
the consciousness that *I can* is what brings happiness to men
of our sort. You know that feeling, and I experience it with
particular force this year.

The year 1864 saw the publication of the first collected
edition of Tolstoy's works. and though they have been
already mentioned, it may be as well to give a complete
list of those twenty 'trials of the pen' which preceded the
appearance of *War and Peace*, and had already sufficed to
place Tolstoy in the front rank of Russian writers. The
following are their titles, with the years in which they
were first published. They suffice to fill four very substantial volumes.

1852 *Childhood.*

1853 *The Raid : A Volunteer's Story.*

1854 *Boyhood.*

1855 *Memoirs of a Billiard-Marker.*

1855 *Sevastopol in December.*

„ *Sevastopol in May.*

„ *The Wood-Felling.*

1856 *Sevastopol in August.*

„ *The Snow Storm.*

„ *Two Hussars.*

„ *Meeting a Moscow Acquaintance in the Detachment.*

„ *A Squire's Morning.*

1857 *Youth.*

„ *Lucerne.*

1858 *Albert.*

1859 *Three Deaths.*

„ *Family Happiness.*

1862 Educational articles in *Yásnaya Polyána.*

1863 *The Cossacks.*

„ *Polikoúshka.*

As I am sometimes asked where satisfactory versions of these stories can be found, I may say that I think the best version of *Childhood, Boyhood and Youth* [1] is Miss Isabel Hapgood's, and I make no apology for quoting a letter Tolstoy wrote me on 23rd December 1901, concerning the volume, *Sevastopol,*[2] translated by my wife and myself, and containing the six stories marked * in the above list. I do this with less hesitation, because his letter illustrates the cordial way in which he encourages those who do any work he can approve of, in connection with his own activity :

I think I already wrote you how unusually the volume pleases me. All in it is excellent : the edition and the foot-notes, and chiefly the translation, and yet more the conscien-

[1] Published by Walter Scott, Ltd., London, and by T. Y. Crowell and Co., New York.

[2] Published by Messrs. A. Constable and Co., London, and Funk and Wagnalls Co., New York.

tiousness with which all this has been done. I happened to open it at *Two Hussars* and read on to the end just as if it were something new that had been written in English.

One day in October Tolstoy went out for a ride on his favourite horse, an English thoroughbred named Máshka. His borzoi dogs Lúbka and Krylát accompanied him. After he had ridden some way, a hare suddenly started up and the dogs rushed after it. Tolstoy had not come out with the idea of hunting, but on seeing the dogs chasing the hare he could not restrain himself, and galloped after them, uttering the hunting cry, ' Atoú ! ' The weather was bad, the ground slippery, and the horse stumbled at a narrow ravine and fell, dislocating and breaking its rider's arm. The horse ran away, and Tolstoy, who was quite alone and several miles from home, fainted. When he came to, he managed to drag himself a distance of more than half a mile to the high-road, where he lay in great pain. Some peasant carts passed by, but at first he could not attract any one's attention. When at last he was noticed, in order not to alarm his wife, he asked to be taken to the hut of an old wife, Akoulína, famed as a bone-setter. In spite of all that she and her son Iván could do—soaping, pulling, twisting and bandaging the arm—they could not set it, and Tolstoy continued to suffer the greatest pain.

The Countess, who had meanwhile heard of the accident, reached the hut late at night. She at once arranged to have her husband taken home, and sent to Toúla for a doctor. The latter arrived about 3 A.M., and after administering chloroform, succeeded, with the aid of two labourers who were called in to assist, in setting the arm. On coming to, Tolstoy's profound disbelief in the efficiency of doctors, prompted him to send for another surgeon. After a consultation the two physicians decided that everything had been done properly, and that Tolstoy must lie up for six weeks to allow the arm to recover. When that time was up, Tolstoy asked for his gun and fired it off to test his arm. No sooner had he done so than he again felt great pain. He thereupon wrote to his father-in-law, Dr. Behrs, and on his advice went to Moscow to consult the specialists. These differed among themselves, but after a week's hesitation a fresh operation was decided upon, and was carried out by two competent surgeons. This time it was quite successful, and in due course the patient completely recovered the use of his arm.

Meanwhile the Countess (now nursing her second child, a daughter named Tatiána, who had been born on 4th October) remained at Yásnaya, where her eldest child, Sergius, was taken dangerously ill with smallpox and diarrhœa. This was the first occasion on which Tolstoy and his wife had been separated.

While in Moscow he concluded an arrangement with Katkóf by which he received Rs. 500 (£75) per printed sheet of sixteen pages for the serial rights in *War and Peace*, which appeared in the *Russian Messenger*. This was just ten times the amount which, when he wrote his first stories, Nekrásof had mentioned as the highest rate paid to any one for the magazine rights in a story.

On 23rd January 1865, when Tolstoy had got over his accident, he wrote Fet another of those jocular letters which sometimes contain more of the real truth than will bear saying seriously :

1865

Shall I tell you something surprising about myself? When the horse threw me and broke my arm, and when I came to after fainting, I said to myself: ' I am an author.' And I am an author, but a solitary, on-the-quiet kind of author. . . . In a few days the first part of ' The Year 1805 ' [so the first part of *War and Peace* was originally called] will appear. Please write me your opinion of it in detail. I value your opinion and that of a man whom I dislike the more, the more I grow up— Tourgénef. He will understand. All I have printed hitherto I consider but a trial of my pen ; what I am now printing, though it pleases me better than my former work, still seems weak—as an Introduction must be. But what follows will be—tremendous !!! . . . Write what is said about it in the different places you know, and especially how it goes with the general public. No doubt it will pass unnoticed. I expect and wish it to do so; if only they don't abuse me, for abuse upsets one. . . .

I am glad you like my wife; though I love her less than my novel, still, you know, she is my wife. Be sure you come to visit us; for if you and Márya Petróvna do not stay here on your return from Moscow it will really, without a joke, be too stupid !

In May 1865 one sees by a letter of Tolstoy's to Fet that one of the children had been ill and he himself had been in bed for three days and barely escaped a fever. His wife's younger sister, Tánya, she of the contralto voice who (with some admixture of his wife) served Tolstoy as model for Natásha in *War and Peace*, was spending the summer at Yásnaya, as she had done each year since her sister's marriage. The Countess Mary and her children were also there. The children, he says, were well, and out all day in the open air. He adds:

I continue to write little by little, and am content with my work. The woodcock still attract me, and every evening I shoot *at them*, that is, generally, past them. My farming goes on well, that is to say, it does not disturb me much—which is all I demand of it. . . .

In reply to a suggestion from Fet, he goes on to say that he will not write more about the Yásno-Polyána school, but hopes some day to express the conclusions to which his three years' ardent passion for that work had brought him. Then comes a reference to the state of agricultural affairs after the Emancipation, and a passing allusion to the question of famine—a subject destined to make great demands on Tolstoy's attention in later years:

Our affairs as agriculturists are now like those of a shareholder whose shares have lost value and are unsaleable on 'Change. The case is a bad one. Personally I only ask that it should not demand of me so much attention and participation as to deprive me of my tranquillity. Latterly I have been content with my private affairs; but the general trend—with the impending misery of famine—torments me more and more every day. It is so strange, and even good and terrible. We have rosy radishes on our table, and yellow butter, and well-baked, soft bread on a clean tablecloth; the garden is green, and our young ladies in muslin dresses are glad it is hot and shady; while *there* that evil hunger-devil is already at work, covering the fields with goose-weed, chafing the hard heels of the peasants and their wives, and cracking the hoofs of the cattle. Our weather, the corn, and the meadows, are really terrible. How are they with you?

The letter closes with advice to Fet to transfer his chief attention from the land to literature, and a statement that Tolstoy himself has done so, and is finding life less difficult.

When Tolstoy went out hunting hares and foxes with borzoi dogs, Miss Tatiána Behrs (the Tánya alluded to above) used often to accompany him.

Between this lady and Count Sergius Tolstoy (Leo's elder brother) an attachment had grown up which caused great distress to them both, for, besides being twenty-two years older than the lady, Sergius was living with, and had a family by, the gipsy mentioned in a previous chapter, though he was not legally married. His affection for his family prevented his yielding completely to his love for Tánya and asking her to be his wife. The Behrs were quite willing that he should do so, and the young lady would have accepted him, and was much pained by the vacillation that resulted from the battle between his love for her and his affection for his family. Ultimately he resolved to be faithful to the union he had formed, and, in order to legitimise his children, went through the form of marriage with their mother in 1867. Almost at the same time, Tánya, having recovered from her disappointment, married a Mr. Kouzmínsky.

Here again one gets a slight glimpse of the experience of life which has led Tolstoy, contrary to the opinion general among the Russian 'intelligents,' to advocate faithfulness at all costs to the woman with whom one has once formed a union.

A knowledge of Tánya's story adds to the interest with which, in Tolstoy's great novel, one reads of Natásha Róstof's troubles and ultimate happiness.

Towards the end of May, Tolstoy visited the estate of Nikólsky (which after the death of his brother Nicholas had become his), and had the house there repaired. In June the whole family moved to Nikólsky, where they lived very quietly; Tolstoy continuing to write *War and Peace*. His friend D. A. Dyákof's estate was only ten miles away, and Tolstoy saw much of him at this time, besides having him at other times as a frequent visitor at Yásnaya. Dyákof was his chief adviser in agricultural matters, as well as in his efforts to improve the stock of his cattle, pigs and poultry. Almost the only other visitors at Nikólsky were the Fets; and the poet records meeting there the Countess's 'charming sister,' Tánya, and experiencing violent antipathy for the sour koumýs, about which Tolstoy was enthusiastic, and a large tub of which stood near the front door.

While living at Nikólsky Tolstoy was invited for a fortnight by a neighbouring landlord, Kiréyevsky, to a grand hunt, in which the huntsmen wore special costumes, and luxurious dinners were served in the woods. What interested Tolstoy most in all this was not the hunt, but the opportunity it afforded him of studying types of the old and new aristocracy.

At this period of his life one hears of his playing the guitar and singing passionate love-songs.

During the autumn of 1865 Tolstoy, accompanied by his eleven-year-old brother-in-law, visited the battlefield of Borodinó. They left Moscow in Dr. Behrs' carriage, with post-horses. When the time came for them to have something to eat, they found that the lunch basket had been left behind, and they had only a small basket of grapes.

Thereupon Tolstoy remarked to his companion, 'I am sorry, not that we have left the basket of food behind, but because your father will be upset and will be angry with his man.' The journey took only one day, and they stayed at the monastery erected in memory of those who fell in the great fight. For two days Tolstoy investigated the scene of the conflict which he was about to describe in his novel, and he then drew the plan of the fight which appears in that work. Even in 1865 there were but few survivors of the campaign of 1812 to be found in the neighbourhood.

Tolstoy used at this time to spend whole days in the Roumyántsef Museum in Moscow, studying books and manu scripts relating to the times of Alexander I, and especially to the reformatory and Masonic movements which then sprang up in Russia, but were subsequently suppressed on political grounds.

S. A. Behrs tells us that Tolstoy

was always fond of children, and liked to have them about him. He easily won their confidence, and seemed to have found the key to their hearts. He appeared to have no difficulty in suiting himself to a strange child, and with a single question set it completely at ease, so that it began at once to chat away with perfect freedom. Independently of this, he could divine a child's thought with the skill of a trained educationalist. I remember his children sometimes running up to him, and telling him they had a great secret; and when they persisted in refusing to divulge it, he would quietly whisper in their ears what it was. 'Ah, what a papa ours is! How did he find it out?' they would cry, in astonishment.

He also says:

Gifted by nature with rare tact and delicacy, he is extremely gentle in his bearing and conduct to others. I never heard him scold a servant. Yet they all had the greatest respect for him, were fond of him, and seemed even to fear him. Nor, with all his zeal for sport, have I ever seen him whip a dog or beat his horse.

A servant who lived with him more than twenty years has said : ' Living in the Count's house from my childhood, I loved Leo Nikoláyevitch as though he were my father' ; and in another place he remarks :

The Count had a stern appearance, but treated the servants excellently, and made things easy for all strangers whom he met. He has a very good heart, and when he was cross with me for anything, I, knowing his character, used at once to leave the room, and when next he called me, it was as though nothing unpleasant had happened.

Speaking of Tolstoy's later years the same servant says :

Leo Nikoláyevitch has now become quite a different man. From 1865 to 1870 he was active in managing the estate, and was fond of cows, bred sheep, looked after the property, and, in a word, attended to everything. At that time he was hot-tempered and impulsive. He would order the trap to be brought when he wanted to go hunting. His man, Alexis, would bring him his hunting-boots, and the Count would shout at him, ' Why have you not dried them? You are not worth your salt!' Alexis, knowing the Count's character, would take the boots away, and bring them back almost directly. ' There! now they're all right,' the Count would say, and would brighten up instantly.

His love of the country and his dislike of towns sprang partly from his keen appreciation of the charm and loveliness of Nature. He saw fresh beauty every day, and often exclaimed : ' What wealth God has! He gives each day something to distinguish it from all the rest.'

Sportsman and agriculturist himself, he maintains that sportsmen and agriculturists alone know Nature. To quote Behrs again :

No bad weather was allowed to interfere with his daily walk. He could put up with loss of appetite, from which he occasionally suffered, but he could never go a day without a sharp walk in the open air. In general, he was fond of active movement, riding, gymnastics, but particularly walking. If his literary work chanced to go badly, or if he wished to throw off the effects of any unpleasantness, a long walk was his sovereign remedy. He could walk the whole day without fatigue; and we have frequently ridden together for ten or twelve hours. In his study he kept a pair of dumb-bells, and sometimes had gymnastic apparatus erected there.

All luxury was distasteful to him; and much that ordinary people regard as common comforts, seemed to him harmful indulgences, bad for the souls and bodies of men. Nothing could well be more simple than the arrangement of his house at Yásnaya, substantial and solidly built as it was, with its double windows, and the Dutch stoves so necessary to warm a Russian house.

He was not at all particular about what he ate, but objected to a soft bed or spring mattress, and at one time he used to sleep on a leather-covered sofa.

He dressed very simply, and when at home never wore starched shirts or tailor-made clothes, but adapted to his own requirements the ordinary Russian blouse, having it made of woollen stuff for winter, and of linen for summer. His out-door winter dress was also an adaptation of the sheepskin *shoúba* and peasants' *caftán*, made of the plainest material; and these afforded such good protection from the weather that they were often borrowed by members of the household as well as by visitors.

During the writing of *War and Peace* Tolstoy generally enjoyed good spirits, and on days when his work had gone well, he would gleefully announce that he had left 'a bit of my life in the inkstand.' One of his chief recreations was to go out hare-hunting with borzoi dogs, and this he often did in company with a neighbouring landed proprietor, Bíbikof.

From October 1865 he ceased to keep his Diary, and did not renew it during the period covered by this volume.

On Twelfth Night a grand masquerade was held at Yásnaya, and the festivities were kept up till past two in the morning, and were followed by a troika drive next day.   1866

That same January the family moved to Moscow, where they hired a six-roomed apartment for Rs. 155 a month (say about £23); and there they remained for six weeks while the second part of *War and Peace* was being printed for the *Russian Messenger*.

Among the friends Tolstoy saw most of at this time were Aksákof and Prince Obolénsky. He also attended the Moscow drawing school, and he tried his hand at sculpture—modelling a bust of his wife. It does not appear, however, that he continued this occupation long.

In May 1866 a second son, Ilyá, was born, and an English nurse introduced into the family.

During this summer an infantry regiment was stationed near Yásnaya, in which a young Sub-Lieutenant named Kolokóltsef was serving, whom the Countess Tolstoy had known in Moscow. He visited the Tolstoys, and introduced to them his Colonel Únosha, and his fellow-officer Ensign Stasulévitch (brother of the Liberal editor of the monthly magazine, *The Messenger of Europe*), who had been degraded to the ranks because, while he was on prison-duty, a prisoner had escaped. Ensign Stasulévitch was middle-aged, but he had only recently regained his rank as officer and joined the regiment commanded by his former comrade, Colonel Únosha.

One day Stasulévitch and Kolokóltsef called on Tolstoy and told him that a soldier, serving as secretary in one of the companies of the regiment, had struck his Company Commander, and was to be tried by court-martial. They asked Tolstoy to undertake the man's defence, and he, having always regarded capital punishment with abhorrence, readily agreed to do so.

The circumstances of the case were these. The soldier, Shibóunin, was a man of very limited intelligence, whose chief occupation was writing out reports. When he had any money he spent it on solitary drinking. The Captain in command of his company, a Pole, apparently disliked him, and frequently found fault with his reports and made

him rewrite them. This treatment Shiboúnin bitterly
resented; and one day, when he had been drinking, on
being told to rewrite a document he had prepared, he
insulted and struck the Captain. By law the penalty for
a private who strikes his officer is death. Tolstoy nevertheless hoped to save the man's life, and obtained permission
to plead on his behalf. The trial took place on 6th June,
and the members of the court-martial were Colonel Únosha,
Stasulévitch, and Kolokóltsef; the latter being merely a
light-headed youngster.

Tolstoy, when telling me of the incident, remarked that
of the four occasions on which he has spoken in public,
this was the time that he did so with most assurance and
satisfaction to himself. He had written out his speech; the
main point of which was that Shiboúnin was not responsible
for his actions, being abnormal, and having from the combined effect of intemperance and the monotony of his
occupation, become idiotic and obsessed by an idea that
his Company Commander did not understand report writing,
and unfairly rejected work faultlessly done. The law de-
crees a mitigation of sentence for crimes committed by
those who are not in the full possession of their senses; and
as this contradicts the paragraph allotting death as the sole
punishment for a soldier who strikes his officer, Tolstoy
argued that mercy should be extended to the prisoner.

The Court adjourned to consider its verdict, and (as
Tolstoy subsequently learnt) Stasulévitch was in favour of
mercy. The Colonel, who was more of a military machine
than a human being, demanded the death sentence, and the
decision therefore rested with the boyish Sub-Lieutenant,
who (submitting to his Colonel) voted for death.

Tolstoy wished to appeal (through his aunt, the Countess
A. A. Tolstoy) to Alexander II for a pardon; but with
characteristic disregard of details, he omitted to mention the
name of the regiment in which the affair had occurred, and
this enabled the Minister of War, Milútin, to delay the
presentation of the petition until Shiboúnin had been shot;

which occurred on 9th August. Tolstoy's appeal never, therefore, reached the Emperor.

In contrast with the action of the Colonel and the Minister, was that of the peasants of the district, who flocked in crowds to see the prisoner; bringing him milk, eggs, home-made linen and all the gifts their poverty could afford. When the day of execution arrived, Shiboúnin went quite impassively to his death; to all appearance incapable of understanding what was happening. The people thronged around the post to which he was to be tied—the women weeping and some of them fainting. They fetched a priest to perform Masses at his grave, and paid for the service to be repeated all day. At night contributions of copper money, linen, and candles such as are burnt in Russian churches, were laid upon his grave. Next day the Masses were recommenced, and were continued until the local police forbade any more religious services, and levelled the grave that the people might not continue to visit it.

The knowledge of such a difference between the spirit of the governors and the governed, helps us once again to understand Tolstoy's ultimate conviction that Government and the administration of law are essentially evil things, always tending to make the world worse and not better. In later life we may be sure he would not have been content to base his plea for mercy on merely legal grounds.

From time to time he continued to be troubled with ill-health; for instance, in July 1866 he writes that he is confined to the house with pains in the stomach which make it impossible for him to turn quickly.

In November—contrary to what he had often said in the past and was to return to in later life—he expresses his sense of the importance of authorship. Fet, criticising something in *War and Peace*, had quoted the words, *irritabilis poetarum gens*, and Tolstoy, replying ' Not I,' welcomes the criticism, begs for more, and goes on to say :

What have you been doing? Not on the Zémstvo [County Council] or in farming (all that is compulsory activity such as we do elementally and with as little will of our own as the ants who make an ant-hill; in that sphere there is nothing good or bad), but what are you doing in thought, with the mainspring of your being, which alone has been, and is, and will endure in the world? Is that spring still alive? Does it wish to manifest itself? How does it express its wish? Or has it forgotten how to express itself? That is the chief thing.

By the autumn of this year the railway southwards from Moscow to Koursk had been constructed as far as Toúla, making it easier to get from Yásnaya to Moscow, and to the rest of Europe. Yet Tolstoy comparatively seldom felt tempted to leave his much-loved, tranquil, busy, country life, in which alone he found himself able to work with the maximum of efficiency.

About this time he undertook the planting of a birch wood, which has since grown up and become valuable.

During the summer of 1867 Tolstoy, despite the dislike and distrust of doctors—which he shares with Rousseau, and which he has again and again expressed in his works—was induced by the state of his health and 1867 by his wife's persuasion, to consult the most famous Moscow doctor of the time, Professor Zahárin, on whose advice he drank mineral water during several weeks

Writing to Fet he says:

If I wrote to you, dear friend, every time I think of you, you would receive two letters a day from me. But one cannot get everything said, and sometimes one is lazy and sometimes too busy, as is the case at present. I have recently returned from Moscow and have begun a strict cure under the direction of Zahárin; and most important of all, I am printing my novel at Ris's, and have to prepare and send off MSS. and proofs every day under threat of a fine and of delayed publication. That is both pleasant and also hard, as you know.

He goes on to criticise Tourgénef's novel, *Dym* (*Smoke*), which had appeared that year:

About *Smoke* I meant to write long ago, and, of course, just what you have now written. That is why we love one another—

because we think alike with the ' wisdom of the heart ' as you call it. (Thank you very much for that letter also : ' the wisdom of the heart ' and ' the wisdom of the mind ' explain much to me.) About *Smoke*, I think that the strength of poetry lies in love ; and the direction of that strength depends on character. Without strength of love there is no poetry ; but strength falsely directed—the result of the poet's having an unpleasant, weak character—creates dislike. In *Smoke* there is hardly any love of anything, and very little poetry. There is only love of light and playful adultery, and therefore the poetry of that novel is repulsive. That, as you see, is just what you write about it. Only I fear to express this opinion because I cannot look soberly at the author, whose personality I do not like ; but I fancy my impression is the general one. One more writer played out !

In November 1867 we find the whole family again established for a while in a lodging in Moscow, where they seem to have remained for a large part of the winter.

Here Fet visited Tolstoy and announced to him that he had decided to arrange a Literary Evening for the benefit of the famine-stricken peasants of Mtsensk, the district in which Fet's estate lay. Tolstoy met the suggestion with irony, maintaining that Fet had invented the famine ; and in reply to a request that he would ensure the success of the evening by reading something, flatly refused to do so, declaring that he never had and never could do such a thing as read in public. Still, he lent Fet the chapter of *War and Peace* containing the wonderful description of the retreat of the Russian army from Smolénsk in fearful drought. This as yet existed only in proof, not having been published. (It forms Chapter V of Part X of Volume II in Mrs. Constance Garnett's version : the best English rendering of that novel.) Read by Prince Kougoúshef, the poet and dramatist, it evoked thunders of applause.

1868   On 12th April 1868 Tourgénef, writing to Fet, said :

I have just finished the fourth volume of *War and Peace*.

There are things in it that are unbearable, and things that are wonderful; and the wonderful things (they predominate) are so magnificently good that we have never had anything better written by anybody; and it is doubtful whether anything as good has been written.

About the same time V. P. Bótkin wrote from Petersburg: 'Tolstoy's novel is having a really remarkable success; every one here is reading it, and they not merely read it but become enthusiastic about it.'

The Epilogue was not completed till late in 1869. On 30th August Tolstoy writes: 'Part VI [*i.e.* Part II of the Epilogue] which I expected to have finished a month ago, is not ready'; and then in the next sentence, he goes into ecstasies over Schopenhauer:

1869

Do you know what this summer has been for me? An unceasing ecstasy over Schopenhauer, and a series of mental enjoyments such as I never experienced before. I have bought all his works, and have read and am reading them (as well as Kant's). And assuredly no student in his course has learnt so much and discovered so much as I have during this summer. I do not know whether I shall ever change my opinion, but at present I am confident that Schopenhauer is the greatest genius among men. You said he had written something or other on philosophic subjects. What do you mean by 'something or other'? It is the whole world in an extraordinarily vivid and beautiful reflection. I have begun translating him. Won't you take up that work? We would publish it together. After reading him I cannot conceive how his name can remain unknown. The only explanation is the one he so often repeats, that except idiots there is scarcely any one else in the world. . . .

He goes on to say that he was starting next day for the Government of Pénza to look at an estate he meant to buy 'in those out-of-the-way parts.' The servant who accompanied Tolstoy has told how they travelled third class from Moscow to Nízhni, and how Tolstoy chatted with his fellow-travellers, so that many of them took him 'for a common man.' The idea of buying the estate in Pénza was ultimately abandoned.

He had by then completed the last part of *War and Peace*, which was to appear complete in book form in November. Two volumes had been published in 1866, three more in 1868, and the sixth was not ready till this year, 1869. (In subsequent editions the book was re-arranged, first into five and then into four volumes.)

Though he had so completely conquered the laziness of which he accused himself in early manhood as to have become a regular, indefatigable and extremely hard worker, yet after the completion of so gigantic a task he felt the need of recuperation and in summer wrote to Fet : ' It is now my deadest time : I neither write nor think, but feel happily stupid,' and he adds that he goes out shooting woodcock and has killed eight at an outing.

That at this time he already felt something of the strong repugnance he so strenuously expressed in later years for luxury and profuse expenditure, is indicated by his comment on the death of his acquaintance, the author V. P. Bótkin, which took place in 1869. The latter, a member of a wealthy family of tea-merchants, having lived with economy till he knew his death was approaching, then hired a splendid lodging in Petersburg, fitted it up with all possible comfort and luxury, engaged a *chef* from the kitchen of the Tsarévitch, paid daily attention to the dinner *menu*, and engaged famous musicians to perform quartets at his lodgings. To the magnificent feasts he gave every day (at which, owing to the state of his health, he himself participated chiefly as a spectator) he gathered a select circle of those friends whose conversation interested him. He told his brother that these arrangements for the close of his life gave him the keenest pleasure, and that ' birds of Paradise are singing in my soul.' On 4th October a quartet and a banquet had been arranged as usual, and many guests were expected—but V. P. Bótkin lay dead in his bed.

Tolstoy, hearing of this, wrote to Fet :

I was terribly shocked by the character of V. P. Bótkin's death. If what is told of it is true, it is terrible. How is it that among his friends not one was found to give to that supreme moment of life the character suitable to it?

Before *War and Peace* was finished, the Countess had borne four children, the fourth being a boy, born on 20th May 1869, and christened Leo—nursing them all herself, as she did her subsequent children, with two exceptions mentioned later on. Her willingness to do her duty in this respect was exceptional among women of her class, for the employment of wet-nurses was extremely common in Russia.

Up to the age of ten, the children were taught Russian and music by the Countess, and she even found time to make their clothes herself till they reached that age. Besides managing the household, her brother tells us that during the composition of *War and Peace* she found time to copy it out no less than seven times, a statement not to be taken literally: for greatly as Tolstoy believes in the proverb that 'Gold is got by sifting,' and indefatigably as he revises his work, not all the chapters of *War and Peace* will have been altered that number of times. With Tolstoy the children learnt arithmetic; and they learnt to read French out of illustrated volumes of Jules Verne.

In all that concerned the education of the children, his wife at this time willingly constituted herself the executant of her husband's decisions, which were based largely on J. J. Rousseau's *Émile*, and were relaxed only in so far as the Countess was unable to carry them out, and as Tolstoy found himself too much occupied with other affairs to attempt to do so. Later on there was less accord between the parents.

With the first child they tried to do without a nurse, but the attempt was unsuccessful, and subsequently Russian nurses and foreign *bonnes* were employed.

Toys were not allowed in the nursery, but much liberty was given to the children. No violent or severe punishments were inflicted on them, and none but their parents might award the punishments that were administered. They aimed at gaining their children's confidence by timely petting and kindly treatment.

If one of the children told a falsehood, this was treated as a serious matter, and the punishment usually consisted in the parents treating the child coldly.   As soon, however, as it showed that it was really sorry, the punishment ceased; but a child was never persuaded to say it was sorry or to promise not to repeat its fault.

All the grown-up people in the house were expected to remember that children are apt to copy and imitate all that they see and hear; and the children were not kept away from the adults, except at lesson time.   Consequently when eight o'clock came and the children went to bed, Tolstoy would often remark : ' Now, we are freer ! '

Partly that they might learn English, partly because Tolstoy believed that education was freer in England than elsewhere, young English governesses were engaged to take charge of his children from the age of three to nine.   He was extremely fortunate in his first choice, for the young lady remained with the Tolstoys for six years, and after her marriage continued in most friendly relations with the whole family.

He aimed at acquainting the children with Nature, and developing their love of it, of animals, and of insects.   He liked to let them realise their impotence and their complete dependence on their elders, but he always did this with kindly consideration.

The children were not allowed to order the servants about, but had to *ask* them for anything they wanted ; and that a good example might be set, every one in the house was expected to do the same.   This was the more important, because the peasant servants in Russia, even after the Emancipation, were scarcely regarded as belonging to the same race of human beings as their masters, and a famous Russian author could say without any exaggeration, ' The balcony was rotten.   Only servants went there; the family did not go there.'   But, to avoid giving a wrong impression, I must here make a reservation. Just because there was no idea of the two classes overlapping, and because so wide a gap existed between them that they dressed quite differently (the peasants having their own costume and style of garments) very cordial and sincere good feeling often grew up between master and man, or between proprietress and servant, and real human interest, such as is shown in Tolstoy's descriptions of the servants in *Childhood*, and in his other stories. It was, and is, not at all unusual for Russian servants to intervene in the conversation of the family or visitors; and the whole relation between employers and employed was quite different to what it is in England, where on Sundays the maid might be mistaken for her mistress, except that she often looks more attractive than the latter.

The plan adopted in the Yásno-Polyána school, where no child was obliged to learn anything it did not care to learn, had to be abandoned in the family; but some scope was allowed to the children to reject what they had no capacity for, and they were never punished for neglecting to prepare lessons, though they were rewarded when they learnt well.

To illustrate Tolstoy's way of developing the minds of those about him, Behrs tells of his own case when, as a youth, he stayed at Yásnaya:

Regardless of my youth at the time, I remember that Tolstoy discussed quite seriously with me all the scientific and philosophic questions it came into my head to put to him. He always answered simply and clearly, and never hesitated to admit the fact if he himself did not understand this or that matter. Often my talk with him took the form of a dispute, on which I embarked in spite of my consciousness of his immense superiority.

The children were always eager to go for walks with their father, to answer his call to practise Swedish gymnastics, and to be on his side in any game he taught them. In winter they skated a good deal; but clearing the snow off the pond under his leadership was an even greater pleasure than the skating itself.

Before breakfast he would go for a walk with his brother-in-law, or they would ride down to bathe in the river that flows by one side of the estate. At morning coffee the whole family assembled, and it was generally a very merry meal, Tolstoy being up to all sorts of jokes, till he rose with the words, ' One must get to work,' and went off to his study, taking with him a tumbler full of tea. While at work in his room not even his wife was allowed to disturb him; though at one time his second child and eldest daughter, Tatiána, while still quite a little girl, was privileged to break this rule. The rare days (generally in summer) when he relaxed, were very welcome to the children, for their father's presence always brought life and animation with it. Generally after dinner, before resuming work, he would read a book not directly connected with the task he had in hand. It was often an English novel; and we hear of his reading Anthony Trollope with approval, Mrs. Henry Wood, who, he says, made a great impression on him, and Miss Braddon. His dislike of George Sand remained unshaken, and he considered *Consuelo* to be a mixture of the pretentious and the spurious. Goethe (especially *Faust*) he admired; while Molière's plays and Hugo's *Les Misérables* appealed to him very strongly indeed. In the evening he was fond of playing duets with his sister. He used to find it hard to keep up with her in playing long pieces with which he was not quite familiar, and when in difficulties he would say something to make her laugh, and cause her to play slower. If he did not succeed by means of this ruse, he would sometimes stop and solemnly take off one of his boots, as though that must infallibly help him out of the difficulty; and he would then recommence, with the remark, ' Now, it will go all right ! '

During the early years of his married life few visitors came to Yásnaya, except the numerous members of the

Tolstoy-Behrs families, who stayed there chiefly in summer. The poet A. A. Fet, D. A. Dyákof, whom he had known from boyhood and had described in *Youth*, N. N. Stráhof, the philosopher and critic, for whose judgment he had great respect and whom he frequently consulted throughout his literary career, and Prince L. D. Ouroúsof, a cousin of the Prince Ouroúsof he had known during the siege of Sevastopol, seem to have been almost the only friends who visited him in the years first following his marriage; and this suited Tolstoy very well, for to entertain many visitors would have seriously interrupted the absorbing work in which he was continually engaged.

Fet has so often been mentioned in this volume that it is time to devote a few lines to describing a man who has come in for much abuse on account of the anti-Emancipationist sympathies expressed in some of his writings. Like Tolstoy, he had grown up with no idea that it is incumbent on men of education and capacity to organise the society of which they are members, or by political action to remedy such abuses as inevitably arise among human beings who do not keep the task of systematic social organisation constantly in view. Of the impression Fet's political opinions made on the Liberals, one may judge by a remark Tourgénef addressed to him in a letter written in 1874: 'Twenty years ago, at the height of Nicholas I's *régime*, you dumbfounded me by announcing your opinion that the mind of man could devise nothing superior to the position of the Russian aristocracy of that day, nor anything nobler or more admirable.' The Liberals saw in Fet a political reactionary —and so he was; but any one who reads his *Recollections* may also see how large a measure of personal worth can be combined with political indifferentism—a quality many Russians of his generation were brought up to regard as a virtue. In private life he was a really worthy man, and Tolstoy once very truly remarked to him:

There are some people whose talk is far above their actual morality; but there are also some whose talk is below that

x

level. You are one who is so afraid of his sermon being above his practice, that you intentionally talk far below your actual practice.

While still a young cavalry officer Fet began to write poetry, for which he had real talent; and after leaving the army he continued his literary career as an Art-for-Art's - sake - ist, producing verse translations of Virgil, Horace, Ovid, Juvenal, Catullus, Tibullus, Propertius, and Persius, besides original works of his own in prose and verse, and (after Tolstoy's suggestion, already recorded) translations from the German of Schopenhauer's *The World as Will and Idea*, and Goethe's *Faust*.

In his dislike, or perhaps one should say ignorance, of politics, commerce, and that great industrial revolution of the Western world that has been the most conspicuous achievement of the last one hundred and fifty years, as well as in his love of pure art, chiefly literary, he had much in common with Tolstoy. They could talk with profound sympathy of all that related to art, and they were alike in their love of country life and in their relation to agriculture, as well as in the fact that the great problems of life centred for them round their own personality rather than around the community to which they belonged. Patriotic by instinct, it was no part of their philosophy to be so; at least they never dreamed of that newer patriotism which seeks to manage the production and distribution of the national wealth so that every member of the community may have an opportunity to live in decent conditions. They had therefore at this period much in common; and one sees by Tolstoy's letters how greatly they enjoyed each other's society, though a time was coming when their friendship would wane.

Tolstoy had a strong dislike of leaving home even for a few days. When it was absolutely necessary for him to go to Moscow he would grumble at his hard fate, and Behrs, when he accompanied him, noticed how town life depressed Tolstoy, making him fidgety and even irritable.

When returning from a journey, or a hunting expedition, he would express his anxiety by exclaiming, 'If only all's well at home!' After he had been away from Yásnaya, Tolstoy never failed to give the home party full and amusing accounts of what he had seen and heard.

A distinguishing feature of Tolstoy, already remarked upon, but so strongly marked that it can hardly be insisted on too much, was the ardent and whole-hearted way in which he threw himself into whatever occupation he took up. On this point Prince D. D. Obolénsky says: 'I have seen Count L. N. Tolstoy in all phases of his creative activity. . . . Whatever his occupation, he did it with conviction, firmly believing in the value of what he was doing, and always fully absorbed by it. I remember him as a man of the world, and have met him at balls, and I remember a remark he once made, "See what poetry there is in women's ball-dresses, what elegance, how much thought, how much charm even in the flowers pinned to the dresses!" I remember him as an ardent sportsman, as a beekeeper, as a gardener; I remember his enthusiasm for farming, for tree planting, fruit culture, horse breeding, and much else.'

A housekeeper who was with him for nine years, said of him:

The Count himself looked after everything, and demanded extreme cleanliness in the cowhouse and in the pig-styes and in the sheep-cot. In particular he delighted in his pigs, of which he had as many as 300, paired off in separate styes. . . . There the Count would not allow the least dirt. Every day I and my assistants had to wash them all, and wipe the floor and walls of the styes; then the Count, on passing through the piggery of a morning, would be very pleased, and would remark aloud: 'What management! . . . What good management!' But God have mercy on us if he noticed the least dirt! That at once made him shout out angrily. . . . The Count was very hasty, and a doctor who used to come to Yásnaya said to him more than once in my presence: 'You must not get so angry, Count, it is very bad for your health. . . .' 'I can't help it,' he would reply. 'I want to restrain myself, but can't do it. That, it seems, is the way I am made!' . . . His farming gave the Count a good revenue in those days. Besides the pigs and their litters, he had 80 cows, 500 good sheep, and very many fowls. We used to make excellent butter, which we sold in Moscow at 60 copecks [about 19 pence] a lb.

His management of property was characteristically personal. He never took shares in any joint-stock company, but he bought land, bred cattle and horses of good quality, planted a large apple-orchard, as well as a quantity of other trees, and in general he acquired property he could manage himself, or (for he entrusted the management of his Samára estates to stewards) over which he had full control. He has always been more alive to the dangers and evils of commercial companies and large engineering and industrial undertakings, than to the good they have achieved by irrigating arid lands, uniting distant realms, and lightening man's toil by making iron bear some of his burdens for him.

Tolstoy furnishes an example of the well-known fact that men of artistic temperament are often untidy. Though he acknowledges the advantages of neatness in general, he often remarked that it is a quality most frequently found in shallow natures. He himself simply could not, and therefore did not try to, keep his things in order. When he undressed he let his clothes or boots drop where he stood; and if he happened to be moving from place to place, his garments remained strewn about the room, and sometimes on the floor. Behrs remarks.

I noticed that to pack his things for a journey cost him great effort, and when I accompanied him I used very willingly to do it for him, and thereby pleased him very much. I remember that once, for some reason, I did not at all wish to pack for him. He noticed this, and with characteristic delicacy did not ask me to, but put his things into his portmanteau himself; and I can assert positively that no one else, were they to try, could have got them into such fearful disorder as they were in, in that portmanteau.

It was a peculiarity of Tolstoy's that he not only liked to have his own sleep out without being disturbed, but that he never could or would wake any one from sleep, and in cases of absolute necessity would ask some one else to relieve him of that disagreeable task.

Behrs recounts that when they sat up late, the man-servant sometimes fell asleep in his chair and omitted to serve up the cold supper. Tolstoy would never allow him to be disturbed on these occasions, but would himself go to the pantry to fetch the supper, and would do this stealthily, and with the greatest caution, so that it became a kind of amusing game. He would get quite cross with Behrs if the latter accidentally let the plates clatter or made any other noise.

Many years later, alluding in my presence to this peculiarity of his, Tolstoy remarked, 'While a man is asleep he is at any rate not sinning.'

On 4th February 1870 Tolstoy wrote to Fet : 1870

I received your letter, dear Afanásy Afanásyevitch, on 1st February, but even had I received it somewhat sooner I could not have come. You write, ' I am *alone, alone* ! ' And when I read it I thought, What a lucky fellow—*alone* ! I have a wife, three children, and a fourth at the breast, two old aunts, a nurse, and two housemaids. And they are all ill together : fever, high temperature, weakness, headaches, and coughs. In that state your letter found me. They are now beginning to get better, but out of ten people, I and my old aunt alone turn up at the dinner table. And since yesterday I myself am ill with my chest and side. There is much, very much, I want to tell you about. I have been reading a lot of Shakespear, Goethe, Poúshkin, Gógol, and Molière, and about all of them there is much I want to say to you. I do not take in a single magazine or newspaper this year, and I consider it very useful not to.

S. A. Behrs tells us that Tolstoy ' never read newspapers, and considered them useless, and when they contain false news, even harmful. In his humorous way he would sometimes parody a newspaper style when speaking of domestic affairs.' His attitude towards journalists and critics (except his friend Stráhof) was rather scornful, and he was indignant when any one classed them even with third-rate authors. He considered that it is a misuse of the printing-press to publish so much that is unnecessary, uninteresting, and worst of all, inartistic. He seldom read criticisms of his own work. 'His feeling towards periodicals in general had its source in his intense dislike of the exploitation of works of art. He would smile contemptuously at hearing it suggested that a real artist produces his works for the sake of money.'

Having said this much about his characteristics and peculiarities, let us note the extent to which his life and mode of thought at this time approximated to his later teaching. His humane relations towards the peasants, his condemnation of many of the manifestations of modern civilisation, his simplicity in household matters and dress, his exemplary family life, humane educational ideals, deep love of sincerity and of industry (including physical labour), his ardent search for truth and for self-improvement, his gradually increasing accessibility to and regard for others, his undoubted love of family and his hatred of violence—indicate that the ideals of his later life were not very far from him, even before the commencement of the conversion told of in his *Confession*.

On 17th February Tolstoy writes to Fet:

I hoped to visit you the night of the 14th, but could not do so. As I wrote you, we were all ill,—I last. I went out yesterday for the first time. What stopped me was pain in the eyes, which is increased by wind and sleeplessness. I now, to my great regret, have to postpone my visit to you till Lent. I must go to Moscow to take my aunt to my sister's, and to see an oculist about my eyes.

It is a pity that one can only get to your place after passing a sleepless, cigarette-smoky, stuffy, railway-carriage, conversational night. You want to read me a story of cavalry life. . . .

And I don't want to read you anything, because I am not
writing anything; but I very much want to talk about Shakespear and Goethe and the drama in general. This whole winter
I am occupied only with the drama; and it happens to me, as
it usually happens to people who till they are forty have not
thought of a certain subject or formed any conception of it,
and then suddenly with forty-year-old clearness turn their
attention to this new untasted subject—it seems to them that
they discern in it much that is new. All winter I have enjoyed
myself lying down, drowsing, playing bézique, going on snow-
shoes, skating, and most of all lying in bed (ill) while characters
from a drama or comedy have performed for me. And they
perform very well. It is about that I want to talk to you. In
that, as in everything, you are a classic, and understand the
essence of the matter very deeply. I should like also to read
Sophocles and Euripides.

There we see Tolstoy, as always, ardently devoting his
attention to some great subject—which happens, this time,
to be dramatic art. So keen is he, that his mind is full
of it whatever else he may be doing; and so vivid is his
imagination that the characters of the plays perform
for him whether he is standing up or lying down. How
real a grip he obtained of the subject with very little
theatre-going, was shown seventeen years later, when he
wrote one of the most powerful dramas ever produced,
and followed it up by an excellent comedy: both pieces
being so good that they are constantly revived in
Russian theatres, besides having achieved success in other
countries.

At the point we have reached there was no break in the
manner of Tolstoy's life. He continued to live quietly at
Yásnaya, and to concern himself chiefly with literature,
and also with the management of his estates and the welfare
of his family. Children continued to be born in rapid
succession, and with the increasing family his means also
increased. But we have come to the middle of that tranquil
period of sixteen years which succeeded his marriage, and

here, while—as one would say of another man—he was indefatigably studying the drama; or while—as one is inclined to say of him—he was resting and recuperating before undertaking his next great work, it is convenient to close this chapter.

CHIEF AUTHORITIES FOR CHAPTER IX

Birukof.

Fet.

Behrs.

Bitovt.

Yasnaya Polyana, P. A. Sergeyenko : *Niva*, No. 34, 1908.

L. N. Tolstoy ; Monografiya Andreevitcha : Petersburg, 1905.

For much information in this chapter as well as elsewhere I am indebted to Tolstoy himself, to the Countess S. A. Tolstoy, to his sister, and particularly to his daughter, Mary Lvovna, Princess Obolensky.

Information concerning the execution of the soldier is given in *Pravo* for 1903.

Prince D. D. Obolensky's *Vospominaniya* appeared in *Roussky Arhiv*, 1896.

See also, *Graf L. N. Tolstoy, Vospominaniya S. P. Arbouzova* : Moscow, 1908.

Arbouzof was in Tolstoy's service twenty-two years. He gives his master an excellent character ; and though very inaccurate, his naive chatter is readable, and throws light on Tolstoy's character.

CHAPTER X

NEARING THE CRISIS

Fet's poem. Franco-Prussian war. Studies Greek. Effect on health. Railways. Koumýs cure in Samára. Mouhamet-Dzhan. An expedition. 'Milk-loving Scythians.' Buys estate. Molokáns. Tourgénef's interest. *ABC* Book. House enlarged. On future life. Re-starts school. Preparation of *ABC* Book. Astronomy. *A Prisoner in the Caucasus. God Sees the Truth.* Ceremonial rites. Stráhof and the *ABC* Book. Samára. Bull kills keeper. Teachers' Congress at Yásnaya. A letter in verse. Peter the Great. A suicide. *Anna Karénina.* Mouhamed Shah. Samára famine. Kramskóy's portrait. Death of son, Peter. Addresses Moscow Society of Literacy. A practical demonstration. Test schools. *The Fatherland Journal: On the Education of the People.* Mihaylóvsky. 'A University in bark shoes.' Toúla Zémstvo Education Committee. Tourgénef translates Tolstoy. Birth of a son. Death of Aunt Tatiána. *ABC* Book approved. Wife's health. *Anna Karénina.* Death of a son. Tourgénef on Tolstoy's writings. Samára. Primitive agriculture. Fête and horse races. Bashkír life. Education of his children. Exercises and playfulness. Croquet. 'Numidian cavalry.' Birth and death of a daughter. Aunt P. I. Úshkof dies. Letters to Fet. Nirvana and Sansara. *Anna Karénina.* 'Summer condition.' Horse-breeding. Loss of Gouneba. Music. P. I. Tschaikóvsky. At the Conservatoire. Folk-songs. Beethoven. Tolstoy on art. Approach of war. Rupture with Katkóf. The Evangelicals. An epitaph. Professor Boutleróf. The Deity. Óptin Monastery. A folk-story teller. Turkish prisoners. Son, Andrew, born. Ill-health. *The Decembrists.* 'Martha is troubled.' Reconciliation with Tourgénef. Samára. Tourgénef at Yásnaya. Their relations

still not cordial. Pilgrims. N. Tchaykóvsky. Mihaylóvsky's forecast. V. I. Alexéyef.

As he grew older Tolstoy's love of outdoor exercise tended
more towards activity serving a useful productive
purpose, and one finds a hint of this in the following
letter to Fet, dated 11th May 1870:

1870

I received your letter, dear friend, when returning perspiring home from work, with axe and spade, and when therefore I was a thousand miles from things artistic in general,
and from our business in particular. On opening the letter
I first read the poem and felt a sensation in my nose. On
coming home to my wife I tried to read it to her, but could not
do so for tears of emotion. The poem is one of those rare ones
in which not a word could be added or subtracted or altered:
it is a live thing, and admirable. . . .

I have just served for a week as juryman, and found it very
interesting and instructive.

The next letter refers to the fact that Tolstoy did his
best literary work in winter, when he often spent almost
the whole day, and sometimes part of the night, at it; that
was the time when his 'sap flowed':

2 *Oct.* 1870.

It is long since we met, and in my winter condition, which
I am now entering, I am specially glad to see you. I have been
shooting; but the sap is beginning to flow, and I am collecting
it as it drips. Whether it be good or bad sap, it is pleasant to
let it flow in these long wonderful autumn evenings. . . . A
grief has befallen me; the mare is ill. The veterinary says her
wind has been broken, but I cannot have broken it.

The Franco-Prussian war, which commenced at this time,
interested Tolstoy keenly. He had come into contact with
the French, in the Crimea, before the Napoleonic autocracy
had long held sway; and he had visited France in 1857
and 1860, before the effect of that putrescent influence had

become fully apparent. Neither the idea of German national unity, nor Bismarck's and Moltke's ideal of efficient organisation and discipline, were things that much appealed to Tolstoy. So it happened that not only were all his sympathies on the side of the French, but he also felt assured of their triumph. His friend Prince Ouroúsof used to write letters to Katkóf's *Moscow Gazette* demonstrating by analogies with games of chess, that the French were continually drawing the German armies into more and more desperate positions in which they must soon be quite destroyed. When, on the contrary, the French were utterly defeated, it came to him as a complete surprise; which all tends to illustrate the fact that men of great intellectual power, living isolated on their country estates, may at times go very considerably wrong in their estimate of the trend of some of the forces that influence the world.

On 12 February 1871 a daughter was born, who was christened Mary. In later life she, of all his children, was the one most deeply influenced by her father's teaching. The Countess, who, as already mentioned, made a point of nursing her own children, owing to the neglect of an attendant, became unable to do so in this instance before the child was many weeks old, and a wet-nurse was engaged; but as soon as the mother saw her child at a stranger's breast she burst into a flood of jealous tears, dismissed the nurse on the spot, and ordered the child to be fed with a bottle. Tolstoy, when he heard what had happened, declared that his wife had only shown the jealous affection natural to a true mother.

During that winter Tolstoy devoted himself strenuously to the study of Greek. On hearing of this, Fet felt so sure that Tolstoy would not succeed, that he 1870- announced his readiness to devote his own skin 1871 for parchment for Tolstoy's diploma of proficiency when the latter should have qualified himself to receive it. Accordingly, in December, Tolstoy wrote him as follows:

I received your letter a week ago, but have not answered because from morning to night I am learning Greek. I am writing nothing, only learning; and to judge by information reaching me through Borísof, your skin (to be used as parchment for my diploma in Greek) is in some danger. Improbable and astounding as it may seem, I have read Xenophon, and can now read him at sight. For Homer, a dictionary and some effort is still necessary. I eagerly await a chance of showing this new trick to some one. But how glad I am that God sent this folly upon me! In the first place I enjoy it; and secondly, I have become convinced that of all that human language has produced truly beautiful and simply beautiful, I knew nothing (like all the others who know but do not understand); and thirdly, because I have ceased to write, and never more will write, wordy rubbish. I am guilty of having done so; but by God I won't do it any more! Explain to me, for Heaven's sake, why no one knows Esop's fables, or even delightful Xenophon, not to mention Plato and Homer, whom I still have before me? In so far as I can as yet judge, our translations, made on German models, only spoil Homer. To use a banal but involuntary comparison: they are like boiled and distilled water, while he is like water fresh from the spring, striking the teeth with its sun-lit sparkle: even its specks only making it seem still clearer and fresher. . . . You may triumph: without a knowledge of Greek, there is no education. But what kind of knowledge? How is it to be got? What is the use of it? To this I have replies clear as daylight.

S. A. Behrs tells us, 'I know for a fact that he learnt the language and read Herodotus in three months.' While

1871

in Moscow that winter, he visited Leóntief, then Professor of Greek at the Katkóf Lyceum, to talk about Greek literature. Leóntief did not wish to believe in the possibility of his having learnt Greek so rapidly, and proposed that they should read something at sight. It happened that they differed as to the meaning of three passages; but after a little discussion the Professor admitted that the Count's interpretations were right.

Tolstoy felt the charm of the literary art of the ancient

world, and so keen was his power of entering into the minds of those of whom he read, and so different to his own was the Greek outlook upon life, that the contradiction produced in him a feeling of melancholy and apathy profound enough to affect his health.

What clash of ideals it was that produced this result we may guess when we consider how from his earliest years he had been attracted by the Christian ideal of meekness, humility, and self-sacrifice, and how little this accords with the outlook on life of the ancient Greeks. In a book written nearly forty years later, Tolstoy tells us that 'If, as was the case among the Greeks, religion places the meaning of life in earthly happiness, in beauty and in strength, then art successfully transmitting the joy and energy of life, would be considered good art' [good, that is, in its subject-matter of feeling conveyed] but art transmitting the opposite feelings would be bad art.[1] Again in the same work he says that the esthetic theory he is combating, seeks to make it appear 'that the very best that can be done by the art of nations after 1900 years of Christian teaching, is to choose as the ideal of life the ideal held by a small, semi-savage, slave-holding people who lived 2000 years ago, imitated the nude human body extremely well, and erected buildings pleasant to look at.'[2]

To wean him from his absorption in Greek literature, his wife at first urged him to take up some fresh literary work ; and finally, becoming seriously alarmed for his health, induced him to go eastward for a koumýs cure. He wrote to Fet at this time :

10 *June* 1871.

DEAR FRIEND,—I have long not written to you, nor been to see you, because I was, and still am, ill. I don't myself know what is the matter with me, but it seems like something bad or good, according to the name we give to our exit. Loss of strength, and a feeling that one needs nothing and wants

[1] *What is Art?* p. 54 : Constable, London, and Funk and Wagnalls Co., New York.　　　　　[2] *Ibid.*, p. 65.

nothing but quiet, which one has not got. My wife is sending me to Samára or Sarátof for two months for a koumýs cure. I leave for Moscow to-day, and shall there learn where I am to go to.

In Moscow it was decided that he should go to the part of Samára he had visited before.

Railways have always been an affliction to Tolstoy. Civilisation has forced them on him without his wish, and, as he argued in his educational articles, to the detriment of the peasant population. Personally, he complained of disagreeable sensations he experienced when travelling by rail, and compared these discomforts with the pleasure of riding on horseback. He objected both to the officious politeness of the conductors and to the way in which the passengers suspiciously shun one another. (This latter complaint is not one a Westerner would bring against Russians, for they appear to us the most friendly and sociable of fellow-travellers.) He used to insist on his wife always travelling first class. He himself went either first or third, but seldom second. To travel third is a more serious matter in Russia than in England ; and he used purposely to choose a car in which there were peasants, and talked to all whom he met.

On this outward journey he went third class, by rail to Nízhni Nóvgorod and by steamer down the Vólga to the town of Samára. On the boat he took the opportunity to study the manners and customs of his fellow-passengers, natives of the Vólga district, and displayed his remarkable gift of making friends with people of all kinds. Before he had been two days on the boat he was on the friendliest terms with everybody, including the sailors, among whom he slept each night in the fore part of the vessel. Even when he met reserved or surly characters, it was not long before he drew them out of their shells, and set them chatting at their ease. One secret of this success was the unaffected interest he took in learning about other people's lives and affairs.

From Samára Tolstoy went eastward for eighty miles on

horseback, following the banks of the river Karalýk till he reached the village of that name. He had lived there in 1862, and was welcomed as an old acquaintance and friend by the Bashkírs, who always spoke of him as 'The Count.' The reader will remember that at the University Tolstoy had studied oriental languages. His knowledge of Tartar no doubt increased his popularity with the Bashkírs. He had with him a man-servant, and his brother-in-law, Stepán Andréyevitch Behrs, then a lad of about sixteen, who subsequently in his *Recollections* gave many particulars about this outing. They lived, not in the 'winter village' of Karalýk, but about one-and-a-half miles away, in a *kotchévka* on the open steppe. A *kotchévka* is a conical tent, made of a collapsible wooden frame covered with large sheets of felt. It has a small painted door, and is usually carpeted with soft feather grass. The one in which Tolstoy's party lived, was a very large one which he hired from the Mullah (priest). It had formerly been used as a mosque, but had the practical disadvantage of not being rain-proof. There were four *kotchévki* in the neighbourhood, one of which was occupied by the Mullah.

On first arriving at Karalýk, Tolstoy for some days felt very depressed and unwell. He complained that he lacked capacity to feel either mental or physical pleasure, and looked at everything 'as though he were a corpse': a characteristic usually most foreign to him, and which in other people always evoked his dislike. It was, however, not long before he recovered his spirits and energy.

There were other visitors at Karalýk, who had also come to benefit by a koumýs cure. They neither associated with the Bashkír nomads, nor adopted their customs; but Tolstoy was extremely fond of the Bashkírs, associated much with them, and strictly followed their diet: avoiding all vegetable foods and restricting himself to meat and animal products. Dinner every day consisted chiefly of mutton eaten with the fingers out of wooden bowls.

Some of the Russian visitors lived in one of the *kotchévki*,

but most of them lodged in the 'winter village.' Tolstoy
soon made friends with them all, and thanks to his genial
influence the whole place grew gay and lively. A professor of
Greek from a Seminary for the education of priests might be
seen trying a skipping-rope match with him; a procureur's
assistant discussed legal and other questions, and there was
a young Samára farmer who became his devoted follower.

Among those who specially interested Tolstoy was
Mouhamet-Dzhan, the Bashkír Elder, whom the Russian
peasants called Michael Ivánovitch. This man was very
nimble and active, full of humour, fond of a joke, and a
very strong player at draughts.

Accompanied by Behrs and two of their new acquaintances, and taking a supply of guns and presents, Tolstoy
went for a four days' drive through the neighbouring villages.
The party had splendid duck-shooting by the lakes they
passed; and they were entertained and treated to koumýs
by the Bashkírs at the *kotchévkas* in which they rested. As
opportunity presented itself, they made suitable acknowledgment for their entertainment by giving presents to
their hosts. One serious drawback to the hospitality they
enjoyed was the fact that their hosts insisted on feeding
them with mutton and fat with their own hands, without
the intermediacy of fork or spoon, and it was out of the
question to insult them by refusing such well-meant though
quite undesired attentions.

On one occasion Tolstoy happened to admire a horse that
had separated from its herd, and remarked to Behrs, 'See
what a beautiful specimen of milking mare that is.' When,
an hour later, they were taking leave, their host tied this
animal to their conveyance, thus presenting it to his visitor.
Of course, on the return journey, Tolstoy had to make an
equivalent present in return.

Another incident of this stay in the Government of
Samára, was a visit to the Petróvsky Fair, which is held once
a year at Bouzoulouk, a small town some fifty miles from
Karalýk. Here Russians, Bashkírs, Oural Cossacks, and

Kirghiz mingled with one another; and Tolstoy was soon on a friendly footing with them all. He would chat and laugh with them even when they were drunk; but when one in that condition took it into his head to embrace the Count, Tolstoy's look was so stern and impressive that the fellow drew back his hands and let them fall, saying, 'No, never mind, it's all right!'

The following letter of 18th July 1871, to Fet, relates to Tolstoy's experience of the nomadic Bashkírs:

Thank you for your letter, dear friend! It seems that my wife gave a false alarm when she packed me off for a koumýs cure and persuaded me that I was ill. At any rate now, after four weeks, I seem to have quite recovered. And as is proper when one is taking a koumýs cure, I am drunk and sweat from morn to night, and find pleasure in it. It is very good here, and were it not for family home-sickness, I should be quite happy. Were I to begin describing, I should fill a hundred pages with this country and my own occupations. I am reading Herodotus, who describes in detail and with great accuracy these same galactophagous [gluttonous-for-milk] Scythians among whom I am living.

I began this letter yesterday, and wrote that I was well. To-day my side aches again. I do not myself know in how far I am ill, but it is bad that I am obliged to think—and cannot help thinking—about my side and my chest. This is the third day that the heat has been terrible. In the *kibítka* [tent] it is as hot as on the shelf of a Russian bath, but I like it. The country here is beautiful—in its age just emerging from virginity, in its richness, its health, and especially in its simplicity and its unperverted population. Here as everywhere I am looking round for an estate to buy. This affords me an occupation, and is the best excuse for getting to know the real condition of the district.

After a six weeks' stay Tolstoy returned to Yásnaya, travelling first class on the return journey.

His search for an estate had been successful, and after persuading his wife that the investment was a sound one, he purchased two thousand acres on his return to Moscow.

The change of scene, or some other influence, weakened

Y

Tolstoy's absorption in Greek literature; and a huge dictionary he had taken with him, was used by his brother-in-law to press a collection of local wildflowers.

During his wanderings on the steppe, Tolstoy met many Molokáns, members of a kind of Bible-Christian peasant sect. They base their faith on the Bible, reject the Greek Church with its traditions, priesthood, dogmas, ritual, sacraments, and icons. The name Molokán, or Milk-Drinker, probably arose from the fact that, not observing the Russian fasts, these people do not scruple to drink milk in Lent. They are said to be distinguished by an honesty and industry not found among their Orthodox neighbours; and they abstain from all intoxicants.

It interested Tolstoy to mix with these people, and he liked to discuss their beliefs, especially with a venerable leader of theirs, named Aggéy. It so happened that in the neighbouring village of Pátrovka there was a very worthy young Russian priest, who was eager to convert the Molokáns, and occasionally arranged debates with them on religious subjects. Tolstoy sometimes attended these debates : his object being not so much to convert the Molokáns, as to understand the points on which they differed from the Russo-Greek Church. He also took an interest in the Mohammedan faith of his Bashkír friends, and on his return to Yásnaya read through a French translation of the Koran.

A few years later Tolstoy associated much with the representatives of various sects and faiths, being then profoundly interested in their beliefs; but at this time, his interest in such matters was only beginning to make itself felt.

A letter of Tourgénef's written at this period, indicates how little he allowed his quarrel with Tolstoy the man, to warp his appreciation of Tolstoy the artist. Writing to Fet on 2nd July 1871, he says:

Your letter again grieves me—I refer to what you write about L. Tolstoy. I have great fears on his account, for two of his brothers died of consumption, and I am very glad he is taking a koumýs cure, in the reality and efficacy of which I have faith.   L. Tolstoy is the only hope of our orphaned literature; he cannot and must not vanish from the face of the earth as prematurely as his predecessors: Poúshkin, Lérmontof and Gógol.

Again in November, writing from Paris, he says:

I am very glad that Tolstoy's health is now satisfactory and that he is at work.   Whatever he does will be good, if only he does not himself mutilate his own handiwork.   Philosophy, which he hates, has revenged herself on him in a strange way: she has infected him, and the enemy of rationalising has plunged head over ears into rationalisation!   But perhaps all *that* has fallen away from him by now, and left only the pure and powerful artist.

On returning home from Samára improved in health, Tolstoy turned his thoughts once more to matters educational: especially to the crying want of good primers for those beginning to read.   We have seen how strongly, in 1862, he had felt the need of well-written books simple enough for beginners and peasant readers, and how he resented the monopolisation of knowledge by the cultured classes entrenched behind barriers of pedantry.   We have seen, too, how under the influence of Homer he swore he would no more write 'wordy rubbish'; and the time had now come for this feeling to bear fruit.   The task to which he devoted his powers at their zenith, was the production of an *ABC* Book for beginners, which was to be as simple, sincere and perfect in form and in subject-matter as possible.

We know from the writings of the American Consul, Mr. Eugene Schuyler, who visited Tolstoy in 1868, and at his request obtained for him a collection of American school primers, that Tolstoy was even then meditating a work of the kind to which he now devoted himself ardently for a whole year.   By September he was hard at work, the Countess as usual acting as his amanuensis.

Of her we hear that in an impulsive, kindhearted way, she often rendered assistance to the poor, not merely among the Yásnaya Polyána peasants, but to others from a distance as well; and that the neighbouring peasants thought well of her.

The increase in the Tolstoy family was met this year by a considerable enlargement of their domicile. By way of a house-warming to celebrate the completion of the building, a masquerade was arranged at Christmas, at which Tolstoy evoked great enthusiasm by appearing as a goat.

About this time, at the age of sixteen, Behrs and a school friend of his became sorely troubled as to the state of their souls, and thought of entering a monastery. This is what he tells us of Tolstoy's relation to the matter:

His attitude towards my inclination was a most cautious one. I often went to him with my doubts and questions, but he always managed to avoid expressing his opinion, knowing how very great an influence it would have with me. He left it to me to work out my own convictions. Once, however, he spoke out with sufficient plainness. We were riding past the village church where his parents lie buried. Two horses were grazing in the churchyard. We had been talking over the only subject that then interested me.

'How can a man live in peace,' I asked, 'so long as he has not solved the question of a future life?'

'You see those two horses grazing there,' he answered; 'are they not laying up for a future life?'

'But I am speaking of our spiritual, not our earthly life.'

'Indeed? Well, about that, I neither know nor can know anything.'

Immediately after New Year he re-started his school; and the children (who often numbered thirty to thirty-five) met, 1872 not as formerly in another building, but in the hall of the Tolstoys' enlarged house. In the mornings the Countess taught her own children, and in the afternoon she, her husband, and even seven-year-old Tánya and eight-year-old Sergius, taught the peasant children, who came only then, but yet made satisfactory progress, being stimulated by the personal interest the Tolstoys took in them, by the pedagogic genius of the Count, and by a perception that education is a rare and valuable luxury, which seldom comes within the reach of Russian peasants.

In the *ABC* Book Tolstoy gives several autobiographical stories of how he learned to ride, and of his dogs Milton and Boúlka. Easy as these are, they are admirably written, and combine brevity and simplicity with sincerity ; though their sincerity lies not in telling the facts just as they occurred, but in the truth of the feeling conveyed to the reader. Besides these and other stories, popular historical sketches, and a number of translations and adaptations from *Esop's Fables* and from Indian, Hebrew and Arabic sources, the work contains some popular ballads or folk-stories in verse. To get these poems as perfect as possible, he studied and collated all the versions of them he could collect.

The section on Arithmetic gave him an immense amount of work, for he would not content himself with the usual explanations of the various operations, but devised explanations of his own.

The book contains some elementary natural science, and for the preparation of this, Tolstoy, besides examining all sorts of text-books, consulted specialists on the various subjects, and himself carefully performed most of the experiments he described.

To select the readings in the Church-Slavonic language, he perused the monkish chronicles and the Lives of the Saints.

Intending to include some readings on astronomy, he took up that study himself, and became so interested in it that he sometimes sat up all night examining the stars.

When the news spread that Tolstoy was writing stories for his *ABC* Book, the magazine editors besieged him with demands, and the first bits of the book to see the light were *A Prisoner in the Caucasus,* which appeared in one of the monthlies in February, and *God Sees the Truth*, which came out in another monthly in March.

Owing to some mismanagement, Tolstoy received nothing for the periodical rights of either of these stories, which in *What is Art?* he names as the best of all his works. They (as well as *The Bear Hunt*, also from the *ABC* Book) are given in English in *Twenty-three Tales*, previously referred to. ¹ In rendering them, I did my best to retain the brief simplicity of the originals; but where Russian customs were alluded to, some of that simplicity was inevitably lost.

With what pleasure Tolstoy looks back to this part of his life's work, was indicated by a remark he made to me in 1902. Speaking of the popularity of *A Prisoner in the Caucasus* for public readings to the peasants, he added with evident satisfaction, that when *A Prisoner in the Caucasus* is now mentioned, it is always taken for granted that it is his little story, and not Poúshkin's famous poem of the same name, that is referred to.

Since their first appearance, these two stories have sold by hundreds of thousands in separate editions at three to ten copecks (about a penny or twopence) each, besides appearing in the *Readers* and among Tolstoy's collected works.

In the following letter to Fet we get a vivid glimpse of the thoughts on life's deepest problems, which were before long to fill Tolstoy's mind completely .

30 Jan. 1872.

It is some days since I received your kind but sad letter, and not till to-day do I settle down to answer it.

It is a sad letter, for you write that Tútchef is dying, and that there is a rumour that Tourgénef is dead ; and about yourself you say the machine is wearing out and you want quietly to think of Nirvana. Please let me know quickly whether this is a false alarm. I hope it is, and that, in the absence of Márya Petróvna, you have taken slight symptoms for a return of your terrible illness.

In Nirvana there is nothing to laugh at; still less is there cause for anger. We all (I, at least) feel that it is much more interesting than life; but I agree that however much I may think about it, I can think of nothing else than that Nirvana is nothingness. I only stand up for one thing: religious reverence —awe of that Nirvana.

There is, at any rate, nothing more important than it.

What do I mean by religious reverence? I mean this: I lately went to see my brother, and a child of his had died and was being buried. The priests were there, and a small pink coffin, and everything as it should be. My brother and I involuntarily confessed to one another that we felt something like repulsion towards ceremonial rites. But afterwards I thought, 'Well, but what should my brother do to remove the putrefying body of the child from the house? How is one to finish the matter decently?' There is no better way (at least, I could devise none) than to do it with a requiem and incense. How is it to be when we grow weak and die? Is nature to take her course, are we to . . . and nothing else? That would not be well. One wishes fully to express the gravity and importance, the solemnity and religious awe of that occurrence, the most important in every man's life. And I also can devise nothing more seemly for people of all ages and all degrees of development, than a religious observance. For me at least those Slavonic words evoke quite the same metaphysical ecstasy as one experiences when one thinks of Nirvana. Religion is wonderful, in that she has for so many ages rendered to so many millions of people these same services—the greatest anything human can render in this matter. With such a task, how can she be logical? Yes—there is something in her. Only to you do I allow myself to write such letters; but I wished to write, and I feel sad, especially after your letter.

Please write soon about your health.—Your

LEO TOLSTOY.

I am terribly dispirited. The work I have begun is fearfully hard, there is no end to the preparatory study necessary. The plan of the work is ever increasing, and my strength, I feel, grows less and less. One day I am well, and three days I am ill.

The work here referred to as 'fearfully hard' was a study of the reign of Peter the Great, in preparation for a novel treating of that period.

On 20th February he again wrote to Fet:

I may not correspond with my friends for years at a time, but when my friend is in trouble, it is terribly shameful and painful not to know of it. . . . Now, being in Moscow, I wished to call on the Bótkins to hear about you, but I fell ill myself, took to my bed, and it was all I could do to get home. Now I am better. At home all is well; but you will not recognise our house: we have been using the new extension all winter. Another novelty is that I have again started a school. My wife and children and I all teach and are all contented. I have finished my *ABC* Book and am printing it. . . .

The next letter shows that his hope that he had finished the *ABC* Book was premature:

16 March 1872.

How I wish to see you; but I cannot come, I am still ill. . . . My *ABC* Book gives me no peace for any other occupation. The printing advances on the feet of a tortoise, and the deuce knows when it will be finished, and I am still adding and omitting and altering. What will come of it I know not; but I have put my whole soul into it.

In May 1872 the Countess gave birth to another boy, who was christened Peter.

The Moscow firm who were printing the book for Tolstoy were not able to give him satisfaction. Not only was the printing a matter of difficulty owing to the variety of type required for a school-book of this kind, but Tolstoy, in accord with his invariable practice, revised the work time after time while it was going through the press. At last, in May, he wrote to his trusty friend and admirer, N. Stráhof, saying that after four months' labour the printing was 'not only not finished, but had not even begun,' and begging Stráhof to have the book printed in Petersburg, and to take on himself for ample payment the whole task of revising the proofs. After some correspondence matters were arranged, though Stráhof declined to accept any payment for the help he rendered.

Tolstoy explained to his friend that he wanted to make a profit on the book if possible. As a rule, all Tolstoy's later teaching seems to grow out of his experience of life; but it would be hard for any one to work more conscientiously than Tolstoy laboured over this book, and yet in later life he speaks as though any admixture of mercenary motives is sure to be fatal to good literary work. We here seem, therefore, to come upon an exception to that rule.

Stráhof's assistance enabled Tolstoy (though he continued to give most careful instructions with regard to the treatment of the various sections of the book) to get a much needed change; and after having as usual worked during the winter and spring up to the very limit of his strength, he went for a short visit to his Samára estate, where he arranged about building, and about breaking up the virgin soil. A peasant from Yásnaya village was appointed steward of the new estate, and was instructed to see to the building of the house there. Being far away from home Tolstoy was anxious about his *ABC* Book; so he cut short his stay, and returned to Yásnaya before the end of July. There he learned that a fine young bull of his had gored its keeper to death. The unpleasantness of such an occurrence and of the legal investigation consequent on the man's death, was greatly increased by the fact that the Investigating Magistrate, an incompetent and arrogant young official, wrongly held Tolstoy responsible for 'careless holding of cattle,' and, besides commencing criminal proceedings against him, obliged him to give a written undertaking not to leave Yásnaya. Prince D. D. Obolénsky tells how Tolstoy arrived one day at a meet at the Prince's estate of Schahovskóy (some thirty miles from Yásnaya) late and much upset, and told of an examination he had that morning undergone at the hands of the Investigating Magistrate, whose duties included those of Coroner. 'Being an excitable man,' says Obolénsky, ' Tolstoy was extremely indignant at the Magistrate's conduct, and told how the latter had kept a Yásno-Polyána peasant in prison for a year-and-a-half on suspicion of having stolen a cow, which then turned out to have been stolen by some one else. " He will confine me for a year," added Tolstoy. " It is absurd, and shows how utterly arbitrary these gentlemen are. I shall sell all I have in Russia and go to England, where every man's person is respected. Here every police-officer, if one does not grovel at his feet, can play one the dirtiest tricks ! " '

P. F. Samárin, who had also come to the hunt, opposed Tolstoy with animation, arguing that the death or even the mutilation of a man, was so serious a matter that it could not be left without judicial investigation. After long argument Samárin more or less convinced Tolstoy, and the latter before retiring to rest remarked to Obolénsky, ' What a wonderful power of calming people Samárin has ! '

The judicial proceedings dragged on for more than a month, and it was not till late in September that Tolstoy was again free to take a journey to Moscow. The proceedings, first against him and then against his steward, were abandoned ; but not before the newspapers had taken the matter up and made a fuss about it.

At last, in November, the *ABC* Book was published. It sold slowly, and was attacked by some of the papers. Tolstoy however was not discouraged, but held to his belief that (as he expressed it to Stráhof) he had ' erected a monument ' —a conviction amply justified by the ultimate success of the work. He had indeed produced a reading-book far superior to anything that had previously existed in Russia, and that is probably unmatched in any language. With certain modifications to be mentioned later on, it continues to circulate throughout Russia to the present day.

In connection with his other efforts to popularise his system of instruction, Tolstoy, in October 1872, invited a dozen teachers from neighbouring schools to visit him for a week at Yásnaya. They were accommodated in his second house (called, as is customary in Russian when speaking of a subsidiary residence, 'the wing'); and a number of illiterate boys were collected from villages within reach, to be taught on Tolstoy's lines. He also formed a project of establishing a 'University in bark shoes' [the country peasants wear bark shoes] or in other words, a training college in which peasants could become teachers without ceasing to be peasants. This plan occupied his attention, off and on, for some years; but (owing to causes which will be related later) never came to fruition.

In December Tourgénef writes from Paris, to Fet:

I got a copy of L. Tolstoy's ABC, but except the beautiful story, *A Prisoner in the Caucasus,* I did not find anything interesting in it. And the price is absurdly dear for a work of that kind.

The price of the first edition of 3000 copies of the *ABC* was Rs. 2 (about 5s. 6d.). Tourgénef probably had no idea of the immense labour, or of the typographical difficulties, involved in its production. The subsequent editions were much cheaper.

About this time Fet sent Tolstoy a letter in rhyme, to which the latter replied as follows:

12 *November* 1872.

The causeless shame felt by the onion
    Before the sweetly-scented rose,
My dearest Fet, I should be feeling,
    Were I to answer you in prose.

And yet in maiden verse replying,
    By sad misgivings I'm beset:
The when and where, yourself please settle—
    But come and visit us, dear Fet.

Tho' drought may parch the rye and barley,
    Yet still I shall not feel upset
If I but spend a day enjoying
    Your conversation, dearest Fet!

> Too apt we often are to worry;
>   O'er future ills let us not fret:
> Sufficient for the day, its evil—
>   It's best to think so, dearest Fet!

Joking apart, write quickly and let me know when to send horses to the station to meet you. I want to see you terribly.

Having at last got his *ABC* off his hands, Tolstoy resumed his preliminary labours for a large novel, which was to deal with the period of Peter the Great. On 19th November 1872 the Countess wrote to her brother:

Our life just now is very, very serious. All day we are occupied. Leo sits surrounded by a pile of portraits, pictures and books, engrossed in reading, marking passages and taking notes. In the evening, when the children have gone to bed, he tells me his plans, and what he means to write. At times he is quite discouraged, falls into despair, and thinks nothing will ever come of it. At other times he is on the point of setting ardently to work; but as yet I cannot say he has actually written anything, he is still preparing.

A month later she wrote:

As usual we are all of us very busy. The winter is the working time for us proprietors, just as much as summer is for the peasants. Leo is still reading historical books of the time of Peter the Great, and is much interested in them. He notes down the characters of various people, their traits, as well as the way of life of the boyars and the peasants, and Peter's activity. He does not yet know what will come of it all, but it seems to me we shall have another prose poem like *War and Peace*; but of the time of Peter the Great.

A few months later he definitely abandoned the project. His opinion of Peter the Great ran directly counter to the popular one, and he felt out of sympathy with the whole epoch. He declared there was nothing great about the personality or activity of Peter, whose qualities were all bad. His so-called reforms, far from aiming at the welfare of the people, aimed simply at his own personal

1873

advantage. He founded Petersburg because the boyars, who were influential and consequently dangerous to him, disapproved of the changes he made, and because he wished to be free to follow an immoral mode of life. The changes and reforms he introduced were borrowed from Saxony, where the laws were most cruel, and the morals most dissolute—all of which particularly pleased him. This, Tolstoy holds, explains Peter's friendship with the Elector of Saxony, who was among the most immoral of rulers. He also considers that Peter's intimacy with the pieman Ménshikof and with the Swiss deserter Lefort, is explained by the contempt in which Peter was held by all the boyars, among whom he could not find men willing to share his dissolute life. Most of all, Tolstoy was revolted by the murder of Peter's son Alexis, in which crime Tolstoy's own ancestor had played a very prominent part.

Almost simultaneously with the abandonment of the project to which he had devoted so much time and attention, Tolstoy, without any special preparation, began to write his second great novel, *Anna Karénina*.

The year before, a lady named Anna who lived with Bíbikof, a neighbouring squire mentioned on a previous page, had committed suicide by throwing herself under a train, out of jealousy of Bíbikof's attentions to their governess. Tolstoy knew all the details of the affair, and had been present at the post-mortem. This supplied him with a theme; but it was not till March 1873, and then as it were by accident, that he actually began to write the book. One day a volume of Poúshkin happened to be lying open at the commencement of *A Fragment*, which begins with the words, 'The guests had arrived at the country house.' Tolstoy, noticing this, remarked to those present that these words, plunging at once into the midst of things, are a model of how a story should begin. Some one then laughingly suggested that he should begin a novel in that way; and Tolstoy at once started on *Anna Karénina*, the second sentence, and first narrative sentence, of which is, ' All was in confusion in the Oblónskys' house.'

In May Tolstoy and his whole family went for a three months' visit to Samára, where he had recently purchased some more land.

This summer he hired a Bashkír named Mouhamed Shah, who owned and brought with him a herd of milking mares. This Mouhamed Shah, or Románovitch as he was called in Russian, was polite, punctual, and dignified. He had a workman to drive the herd, and a wife (who retired behind a curtain in his *kotchévka* when visitors came to see him) to wait upon him. In subsequent years this worthy man repeatedly resumed his engagement with the Tolstoys.

This was the first year the whole estate had been ploughed up and sown. It was fortunate for the district that some one who had the ear of the public, happened to be there; for the crops in the whole neighbourhood failed utterly, and a famine ensued. So out-of-the-world were the people and so cut off from civilisation, that they might have suffered and died without the rest of Russia hearing anything about it, had not Tolstoy been at hand to make their plight known in good time by an appeal for help, which the Countess prompted him to draw up, and which appeared on 17th August, in Katkóf's paper, the *Moscow Gazette*.

In this article on the Samára Famine, Tolstoy describes how the complete failure of the harvest, following as it did on two previous poor harvests, had brought nearly nine-tenths of the population to destitution and hunger.

To ascertain the real state of things Tolstoy took an inventory at every tenth house in the village of Gavrílovka —the one nearest his estate; and of the twenty-three families so examined, all but one were found to be in debt, and none of them knew how they were to get through the winter. Most of the men had left home to look for work, but the harvest being bad everywhere, and so many people being in search of work, the price of labour had fallen to one-eighth of what it had previously been.

Tolstoy visited several villages and found a similar state of things everywhere. Together with his article, he sent Rs. 100 (then equal to about £14) as a first subscription to a Famine Fund. This was only a small part of what he spent in relief of the impoverished peasants, for when Prougávin (well known for his valuable descriptions of Russian sects) visited the district in 1881, many of the inhabitants spoke to him of Tolstoy's personal kindness to the afflicted, and of his gifts of corn and money during the famine.

The subscription proved a success. Tolstoy's aunt, the Countess A. A. Tolstoy (who had charge of the education of Marie Alexándrovna, subsequently Duchess of Edinburgh), mentioned the matter to the Empress, who was one of the first to contribute. Her example was largely followed, and altogether, in money and in kind, something like Rs. 2,000,000, or about £270,000, was contributed during 1873-4. Within a year or two, good harvests again completely changed the whole appearance of the district.

This was the first, but neither the last nor the worst, of the famines in which Tolstoy rendered help.

Before the end of August 1873 he was back at Yásnaya, and wrote to Fet:

On the 22nd we arrived safely from Samára. . . . In spite of the drought, the losses and the inconvenience, we all, even my wife, are satisfied with our visit, and yet more satisfied to be back in the old frame of our life; and we are now taking up our respective labours. . . .

A month later he writes again, referring to Kramskóy's portrait of himself, a photogravure of which forms the frontispiece of this volume, and shows the blouse which even in those days, before his Conversion, he wore when at home, instead of a tailor-made coat:

25 *September* 1873.

I am beginning to write. . . . The children are learning; my wife is busy and teaches. Every day for a week Kramskóy has been painting my portrait for Tretyakóf's Gallery, and I sit and chat with him, and try to convert him from the Petersburg faith to the faith of the baptized. I agreed to this, because Kramskóy came personally, and offered to paint a second portrait for us very cheaply, and because my wife persuaded me.

Up to this time Tolstoy, sensitive about his personal appearance, and instinctively disliking any personal advertisement, had always had an objection to having his portrait painted; and if he ever allowed himself to be photographed, was careful to have the negative destroyed that copies might not be multiplied. This prejudice he abandoned in later life; and after Kramskóy had broken the ice, portraits and photographs of Tolstoy became more and more common.

Kramskóy's acquaintance with the Tolstoys came about in this way. He was commissioned to paint a portrait of the great novelist, for the collection of famous Russians in Tretyakóf's picture gallery in Moscow; but sought in vain in that town for his photograph, and was too modest to ask Tolstoy (who, he knew, was living a secluded life at Yásnaya) to give him sittings. He therefore hired a *dátcha*, some three miles from Yásnaya, with the intention of painting Tolstoy, who often rode past on horseback. His intention, however, became known, and the Tolstoys at once sent him a friendly invitation to visit them. Of the two very similar portraits of Tolstoy which Kramskóy painted, one has remained at Yásnaya.

Before Tolstoy's next letter to Fet, the angel of death had crossed the threshold of his house for the first time in his married life. On 11th November he wrote:

We are in trouble: Peter, our youngest, fell ill with croup and died in two days. It is the first death in our family in eleven years, and my wife feels it very deeply. One may console oneself by saying that if one had to choose one of our eight, this loss is lighter than any other would have been; but the heart, especially the mother's heart—that wonderful and highest manifestation of Divinity on earth—does not reason, and my wife grieves.

During the whole of 1874 Tolstoy made strenuous efforts to get his system of education more generally adopted. On 15th January, overcoming his dislike of speaking in public, he addressed the Moscow Society of Literacy 1874 on the subject of the best way to teach children to read. The details of his argument need not here detain us, as it will fall to the lot of few of my readers to teach Russian children to read Russian ; but briefly, the German *Lautiermethode* had been adopted by Russian pedagogues in a way that Tolstoy considered arbitrary and pedantic, and his appeal, which in the main has not carried conviction to the educationalists, was against that method.

The large hall in which the meeting took place was crowded. The President of the Society, Mr. Shatílof, invited Tolstoy to open the debate, but Tolstoy preferred to reply to what questions and remarks the other speakers might put. In the course of the animated proceedings, in which several men well known in the Russian educational world took part, the discussion widened out till it covered the question of the whole direction of elementary education ; and Tolstoy, from the standpoint of his belief that it is harmful to force upon the people a culture they do not demand and are not prepared for—and much of which, though considered by us to be science, may yet turn out to be no better than the alchemy and astrology of the Middle Ages—denounced the education forced upon the children in elementary schools, and declared that this should be confined in the first place to teaching the Russian language and arithmetic, leaving natural science and history alone. To prove the advantage of his way of teaching reading, Tolstoy offered to give a practical demonstration in one of the schools attached to some of the Moscow mills. Accordingly it was arranged that this should take place the next day and the day after, at the mills owned by Mr. Ganéshin, on the Devítche Pólye just outside Moscow. On the morrow Tolstoy was unwell, and did not appear; but he gave his demonstration on the evening of the following day,

z

with the result that, on the suggestion of Mr. Shatílof, the Society of Literacy decided to start two temporary schools for the express purpose of testing the rival methods during a period of seven weeks. The one school was taught by Mr. M. E. Protopópof, an expert in the *Lautiermethode*, while in the other school Tolstoy's method was taught by Mr. P. V. Morózof. After seven weeks the children were examined by a Committee, which had to report to the Society at a meeting held on 13th April. The members of the Committee however could not agree, and handed in separate and contradictory reports. At the meeting of the Society there was again a great divergence of opinion; and Tolstoy, who considered that the test had not been made under proper conditions (most of the pupils being too young, and the continual presence of visitors preventing the teacher from holding the children's attention), but that nevertheless his method had shown its superiority, decided to appeal to a wider public, and did so in the form of a letter addressed to Mr. Shatílof.

A full account of what happened from the time the dispute passed into the press, has been given by that powerful and popular critic and essayest, N. K. Mihaylóvsky, who was at this time a colleague of Nekrásof. In 1866 the *Contemporary* had been prohibited, as a punishment for its too Liberal tendencies. In 1868 Nekrásof and Saltykóf (Stchedrín) had taken over the management of the *Fatherland Journal*. Tolstoy, who had long dropped out of touch with Nekrásof, now addressed to him a request that the *Fatherland Journal* should take a hand in his fight with the pedagogic specialists, and should interest a wider public in his educational reforms. As an inducement, he held out a prospect (never fulfilled) that he would contribute some of his works of fiction to their magazine. The outcome of his correspondence with Nekrásof was, that though the whole question of elementary education was somewhat foreign to a literary magazine such as the *Fatherland Journal*, a long article by Tolstoy (his letter to Shatílof) appeared in the

September number, under the title of *On the Education of the People*.

Tolstoy's educational articles in 1862, when he issued them in his own magazine, had fallen quite flat and attracted no attention, but this article, by the author of *War and Peace*, in a leading Petersburg magazine, though expressing very similar views, received very much attention, and was criticised, favourably or adversely, in a large number of other publications. Though his views were only adopted to a small extent, yet the severe shock which he administered to the professional pedagogues who looked on school-children as 'a flock existing for the sake of its shepherds,' had a most healthy influence, and that it did not pass without some immediate practical effect is indicated by the rejection from the Moscow Teachers' Seminary of one of the text-books Tolstoy attacked most fiercely.

Following on the storm raised in the press by Tolstoy's article, Mihaylóvsky, in the *Fatherland Journal* for January 1875, published a long article entitled *An Outsider's Notes*, in which he took Tolstoy's part against the pedagogues, and said : 'Though I am one of the profane in philosophy and pedagogics, and am writing simply a *feuilleton*, I nevertheless advise my readers to peruse this *feuilleton* with great attention, not for my sake, but for Tolstoy's, and for the sake of those fine shades of thought on which I do but comment.'

Before this, however, Tolstoy had made another attempt to improve the state of elementary education, by promoting the establishment of that 'University in bark shoes' to which I have already alluded.

He had found some of the boys in the Yásno-Polyána school anxious to continue their studies after finishing the school course ; and an experiment in teaching these lads algebra had been highly successful.

In his last article on Education, Tolstoy had pointed out that a great obstacle to the spread of efficient elementary instruction lay in the fact that the peasants could not afford the salaries (extremely modest as these sound to Western ears) demanded by Russian teachers of the non-peasant classes. It was therefore quite natural that he should now devise a scheme for preparing teachers from among the peasants themselves; and he drew up a project for a training college to be established at Yásnaya, under his own direction and control.

In the summer of this year Tolstoy paid a brief visit to his Samára estate to look after its management; and he took his son Sergius with him.

On 20th November 1874 the Countess wrote to her brother:

Our usual serious winter work is now in full swing. Leo is quite taken up with popular education, schools, and colleges for teachers, where teachers for the peasants' schools are to be trained. All this keeps him busy from morning till night. I have my doubts about all this. I am sorry his strength should be spent on these things instead of on writing a novel; and I don't know in how far it will be of use, since all this activity will extend only to one small corner of Russia.

P. F. Samárin, the Marshal of the Nobility of Toúla Government, backed Tolstoy cordially, and pointed out that the Zémstvo (County Council) had a sum of Rs. 30,000 available for educational purposes, and that this might be devoted to starting a teachers' Training College. To attain this end Tolstoy, who heretofore had always refused to stand for election, consented to enter the Zémstvo, and after being returned to that body, was unanimously chosen to serve on its Education Committee.

He presented a report in the sense indicated above, which was at first favourably discussed; but unfortunately one of the oldest members rose, and alluding to the fact that a collection was being made all over Russia for a monument to Catherine the Great, and that it was the centenary of the decree by which she had created the Government of Toúla, proposed that the money should be devoted to the monu-ment of their Benefactress. This loyal sentiment met with approval, and though Tolstoy did not at once abandon his plan, the means to carry it out were never forthcoming, and we do not hear much more of it.

If one did not know how stupidly reactionary the governing classes of Russia were at this period, it would seem extraordinary that the central and the local authorities alike should have so constantly balked and hindered Tolstoy's disinterested projects : forbidding the publication of his newspaper for soldiers, mutilating his stories, sending gendarmes to search his schools, looking askance at his school magazine, and defeating his project for a Training College. Can it be wondered at, that he came more and more to identify Government with all that is most opposed to enlightenment? We know that similar causes were, at that very time, driving men and women of a younger generation to undertake dangerous propaganda work, in more or less definite opposition to the existing order of society, among factory workmen and country peasants.

His devotion to educational matters did not entirely supersede, though no doubt it delayed, his activity as a novelist. In the spring of 1874 he had taken the commencement of *Anna Karénina* to Moscow, but for some reason none of it appeared that year.

Tourgénef, in collaboration with Madame Viardot, was at this time translating some of Tolstoy's best stories into French. Writing to Fet in March 1874, he says :

The season is now almost over, but all the same I will try to place his [Tolstoy's] *Three Deaths* in the *Revue des Deux Mondes* or in the *Temps,* and in autumn I will without fail get out *The Cossacks.* The more often I read that story, the more convinced I am that it is the *chef d'œuvre* of Tolstoy and of all Russian narrative literature.

Meanwhile life and death pursued their course. In April a son was born and christened Nicholas; and before long, death, having a few months previously taken the youngest, returned to claim the oldest members of the household.

The first of them to go was his dearly-loved Aunty Tatiána Alexándrovna, to whose good influence through life he owed so much. She died on 20th June, and next year his other aunt followed her.

Tolstoy never refers to his aunt Tatiána without letting us see how he cherishes her memory. Here for instance are one or two of his notes relating to her:

When already beginning to grow feeble, having waited her opportunity, one day when I was in her room she said to us, turning away (I saw that she was ready to cry), 'Look here, *mes chers amis*, my room is a good one and you will want it. If I die in it,' and her voice trembled, 'the recollection will be unpleasant to you; so move me somewhere else, that I may not die here.' Such she always was, from my earliest childhood, before I was able to understand her goodness.

Again referring to her death, and to the love for his father which had played so large a part in her life, he adds:

She died peacefully, gradually falling asleep; and died as she desired, not in the room that had been hers, lest it should be spoilt for us.

She died recognising hardly any one. But me she always recognised, smiling and brightening up as an electric lamp does when one touches the knob, and sometimes she moved her lips trying to pronounce the name Nicholas: thus in death completely and inseparably uniting me with him she had loved all her life.

The opinion the peasants had of her, was shown by the fact that when her coffin was carried through the village, there was not one hut out of the sixty in Yásnaya Polyána, from which the people did not come out asking to have the procession stopped and a requiem sung for her soul. 'She was a kind lady and did nobody any harm,' said they. Tolstoy adds:

On that account they loved her, and loved her very much. Lao-Tsze says things are valuable for what is not in them. So it is with a life. It is most valuable if there is nothing bad in it; and in the life of Tatiána Alexándrovna there was nothing bad.

Except in the case of his brother Nicholas, Tolstoy has usually not been greatly upset even by the deaths of those near and dear to him. The following letter to Fet shows how he took Tatiána's death:

24 *June* 1874.

Two days ago we buried Aunt Tatiána Alexándrovna. She died slowly and gradually, and I had grown accustomed to the process; yet her death was, as the death of a near and dear one always is, a quite new, isolated and unexpectedly-stirring event. The others are well, and our house is full. The delightful heat, the bathing and the fruit have brought me to the state of mental laziness I love, with only enough mental life remaining to enable me to remember my friends and think of them.

The next letter, dated the 22nd October, tells its own tale:

DEAR AFANÁSY AFANÁSYEVITCH,—I have planned to buy, and must buy, some land at Nikólsky, and for that purpose must borrow Rs. 10,000 for one year on mortgage. It may be that you have money you want to place. If so, write to Iván Ivánovitch Orlóf, Nikólsky village, and he will arrange the affair with you independently of our relations to one another. . . . How gladly would I come to see you, were I not so over-whelmed with the school, family and estate business, that I have not even time to go out shooting. . . . I hope to be free when winter comes.

A small second edition of Tolstoy's *ABC* Book, in twelve paper-bound parts, was printed this year; but he did not yet feel quite satisfied with that work, and towards the close of the year he revised it, abbreviating, omitting the arithmetic, and introducing graduated reading exercises. As soon as the pupil has mastered a few of the most necessary letters and can put these together, Tolstoy contrives out of the very simplest syllables to construct sentences that have a meaning and an interest. The *New ABC* Book, apart from the more advanced *Readers*, and consisting of ninety-two pages of elementary matter, was issued in 1875, at the low price of 14 copecks (about 4d.). Since Tolstoy's efforts have seldom been favoured by the Government, it is worth noting that this edition was 'Approved and recommended by the Scholarly Committee of the Ministry of Popular Education.' Between one and two million copies of it have since been sold. The reading matter from his first *ABC* Book was subsequently graded into four cheap *Readers* costing 3d. to 4d. each, and though not honoured by the Ministry of Education, they have from that time to this circulated in increasing quantities, being printed of late years in edition after edition of 50,000 at a time.

The Countess has in general enjoyed good health and worn her years and the cares of her large family very lightly; but during the winter of 1874-5 her condition gave her husband much concern. In January he was able to write to Fet: 'I have ceased to fear for my wife's health'; but in fact for some time longer she continued to be ailing.

The commencement of *Anna Karénina*, appeared in the first four monthly numbers of the *Russian Messenger* for 1875.

By far the best English version of that novel (as also of *War and Peace*) is Mrs. Constance Garnett's, though I do not like her alteration of the title of the book to *Anna Karénin*, nor am I quite satisfied with her treatment of some of the conversations in it; but unquestionably we have much to thank her for.

In February the baby, Nicholas, died of inflammation of the brain, and on 4th March 1875 [1] Tolstoy wrote to Fet:

We have one grief after another; you and Márya Petróvna will certainly be sorry for us, especially for Sónya. Our youngest son, ten months old, fell ill three weeks ago with

---

[1] This letter evidently relates to the year 1875, though in Fet's *Vospomin-dniya* it is given as belonging to 1874.

the dreadful illness called 'water on the brain,' and after three weeks' terrible torture died three days ago, and we have buried him to-day. I feel it hard through my wife; but for her, who was nursing him herself, it is very hard.

In the same letter he mentions *Anna Karénina*, and immediately afterwards he makes an allusion to the first idea of his *Confession*, which was not actually written till 1879:

It pleases me very much that you praise *Karénina* and I hear that she gets praised; but assuredly never was writer so indifferent to his success as I am!

On the one hand what preoccupies me are the school affairs, and on the other, strange to say, the subject of a new work, which took possession of me just at the worst time of the boy's illness,—and that illness itself and death. . . .

From Tourgénef I have received the translation, printed in the *Temps*, of my *Two Hussars*, and a letter written in the third person asking to be informed that I have received it, and saying that other stories are being translated by Madame Viardot and Tourgénef,—both of which were unnecessary. [Tolstoy means that they need neither have sent him the translation, nor informed him of what they were doing.]

The commencement of *Anna Karénina* did not find favour with Tourgénef, who on 14th March wrote from Paris to A. S. Souvórin, the novelist and proprietor of the *Nóvoye Vrémya* (*New Times*):

His [Tolstoy's] talent is quite extraordinary, but in *Anna Karénina* he, as one says here, *a fait fausse route*; one feels the influence of Moscow, Slavophil nobility, Orthodox old maids, his own isolation, and the absence of real artistic freedom. Part II is simply dull and shallow—that's what's the matter.

And writing in similar strains to Polónsky the poet, Tourgénef said:

Anna Karénina does not please me, though there are some truly splendid pages (the steeplechase, the mowing, and the hunt). But it is all sour: smells of Moscow, holy oil, old maidishness, Slavophilism, and the aristocracy, etc.

The cordiality of Tourgénef's appreciation of Tolstoy's writings in general, is sufficient guarantee that it was no personal prejudice that led him to speak in this way of a book which is one of Tolstoy's three most important novels, and which many people hold to be the best of them all. What really caused his harsh judgment, is a matter I will deal with later on.

This summer the whole Tolstoy family went to the Samára estates, which had already been considerably increased by the last purchase, and which ultimately exceeded 16,000 acres. Mouhamed Shah with his herd of mares and his *kotchévka*—which Tolstoy called ' our saloon '—again appeared on the scene. A second *kotchévka* was set up for the use of the Tolstoys themselves, and was so much in favour that all the members of the family were eager to occupy it.

The novelty and the peculiarities of steppe farming interested Tolstoy, and he, as well as other members of his household, took an active part in harvesting and winnowing. How primitive were the Samára methods of agriculture may be shown by mentioning their manner of threshing. A ring of horses was formed, tied head to tail. In the centre of the ring stood a driver with a long lash, and the horses were set trotting round a corresponding circle of sheaves, out of which they trod the grain.

The virgin soil was ploughed up by five or even six pair of oxen, wearing round their necks deep-toned bells, sounding in a minor key. These things, together with the pipes of the boys who watched the herds, the sultry days, and the marvellously clear moonlit nights, had a wonderful charm for the whole party, and this charm was increased by Tolstoy's capacity to notice and direct attention to whatever was interesting or beautiful.

The whole family became interested, Behrs tells us, in their new farming, and some of them went with Tolstoy as far afield as Orenbourg to purchase cattle and horses.

He bought about a hundred Bashkír mares and crossed

them with an English trotter and with horses of other breeds, hoping to obtain a good new type.

One evening his whole herd, and Mouhamed Shah's as well, were very nearly driven off by some Kirghiz nomads who were passing. The invaders were, however, pursued and driven off by two mounted Bashkír labourers.

Tolstoy declared farming in Samára to be a game of chance. It cost nearly three times as much to plough up the land, sow it, and gather in a harvest, as it did to purchase the freehold of the estate; and if during May and June there was not at least one good fall of rain, everything perished; whereas if it rained several times, the harvest yielded thirty to forty-fold.

One day, at harvest time, a poor wandering Tartar, drawing two little children in a tiny cart, came up to the balcony on which the Tolstoys were sitting, and asked to be hired as a labourer. He was allowed to set up his wigwam in a field close by, and the Tolstoy children used to go there every day to feed the little Tartars.

In the neighbouring village lived several well-to-do Russian peasants with whom Tolstoy was on very good terms. Either because they were economically independent and lived in a province where serfdom had not prevailed, or as a result of Tolstoy's tact and ability to set people at their ease, these peasants always behaved with dignity and self-respect. They shook hands when they said 'How do you do?' and seemed quite at home with the Count.

He used to notice with pleasure the good relations and complete religious toleration that existed in those parts between the Orthodox peasants and their Mohammedan neighbours; and he was also delighted that the priest at Pátrovka was on friendly terms with the Molokáns he was trying to convert.

One rainy night, after staying late at this priest's house, Tolstoy and his brother-in-law completely lost their way. It was so dark that they could not see their horses' heads. Behrs was riding an old working horse, which kept pulling to the left. Tolstoy, on hearing this, told him to let the horse follow its bent. Behrs therefore tied his reins so that they hung loose, and wrapping himself in his cloak from the drenching rain, allowed the horse to go where it liked. Carefully avoiding the ploughed land, it soon brought them out on to the road, and, curiously enough, to just the one part of it which was distinguishable from the extraordinary sameness of the rest, so that the riders knew just where they were.

The most striking event of this year's stay in Samára was a horse race, arranged by Tolstoy. Mouhamed Shah was authorised to announce to the peasants and neighbours that races would be held on the Count's estate; and invitations were sent to all likely to take part. Bashkírs and Kirghiz assembled, bringing with them tents, portable copper boilers, plenty of koumýs, and even sheep. Oural Cossacks and Russian peasants also came from the whole surrounding neighbourhood. In preparation for the race, says Behrs:

We ourselves chose a level place, measured out a huge circle three miles in circumference, marked it by running a plough round, and set up posts. Sheep and even one horse were prepared with which to regale visitors. By the appointed day some thousands of people had collected. On the wild steppe, covered with feather grass, a row of tents appeared, and soon a motley crowd enlivened it. On the conical hillocks (locally called 'cones') felt and other carpets were spread, on which the Bashkírs sat in circles, their legs tucked under them. In the centre of the circle, out of a large *toursouk* [a leather bottle made of an animal's leg] a young Bashkír poured koumýs, handing the cup to each of the company in turn. Their songs, and the tunes played on their pipes and reeds, sounded somewhat dreary to a European ear. Wrestling, at which the Bashkírs are particularly skilful, could be seen here and there. Thirty trained horses were entered for the chief race. The riders were boys of about ten years, who rode without saddles.

This race was for thirty-three miles, and it took exactly an hour and forty minutes; consequently it was run at the rate of three minutes a mile. Of the thirty horses, ten ran the whole distance, the others giving up. The principal prizes were a horse, an ox, a gun, a clock, and a dressing-gown. The festival lasted two days, and passed off in perfect order and very gaily. To Tolstoy's delight no police were present. The guests all politely thanked their host and departed highly satisfied. 'Even in the crowd,' says Behrs, 'it seemed to me that Leo Nikoláyevitch knew how to evoke *entrain* combined with respect for good order.'

Tolstoy visited the Petróvsky Fair, as was his yearly custom, and stayed at the Bouzouloúk Monastery, where a hermit resided who was 'saving his soul' by a solitary and ascetic life. This man lived in an underground catacomb. When he came out he walked about the garden and showed his visitors an apple-tree he had planted forty years before, under which it was his custom to sit when receiving pilgrims. He spoke to Tolstoy about the Scriptures, and showed him his catacomb-home, the coffin in which he slept, and the large crucifix before which he prayed.

Tolstoy considered that the respect paid to this man by pilgrims and other visitors, was the outcome of genuine religious feeling, and proved that the hermit, by giving the example of a pure, unworldly life, supplied a real want.

Readers of Tolstoy's short stories will be aware of the use to which he subsequently put his knowledge of the Bashkírs and of the hermit.

On 26th August, after reaching Yásnaya, he wrote to Fet:

Two days ago we arrived home safely. . . .

We have had an average harvest, but the price of labour has been enormous, so that finally ends only just meet. For two months I have not soiled my hands with ink nor my heart with thoughts. Now I am settling down again to dull, common-place *Anna Karénina* with the sole desire to clear a space quickly, and obtain leisure for other occupations—only not for the educational work I love but wish to abandon. It takes too much time.

His Samára experiences confirmed in him the feeling that not the civilisation and progress and political struggles of the Western world and of the small Westernised section of Russians, were really important, but the great primitive struggle of plain people to obtain a subsistence in healthy natural conditions; and he adds in the same letter:

Why fate took me there [to Samára] I do not know; but I know that I have listened to speeches in the English Parliament, which is considered very important, and it seemed to me dull and insignificant; but there, are flies, dirt, and Bashkír peasants, and I, watching them with intense respect and anxiety, became absorbed in listening to them and watching them, and felt it all to be very important.

One must live as we lived, in a healthy out-of-the-way part of Samára, and see the struggle going on before one's eyes of the nomadic life (of millions of people on an immense territory) with the primitive agricultural life, in order to realise all the importance of that struggle.

After their return from the Government of Samára, all the children got hooping-cough. The Countess caught it from them, and, being in the sixth month of pregnancy, was very ill. This resulted in the premature birth of a girl, Varvára, who lived less than two hours.

Tolstoy's eldest son, Sergius, had now reached the age of twelve. Besides their English governess and a Swiss lady, the children had at different times a Swiss, a Frenchman, and a German as tutors for modern languages. Tutors and students who acted as tutors, also lodged at Yásnaya and taught other subjects. A music master came over from Toúla. The eldest boy had considerable musical talent, and the family as a whole were musical. As soon as they had mastered their finger exercises, the Count insisted on their at once being allowed to learn serious pieces.

Every effort was made to awaken and foster the talent for drawing and painting which some of the children, and especially the eldest daughter, Tatiána, possessed; but lessons in these subjects were only given to those who showed real capacity for them.

Much as Tolstoy disliked the curriculum of the Grammar Schools ('Gymnasiums,' as they are called in Russia), he did, not wish to make it impossible for his sons to enter the University, and they followed the usual classical course. Sergius passed his examinations each year in Toúla Gymnasium, being carefully coached at home.

In his *Recollections* Behrs tells us of Tolstoy's enlivening influence in the family:

I cannot sufficiently describe the joyous and happy frame of mind that usually reigned at Yásnaya Polyána. Its source was always Leo Nikoláyevitch. In conversation about abstract questions, about the education of children, about outside matters—his opinion was always most interesting. When playing croquet, or during our walks, he enlivened us all by his humour and his participation, taking a real part in the game or the walk.

With me, he liked to mow, or use the rake; to do gymnastics, to race, and occasionally to play leap-frog or *gorodkí* [a game in which a stick is thrown at some other shorter sticks placed in a pattern], etc. Though far inferior to him in strength, for he could lift 180 lbs. with one hand, I could easily match him in a race, but seldom passed him, for I was always laughing. That mood accompanied all our exercises. Whenever we happened to pass where mowers were at work, he would go up to them and borrow a scythe from the one who seemed most tired. I of course imitated his example. He would then ask me, Why we, with well-developed muscles, cannot mow six days on end, though a peasant does it on rye-bread, and sleeping on damp earth? 'You just try to do it under such conditions,' he would add in conclusion. When leaving the meadow, he would take a handful of hay from the haycock and sniff it, keenly enjoying its smell.

Children and grown-ups alike played croquet at Yásnaya. The game generally began after dinner in the evening, and only finished by candlelight. Behrs says that, having played it with Tolstoy, he considers croquet to be a game of chance. Tolstoy's commendation of a good shot always pleased the player and aroused the emulation of his opponents. The kindly irony of his comments on a miss, also acted as a spur. A simple word from him, uttered just at the right moment and in the right tone, produced that *entrain* which makes any occupation interesting and infects all who come under its influence.

The sincerity of Tolstoy's nature showed itself in the frank expression of his passing mood. If, when driving to the station, he saw that they had missed the train, he would exclaim, ' Ach ! we 've missed it ! ' with such intensity that every one within earshot would first feel as though a calamity had occurred, and would then join in the hearty laughter which his own vehement exclamation evoked in Tolstoy. It was the same when he made a bad miss at croquet; and also if, when sitting at home, he suddenly remembered some engagement he had forgotten to keep. If, as sometimes happened, his exclamation alarmed his wife, he would half-jokingly add, like a scolded child, ' I 'll never do it again ! '

His laughter, which began on a high note, had something wonderfully infectious about it. His head would hang over on one side, and his whole body would shake.

His good-natured irony constantly acted as a stimulant to those about him. If, for instance, some one was in the dumps about the weather, Tolstoy would say : ' Is your weather behaving badly ? ' Or when Behrs was sitting comfortably listening to a conversation, he would say to him : ' As you are on the move, you might please bring me so-and-so.'

When he felt it wise to reject an extra cigar or a second helping of some favourite dish, he would remark to those present : ' Wait till I am grown up, and then I will have two helpings,' or ' two cigars,' as the case might be.

If, says Behrs, ' he noticed any of the children making a wry or affected face, he generally called out, " Now then, no grimacing; you 'll only spoil your phiz." '

Behrs also tells us that .

What he called ' the Numidian cavalry ' evoked our noisiest applause. He would unexpectedly spring up from his place and, raising one arm in the air with its hand hanging quite loose from the wrist, he would run lightly through the rooms. All the children, and sometimes the grown-ups also, would follow his example with the same suddenness.

Tolstoy read aloud very well, and would often read to the family or to visitors.

His contempt for doctors and medicine is plainly indicated both in *War and Peace* and *Anna Karénina*. Like Rousseau he considered that the practice of medicine should be general and not confined to one profession; and this opinion inclined him to approve of the folk-remedies used by the peasants. But he did not go the length of refusing to call in a doctor when one of the family was seriously ill.

Before the year closed, Tolstoy's aunt, Pelagéya Ilýnishna Úshkof, with whom he had lived in his young days in Kazán, also passed away. She had been separated from her husband before his death in 1869, and had long not even seen him, though they remained quite friendly towards one another. She was very religious in an Orthodox Church way, and after her husband's death retired to the Óptin nunnery. Subsequently she moved to the Toúla nunnery, but arranged to spend much of her time at Yásnaya; where in her eightieth year she fell ill and died. She was in general a good-tempered though not clever woman, and all her life long strictly observed the ceremonies of the Church and thought that she firmly believed its teaching about redemption and resurrection; yet she was so afraid of death that on her death-bed she was reluctant to receive the eucharist, because it brought home to her mind the fact that she was dying; and as a consequence of the sufferings caused by the fear of death, she became irritable with all about her.

A servant who lived in the house at the time, tells that while at Yásnaya she used, on the first of each month, to send for a priest. As soon as he arrived, and began the usual ceremony of blessing with holy water, Tolstoy would escape and hide himself. Not till the gardener, Semyón—whom he used to send into the conservatory to reconnoitre—brought him word that the priest had gone, would Tolstoy reappear in the house.

About that time, however, his attitude towards Church ceremonies altered. His man-servant Sergéy Arboúzof (who saw only the external signs of the complex inner struggle going on in Tolstoy) tells us:

Suddenly a wonderful change came over him, of which I was a witness. In 1875 a priest, Vasíly Ivánovitch, from the Toúla Seminary, used to come to teach theology to Tolstoy's children. At first, Leo Nikoláyevitch hardly ever talked to him, but it once happened that a snow-storm obliged Vasíly Ivánovitch to stop the night at our house. The Count began a conversation with him, and they did not go to bed till daylight. They talked the whole night.

From that day Leo Nikoláyevitch became very thoughtful, and always talked with Vasíly Ivánovitch. When Lent came round, the Count got up one morning and said, ' I am going to do my devotions, and prepare to receive communion. You can go back to bed, but first tell the coachman not to get up. I will saddle Kalmýk (his favourite horse at that time) myself. Forgive me, Sergéy, if I have ever offended you ! ' and he went off to church.

From that day for a couple of years he always went to church, seldom missing a Sunday. The whole village was surprised, and asked, ' What has the priest told the Count, that has suddenly made him so fond of church-going ? '

It used to happen that the Count would come into my hut when I was teaching my little boy religion.

' What are you teaching him ? ' he would ask.

And I used to say, ' To pray.'

' Ah ! ' said he, ' that is right. A man who does not pray to God is not a real man.'

The publication of *Anna Karénina* was renewed in the first four numbers of the *Russian Messenger* for 1876. On 1st March Tolstoy writes to Fet :

1876

Things are still not all right with us. My wife does not get over her last illness, coughs, gets thin, and has first fever and then headaches. And therefore the house lacks well-being, and I lack mental tranquillity, which I now particularly need for my work. The end of winter and beginning of spring is always my chief time for work, and I must finish my novel, which now wearies me. . . . I always hope a tooth will come loose in your jaw, or in your thrashing machine, and cause you to go to Moscow. Then I shall spin a cobweb at Kozlóvka [the nearest station to Yásnaya] and catch you.

In April Fet wrote to Tolstoy to say that he had been seriously ill, had thought he was dying, and ' wished to call you to see how I departed.' On 29th April Tolstoy replies in a letter notable because it gives us a glimpse of the progress he had made in the fierce five-year inner struggle with doubt which preceded the production of his *Confession* :

I am grateful to you for thinking of calling me to see your departure, when you supposed it was near. I will do the same when I get ready to go *thither*, if I am able to think. No one will be so necessary to me at that moment as you and my brother. When death draws near, intercourse with people who in this life look beyond its bounds, is precious and cheering ; and you and those rare *real* people I have met in life, always stand on the very verge and see clearly, just because they look now at Nirvana—the illimitable, the unknown—and now at Sansara ; and that glance at Nirvana strengthens their sight. But worldly people, however much they may talk about God, are unpleasant to you and me, and must be a torment when one is dying, for they do not see what we see, namely the God who ' is more indefinite and distant, but loftier and more indubitable,' as was said in that article.

You are ill and think of death, and I am alive and do not cease thinking of and preparing for the same thing. . . . Much that I have thought, I have tried to express in the last chapter of the April number of the *Russian Messenger* [*Anna Karénina*, Part I, Chap. XX].

The passage referred to, telling of the death of Lévin's brother, is evidently based on the death of Tolstoy's own brother Demetrius; and it may here be mentioned that many characters in *Anna Karénina* are drawn more or less closely from life. For instance, Agáfya Miháylovna, the servant, was a real person, and that was her real name. She died at Yásnaya only a few years ago. Yásnaya Polyána itself, in many of its details, is also described in the novel.

On 12th May Tolstoy again writes to Fet:

It is already five days since I received the horse, and every day I prepare but never make time to write to you. Here the spring and summer life has begun, and our house is full of guests and of bustle. This summer life seems to me like a dream: it contains some slight remains of my real, winter life, but consists chiefly of visions, now pleasant and now unpleasant, from some absurd world not ruled by sane sense. Among these visions came your beautiful stallion. I am very much obliged to you for it. Where am I to send the money to? . . .

An event which occupies me very much at present is Sergéy's examinations, which begin on the 27th. . . . What a terrible summer! Here it is dreadful and mournful to look at the wood, especially at the young trees. They have all perished.

On 18th May he wrote again:

I have been slow in answering your long and cordial letter because I have been unwell and dispirited, as I still am, but I will write at least a few lines. Our house is full of people: my niece Nagórnaya with two children, the Kouzmínskys with four children; and Sónya [the Countess] is still poorly, and I dejected and dull-minded. Our one hope was for good weather, and that we have not got. As you and I resemble one another, you must know the condition in which one feels oneself to be, now a God from whom nothing is hid, and now stupider than a horse. In that state I am at present. So do not be exacting. Till next letter, yours, L. TOLSTOY.

The Kouzmínskys referred to above were Tánya, her husband, and their family. They spent every summer at Yásnaya, in the 'wing' house. When discussing any excursion or other undertaking with Mr. Kouzmínsky, Tolstoy would often say, 'But we must hear what the

Authorities have to say about it,' the Authorities being their wives.

Passing into his 'summer condition,' Tolstoy's attention to *Anna Karénina* slackened; but before the end of the year he set energetically to work to finish it. The interest aroused by the book was extreme, and the story goes that Moscow ladies used to send to the establishment where the novel was being printed, to try to find out what the continuation would be.

On 21st July Tolstoy writes inviting Fet's brother, Peter Afánasyevitch, a great lover of horses, to accompany him to Samára; and in the same letter he makes an allusion to the troubles of the Slavs in Turkey, where fighting had already been going on for a twelvemonth with the Herzegovinians. Peter Afanásyevitch had gone as a volunteer, and had returned after the failure of the insurrection.

21 July 1876.

I am very much to blame, dear Afanásy Afanásyevitch, for having been so slow in writing to you. I prepare to write every day, but cannot find time because I am doing nothing. . . . Stráhof was here a week ago, and we philosophised to the point of weariness. . . .

I press the hand of Peter Afanásyevitch. I should like to hear his stories about Herzegovina, in the existence of which I do not believe !

I am arranging to go to Samára in September. If Peter Afanásyevitch has no plans for September, will not he go with me to see the Kirghiz and their horses? How jolly it would be !

Mention has already been made of the fact that Tolstoy, who understood horses very well, was at this time interested in horse-breeding as a source of revenue. To buy them he visited Orenbourg, where he met General Kryzhanóvsky, a friend who had been one of his superior officers in Sevastopol and was now Governor-General of this northern Province. They spent the time together very pleasantly recalling their past experiences.

To his wife, who had found it hard to consent to his absence, he wrote in September :

I know that it is hard for you, and that you are afraid ; but I saw the effort you made to control yourself and not to hinder me and, were it possible, I loved you yet more on that account. If only God grants you to spend the time well, healthily, energetically and usefully ! . . . Lord have mercy on me and on thee !

In a letter of 13th November Tolstoy writes to Fet :

Pity me for two things : (1) a good-for-nothing coachman took the stallions to Samára and, wishing to take a short cut, drowned Gouneba in a bog within ten miles of the estate ; (2) I sleep and cannot write ; I despise myself for laziness and do not allow myself to take up any other work.

Twenty-eight years after the loss of Gouneba, the Countess, in speaking to me of her husband's qualities as a man of affairs, remarked that his schemes were very good, but that he generally spoilt them by lack of care in details. ' For instance,' she remarked, ' it was quite a good idea of his to send a very fine stallion which cost Rs. 2000 [about £260] to our estate in Samára. There were no such horses in the district ; but he must needs entrust it to a drunken Tartar who made away with it and said he had lost it.'

On 7th December 1876 Tolstoy wrote to Fet acknowledging a poem, ' Among the Stars,' which the latter had sent him :

That poem is not only worthy of you, but is specially, specially good, with that philosophic-poetic character which I expect from you. It is excellent that it is said by the stars. . . . It is also good, as my wife remarked, that on the same sheet on which the poem is written, you pour out your grief that the price of kerosene has risen to 12 copecks. That is an indirect but sure sign of a poet.

The reader is by this time well aware of Tolstoy's devotion to music. Though it was at times crowded out of his life by other interests, he always returned to it with ardour when opportunity offered. Behrs tells us that Tolstoy generally, when playing, chose serious music.

He often sat down to the piano before beginning to work. . . . He always accompanied my youngest sister [Tánya] and enjoyed her singing very much. I noticed that the sensation music evoked in him expressed itself by a slight pallor and a scarcely perceptible grimace, suggestive of something like terror. Hardly a day passed in summer without my sister singing and without the piano being played. Occasionally we all sang together, and he always played the accompaniments.

As Tolstoy's spiritual crisis approached, the attraction of music for him seemed to increase, and it was about this period, that is to say in December 1876, that he made acquaintance with the composer P. I. Tschaikóvsky, who had held the post of Director of the Moscow Conservatoire, the first seeds of which Tolstoy had helped to plant nearly twenty years before.

Tschaikóvsky had from his youth up been a devoted admirer of Tolstoy, whose skill in reading the human heart appeared to him almost superhuman. He was therefore highly gratified when Tolstoy of his own accord sought his acquaintance. At first their personal intercourse did not appear to lessen the composer's reverence for the author, for on 23rd December 1876 he wrote to a friend :

Count L. N. Tolstoy spent some time here recently. He visited me several times and spent two whole evenings with me. I am tremendously flattered, and proud of the interest I have inspired in him, and for my part am completely enchanted by his ideal personality.

Tschaikóvsky induced Nicholas Rubinstein, then Director of the Moscow Conservatoire, to arrange a musical evening solely for Tolstoy, and at this concert, Rubinstein, Fitzenhagen, and Adolph Bródsky, who is now Principal of the Manchester College of Music, were among the chief performers.

One of the pieces performed by a quartet was Tschaikóvsky's 'Andante in D Major,' which so affected Tolstoy that he wept. 'Never, perhaps, in my life,' says Tschaikóvsky, 'was I so flattered, or my vanity as a composer so touched, as when Leo Nikoláyevitch, sitting next to me and listening to the quartet performing my Andante, burst into tears.'

After Tolstoy had returned to Yásnaya he wrote to Tschaikóvsky, sending him a collection of folk-songs, and saying :

I send you the songs, dear Peter Ilyítch. I have again looked them through. They will be a wonderful treasure in your hands. But for God's sake work them up and use them in a Mozart-Haydn style, and not in a Beethoven-Schumann-Berlioz, artificial way, seeking the unexpected. How much I left unsaid to you. I really said nothing of what I wanted to say. There was no time. I was enjoying myself. This last stay of mine in Moscow will remain one of the best of my reminiscences. Never have I received so precious a reward for my literary labours as on that wonderful evening.

Tschaikóvsky replied :

Count, I am sincerely grateful to you for sending the songs. I must tell you candidly that they have been taken down by an unskilful hand, and bear only traces of their pristine beauty. The chief defect is that they have been artificially squeezed and forced into a regular, measured form. Only Russian dance music has a rhythm and a regular and equally accentuated beat; but folk-ballads have of course nothing in common with dance songs. Moreover, most of these songs are, arbitrarily it seems, written in a solemn D Major, which again does not suit a real Russian song, which almost always has an indefinite tonality approximating nearest of all to ancient Church music. In general, the songs you have sent me cannot be worked up in a regular and systematic way : that is to say, one cannot make a collection of them, because for that they would have to be taken down as nearly as possible in the way in which the people perform them. That is an extremely difficult matter, demanding fine musical feeling and great historico-musical erudition.

Except Balakíref, and to some extent Prokoúnin, I do not know any one competent for the task.   But as material for symphonic treatment, your songs can be of use, and are even very good material, which I certainly will avail myself of in one way or other.

It is rather disappointing to find that the intercourse between these two men, each so great in his own way, and each such an admirer of the other's genius, was not continued.

Tschaikóvsky's expectations had been pitched too high, and he felt a certain disappointment that his 'demigod' was, after all, but human.   He had dreaded to meet the novelist lest the latter should penetrate the secret recesses of his soul; but, says Tschaikóvsky:

He who in his writings was the deepest of heart-seers, proved in personal contact to be a man of simple, whole, and frank nature, showing very little of the omniscience I had feared. . . . It was plain he did not at all regard me as a subject for his observation, but simply wanted to chat about music, in which he was then interested.   He took a pleasure in denying Beethoven, and plainly expressed doubts of his genius.   This was a trait not at all worthy of a great man. To pull down a universally acknowledged genius to the level of one's own intelligence, is characteristic of small people.

Feeling thus, Tschaikóvsky purposely avoided meeting Tolstoy again, and even took a temporary aversion to *Anna Karénina*, though eventually he returned to his former admiration of Tolstoy's novels.

Tschaikóvsky was not aware of the reasons Tolstoy had for the unorthodox position he held on art generally and music in particular: reasons which it will be more in place to deal with later on, and which I have in fact already treated of at some length in a previous work, *Tolstoy and his Problems*.   Here let it suffice to say that there is plenty of evidence to show that Tolstoy can enjoy Beethoven, and enjoy even the works of Beethoven's last period, which are the ones he criticises.   There is, for instance, the episode with Mlle. Oberlender, which will be recounted later on, and we have his own statement in *What is Art?* :

I should mention that whatever other people understand of the productions of Beethoven's later period, I, being very susceptible to music, equally understand. For a long time I used to attune myself so as to delight in those shapeless improvisations which form the subject-matter of the works of Beethoven's later period ; but I had only to consider the question of art seriously, and to compare the impression I received from Beethoven's later works with those pleasant, clear, and strong musical impressions which are transmitted, for instance, by the melodies of Bach (his arias), Haydn, Mozart, Chopin (when his melodies are not overloaded with complications and ornamentation), and of Beethoven himself in his earlier period, and above all, with the impressions produced by folk-songs,—Italian, Norwegian, or Russian,—by the Hungarian *tzardas*, and other such simple, clear, and powerful music, and the obscure, almost unhealthy excitement from Beethoven's later pieces that I had artificially evoked in myself was destroyed.

His work among peasant children has convinced him that the normal human being possesses capacities for the enjoyment of art ; and that in most unexpected places the capacity to produce admirable art is now lying latent. That is why he sets up Brevity, Simplicity, and Sincerity as the criterions of art, and why he believes that folk-tales and folk-songs and folk-dances, the Gospel parables, such Old Testament stories as the history of Joseph, the Arabian Nights and the Christmas Carol ; and music such as the *tzardas*, the *Swanee River*, the *Old Hundredth*, and Bach's arias, are infinitely more important to the life and wellbeing of humanity than *King Lear* or the *Ninth Symphony*.

Tolstoy—who had boasted of not reading newspapers, and who had lived so detached from politics and the events of contemporary history—began at this time to feel keenly interested in a question closely connected with Russia's foreign policy.

Following the insurrection in Herzegovina, another had

broken out in Bulgaria in May 1876, but had been quickly suppressed by the Turks, who burnt some sixty-five villages; the Bashi-Bazouks committing unspeakable atrocities on the defenceless inhabitants. At the commencement of July, Servia and Montenegro declared war against Turkey; but, in spite of help rendered by numerous Russian volunteers, they were soon crushed by the Turks, and would have been completely at their mercy had not Russia, on 31st October, issued an ultimatum demanding an armistice, which Turkey conceded. On 10th November Alexander II made a speech in the Moscow Krémlin, in which he declared that he would act independently of the other powers unless satisfactory guarantees of reform were obtained forthwith from the Sultan. These events gradually led to the war which broke out between Russia and Turkey in April 1877.

Before this, however, in the letter of 13th November 1876, already quoted, Tolstoy wrote to Fet :

I went to Moscow to hear about the war. This whole affair agitates me greatly. It is well for those to whom it is clear; but I am frightened when I begin to reflect on all the complexity of the conditions amid which history is made, and how some Madame A.—with her vanity—becomes an indispensable cog in the whole machine !

The Russo-Turkish imbroglio led, early in 1877, to a split between Tolstoy and Katkóf. Tolstoy, at bottom and in his own original way, was certainly a reformer; and his alliance with Katkóf, who was quite reactionary, had always been rather like the yoking of an ox with an ass. At this time Katkóf was ardent for the liberation of the Slavs from Turkish tyranny, laudatory of those who volunteered for the war, and eager for the aggrandisement of Russia. Tolstoy, with his knowledge of the realities of war and his insight into the motives that actuate the men who fight, had his doubts about the heroic and self-sacrificing character of the volunteers and the purity of the patriotism of the press; and he expressed these doubts very plainly in some of the concluding chapters of *Anna Karénina*: as, for instance, where he makes Lévin say of 'the unanimity of the press':

'That's been explained to me: as soon as there's a war their incomes are doubled. So how can they help believing in the destinies of the people and the Slavonic races . . . and all the rest of it?'

The result was that when the final chapters of the novel were appearing in the *Russian Messenger* during the first months of 1877, Katkóf returned some of the MS. to Tolstoy with numerous corrections and a letter saying that he could not print it unless his corrections were accepted.

Tolstoy was furious that a journalist should dare to alter a single word in his book, and in reply sent a sharp letter to Katkóf, which resulted in a rupture. Tolstoy issued the last part of *Anna Karénina* separately in book form and not in the magazine, besides, of course, issuing the whole work in book form, as usual; and, in the May number of his *Russian Messenger*, Katkóf had to wind up the story as best he could, by giving a brief summary of the concluding part.

These events throw light on the following letter to Fet:

23 *March* 1877.

You can't imagine how glad I am to have your approval of my writings, dear Afanásy Afanásyevitch, and in general to receive your letter. You write that the *Russian Messenger* has printed some one else's poem, while your *Temptation* lies waiting. It is the dullest and deadest editorial office in existence. They have become terribly repulsive to me, not on my own account, but for the sake of others. . . .

My head is now better, but as it gets better it has to work that much harder. March and the beginning of April are the months when I work most, and I still continue to be under the delusion that what I am writing is very important, though I know that in a month's time I shall be ashamed to remember that I thought so. Have you noticed that a new line has now been started, and that everybody is writing poetry : very bad poetry, but they all do it. Some five new poets have introduced themselves to me lately.

The dislike Tolstoy felt of the artificially stimulated war fever (though, to do Katkóf and his friends justice, one must admit that no European Power during the last fifty years has had more justification for war than Russia had for intervening in defence of the Slav population of Turkey) was connected with the religious impulse that was beginning to reshape his whole life ; but it does not appear that he actually disapproved of the war after Russia had officially commenced it. What he primarily objected to was, that private individuals should push the Government into a war.

An influence which has left its traces in the latter part of *Anna Karénina* (particularly Part VII, Chap. 21) was Tolstoy's intercourse, about this time, with some of the most prominent followers of Lord Radstock, who frequently visited Russia and obtained considerable influence with a number of people in certain aristocratic Petersburg circles. One of these people, Count A. P. Bóbrinsky, who had been Minister of Ways of Communication, made Tolstoy's acquaintance and had animated religious discussions with him. Both Bóbrinsky and Colonel Páshkof (another very prominent Radstockite) for a while cherished hopes of winning Tolstoy over to Evangelical Christianity, and making him the spokesman of their cause. Tolstoy, as the event proved, was quite capable of throwing himself whole-heartedly into a religious movement ; but he needed a faith much more clear-cut than the scheme of Redemption by the blood of Jesus : one that faced the facts of life, dealt explicitly with the bread-and-butter problem, and told men how to regard the fact that some people have to overtax their strength without ever reaching an assured maintenance, while others have a superabundance provided for them from their birth without ever needing to do a stroke of work. His profound contempt for Evangelical doctrines flashed out twenty years later, in the 17th Chapter of Book II of *Resurrection*.

It was a little before this that Fet told Tolstoy the following story. Sauntering in a churchyard, he had come upon an inscription which touched him more than any epitaph he had ever read. The tombstone was in the form of an obelisk of plain grey sandstone. On one of its four sides were deeply cut the words:

Here is buried the body of the peasant girl Mary;
on another side:
Here also is buried an infant of the female sex.
On the side opposite the name of the deceased stood these words ill-spelt:
This, my dear, is the last adornment I can give thee;
and below stood the name of
Retired non-commissioned officer So-and-so.

In his next letter Tolstoy writes:

18 *October* 1876.
This, my dear, is the last adornment I can give thee is charming! I have told it twice, and each time my voice has broken with tears.

In Tolstoy's next letter to Fet, dated 11th January, we get a glimpse of one of the reasons that led this strenuous worker to prefer a country life:

1877

DEAR AFANÁSY AFANÁSYEVITCH,—One does not strike or cut off the head that owns its fault! I confess that I am quite at fault towards you. But truly, in Moscow I am in a condition of irresponsibility; my nerves are out of order, the hours turn to minutes, and as though on purpose, the people I do not want turn up and prevent my seeing those whom I do want.

Among the people whom in his search for truth Tolstoy did want to know, were some of the leading scientists of that day—a day when many men thought that Darwin had opened the gateway to a knowledge which would gradually solve the mysteries of life and death, the here and the hereafter. The great literary fame Tolstoy now enjoyed made it an easy matter to make such acquaintances.

One of the scientists he got to know, was a celebrated professor of Chemistry, A. M. Boutleróf, whom to his amazement he found to be much concerned with table-turning and spiritualism; occupations Tolstoy held in contempt.

A letter to Fet, dated 14th April, gives some inkling of what was going on in Tolstoy's mind at this time:

I value every letter of yours, especially such as this last! You would hardly believe how pleased I am at what you write 'On the existence of the Deity.' I agree with it all, and should like to say much about it, but cannot in a letter, and am too busy. It is the first time you have spoken to me about the Deity—God. And I have long been thinking unceasingly about that chief problem. Do not say that one cannot think about it! One not only can, but must! In all ages the best, the real people, have thought about it. And if we cannot think of it as they did, we must find out *how*. Have you read *Pensées de Pascal*—*i.e.* have you read it recently with a mature headpiece? When (which God grant) you come to see me, we will talk of many things, and I will give you that book. Were I free from my novel—of which the end is already in type and I am correcting the proofs—I would at once on receipt of your letter have come to you.

In the middle of this summer Tolstoy, bringing with him N. Stráhof, paid Fet an unexpected visit. The latter had at this time engaged as governess a Mlle. Oberlender, an excellent pianist, and in his *Recollections* he tells us that on this visit:

The Count, a sensitive esthete by nature, was greatly taken by the piano playing of Mlle. Oberlender. He sat down to play duets with her, and they played through almost the whole of Beethoven.

Fet quotes Tolstoy's comment on the lady's performance:

'When we were young, such pianists travelled across Europe

giving concerts. She reads any piece of music as you read poetry, finding just the suitable expression for each note.'

Towards the end of July, Tolstoy, accompanied by N. Stráhof, visited for the first time the Monastery of Óptin, which is situated in the Kaloúga Government, and is about 135 miles to the west of Yásnaya. A very prominent figure in the monastic world at that time was the *Staretz* Father Ambrose, with whom Tolstoy had some long conversations. Among others whose acquaintance Tolstoy made there, was a monk who had formerly been an officer in the Horse Guards. One of the most important of the works Tolstoy left for publication after his death, is a remarkable novel called *Father Sergius*, the hero of which is a man of the world who becomes a monk, acquires a reputation for sanctity, and then yields to temptation and ends as an outcast. His visits to the Óptin Monastery, which were repeated three times, supplied Tolstoy with material which many years later he utilised in that work.

At Óptin, Tolstoy had met his friend Prince Obolénsky, to whom on his return journey he paid a visit at the latter's estate of Beryósino. Here he renewed acquaintance with N. Rubinstein, who was staying with Obolénsky, and whose pianoforte playing he enjoyed intensely.

A visit which much interested Tolstoy was paid him about this time by an itinerant story-teller, expert in folk-lore, wielding beautifully the simple language of the people, such as Tolstoy loves and has utilised in his stories. He took down in writing some of this traveller's tales, and from them subsequently worked up into literary form *What Men Live By*, *The Three Hermits* (included in *Twenty-three Tales*), and some others. The root idea of *What Men Live By* is that of an angel sent by God to do penance on earth for a well-intentioned act of disobedience. It seems that it is one of the most widely disseminated of the world's legends, appearing and reappearing in the literature of many countries through many centuries.

In the latter part of 1877 a number of Turkish prisoners

of war were located in an abandoned sugar-factory between Toúla and Yásnaya. Tolstoy visited them there, and found that they were fairly well treated. Being himself greatly concerned about religion, he naturally talked to them on that subject, and was much impressed when he found that each of them had a copy of the Koran in his kit.

On 6th December another son, Andrew (Andréy), was born.

All through this year, amid bustle and activity of various kinds, spiritual problems continued to torment Tolstoy, and his physical health began to show signs of the strain. Here is a note to Fet, dated 2nd September:

Just now I am constantly out hunting and am busy arranging how to place our educational staff for the winter. I have been to Moscow looking for a teacher and a tutor. To-day I feel quite ill.

Nor did matters improve as the months went on, for on 27th January he again writes: 1878

Most unfortunately your suppositions, dear Afanásy Afanásyevitch, are wrong. Not only am I not at work, but the reason I failed to answer you was because I have been ill all this time. Lately I have even been in bed for some days. A chill in various forms: teeth and side, and the result is that time goes by—my best time—and I do no work.

Then follows a touch showing how, in many matters, his wife's mind was still attuned to his own, though she was not sharing his spiritual struggles, and in the matter of the education of the children there was already some disagreement between them:

On reading it I said to my wife, 'Fet's poem is charming, but there is one word that is wrong.' She was nursing and bustling about at the time; but at tea, having quieted down, she took up the poem to read, and at once pointed out the words 'as the Gods'—which I considered bad.

On 25th March 1878 he writes to Fet:

Last week, after seventeen years' absence, I went to Petersburg to purchase some land in Samára from General B. . . .

2 B

There I met a pair of Orlóf Generals who made me shudder: it was just as though one were standing between two sets of rails with goods trains passing. To enter into the minds of these Generals, I had to recall the rare days of drunkenness I have experienced, or the days of my very earliest childhood.

After completing *Anna Karénina* Tolstoy again took up *The Decembrists*, which he had put aside in favour of *War and Peace* fourteen years before. As already mentioned, a second cousin of Tolstoy's mother, Prince S. G. Volkónsky, had been a prominent Decembrist; and Tolstoy had at his disposal a number of family diaries and journals throwing much light on the subject of that conspiracy. While in Petersburg he made personal acquaintance with some of the survivors of the movement, and also applied to the Commandant of the Petropávlof Fortress—who happened to be an officer under whom he had served in the Crimea—for permission to see the Alexis dungeons, in which the Decembrists had been confined. The Commandant received him very politely, allowed him to see over other parts of the fortress, but told him that, though any one could enter the dungeons, only three persons in the whole Empire—the Emperor, the Commandant, and the Chief of the Gendarmes—having once entered them, could again leave them.

Finally, after writing three fragments of it, Tolstoy abandoned this novel, to which he had devoted much time. The subject was one he could hardly have dealt with frankly without getting into trouble with the Censor; and he had been refused permission to study the State Archives; but in the following passage Behrs gives another, and a curiously characteristic, reason for Tolstoy's decision:

He affirmed that the Decembrist insurrection was a result of the influence of French nobles, a large number of whom had emigrated to Russia after the French Revolution. As tutors in aristocratic families, they educated the whole Russian nobility, which explains the fact that many of the Decembrists were Catholics. The belief that the movement was due to foreign influence, and was not a purely national one, sufficed to prevent Tolstoy from sympathising with it.

Another letter to Fet again shows the direction in which Tolstoy's mind was working:

6 *April* 1878.

I have received your delightful and long letter, dear Afanásy Afanásyevitch. Do not praise me. Really you see in me too much good, and in others too much bad. One thing in me is good: that I understand you and therefore love you. But though I love you as you are, I am always angry with you for this, that 'Martha is anxious about many things; but one thing is needful.' And in you that one thing is very strong, but somehow you disdain it and are more concerned about arranging a billiard room. Don't suppose that I refer to poems: though I expect them to come too! But it is not of them I speak; they will come in spite of the billiards; I am speaking of a conception of the world which would make it unnecessary to be angry at the stupidity of mortals. Were you and I to be pounded together in a mortar and moulded into two people, we should make a capital pair. But at present you are so attached to the things of this life, that should they some day fail you, it will go hard with you; while I am so indifferent to them, that life becomes uninteresting, and I depress others by an eternal pouring 'from void into vacuum'! Do not suppose that I have gone mad; I am merely out of sorts, but hope you will love me though I be black.

The prolonged mental struggle through which Tolstoy passed with great suffering during the years 1874-78, was quite evident to those about him, at least from 1876 onward. Not merely did he go regularly to church, and shut himself up in his study morning and evening to pray, but his former high spirits subsided, and his desire to become meek and humble was plainly noticeable. One result of his altered attitude was, that he felt keenly that it was wrong to have an enemy. Accordingly he wrote Tourgénef to that effect, and held out to him the right hand of friendship.

To this Tourgénef replied:

Paris, 8 *May* 1878.

Dear Leo Nikoláyevitch,—I only to-day received your letter, addressed *poste-restante*. It gladdened and touched me very much. With the greatest readiness will I renew our former friendship, and I warmly press the hand you hold out to me. You are quite right in supposing me to have no hostile feelings towards you. If ever they existed they have long since disappeared, and the recollection of you only remains as of a man to whom I am sincerely attached, and of a writer whose first steps it was my good fortune to be the first to hail, and each new work from whom has always aroused in me the liveliest interest. I am heartily glad of the cessation of the misunderstandings that arose between us.

I hope this summer to be in the Government of Orlóf, and in that case we shall of course see one another. Till then, I wish you all that is good, and once more press your hand in friendship.

On 13th June, on the point of starting for Samára with the elder children and their tutor, Tolstoy writes to Fet:

I have seldom so enjoyed a summer as this year, but a week ago I caught cold and fell ill, and only to-day have I come to life again.

Somewhat later in the summer the Countess, with the younger children, joined her husband in Samára.

Hardly were the Tolstoys back from Samára before Tourgénef wrote from Moscow that he would be in Toúla on the following Monday, 7th August. Tolstoy, accompanied by his brother-in-law, drove thither to meet him, and brought him to Yásnaya, where he passed a couple of days. Both writers were delighted to feel that their seventeen-year disagreement was ended; and the Countess, who when a girl had known Tourgénef well, was equally pleased to welcome him to the house.

A lady who was there at the time, tells us that the two writers spent much of their time in philosophic and religious conversation in Tolstoy's study, but:

When they came out into the sitting-room their conversation

became general and took a different turn. Tourgénef told with pleasure of the villa Bougival which he had just bought near Paris, and of its comfort and arrangements, saying, 'We have built a charming conservatory, costing ten thousand francs,' and ' we ' did so-and-so and so-and-so, meaning by ' we,' the Viardot family and himself.

'Of an evening we often play *vint* [a game similar to bridge] —do you ?' he asked Tolstoy.

'No, we never play cards,' replied the Count, and turned the conversation to another topic.

Knowing that he was fond of chess, the Countess Tolstoy asked him to play a game with her eldest son, a lad of fifteen, saying, ' He will all his life remember having played with Tourgénef.'

Tourgénef condescendingly agreed, and began a game, while continuing to talk to us.

' In Paris I often used to play chess and was considered a good player. They called me *le chevalier de pion*. I am fond of pawns. . . . Do you know the new phrase now in fashion among the French—*vieux jeu ?* Whatever you say, a Frenchman replies, " *Vieux jeu !* " '

' Eh ! but one must not joke with you,' he exclaimed suddenly, turning to his youthful opponent. 'You have all but done for me.'

And he began to play carefully, and only won the game with difficulty, for young Tolstoy really played chess excellently.

At evening tea Tourgénef told how he had played the part of a satyr at Mme Viardot's private theatricals, and how some of the audience had gazed at him with amazement. We knew that he had himself written the piece (a sort of operetta) for those theatricals, and knew also that Russians, both abroad and at home, disapproved of his playing the fool for Mme Viardot's amusement ; and we all felt uncomfortable. In telling it he seemed to be trying to justify himself, but he soon passed on to another theme, and we breathed more freely.

He had the gift of words and spoke readily and smoothly, but seemed to prefer narrating to conversing. He told us of his confinement in the Hauptwerk of the Spássky Police-station in Petersburg, for his article on the death of Gógol, and he described how dull it was. . . .

Tolstoy also narrated, and I liked his stories better: they were more strongly sketched, often humorous, and always original. In them much was simple, unexpected and touching. . . . I. S. Aksákof used to say, with reference to Tolstoy's gigantic power, that he had 'a bear-like talent,' but I will add that his soul is as meek 'as a dove,' and as enthusiastic as a youth; and that the union of those two qualities explains the new direction he has since taken, a direction which so distressed Tourgénef.

An hour before midnight Tourgénef rose.

'It is time for me to go to the station,' said he.

We all rose. The railway station was one-and-a-half miles away, and Count Leo Nikoláyevitch drove with him, to see him off.

Behrs also writes of the same visit:

At dinner Tourgénef told many stories, and to the delight of the younger folk mimicked not only persons, but animals also. Thus, placing one hand under the other, he depicted a fowl waddling in the soup, and then imitated a hunting dog at a loss. As I listened to him and watched his tricks I couldn't help thinking that he evidently inherited something of the talent for which one of his ancestors under Peter the Great enjoyed no little fame.

This was the last summer Behrs, now a young man of twenty-three, passed with Tolstoy before taking up official work in the Caucasus. His evidence fully supports that of others who have seen Tolstoy in contact with children, peasants or native races: to all of these Tolstoy extends his charm of comprehension, consideration, and sympathy.

Whenever Tolstoy went out with his gun and his dogs, Behrs used to accompany him; and together they would ride twenty-four miles from Yásnaya to visit Count Sergius Tolstoy at Pirogóvo. Leo Tolstoy took his brother-in-law on these visits, Behrs says, 'for my sake, if not for his own, since he knew what pleasure it gave me to be with him.' The remark he made when he heard that Behrs had obtained an official appointment in the Caucasus is characteristic: 'You are too late for the Caucasus. The whole country already stinks of officials.' Characteristic too of the feeling Tolstoy inspires among those who know him most intimately, is Behrs's concluding remark: 'I at least am aware of nothing in his life that needs to be concealed.'

At the beginning of September Tourgénef, on his return from his estate, again visited Yásnaya, but he arrived at an unfortunate time, when there was illness in the house, and he paid but a short visit.

One sees by a letter to Fet on 5th September that Tolstoy still found himself unable to be quite intimate with his fellow novelist:

Tourgénef on his return journey came to see us and was glad to receive your letter. He is still the same, and we know the degree of nearness possible between us.

I have a terrible desire to write something, but feel a depressing doubt whether this is a false or a true appetite.

The last sentence must refer to the *Confession*, most of which was not written till the next year.

In October he again wrote to Fet:

I do not know how or in what spirit to begin to write to you, dear Afanásy Afanásyevitch; any way, there are no words for it but, 'I am to blame, I am to blame, and I am altogether to blame!' Though it is always superfluous for apologisers to explain their reasons, I will yet write mine because they are true and explain my condition. For a month past, if not more, I have been living amid the fumes not of external occurrences (on the contrary we are by ourselves, living quietly) but of what is going on inside: something I know not how to name. I go out shooting, read, reply to questions put to me, eat, and sleep, but can do nothing, not even write a letter, a score of which have collected.

Apparently while in bad spirits, he wrote to Tourgénef asking him not to refer to his (Tolstoy's) writings—for the latter replies on 15th October, saying: 'I am glad you are all physically well, and hope the " mental sickness " of which you write has now passed.' He then continues :

Although you ask me not to speak of your writings, I must still remark that it has never happened to me to laugh at you ' even a little.' Some of your things pleased me very much; others did not please me at all; while others again, such as *The Cossacks* for instance, afforded me great pleasure and excited my wonder. But what ground was there for laughter? I thought you had long since got rid of such 'reflexive' feelings. Why are they current only among authors, and not among musicians, painters, and other artists? Probably because in literary work more of that part of the soul is exposed, which it is not quite convenient to show. But at our (already mature) age as authors, it is time we were accustomed to it.

This displeased Tolstoy, who in his next letter to Fet expressed his vexation with Tourgénef who, I imagine, had not intended to give offence :

22 *November* 1878.

DEAR AFANÁSY AFANÁSYEVITCH,—I will go to Moscow and have ' I am to blame' printed on my notepaper. But I don't think I am to blame for not replying to the letter in which you promised to come and see us. I remember my joy at that news, and that I replied immediately. If not, still please don't punish me, but come. . . .

Yesterday I received a letter from Tourgénef; and do you know, I have decided that it will be better to 'keep further away from him and from sin' [A common Russian saying]. He is an unpleasant sort of quarrel-maker.

My congratulations to you on your birthday. I will not in future omit to congratulate you on the 23rd, and hope not to forget it for the next dozen times. That will be enough for either of us. *Au revoir !*

Fet was destined to live four years beyond the span Tolstoy allotted him, and Tolstoy himself is still with us, though more than thirty years have passed since that letter was written ; and what strenuous years they have been !

How he has wrestled with life's greatest problems one after another, and how he has flung down before the world his opinions (right, wrong, or motley) on dogmatic theology, Christ's Christianity, religion in general, economic and social problems, famine, the employment of violence, war, conscription, Government, patriotism, the sex problem, art, science, food-reform and the use of stimulants and narcotics, besides producing a series of simple stories for the people, as well as more complex ones for the rest of society, three plays, one great novel, and a stream of weighty and interesting essays and letters which have poured forth from Yásnaya in an increasing stream as the years went by ; not to mention works kept back for posthumous publication, at the mention of which the literary world pricks up its ears!

On 1st October 1878 Tourgénef wrote to Fet from Bougival, again saying that he intended to translate *The Cossacks* into French, and adding, 'It will give me great pleasure to assist in acquainting the French public with the best story that has been written in our language.'

In another letter from Bougival in December, he remarked :

I was very glad to come together with Tolstoy, and I spent three pleasant days with him; his whole family are very sympathetic, and his wife is charming. He has grown very quiet and has matured. His name begins to gain European celebrity : we Russians have long known that he has no rivals.

The course of the story has swept me a little past Tolstoy's fiftieth birthday—the point at which I intended to close this first part of my work. Besides giving some brief survey of his writings during his first twenty-five years of authorship, all that now remains is to give a summary of that remarkable work, his *Confession*, which shows us vividly, though with some amount of involuntary artistic heightening, what had been going on in his mind and soul from 1874 to 1879, the year in which it was written.

By way of brief preface to his *Confession*, it will be in place to say a few words about two different tendencies which, each in its own way, influenced Tolstoy. On the one hand there was the religious life of the people, with all its Medieval traditions. Tolstoy had only to go a short walk from his house to reach the highroad, on which pilgrims going afoot to the shrines of the Saints could always be met; and he had many a conversation with these pilgrims at the rest-house they frequented. Among them there were many to whom the things of this world were certainly less precious than obedience to the will of God as they understood it; and Tolstoy's stories show us how closely he observed these people, and how near some of them came to his soul. On the other hand he was influenced by the quite modern and very remarkable movement that was at this time beginning to make itself felt in Russia; a movement having its roots in conditions of life which greatly disturbed Tolstoy's own mind, and which took as one of its watchwords the motto 'Towards the People'—a sentiment quite in harmony with his own attitude.

In 1875 public attention was aroused by the trial of the Dolgoúshin group of propagandists; and the trial of 'The Moscow 50,' in March 1877, revealed the fact that a number of girls of wealthy families were voluntarily leading the life of factory hands working fourteen hours a day in overcrowded factories, that they might come into touch with working people, to teach them, and to carry on a social and political propaganda among them. Then followed the historic trial of 'The 193' in 1878.

These and many other indications showed that in spite of the repressive measures of the Government, a steadily increasing number of Russians felt (what Tolstoy also felt strongly) that the existing order of society results in the mass of the people having to live in conditions of blighting ignorance and grinding poverty; while the parasitic minority who live in plenty and sometimes in extravagant superfluity, render no service at all equivalent to the cost of their maintenance. The mere statement that those who had received an education thanks to the work of the masses, owe service to the masses in return, sufficed to rouse to action some of the young men and women of that day. They left their wealthy homes, lived the simplest lives, ran fearful risks, and according to their lights—sometimes not very clear ones—devoted themselves to the service of the people.

While this was going on around him, a man with such a temperament as Tolstoy's, could not be at rest.

Already in 1875 Mihaylóvsky had published a remarkable series of articles on *The Right and Left Hand of Count Tolstoy*, in which he pointed out that that author's works reveal the clash of contrary ideals and tendencies in the writer's soul, and that especially his educational articles contain ideas quite in conflict with certain tendencies noticeable in *War and Peace*. With remarkable prevision Mihaylóvsky predicted an inevitable crisis in Tolstoy's life, and added :

One asks oneself what such a man is to do, and how he is to live? . . . I think an ordinary man in such a position would end by suicide or drunkenness ; but a man of worth will seek for other issues—and of these there are several.

One of these he suggested would be, to write for the people (Tolstoy's *Readers* had already been published) or to write so as to remind 'Society' that its pleasures and amusements are not those of the mass of mankind, and thus to arouse the latent feelings of justice in some who now forget the debt they owe to their fellows.

In fact, the trial of 'The 193' or the movement from which it arose, had a vital, though indirect, influence on Tolstoy, who at this time had engaged V. I. Alexéyef, a graduate of Petersburg University, as mathematical master for his son. Alexéyef had been a member of the Tchaykóvsky group which carried on an educational propaganda in elementary Socialism in the early '70's. The activities of this group were so restricted, and they were so hampered by the police, that some of its members, feeling a need of freer activity, migrated to Kansas, where for two years they carried on an agricultural colony. Dissensions arose among them, and their experiment failed. Alexéyef returned to Russia; Tchaykóvsky settled in England, where he spent many years, and only returned to Russia after the amnesty of 1905, to be again arrested and to spend more than a year in prison awaiting a trial which ended in his acquittal. Tolstoy noticed that Alexéyef was a man who shaped his life in accord with his beliefs, and he respected him accordingly, and through him made acquaintance with some of the best representatives of the immature Socialist movement then brewing in Russia. We have here a remarkable example of the indirect way in which thoughts influence the world. Auguste Comte wrote a philosophy. Having filtered through the minds of G. H. Lewes and J. S. Mill, it reached Nicholas Tchaykóvsky when he was a schoolboy of fourteen in the Seventh Gymnasium in Petersburg. 'It fascinated me to such an extent,' says he in the reminiscences contributed to G. H. Perris's interesting book, *Russia in Revolution,* 'that, while sitting in school, I longed to get back to our lodgings and to my chosen reading. The more I progressed, the more I was absorbed. This study powerfully affected my mind and systematised my ideas.' A few years later Tchaykóvsky, having read much meanwhile, formed his group, which sowed the seeds of changes yet to come. Progress, however, was very slow, and he felt 'the ineffectiveness of ordinary political and socialistic propaganda among a deeply religious peasantry, still hopeful of benefits from above.' This forced him to reconsider the whole situation. 'I met,' adds he, 'some friends with whom I began to work upon the rather Utopian idea of formulating a new religion, and, for the sake of more effective experiment, we were soon compelled to transfer ourselves with this stupendous mission, to the steppes of Kansas.'

Wishing to transform society, Tchaykóvsky had seen the need of some systematic outlook on life—'a new religion,' in fact. Dissatisfied with his own outlook on life, Tolstoy was seeking a new religion, and when he found it, it led him to demand great changes in society. The mature novelist and the young propagandist, who have never met in the flesh, had therefore much in common; though Tolstoy dislikes the works of Comte and Mill, which had done so much for Tchaykóvsky, and can hardly speak of them with tolerance (except Mill's *Autobiography*, which interests him). Detesting the methods of violence to which those who succeeded Tchaykóvsky felt themselves driven, Tolstoy could still not doubt the sincerity of the faith that actuated most of them; for they had all to lose and nothing to gain by joining the revolutionary movement. Sophie Peróvsky, one of 'the 193' (subsequently hanged in Petersburg for taking part in the assassination of Alexander II), was the daughter of the Governor-General of that city, and was a niece of the Minister of Education. Demetrius Lisogoúb, a landowner, devoted his whole fortune of some £40,000 to the movement; and was hanged in Odessa. Prince Peter Kropótkin risked his all to give lessons to workmen; and escaped abroad, having lost position, fortune, and the right to live in his native land. Tolstoy, an older man, with a strong character and definite views of his own on many points, could not join the Socialist movement, but that he was influenced by it is beyond doubt.

The state of Russian life was indeed such that men of sensitive consciences could not be at rest (as, indeed, when and where in the wide world can they?), and the work Tolstoy had already done, marked him out as one in whose soul the struggle which was moving others, would assuredly be fought out strenuously. No one however, and certainly not he himself, as yet knew what effect that crisis would have upon him, or what his course of life would be in the years that were to come.

CHIEF AUTHORITIES FOR CHAPTER X

Besides books mentioned in last chapter, information relating to this period is contained in a number of magazines and newspaper articles, of which the following are the most important.

On the Education dispute see :

Moskov. Eparhial. Ved., October 1874.
Rousskiya Vedomosti, 1894, No. 31.
N. K. Mihaylovsky's *Zapiski Profana*, and
E. Schuyler in *Rousskaya Starina*, October 1870, and in *Scribner's Magazine*, May and June, 1889.

About Samara Famine, etc., see :
A. S. Prougavin in *Obrazovaniye*, Nov. 1902.

On Tourgenef's visit to Yasnaya see :
Tobolskiya Goubern. Vedomosti, 1893, No. 26.

The *Rousskoye Obozreniye*, 1896, contains a letter from Tolstoy to Fet.
The *Vestnik Evropy*, June 1904, contains M. Zaharina's *Vospominaniya gr. A. A. Tolstaya*.

Zhisn P. I. Tschaikovskavo.

Pervoe Sobranie pisem Tourgeneva, 1840-1883 ; Petersburg, 1884.
P. A. Sergeyenko in *Niva*, No. 8, 1906.

CHAPTER XI

CONFESSION

What is the meaning of life? Thoughts of suicide. The
traveller in the well. Schopenhauer and Solomon. Four
ways of meeting the problem. The peasants' answer. The
finite linked to the infinite. Faith essential. Faiths that
obscure. Why life seemed meaningless. The search for
God. The infallibility of the Church. Rites and prayers.
Communion. The lives of the Saints. The Orthodox and the
Sectarians. War. The need to unravel truth from error.

THIS chapter is a summary of Tolstoy's *Confession*,[1] or
'Introduction to a Criticism of Dogmatic Theology and to
an Investigation of the Christian Teachings,' as the Russian
title ran, from the first pages of which I have already quoted
freely in the preceding chapters. I have kept as much to
Tolstoy's words as possible, but having to condense, I have
not only omitted much, but have also paraphrased some
passages to avoid repetition. The plan I have adopted,
since this is a *Life* and not a theological treatise, has been
to cut down to a mere skeleton the abstract argument of
Tolstoy's *Confession*, while giving almost in full what he
says about his own experience.

Many men, at the age of puberty, or at any rate while
their minds were still maturing, have experienced the change
known as 'Conversion.' That is to say, they have more or
less suddenly turned round and looked at life from a fresh

---

[1] It is strange that Tolstoy's *Confession* has not yet been put into English
at all reproducing the vigorous simplicity of the original. There is, I think,
nothing better than the threepenny edition issued by the *Free Age Press*
under the title, *How I Came to Believe*; and on looking at that to see if I
could quote from it, I find that it is not good enough.

point of view: what in their nature had been latent or secondary has become dominant and primary, and things temporal and material have become subordinate to things spiritual and eternal.

What is unusual about the story of Tolstoy's conversion is that it came so late in life and so gradually, and that the intellect played so large a part in it.

Some men take to religion at the prompting of the heart, others at the prompting of the brain; and Tolstoy belongs to the latter category, not from lack of heart, but because strong as are his emotions, his intellectual power is stronger still.

His *Confession* was written in 1879, and in it he says:

Five years ago something very strange began to happen to me: At first I experienced moments of perplexity and arrest of life, as though I did not know how to live or what to do; and I felt lost and became dejected. But this passed, and I went on living as before. Then these moments of perplexity began to recur oftener and oftener, and always in the same form. They were always expressed by the questions: What's it for? What does it lead to?

At first it seemed to me that these were aimless and irrelevant questions. I thought that it was all well known, and that if I should ever wish to deal with the solution, it would not cost me much effort; just at present I had no time for it, but when I wanted to I should be able to find the answer. The questions, however, began to repeat themselves frequently, and more and more insistently to demand replies; and like drops of ink always falling on one place, they ran together into one black blot.

That occurred which happens to every one sickening with a mortal internal disease. At first trivial signs of indisposition appear, to which the sick man pays no attention; then these signs reappear more and more often, and merge into one uninterrupted period of suffering. The suffering increases, and before the sick man can look round, what he took for a mere indisposition has already become more important to him than anything else in the world—it is death!

That was what happened to me. I understood that it was no casual indisposition, but something very important, and that if these questions constantly repeated themselves, it would be necessary to answer them. And I tried to do so. The questions seemed such stupid simple childish questions; but as soon as I touched them and tried to solve them, I at once became convinced (1) that they are not childish and stupid, but the most important and the deepest of life's questions; and (2) that, try as I would, I could not solve them. Before occupying myself with my Samára estate, the education of my son, or the writing of a book, I had to know *why* I was doing it. As long as I did not know why, I could do nothing, and could not live. Amid the thoughts of estate management which greatly occupied me at that time, the question would suddenly occur to me: 'Well, you will have 16,000 acres of land in Samára Government and 300 horses, and what next?' . . . And I was quite disconcerted, and did not know what to think. Or, when considering my plans for the education of my children, I would say to myself: What for? Or when considering how the peasants might be prosperous, I suddenly said to myself, 'But what business is it of mine?' Or when thinking of the fame my works would bring me, I said to myself, 'Very well: you will be more famous than Gógol or Poúshkin or Shakespear or Molière, or than all the writers in the world—and what will it lead to?' And I could find no reply at all. The questions would not wait, they had to be answered at once, and if I did not answer them, it was impossible to live. But there was no answer.

I felt that what I had been standing on had broken down, and that I had nothing left under my feet. What I had lived on, no longer existed; and I had nothing left to live on.

My life came to a standstill. I could breathe, eat, drink and sleep, and I could not help doing these things; but there was no life, for there were no wishes the fulfilment of which I could consider reasonable. . . . Had a fairy come and offered to fulfil my desires, I should not have known

2 c

what to ask. . . . If in moments of intoxication I felt something which I cannot call a wish, but a habit left by former wishes, in sober moments I knew this to be a delusion, and that there is really nothing to wish for. I could not even wish to know the truth, for I guessed in what it consisted. The truth was that life is meaningless. I had, as it were, lived, lived, and walked, walked, till I had come to a precipice and saw clearly that there was nothing ahead of me but destruction. It was impossible to stop, impossible to go back, and impossible to close my eyes or avoid seeing that there was nothing ahead but suffering and real death—complete annihilation.

It had come to this, that I, a healthy, fortunate man, felt I could no longer live: some irresistible power impelled me to rid myself one way or other of life. I cannot say I *wished* to kill myself. The power which drew me away from life was stronger, fuller, and more widespread than any mere wish.

The thought of self-destruction now came to me as naturally as thoughts of how to improve my life had come formerly. And it was so seductive that I had to be wily with myself, lest I should carry it out too hastily: ' If I cannot unravel matters, there will always be time.' And it was then that I, a man favoured by fortune, hid a cord from myself, lest I should hang myself from the crosspiece of the partition in my room, where I undressed alone every evening; and I ceased to go out shooting with a gun, lest I should be tempted by so easy a way of ending my life. I did not myself know what I wanted: I feared life, desired to escape from it; yet still hoped something of it.

And all this befell me at a time when all around me I had what is considered complete good fortune. I was not yet fifty; I had a good wife who loved me and whom I loved; good children, and a large estate which without much effort on my part improved and increased. I was respected by my relations and acquaintances more than at any previous time. I was praised by others, and without much self-deception could consider that my name was famous. And

TOLSTOY'S LIBRARY.

(FORMERLY HIS STUDY AND DRESSING-ROOM.) SHOWING THE WOODEN CROSS-PIECE
FROM WHICH HE WISHED TO HANG HIMSELF

far from being insane or mentally unwell,—on the contrary I enjoyed a strength of mind and body such as I have seldom met with among men of my kind: physically I could keep up with the peasants at mowing, and mentally I could work for eight to ten hours at a stretch without experiencing any ill results from such exertion. . . .

My mental condition presented itself to me in this way: my life is a stupid and spiteful joke some one has played on me. Though I did not acknowledge a 'some one' who created me, yet that form of representation—that some one had played an evil and stupid joke on me by placing me in the world—was the form of expression that suggested itself most naturally to me.

Involuntarily it appeared to me that there, somewhere, is some one who amuses himself by watching how I live for thirty or forty years: learning, developing, maturing in body and mind, and how—having now with matured mental powers reached the summit of life, from which it all lies before me, I stand on that summit—like an arch-fool—seeing clearly that there is nothing in life, and that there has been and will be nothing. And he is amused. . . .

But whether that 'some one' laughing at me existed or not, I was none the better off. I could give no reasonable meaning to any single action, or to my whole life. I was only surprised that I could have avoided understanding this from the very beginning—it has been so long known to all. To-day or to-morrow sickness and death will come (they have come already) to those I love or to me; nothing will remain but stench and worms. Sooner or later my deeds, whatever they may have been, will be forgotten, and I shall not exist. Then why go on making any effort? . . . How can man fail to see this? And how go on living? That is what is surprising! One can only live when one is intoxicated with life; as soon as one is sober it is impossible not to see that it is all a mere fraud and a stupid fraud! That is precisely what it is: there is nothing either amusing or witty about it; it is simply cruel and stupid.

There is an Eastern fable, told long ago, of a traveller overtaken on a plain by an enraged beast. Escaping from the beast he leaps into a dry well, but sees at the bottom of the well a dragon that has opened its jaws to swallow him. And the unfortunate man, not daring to climb out lest he should be destroyed by the enraged beast, and not daring to leap to the bottom of the well lest he should be eaten by the dragon, seizes a twig growing in a crack in the well and clings to it. His hands are growing weaker, and he feels he will soon have to resign himself to the destruction that awaits him above or below; but still he clings on; and he sees that two mice, a black and a white one, go regularly round and round the stem of the twig to which he is clinging, and gnaw at it. And soon the twig itself will snap and he will fall into the dragon's jaws. The traveller sees this and knows that he will inevitably perish; but while still hanging he looks around and finds some drops of honey on the leaves of the twig and reaches them with his tongue and licks them. So I too clung to the twig of life, knowing that the dragon of death was inevitably awaiting me, ready to tear me to pieces; and I could not understand why I had fallen into such torment. I tried to lick the honey which formerly consoled me; but the honey no longer gave me pleasure, and the white and black mice of day and night gnawed at the branch by which I hung. I saw the dragon clearly, and the honey no longer tasted sweet. And this is not a fable, but the real unanswerable truth intelligible to all.

The deception of the joys of life which formerly allayed my terror of the dragon, now no longer deceives me. No matter how much I may be told: 'You cannot understand the meaning of life, so do not think about it, but live,' I can no longer do it: I have already done it too long. I cannot now help seeing day and night going round and bringing me to death. That is all I see, for that alone is true. All else is false.

The two drops of honey which diverted my eyes from

the cruel truth longer than the rest : my love of family, and of writing—art as I called it—were no longer sweet to me.

Family . . . said I to myself. But my family : wife and children—are also human. They too are placed as I am : they must either live in a lie, or see the terrible truth. Why should they live? Why should I love them, guard them, bring them up, or watch them ? That they may come to the despair that I feel, or else be stupid ? Loving them, I cannot hide the truth from them : each step in knowledge leads them to that truth. And the truth is death.

' Art, poetry ? ' . . . Under the influence of success and the praise of men, I had long assured myself that this was a thing one could do though death was drawing near— death which destroys all things, including my work and its remembrance ; but I soon saw that that too was a fraud. It was plain to me that art is an adornment to life, an allurement to life. But life had lost its attraction for me ; so how could I attract others? As long as I was not living my own life, but was borne on the waves of some other life— as long as I believed that life had a meaning, though one I could not express—the reflection of life in poetry and art of all kinds, afforded me pleasure : it was pleasant to look at life in the mirror of art. But when I began to seek the meaning of life, and felt the necessity of living on my own account, that mirror became for me unnecessary, superfluous, ridiculous, or painful. I could no longer soothe myself with what I saw in the mirror, for what I saw was, that my position was stupid and desperate. It was all very well to enjoy the sight when in the depth of my soul I believed that my life had a meaning. Then the play of lights— comic, tragic, touching, beautiful and terrible—in life, amused me. But when I knew life to be meaningless and terrible, the play in the mirror could no longer amuse me. No sweetness of honey could be sweet to me when I saw the dragon, and saw the mice gnawing away my support.

Nor was that all. Had I simply understood that life has no meaning, I could have borne it quietly, knowing that

that was my lot. But I could not satisfy myself with that. Had I been like a man living in a wood from which he knows there is no exit, I could have lived; but I was like one lost in a wood who, horrified at having lost his way, rushes about, wishing to find the road, yet knows that each step he takes confuses him more and more; and still cannot help rushing about.

It was indeed terrible. And to rid myself of the terror, I wished to kill myself. I experienced terror at what awaited me—knew that that terror was even worse than the position I was in; but still I could not patiently await the end. However convincing the argument might be that, in any case, some vessel in my heart would give way, or something would burst and all would be over, I could not patiently await that end. The horror of darkness was too great, and I wished to free myself from it as quickly as possible by noose or bullet. That was the feeling which drew me most strongly towards suicide.

.   .   .   .   .   .

' But perhaps I have overlooked something, or misunderstood something ? It cannot be that this condition of despair is natural to man ! ' thought I, and as a perishing man seeks safety, I sought some way of escape.

I sought everywhere; and thanks to a life spent in learning, and thanks also to the relations I had with the scholarly world, I had access to scientists and scholars in all branches of knowledge, and they readily showed me all their knowledge, not only in books, but also in conversation, so that I had at my disposal all that knowledge has to say on this question of life. . . .

The question which at the age of fifty brought me to the verge of suicide, was the simplest of questions lying in the soul of every man, from the foolish child to the wisest elder : it was a question without answering which one cannot live, as I had found by experience. It was, What will come of what I am doing to-day or shall do to-morrow—What will come of my whole life ?

Differently expressed, the question is : Why should I live, why wish for anything, or do anything? It can also be expressed thus : Is there any meaning in life, that the inevitable death awaiting one, does not destroy? All human knowledge I found divided into two kinds. One kind, such as chemistry and mathematics and the exact sciences, did not deal with my question. They were interesting, attractive, and wonderfully definite, but made no attempt to solve the question; while on the other hand the speculative sciences, culminating in metaphysics, dealt with the question, but supplied no satisfactory answer.

Where philosophy does not lose sight of the essential question, its answer is always one and the same : an answer given by Socrates, Schopenhauer, Solomon and Buddha.

'We approach truth only inasmuch as we depart from life,' said Socrates when preparing for death. 'For what do we who love truth, strive after in life? To free ourselves from the body, and from all the evil that is caused by the body! If so, then how can we fail to be glad when death comes to us?'

'The wise man seeks death all his life, and therefore does not fear death.'

And Schopenhauer also says that life is an evil; and Solomon (or whoever wrote the works attributed to him) says :

'Vanity of vanities, all is vanity. What profit hath man of all his labour under the sun? . . . There is no remembrance of former things, neither shall there be any remembrance of things that are to come, with those that shall come after. . . .

'Therefore I hated life, because the work that is wrought under the sun is grievous to me ; for all is vanity and vexation of spirit.'

And Sakya Muni when he learnt what age and sickness and death are, could find no consolation in life, and decided that life is the greatest of evils; and he devoted all the strength of his soul to free himself from it, and to free others; and to do this so that even after death life shall not be renewed any more, but be completely destroyed at its very roots. So speaks all the wisdom of India.

These then are the direct replies that human wisdom gives, when it replies to the question of life:

'The life of the body is an evil and a lie. Therefore the destruction of the life of the body is a blessing, and we should desire it,' says Socrates.

'Life is that which should not be—an evil; and the passage into Nothingness is the only good in life,' says Schopenhauer.

'All that is in the world: folly and wisdom and riches and poverty and mirth and grief—are vanity and emptiness. Man dies and nothing is left of him. And that is stupid,' says Solomon.

'To live in the consciousness of the inevitability of suffering, of becoming enfeebled, of old age and of death, is impossible—we must free ourselves from life, from all possible life,' says Buddha.

And what these strong minds said, has been said and thought and felt by millions upon millions of people like them. And I have thought it and felt it.

One cannot deceive oneself. It is all—vanity! Happy is he who has not been born: death is better than life, and one must free oneself from life.

Then I began to consider the lives of the men of my own kind; and I found that they met the problem in one or other of four ways.

The first way was that of ignorance. Some people—mostly women, or very young or very dull people—have not yet understood the question of life; but I, having understood it, could not again shut my eyes.

The second way was that of the Epicureans, expressed by Solomon when he said: 'Then I commended mirth, because a man hath no better thing under the sun, than to eat, and to drink, and to be merry.'

That is the way in which the majority of people of

our circle make life possible for themselves. Their circumstances furnish them with more of welfare than of hardship,
and their moral dullness makes it possible for them to
forget that the advantage of their position is an accidental
advantage, and that not every one can have a thousand
wives and a thousand palaces like Solomon, and that for
every man with a thousand wives there are a thousand without wives, and that for each palace there are a thousand
people who have to build it in the sweat of their brows; and
that the accident that has to-day made me a Solomon, may
to-morrow make me Solomon's slave. The dullness of these
people's imaginations enables them to forget what gave
no peace to Buddha—the inevitability of sickness, age and
death, which to-day or to-morrow will destroy all these
pleasures. I could not imitate these people: I had not
their dullness of imagination, and I could not artificially
produce it in myself.

The third escape is that of strength and energy. It consists in understanding that life is an evil and an absurdity,
and in destroying it. It is a way adopted by a few ex-
ceptionally strong and consistent people. I saw that it was
the worthiest way of escape, and I wished to adopt it.

The fourth escape is that of weakness. It consists in
seeing the truth of the situation, and yet clinging to life
as though one still hoped something from it; and I found
myself in that category.

To live like Solomon and Schopenhauer, knowing that life
is a stupid joke played upon us, and still to go on living:
washing oneself, dressing, dining, talking and even writing
books, was to me repulsive and tormenting, but I remained
in that position.

I now see that if I did not kill myself, it was due to some
dim consciousness of the invalidity of my thoughts. And
I began to feel, rather than argue, in this way: 'I, my
reason, has acknowledged life to be unreasonable. If there
be no higher reason (and there is not: nothing can prove
that there is) then reason is the creator of life for me. If

reason did not exist, there would be for me no life. How can reason deny life, when it is the creator of life? Or to put it the other way : were there no life, my reason would not exist ; therefore reason is life's son. Life is all. Reason is its fruit, yet reason denies life itself!' I felt that there was something wrong here.

Nothing prevents our denying life by suicide. Well then, kill yourself, and cease discussing. If life displeases you, kill yourself! You live, and cannot understand the meaning of life—then finish it ; and do not fool about in life, saying and writing that you do not understand it. You have come into good company, where people are contented and like what they are doing : if you find it dull and repulsive—go away !

Indeed, what are we who are convinced of the necessity of suicide yet do not decide to commit it, but the weakest, most inconsistent, and to put it plainly, the stupidest of men, fussing about with our own stupidity as a fool fusses about with a painted hussy ?

'There is something wrong,' said I to myself ; but what was wrong, I could in no way make out. It was long before the fog began to clear, and I began to be able to restate my position.

It had seemed to me that the narrow circle of rich learned and leisured people to whom I belonged, formed the whole of humanity, and that the milliards of others who have lived and are living, were cattle of some sort—not real people. . . . And it was long before it dawned upon me to ask : ' But what meaning is, and has been, given to their lives by all the milliards of common folk who live and have lived in the world ? '

I long lived in this state of lunacy, which in fact if not in words is particularly characteristic of us Liberal and learned people. But whether the strange physical affection I have for the real labouring people compelled me to understand them and to see that they are not so stupid as we suppose ; or whether it was due to the sincerity of my conviction that

I could know nothing beyond the fact that the best I could do was to hang myself, at any rate I instinctively felt that if I wished to live and understand the meaning of life, I must seek this meaning not among those who have lost it and wish to kill themselves, but among those milliards of the past and the present who know it, and who support the burden of their own lives and of ours also.

And on examining the matter I saw that the milliards of mankind always have had and still have a knowledge of the meaning of life, but *that* knowledge is their faith, which I could not but reject. 'It is God, one and three, the creation in six days, the devils and angels, and all the rest that I cannot accept as long as I retain my reason,' said I to myself.

My position was terrible. I knew I could find nothing along the path of reasonable knowledge, except a denial of life ; and in faith I could find nothing but a denial of reason, still more impossible to me than a denial of life.

Finally I saw that my mistake lay in ever expecting an examination of finite things to supply a meaning to life. The finite has no ultimate meaning apart from the infinite. The two must be linked together before an answer to life's problems can be reached.

It had only appeared to me that knowledge gave a definite answer—Schopenhauer's answer : that life has no meaning, and is an evil. On examining the matter further, I understood that the reply is not positive : it was only my feeling that made it seem so. The reply, strictly expressed as the Brahmins and Solomon and Schopenhauer express it, amounts only to an indefinite answer, like the reply given in mathematics when instead of solving an equation we find we have solved an identity : $X = X$, or $0 = 0$. The answer is, that life is nothing. So that philosophic knowledge merely asserts that it cannot solve the question, and the solution remains, as far as it is concerned, indefinite. And I understood, further, that however unreasonable and monstrous might be the replies given by faith, they had this advantage, that they introduce into each reply a relation between the finite and the infinite, without which relation no reply is possible.

Whichever way I put the question, that relation appeared in the answer. How am I to live?—According to the law of God. What real result will come of my life?—Eternal torment or eternal bliss. What meaning has life, that death does not destroy?—Union with the eternal God: heaven.

Faith still remained to me as irrational as it was before, but I could not but admit that it alone gives mankind a reply to the questions of life; and that consequently it makes life possible.

Where there is life, there, since man began, faith has made life possible for him; and the chief outline of that faith is everywhere and always one and the same. Faith does not consist in agreeing with what some one has said, as is usually supposed; faith is a knowledge of the meaning of human life in consequence of which man does not destroy himself, but lives. Faith is the strength of life. If a man lives he believes in something. If he does not see and recognise the visionary nature of the finite, then he believes in the finite; if he understands the visionary nature of the finite, he must believe in the infinite. Without faith he cannot live.

. . . . . .

What am I?—A part of the infinite. In those few words lies the whole problem.

I began dimly to understand that in the replies given by faith, is stored up the deepest human wisdom.

I understood this; but it made matters no better for me.

I was now ready to accept any faith, if only it did not demand of me a direct denial of reason—which would be a falsehood. And I studied Buddhism and Mohammedanism from books, and most of all, I studied Christianity both from books and from living people.

Naturally I first of all turned to the Orthodox of my

circle, to people who were learned : to Church theologians, the monks, to the theologians of the newest shade, and even to the Evangelicals[1] who profess salvation by belief in the Redemption. And I seized on these believers and questioned them as to their beliefs, and their understanding of the meaning of life.

But in spite of my readiness to make all possible concessions, I saw that what they gave out as their faith did not explain the meaning of life, but obscured it.

I remember the painful feeling of fear of being thrown back into my former state of despair, after the hope I often and often experienced in my intercourse with these people.

The more fully they explained to me their doctrines, the more clearly did I see their error. . . . It was not that in their doctrines they mixed many unnecessary and unreasonable things with the Christian truths that had always been near to me : that was not what repelled me. I was repelled by the fact that these people's lives were like my own, with only this difference—that such a life did not correspond to the principles they expounded in their teachings.

No arguments could convince me of the truth of their faith. Only deeds which showed that they saw a meaning in life, which made what was so dreadful to me—poverty sickness and death—not dreadful to them, could convince me. And such deeds I did not see among the various bodies of believers in our circle. On the contrary, I saw such deeds done by people of our circle who were the most unbelieving, but never by the so-called believers of our circle.[2]

[1] Readers of *Resurrection* (Book II, Chap. 17) will remember the vivid description of the Evangelical meeting addressed by Kiesewetter, who spoke in English. The original from whom Tolstoy drew Kiesewetter was Baedeker, a well-known Evangelical preacher who lived in England, but visited Russia frequently.

[2] This passage is the more noteworthy because it is almost the only reference (and even this is indirect) made by Tolstoy at this period to the revolutionary or 'To-the-People' movement in which so many young men and women were

And I understood that the belief of these people was not the faith I sought, and that their faith is not a real faith, but an Epicurean consolation in life.

And I began to draw near to the believers among the poor simple unlettered folk : pilgrims monks sectarians and peasants.　Among them, too, I found a great deal of superstition mixed with the Christian truths; but their superstitions seemed a necessary and natural part of their lives. . . . And I began to look well into the life and faith of these people, and the more I considered it, the more I became convinced that they have a real faith, which is a necessity to them and alone gives their life a meaning and makes it possible for them to live. . . . In contrast with what I had seen in our circle, where the whole of life is passed in idleness and amusements and dissatisfaction, I saw that the whole life of these people was passed in heavy labour, and that they were content with life. . . . While we think it terrible that we have to suffer and die, these folk live and suffer, and approach death with tranquillity, and in most cases gladly.

And I learnt to love these people.　The more I came to know their life the more I loved them, and the easier it became for me to live.　So I went on for about two years, and a change took place in me which had long been preparing, and the promise of which had always been in me.　The life of our circle, the rich and learned, not merely became distasteful to me but lost all meaning for me; while the life of the whole labouring people, the whole of mankind who produce life, appeared to me in its true light.　I understood that *that* is life itself, and that the meaning given to that life is true ; and I accepted it.

I then understood that my answer to the question, ' What is life?' when I said that life is ' evil,' was quite correct.

risking and sacrificing home, property, freedom, and life itself, from motives which had much in common with his own perception that the upper layers of ' Society' are parasitic, and prey on the vitals of the people who support them.

The only mistake was, that that answer referred to *my* life, but not to life in general. My life, a life of indulgence and desires, was meaningless and evil. . . . And I understood the truth, which I afterwards found in the Gospels, that men love darkness rather than the light because their deeds are evil; and that to see things as they are, one must think and speak of the life of humanity, and not of the life of the minority who are parasites on life.

And indeed, the bird lives so that it must fly, collect food and build its nest; and when I see the bird doing that, I joy in its joy. The goat, hare and wolf live so that they must feed themselves, and propagate and feed their families, and when they do so, I feel firmly assured that they are happy and that their life is a reasonable one. And what does man do? He should earn a living as the beasts do, but with this difference—that he would perish if he did it alone; he has to procure it not for himself but for all. When he does *that*, I have a firm assurance that he is happy and that his life is reasonable. And what had I done during the whole thirty years of my conscious life? I had not only not been earning a living for all, I had not even earned my own living. I had lived as a parasite, and when I asked myself what use my life was, I found that my life was useless. If the meaning of human life lies in supporting it, how could I, who for thirty years had occupied myself not with supporting life but with destroying it in myself and in others—how could I obtain any other reply than that my life was senseless and an evil? It was both senseless and evil.

The conviction that a knowledge of life can only be found by living, led me to doubt the goodness of my own life. . . . During that whole year, when I was asking myself almost every moment, whether I should not end matters with a noose or a bullet—all that time, alongside the course of thought and observation about which I have spoken, my heart was oppressed with a painful feeling which I can only describe as a search for God.

I went over in my mind the arguments of Kant and Schopenhauer showing the impossibility of proving the existence of a God, and I began to refute them. Cause, said I to myself, is not a category such as are Time and Space. If I exist, there must be some cause for it, and a cause of causes. And that first cause of all, is what men have called 'God.' And as soon as I acknowledged that there is a force in whose power I am, I at once felt that I could live. But I asked myself: What is that cause, that force? How am I to think of it? What are my relations to that which I call 'God'? And only the familiar replies occurred to me: 'He is the Creator and Preserver.' This reply did not satisfy me, and I felt I was losing within me what I needed for my life. I became terrified and began to pray to him whom I sought, that he should help me. But the more I prayed the more apparent it became to me that he did not hear me, and that there was no one to whom to address myself. And with despair in my heart that there is no God at all, I said: 'Lord, have mercy, save me! Lord, teach me!' But no one had mercy on me, and I felt that my life was coming to a standstill.

But again and again I returned to the same admission that I could not have come into the world without any cause or reason or meaning; I could not be such a fledgling fallen from its nest as I felt myself to be. Or, granting that I be such, lying on my back in the high grass, even then I cry because I know that a mother has borne me within her, has hatched me, warmed me, fed me and loved me. Where is she—that mother? If she has deserted me, who is it that has done so? I cannot hide from myself that some one bore me, loving me. Who was that some one? Again 'God'?

'He exists,' said I to myself. And I had only for an instant to admit that, and at once life rose within me, and I felt the possibility and joy of being. But again, from the admission of the existence of a God I went on to seek my relations with him; and again I imagined *that* God—our

creator in three persons who sent his son, the Saviour—
and again *that* God, detached from the world and from me,
melts like a block of ice, melts before my eyes, and again
nothing remains, and again the spring of life dries up
within me, and I despair, and feel that I have nothing to
do but to kill myself. And the worst of all is, that I feel
I cannot do it.

Not twice or three times, but tens and hundreds of times,
I reached those conditions first of joy and animation,
and then of despair and consciousness of the impossibility
of living.

I remember that it was in early spring : I was alone in
the wood listening to its sounds. I listened and thought
ever of the same thing, as I had constantly done during
those last three years. I was again seeking God.

'Very well, there is no God,' said I to myself; 'there is
no one who is not my imagination but a reality like my
whole life. He does not exist, and no miracles can prove
his existence, because the miracles would be my perceptions,
besides being irrational.'

'But my *perception* of God, of him whom I seek,' asked I
of myself, 'where has that perception come from?' And
again at this thought the glad waves of life rose within me.
All that was around me came to life, and received a meaning. But my joy did not last long. My mind continued
its work.

'The conception of God, is not God,' said I to myself.
'The conception, is what takes place within me. The conception of God, is something I can evoke or can refrain from
evoking in myself. That is not what I seek. I seek that,
without which there can be no life.' And again all around
me and within me began to die, and again I wished to kill
myself.

But then I turned my gaze upon myself, on what went on
within me, and I remembered that I only lived at those
times when I believed in God. As it was before, so it was
now ; I need only be aware of God to live ; I need only

manners, tones and gestures, besides being possessed of a yet more wonderful knowledge of the hearts and minds of all sorts and conditions of men, from the shamefaced child to the officer dying on the field of battle. He is so concerned with the interest and importance of life, that he can hold his reader's attention without having to tell his stories so that they must be guessed like riddles, and he never makes use of elaborate plots. He needs no tricks of that sort. Nor does he strive after effect by the use of pornographic details, the introduction of extraordinary events, or the piling up of many horrible details. His stories are as straightforward as everyday life.

His great novels bear out all the promise of his short stories, with the added power of maturity.

Though highly original and of strong individuality, he stands none the less in the line of succession of great writers which began with Poúshkin, whose genius for simple sincere and direct narrative gave an invaluable direction to Russian literature, was continued by Gógol whose biting irony and remorseless exposure of shams and hypocrisies completed the emancipation from romanticism, and was carried on by Tourgénef, whose art, conscious of and not indifferent to the trend of thought and feeling in the society it describes, reached an extraordinary pitch of artistic perfection.

Tolstoy's works have from the first interested Russia, and now interest the world, because in greater measure than any of his predecessors he possesses the capacity to feel intensely, note accurately, and think deeply. The combination which makes Tolstoy the most interesting of writers, is the scientific accuracy of his observation (which never allows him to take liberties with his characters or events in order to make out a case for the side he sympathises with) and the fact that he is mightily in earnest. Life to him is important, and art is the handmaid of life. He wants to know what is good and what is bad; to help the former and to resist the latter. His work tends to evolve order out of life's chaos; and as that is the most important thing a man can do, his books are among

creator in three persons who sent his son, the Saviour—
and again *that* God, detached from the world and from me,
melts like a block of ice, melts before my eyes, and again
nothing remains, and again the spring of life dries up
within me, and I despair, and feel that I have nothing to
do but to kill myself. And the worst of all is, that I feel
I cannot do it.

Not twice or three times, but tens and hundreds of times,
I reached those conditions first of joy and animation,
and then of despair and consciousness of the impossibility
of living.

I remember that it was in early spring : I was alone in
the wood listening to its sounds. I listened and thought
ever of the same thing, as I had constantly done during
those last three years. I was again seeking God.

'Very well, there is no God,' said I to myself; 'there is
no one who is not my imagination but a reality like my
whole life. He does not exist, and no miracles can prove
his existence, because the miracles would be my perceptions,
besides being irrational.'

'But my *perception* of God, of him whom I seek,' asked I
of myself, 'where has that perception come from?' And
again at this thought the glad waves of life rose within me.
All that was around me came to life, and received a meaning. But my joy did not last long. My mind continued
its work.

'The conception of God, is not God,' said I to myself.
'The conception, is what takes place within me. The conception of God, is something I can evoke or can refrain from
evoking in myself. That is not what I seek. I seek that,
without which there can be no life.' And again all around
me and within me began to die, and again I wished to kill
myself.

But then I turned my gaze upon myself, on what went on
within me, and I remembered that I only lived at those
times when I believed in God. As it was before, so it was
now ; I need only be aware of God to live ; I need only

forget him, or disbelieve in him, and I die. . . . 'What more do you seek?' exclaimed a voice within me. 'This is he. He is that without which one cannot live. To know God and to live is one and the same thing. God is life. Live seeking God, and then you will not live without God.' And more than ever before, all within me and around me lit up, and the light did not again abandon me.

And I was saved from suicide. . . . And strange to say, the strength of life which returned to me was not new, but quite old—the same that had borne me along in my earliest days.

I quite returned to what belonged to my earliest child-hood and youth. I returned to the belief in that Will which produced me, and desires something of me. I returned to the belief that the chief and only aim of my life is to be better, *i.e.* to live in accord with that Will. And I returned to the belief that I can find the expression of that Will, in what humanity, in the distant past hidden from me, has produced for its guidance: that is to say, I returned to a belief in God, in moral perfecting, and in a tradition transmitting the meaning of life. . . .

I turned from the life of our circle: acknowledging that theirs is not life but only a simulacrum of life, and that the conditions of superfluity in which we live deprive us of the possibility of understanding life. . . . The simple labouring people around me were the Russian people, and I turned to them and to the meaning which they give to life. That meaning, if one can put it into words, was the following. Every man has come into this world by the will of God. And God has so made man that every man can destroy his soul or save it. The aim of man in life is to save his soul; and to save his soul he must live 'godly,' and to live 'godly' he must renounce all the pleasures of life, must labour, humble himself, suffer and be merciful. . . . The meaning of this was clear and near to my heart. But together with this meaning of the popular faith of our non-sectarian folk among whom I live, much was inseparably bound up that revolted me and seemed to me inexplicable: sacraments,

Church services, fasts, and the adoration of relics and icons. The people cannot separate the one from the other, nor could I. And strange as much of it was to me, I accepted everything; and attended the services, knelt morning and evening in prayer, fasted, and prepared to receive the eucharist; and at first my reason did not resist anything. What had formerly seemed to me impossible, did not now evoke in me any resistance. . . .

I told myself that the essence of every faith consists in its giving life a meaning which death does not destroy. Naturally, for a faith to be able to reply to the questions of a king dying in luxury, of an old slave tormented by overwork, and of all sorts of people, young and old, wise and foolish,—its answers must be expressed in all sorts of different ways. . . . But this argument, justifying in my eyes the queerness of much on the ritual side of religion, did not suffice to allow me, in the one great affair of life —religion—to do things which seemed to me questionable. With all my soul I wished to be in a position to mingle with the people, fulfilling the ritual side of their religion; but I could not do it. I felt that I should lie to myself, and mock at what was sacred to me, were I to do so. At this point, however, our new Russian theological writers came to my rescue.

According to the explanation these theologians gave, the fundamental dogma of our faith is the infallibility of the Church. From the admission of that dogma follows inevitably the truth of all that is professed by the Church. The Church as an assembly of true-believers united by love, and therefore possessed of true knowledge, became the basis of my belief. I told myself that divine truth cannot be accessible to a separate individual; it is revealed only to the whole assembly of people united by love. To attain truth one must not separate; and not to separate, one must love and must endure things one may not agree with.

Truth reveals itself to love, and if you do not submit to the rites of the Church, you transgress against love; and by transgressing against love you deprive yourself of the possibility of recognising the truth. I did not then see the sophistry contained in this argument. I did not see that union in love may give the greatest love, but certainly cannot give us divine truth expressed in the definite words of the Nicene Creed. I also did not perceive that love cannot make a certain expression of truth an obligatory condition of union. I did not then see these mistakes in the argument, and thanks to it, was able to accept and perform all the rites of the Orthodox Church without understanding most of them.

When fulfilling the rites of the Church I humbled my reason, submitted to tradition, united myself with my forefathers: the father, mother and grandparents I loved, and with all those millions of the common people whom I respected. When rising before dawn for the early Church services, I knew I was doing well, if only because I was sacrificing my bodily ease to humble my mental pride, and for the sake of finding the meaning of life. However insignificant these sacrifices might be, I made them for the sake of something good. I fasted, prepared for communion, and observed the fixed hours of prayer at home and in church. During Church service I attended to every word, and gave them a meaning whenever I could.

But this reading of meanings into the rites had its limits. . . . If I explained to myself the frequent repetition of prayers for the Tsar and his relatives, by the fact that they are more exposed to temptation than other people and therefore more in need of being prayed for, the prayers about subduing enemies and foes under his feet (even though one tried to say that sin was the foe prayed against) and many other unintelligible prayers—nearly two-thirds of the whole service—either remained quite incomprehensible or, when I forced an explanation into them, made me feel that I was lying, and thereby quite destroying my relation to God and losing all possibility of believing. . . .

Never shall I forget the painful feeling I experienced the day I received the eucharist for the first time after many years. The service, confession and prayers were quite intelligible and produced in me a glad consciousness that the meaning of life was being revealed to me. The communion itself I explained as an act performed in remembrance of Christ, and indicating a purification from sin and the full acceptance of Christ's teaching. If that explanation was artificial I did not notice its artificiality : so happy was I at humbling and abasing myself before the priest—a simple timid country clergyman—turning all the dirt out of my soul and confessing my vices, so glad was I to merge in thought with the humility of the Fathers who wrote the prayers of the Office, so glad was I of union with all who have believed and now believe, that I did not notice the artificiality of my explanation. But when I approached the altar gates, and the priest made me say that I believed that what I was about to swallow was truly flesh and blood, I felt a pain in my heart : it was not merely a false note, it was a cruel demand made by some one or other who evidently had never known what faith is.

I now permit myself to say that it was a cruel demand, but I did not then think so : only it was indescribably painful to me. At the time, I found in my soul a feeling which helped me to endure it. This was the feeling of self-abasement and humility. I humbled myself, swallowed that flesh and blood without any blasphemous feelings, and with a wish to believe. But the blow had been struck, and knowing what awaited me, I could not go a second time.

I continued to fulfil the rites of the Church and still believed that the doctrine I was following contained the truth, when something happened to me which I now understand but which then seemed strange.

I was listening to the conversation of an illiterate peasant, a pilgrim, about God, faith, life and salvation, when a knowledge of faith revealed itself to me. I drew near to

explain the matter to me, except one man, who explained it all, and explained it so that I never asked any one any more about it.

I asked him why we should not unite on those main points on which we could agree, and leave the rest for each to decide as he pleases. My collocutor agreed with my thoughts, but told me that such concessions would bring reproach on the spiritual authorities for deserting the faith of our forefathers, and this would produce a split; and the vocation of the spiritual authorities is to safeguard in all its purity the Greco-Russian Orthodox faith inherited from our forefathers.

And I understood it all. I am seeking a faith, the power of life; and they are seeking the best way to fulfil before men certain human obligations. . . . And I noticed what is done in the name of religion, and was horrified; and I almost entirely abjured Orthodoxy.

The second relation of the Church to a question of life, was with regard to war and executions.

At that time Russia was at war. And Russians, in the name of Christian love, began to kill their fellow-men. It was impossible not to think about this, and not to see that killing is an evil, repugnant to the first principles of any faith. Yet they prayed in the churches for the success of our arms, and the teachers of the faith acknowledged killing to be an act resulting from the faith. And besides the murders during the war, I saw during the disturbances which followed the war, Church dignitaries and teachers and monks of the lesser and stricter Orders, who approved the killing of helpless erring youths. And I took note of all that is done by men who profess Christianity, and I was horrified.

And I ceased to doubt, and became fully convinced that not all was true in the religion I had joined. Formerly I should have said that it was all false; but I could not say so now, for I had felt its truth and had lived by it. But I no longer doubted that there is in it much that is false.

And though among the peasants there was less admixture of what repelled me, still I saw that in their belief also, falsehood was mixed with the truth.

But where did the truth and where did the falsehood come from? Both the falsehood and the truth were contained in the so-called holy tradition and Scriptures. Both the falsehood and the truth had been handed down by what is called the Church.

And whether I liked to or not, I was brought to the study and investigation of these writings and traditions—which till now I had been so afraid to investigate.

And I turned to the examination of that same theology which I had once rejected with such contempt. . . . On it religious doctrine rests, or at least with it the only knowledge of the meaning of life that I have found, is inseparably connected. . . . I shall not seek the explanation of everything. I know that the explanation of everything, like the commencement of everything, must be concealed in infinity. But I wish to understand in a way which will bring me to what is inevitably inexplicable. I wish to recognise anything that is inexplicable, as being so, not because the demands of my reason are wrong (they are right, and apart from them I can understand nothing), but because I recognise the limits of my intellect. I wish to understand in such a way that everything that is inexplicable shall present itself to me as being necessarily inexplicable, and not as being something I am under an arbitrary obligation to believe. I must find what is true and what is false, and must disentangle the one from the other. I am setting to work upon this task. What of falsehood I find in the teaching, and what I find of truth, and to what conclusions I come, will form the following parts of this work, which if it be worth it, and if any one wants it, will probably some day be printed somewhere.

. . . . . .

These closing words in which Tolstoy expresses the hope that his work 'will probably some day be printed some-

where,' are a reminder of the difficulties and dangers that
had to be encountered in Russia by any man who set out to
challenge the authority of the Orthodox Church, whose
affairs were managed by the Holy Synod, presided over by a
Procurator able to call on the secular powers to enforce his
decisions.

AUTHORITY FOR CHAPTER XI

Tolstoy's *Ispoved* : Christchurch, 1901.

Tolstoy's *Confession* being prohibited in Russia, had to be printed
abroad. The edition mentioned above is a reliable one.

CHAPTER XII

Tolstoy's first nineteen stories. Stands in a line of succession. Quality as writer. *War and Peace.* 'Great' men. Napoleon. The battles of Schöngraben and Borodinó. Tolstoy's influence on war-correspondence. Serfdom. The organisation of society. Characters in *War and Peace.* Its range. *Anna Karénina* : Matthew Arnold's essay. Translations. The tendency of the book. Kropótkin's criticism. The volunteers. Tolstoy's attitude towards Government. W. D. Howells's appreciation. Tolstoy's Last Three Decades of work : the magnitude and nature of his effort.

TOLSTOY's writings during the first twenty-five years of his literary career divide up into six sections.

First came a series of seventeen stories and sketches, beginning with *Childhood* and ending with *Family Happiness.* Next came his series of educational articles in the *Yásnaya Polyána* magazine. Third came *The Cossacks* (the finest story he had yet written) and *Polikoúshka.* Fourth, came *War and Peace.* Fifth, came the *ABC* Book, the *Readers,* and another article on Education ; and sixth, came *Anna Karénina.*

Leaving the educational works out of account, the list can be reduced to nineteen stories and sketches, followed by two great novels.

The nineteen sketches and stories, 'trials of the pen,' as Tolstoy called them, covered a wide range of subjects, from charmingly realistic sketches of childhood to vigorous depictions of Cossack life, and showed their writer to be an amazingly accurate observer of physical facts and qualities, manners, tones and gestures, besides being possessed of a yet more wonderful knowledge of the hearts and minds of all sorts and conditions of men, from the shamefaced child to the officer dying on the field of battle. He is so concerned with the interest and importance of life, that he can hold his reader's attention without having to tell his stories so that they must be guessed like riddles, and he never makes use of elaborate plots. He needs no tricks of that sort. Nor does he strive after effect by the use of pornographic details, the introduction of extraordinary events, or the piling up of many horrible details. His stories are as straightforward as everyday life.

His great novels bear out all the promise of his short stories, with the added power of maturity.

Though highly original and of strong individuality, he stands none the less in the line of succession of great writers which began with Poúshkin, whose genius for simple sincere and direct narrative gave an invaluable direction to Russian literature, was continued by Gógol whose biting irony and remorseless exposure of shams and hypocrisies completed the emancipation from romanticism, and was carried on by Tourgénef, whose art, conscious of and not indifferent to the trend of thought and feeling in the society it describes, reached an extraordinary pitch of artistic perfection.

Tolstoy's works have from the first interested Russia, and now interest the world, because in greater measure than any of his predecessors he possesses the capacity to feel intensely, note accurately, and think deeply. The combination which makes Tolstoy the most interesting of writers, is the scientific accuracy of his observation (which never allows him to take liberties with his characters or events in order to make out a case for the side he sympathises with) and the fact that he is mightily in earnest. Life to him is important, and art is the handmaid of life. He wants to know what is good and what is bad; to help the former and to resist the latter. His work tends to evolve order out of life's chaos; and as that is the most important thing a man can do, his books are among the most interesting and important books of our time. He makes no pretence of standing aloof, cutting off his art from his life, or concealing his desire that kindness should prevail over cruelty. Life interests him, and therefore the reflection of life interests him, and the problems of art are the problems of life: love and passion and death and the desire to do right.

The chief subject reappearing again and again throughout the stories he wrote before *War and Peace*, is the mental striving of a young Russian nobleman to free himself from the artificial futilities of the society in which he was born, and to see and do what is right. The search is only partially successful. The indictment of society is often convincing, but the heroes' failures and perplexities are frankly admitted. Sometimes there is no hero. In *Sevastopol*, for instance, he exclaims : ' Where in this tale is the evil shown that should be avoided ? Where is the good that should be imitated ? Who is the villain, who the hero of the story ? All are good and all are bad '; and in *Lucerne* he says : ' Who will define for me what is freedom, what despotism, what civilisation and what barbarism ? Or tell me where are the limits of the one or the other ? Who has in his soul so immovable a *standard of good and evil* that by it he can measure the passing facts of life ? '

This searching for what is good and rejecting what is false —resulting in a strong distrust and dislike of the predatory masterful domineering types of humanity, and in general of what has usually been regarded as the heroic type, and also in a friendly compassion for all that is humble simple forbearing and sincere—is the keynote of Tolstoy's early tales. They are studies of life, so truthful that the characters seem to have an independent life of their own. They speak for themselves, and at times, like Balaam, bless what they were apparently expected to curse. For instance, when Prince Nehlúdof insists on bringing the wandering musician into the Schweizerhof Hotel in *Lucerne*, we feel how uncomfortable he thereby makes the poor singer, though that is evidently not what Tolstoy originally set out to make us feel.

War and Peace, besides being maturer than the preceding tales, was composed during the early years of Tolstoy's married life, when he felt more content with himself and with life in general, and when his attitude towards existing things was more tolerant and sympathetic than it had been, or than it became in later years.

He told me that in *War and Peace* and *Anna Karénina* his aim was simply to amuse his readers. I am bound to accept his statement; but one has only to read either of those books to see that through them Tolstoy's ardent nature found vent, with all its likes and dislikes, strivings, yearnings, hopes and fears.

I asked Tolstoy why in *What is Art?* he relegates these great novels to the realm of 'bad art'; and his answer showed, as I expected it would, that he does not really consider them at all bad, but condemns them merely as being too long, and written in a way chiefly adapted to please the leisured well-to-do classes, who have time for reading novels in several volumes, because other people do their rough work for them. Of *War and Peace* he said, 'It is, one would think, harmless enough, but one never knows how things will affect people,' and he went on to mention, with regret, that one of Professor Zahárin's daughters had told him that from his novels she had acquired a love of balls and parties; things of which, at the time of our conversation, he heartily disapproved.

In form, *War and Peace* is unlike any English novel, but it resembles Poúshkin's *The Captain's Daughter* (though the latter is a much shorter story) in that both works are chronicles of Russian families, round whom the stories centre. In *War and Peace* there are two families, the Rostófs and the Bolkónskys.

The mighty drama of the Napoleonic advance from 1805 to 1812 comes into the novel, in so far as it affects the members of those two families. But Tolstoy is not content

merely to tell us of historic events. He introduces a whole
philosophy of history, which is sound at bottom though no
doubt he somewhat overstates his case, as is his habit.
The theory is that the 'great' men of history count for very
little. They are the figureheads of forces that are beyond
their control. They do most good and least harm when,
like Koutoúzof, they are aware of the true direction of the
great human forces and adapt themselves to them; but
then they are modest, and the world does not esteem them
great. The typical case of the impotent 'great' man is
Napoleon in 1812, at the time of his invasion of Russia.
He posed before the world as a man of destiny whose will
and intellect decided the fate of empires. Yet from first to
last, during that campaign, he never in the least knew what
was about to happen. The result was decided by the spirit
of the Russian nation, and by its steadfast endurance. Every
common Russian soldier who understood that the Russian
people dreaded and detested the thought of a foreign yoke,
and who therefore co-operated with the natural course of
events, did more to further the result than Napoleon, that
'most insignificant tool of history,' as Tolstoy calls him,
who even in St. Helena was never able to understand what
had caused his overthrow.

The main theme of the novel, if it be permissible to select
a main theme out of the many latent in the story, is Tolstoy's
favourite thesis. He tacitly asks: What is good and what
is bad? With what must we sympathise and what must we
reject? And the reply is that the predatory, artificial and
insincere types, exemplified historically by the invading
French, as well as by such characters among the Russians as
Ellen, Anatole and Dólohof, are repugnant to him, while
he loves the humble, the meek and the sincere: Marie and
Platon Karatáef, Natásha (so impulsive and charming in her
youth, so absorbed in her family later on), and Pierre (who is
often humble and always sincere, and loves ideas and ideals).

It is impossible to do justice to this wonderful book in
any brief summary. It is not a work to be summed up in a

few pages. It has many characters, all of them so distinctly drawn that we know them better than we know our personal acquaintances. It treats of life's deepest experiences from the cradle to the grave; and to read it with the care it deserves is to know life better and see it more sanely and seriously than one ever did before. Some foolish people think that reading novels is a waste of time; but there are hardly any books—at any rate hardly any big books—that are better worth reading than Tolstoy's novels.

He is probably justified in claiming that his history is truer than the historians' history of the battles of Schöngraben, Austerlitz, and Borodinó. The historians, from mendacious military reports drawn up after the action, try to discover what the Commanders-in-Chief meant to do; and to tell their story within moderate limits they have to systematise what was really a huge disorder; thereby giving their readers a completely wrong impression of what a battle is like.

N. N. Mouravyóf, a Commander-in-Chief who distinguished himself in more than one war, declared he had never read a better description of a battle than Tolstoy's account of Schöngraben; and added that he was convinced from his own experience that during a battle it is impossible to carry out a Commander-in-Chief's orders.

Tolstoy, when he wrote the book, was convinced that war is inevitable. The idea that it is man's duty to resist war and to refuse to take part in it, came to him later.

In an article entitled 'Some Words about *War and Peace*,' which he wrote in 1868 for one of the periodicals, he says:

'Why did millions of people kill one another, when since the foundation of the world it has been known that this is both physically and morally bad?

'Because it was so inevitably necessary, that when doing it they fulfilled the elemental zoological law bees fulfil when they kill one another in autumn, and male animals fulfil when they destroy one another. No other reply can be given to that dreadful question.'

Yet his inveterate truthfulness, and his personal knowledge of war, caused him to describe it so exactly, that the result is tantamount to a condemnation. As Kropótkin says, *War and Peace* is a powerful indictment of war. The effect which the great writer has exercised in this direction upon his generation can be actually seen in Russia. It was already apparent during the Russo-Turkish war of 1877-8, when it was impossible to find in Russia a correspondent who would have described how ' *we* peppered the enemy with grape-shot,' or how ' we knocked them down like ninepins.' If any one could have been found to use in his letters such survivals of barbarism, no paper would have dared to print them. The general character of the Russian war-correspondent had totally changed ; and during that war there appeared Gárshin the novelist, and Verestchágin the painter, ' with whom to combat war became a life work.'

It has been charged against *War and Peace* that it neglects to show the evil side of serfdom : the brutality, the cruelty, the immurement of women, the flogging of grown-up sons, the torture of serf girls by their mistresses, etc. But Tolstoy studied the period closely from letters, diaries and traditions, especially from the records of his own grandparents, the Tolstoys and the Volkónskys ; and he says he did not find horrors worse than are to be found now, or at any other period. People then loved and envied, and sought for truth and virtue, and were swayed by passions, as now. Their mental and moral life was just as complex, and in the upper circles it was sometimes even more refined than now. . . . No doubt the greater remoteness of the higher circle from the other classes gave a special character to the period, but not the character of brutal violence.

Tolstoy is in sympathy with that time, sees the poetry of it, and knows how much of goodness, courage, kindliness and high aspiration existed among those politically unen-

2 K

franchised serf-owners. With our modern, Western desire to *organise society efficiently*, he never has sympathised. The state of a man's mind has always been to him more important than the conditions of his life, and it seems to him as though there were some antithesis between the two: as though, if you organised your society, it would cease to think truly or feel deeply. We in the West are beginning to believe the opposite, and to suspect that to leave society unorganised or disorganised has an inevitable tendency to blunt our minds and souls. But not the less is it valuable to have so wonderful a picture of Russia as it was at the commencement of the nineteenth century, painted by one who sees it as the best Russians of that period saw it themselves.

Of the history part of the book, it should be noted that Tolstoy says: 'Wherever in my novel historic characters speak or act, I have not invented, but have made use of materials which during my work have accumulated till they form a whole library.'

He told me he considered the defect of the book, besides its size, to be the intrusion of a long philosophic argument into the story. He still holds the opinions he held when he wrote it, as to the influence or impotence of 'great' men, as well as all that he then said about destiny and free will; but he now realises that his novel would have been a better novel without these abstract disquisitions.

The characters in the book are not strictly copied from life, but in the main Tolstoy's father's family are represented by the Rostófs and his mother's by the Bolkónskys. In the magazine article already referred to, Tolstoy says that only two minor characters are taken from life, and 'all the other characters are entirely invented, and I have not even for them any definite prototypes in tradition or in reality.' But when he said that, he was defending himself from the charge of having copied actual people who had played a part in the society of the time, and he clearly overstates his case, for to a considerable extent the characters in the novel correspond to the people mentioned in the following list:

CHARACTERS IN *War and Peace*:	MEMBERS OF THE TOLSTOY OR VOLKÓNSKY FAMILIES:
The old Prince N. Bolkónsky	= Tolstoy's grandfather, Prince N. Volkónsky.
His daughter, Princess Marie N. Bolkónsky	= Tolstoy's mother, the Princess Marie N. Volkónsky.
The old Count Ilyá A. Rostóf	= Tolstoy's grandfather, Count Ilyá A. Tolstoy.
Count Nicholas I. Rostóf	= Tolstoy's father, Count Nicholas I. Tolstoy.
Countess Natálya Rostóf	= Tatiána Behrs, Tolstoy's youngest sister-in-law.
Sónya	= Tatiána A. Érgolsky.

Dólohof is made up of a combination of Count Theodore Tolstoy, a famous traveller, with R. I. Dórohof, a notorious dare-devil of Alexander I.'s days.

Many even of the minor characters, such as Mlle. Bourienne, and Ivánushka the woman pilgrim in man's clothes, are copied more or less closely from people connected with the Volkónskys' home at Yásnaya Polyána.

Tolstoy's sympathies and antipathies in this novel: his appreciation of affection, kindliness, simplicity and truthfulness, and his dislike of what is cruel, pompous, complicated or false, are the same as in his earlier stories, but mellowed and wiser; they are also the same as in his later didactic writings, though there they are formulated, dogmatic and rigid.

The novel covers nearly the whole range of Tolstoy's experience of life: in it we have the aristocracy and the peasants; town life and country life; the Commanders, officers and privates of the army, in action and out of action; the diplomatists and courtiers; flirtation, love, balls, hunting, and a reform movement which is all talk.

What Tolstoy does not show, is what he did not know—the middle-class world : the world of merchants, manufacturers, engineers and men of business. Of course these in Russia a hundred years ago, played a comparatively small part ; and there was practically no political activity such as that of our County Councils, Borough Councils and Parliament. But that all this was absent from Tolstoy's mind, and that his outlook on life was confined to the aristocracy which consumed and the peasantry which produced, will, in the sequel, help us to understand the social teaching to which he ultimately came. His brother-in-law tells us that Leo Tolstoy 'has in my presence confessed to being both proud and vain. He was a rampant aristocrat, and though he always loved the country folk, he loved the aristocracy still more. To the middle class he was antipathetic. When, after his failures in early life, he became widely famous as a writer, he used to admit that it gave him great pleasure and intense happiness. In his own words, he was pleased to feel that he was both a writer and a noble.

'When he heard of any of his former comrades or acquaintances receiving important appointments, his comments reminded one of those of Souvórof [a Field-Marshal of Catherine the Great's time], who always maintained that at Court one receives promotion for cringing and flattery, but never for good work. Sometimes he would ironically remark that, though he had himself not earned a Generalship in the artillery, he had at any rate won his Generalship in literature.'

A simple world of nobles and peasants, with little organisation, and that of a poor kind : a world the evils of which were mitigated by much kindliness and good intention, and in which, on the whole, the less the Government interfered with anybody or anything, the better—was old Russia as it existed under Alexander I and as it still existed when Tolstoy was young. He has described it with extraordinary vividness, and has made it possible for us to picture to ourselves a country and an age not our own. What effect the limitation of his outlook, referred to above, had on the subsequent development of his opinions, need not here be considered. It does not spoil the novel, for no novel can show us the whole of life; but it had a very serious effect on the formulation of his later philosophy of life. Of certain important types of humanity he has hardly any conception. Of the George Stephenson type, for instance, which masters the brute forces of nature and harnesses them to the service of man—doing this primarily from love of efficient work—he knows nothing; nor does he know anything of the Sidney Webb type, which sets itself the yet more difficult task of evolving social order out of the partial chaos of modern civilisation; or of the best type of organisers in our great industrial undertakings: the men whose hearts are set on getting much work well done, with little friction and little waste, and to whom the successful accomplishment of a difficult project gives more satisfaction than any effortless acquisition of wealth would do. Tolstoy oversimplifies life's problems. He makes a sharp contrast between the predatory and the humble types; and there is a measure of truth in his presentation. He is right that life is supported by the humble, and is rendered hard by the predatory types; but he has omitted from his scheme of things the man of organising mind: the man who knows how to get his way, and generally gets it (or a good deal of it) but does this mainly from worthy motives; the man who is not perfect, and may take more than is good for him, and may have some of the tendencies of the predatory type, but who still, on the whole, is worth, and more than worth, his salt, and but for whom there would be more of chaos and less of order in the world. Tolstoy has said in one of his later writings that the cause of the Russian famines is the Greek Church; and he is right. All that stupefies, all that impedes thought, tends to make men inefficient even in their agricultural operations. But by parity of reasoning he should see that the introduction of thought into methods of production, distribution and exchange, which has, during the last hundred and fifty years, so revolutionised our Western world, should not be condemned as bad in itself, however ugly many of its manifestations may be; and however often we may see the organising and the predatory types exemplified in one and the same person.

Outside Russia, *Anna Karénina* is perhaps more popular than *War and Peace*. The former is a long novel, but not nearly as long as the latter; and though it contains philosophic disquisitions, these fit better into the story and are shorter and clearer than the philosophic chapters in *War and Peace*. In arrangement, again, *Anna Karénina* is more like the novels we are accustomed to, though instead of one hero and heroine it has two pairs of lovers, living quite different lives, and not very closely connected.

It deals with the passionate love of a beautiful and attractive woman; and it has a further interest in the fact that Lévin, to a greater degree than any of the author's other characters, represents Tolstoy himself; though Tolstoy made Lévin a very simple fellow in order to get a more effective contrast between him and the representatives of high life in Moscow and Petersburg.

Anna Karénina had the advantage of being introduced to the English reading public by Matthew Arnold in an essay which is one of the very best any one has ever written about Tolstoy. It is so good, and still carries so much weight, that I may be excused for mentioning three points on which it seems to me misleading. First, Arnold's ground for preferring *Anna Karénina* to *War and Peace* is ill chosen. He says: 'One prefers, I think, to have the novelist dealing with the life which he knows from having lived it, rather than with the life which he knows from books or hearsay. If one has to choose a representative work of Thackeray, it is *Vanity Fair* which one would take rather than *The Virginians*.'

This surely is misleading. War in Russia in 1812 was very similar to war in Russia in 1854, and the son who had fought in the latter war, describing the war in which his father had fought, was not at all in the position of Thackeray describing the life of the Virginians. Tolstoy depicting the homes of his parents and grandparents, which he in part remembered, and which he at any rate knew well from those who had formed part of them, was as close to first-hand experience as he was when describing the life of Karénin the pedantic Petersburg statesman, who belonged to a world which was essentially foreign to Tolstoy, though he had occasionally glanced at it.

But the sentence in Arnold's essay which has done most harm, is that in which he speaks about translations: 'I use the French translation; in general, as I long ago said, work of this kind is better done in France than in England, and *Anna Karénine* is perhaps also a novel which goes better into French than into English.'

It is true enough that the first English translations of Tolstoy were very poor, and it is also true that the French versions, so long as Tourgénef attended to them, were really good. But Arnold was wrong in supposing that *Anna Karénina* would naturally go better into French than into English. Had he been able to read the original, or had he been acquainted with Russian life, he would have seen that in Tolstoy's novels there are two sets of people: a Court, Petersburg set, who continually speak French and are Frenchified; and a plain, homely, straight-forward Russian (I had almost said, English) set who do not use French phrases, and who are sharply contrasted with the others. This contrast can be made quite clear in an English version, but it is difficult to make it clear in a version where even the most Russian characters have to speak French. The case is worse than that, however: Arnold did not say, as he fairly might have said, that up to his time the French versions were better than the English; he speaks as though it were in the nature of things that any translation into French must be better than any possible translation into English. A prejudice of that kind tends to divert attention from the fact that some

French translations are bad, and some English translations are good. As a matter of fact, since Arnold's time the position has been largely reversed. When staying at Yásnaya Polyána in 1902, I heard Tolstoy express considerable dissatisfaction with the new collected French edition of his works, the first volumes of which had then recently appeared, while he commended some recent English versions, including work done by Mrs. Garnett and by my wife.

A grave error, again, is made by Arnold in speaking of Tolstoy's later life, where he says that he ' earns his bread by the labour of his own hands.' Tolstoy never did that, and never claimed to have done it; though it is extraordinary how often and how confidently the statement has been repeated. It is a matter however which need not detain us, for it does not relate to the period with which this volume deals.

Arnold's summary of the story of the novel is excellent, but I can here only quote one more passage from his essay. ' We have,' he says, ' been in a world which misconducts itself nearly as much as the world of a French novel all palpitating with " modernity." But there are two things in which the Russian novel—Count Tolstoi's novel at any rate—is very advantageously distinguished from the type of novel now so much in request in France. In the first place, there is no fine sentiment, at once tiresome and false. We are not told to believe, for example, that Anna is wonderfully exalted and ennobled by her passion for Vrónsky. The English reader is thus saved from many a groan of impatience. The other thing is yet more important. Our Russian novelist deals abundantly with criminal passion and with adultery, but he does not seem to feel himself owing any service to the goddess Lubricity, or bound to put in touches at this goddess's dictation. Much in *Anna Karénine* is painful, much is unpleasant, but nothing is of a nature to trouble the senses, or to please those who wish their senses troubled. This taint is wholly absent.'

W. D. Howells, who has stood sponsor for Tolstoy in

America as Matthew Arnold has done in England, similarly says: 'It is Tolstoy's humanity which is the grace beyond the reach of art in his imaginative work. It does not reach merely the poor and the suffering; it extends to the prosperous and the proud, and does not deny itself to the guilty. There had been many stories of adultery before *Anna Karénina*, nearly all the great novels outside of English are framed upon that argument, but in *Anna Karénina*, for the first time the whole truth was told about it. Tolstoy has said of the fiction of Maupassant that the whole truth can never be immoral; and in his own work I have felt that it could never be anything but moral.'

Tolstoy never fears to deal with the real problems of life, and never fears to call a spade a spade; but he also never panders to the animal passions. In a letter relating to *Resurrection* he remarked: 'When I read a book, what chiefly interests me is the *Weltanschauung des Autors*: what he likes and what he hates. And I hope that any one who reads my book with that in view will find out what the author likes and dislikes, and will be influenced by the author's feelings.' What is important is not the subject treated of, but the feeling the author imparts when dealing with it.

Arnold, it is true, is rather shocked that Anna should yield so quickly and easily to the persuasions of Vrónsky. He is quite sure that she ought to have resisted. But here we come to a matter on which many Russians disapprove of Tolstoy on quite the opposite ground. Kropótkin in his interesting work *Ideals and Realities in Russian Literature*, has stated their case very clearly, and this is the substance of what he says:

Anna Karénina produced in Russia an impression which brought Tolstoy congratulations from the reactionary camp and a very cool reception from the advanced portion of society. The fact is that the question of marriage and of the separation of husband and wife, had been most earnestly debated in Russia by the best men and women, both in

literature and in life. Levity towards marriage such as is
continually unveiled in the Divorce Courts, was decidedly
condemned, as also was any form of deceit such as supplies
the subject for countless French novels and plays. But
after levity and deceit had been condemned, the right of a
new love—appearing perhaps after years of happy married
life — was seriously considered. Tchernyshévsky's novel,
What Is To Be Done? may be taken as the best expression
of the opinions on marriage which became current among
the better portion of the young generation. Once married,
it was said, don't take lightly to love affairs or flirtation.
Not every fit of passion deserves the name of a new love;
and what is called love is often merely temporary desire.
Even if it be real, before it has grown deep there is
generally time to reflect on the consequences that would
result were it allowed to grow. But when all is said and
done, there are cases when a new love does come, and comes
almost inevitably: as for instance when a girl has been
married almost against her will under the continued in-
sistence of her lover, or when the two have married without
properly understanding one another, or when one of the
two has continued to progress towards an ideal, while the
other, after having worn the mask of idealism, falls back
into the Philistine happiness of warmed slippers. In such
cases separation not only becomes inevitable, but is often to
the interest of both. It would be better for both to live
through the suffering a separation involves (honest natures
are improved by such suffering) than to spoil the entire
subsequent life of one—or both in most cases—and to face
the evil consequences which living together under such
circumstances would be sure to produce on the children.
That at any rate was the conclusion to which, both in
literature and in life, the best portion of Russian society
came.

And into the society Kropótkin describes in the above
statement, comes Tolstoy with *Anna Karénina*. The
epigraph of the book is 'Vengeance is mine, I will repay,'

and death by suicide is the fate of poor Anna, who was married young to an old and unattractive man, and who had never known love till she met Vrónsky. Deceit was not in her nature. To maintain a conventional marriage would not have made her husband or child happier. Separation and a new life with Vrónsky, who seriously loved her, was the only possible outcome. At any rate, continues Kropótkin, if the story of *Anna Karénina* had to end in tragedy, it was not in consequence of an act of supreme justice. The artistic genius of Tolstoy, honest here as everywhere, itself indicated the real cause, in the inconsistency of Vrónsky and Anna. After leaving her husband and defying public opinion—that is, as Tolstoy shows, the opinion of women not honest enough to have a right to a voice in the matter — neither she nor Vrónsky had the courage to break right away from that society, the futility of which Tolstoy describes so exquisitely. Instead of that, when Anna returns with Vrónsky to Petersburg, their chief preoccupation is, how Betsy and other such women will receive her if she reappears among them? 'And it was the opinion of the Betsies—surely not Superhuman Justice— which brought Anna to suicide.'

Whether Matthew Arnold's view or Kropótkin's view be accepted, Tolstoy at any rate does full justice to Anna's charm : 'her large, fresh, rich, generous, delightful nature which keeps our sympathy' and even our respect ; there is no nonsense about her being a degraded or vile person. And after all, Tolstoy's view of marriage sanctity is a very old and a very widely held one ; and it is surely good to have that side of the case put so artistically, so persuasively, so well, as he puts it. If ultimately the idea that two uncongenial people ought to live out their lives together because they have married, has to be abandoned, let it not be abandoned without the very best advocates being heard on its behalf.

Anna Karénina contains passages : the ball, the officers' steeplechase, the mowing, the death of Lévin's brother, and others, which for artistic beauty are unsurpassed and, one is tempted to add, unsurpassable. It also, towards the end, contains in admirably concise form much of what Tolstoy has told in his *Confession*, of his quest after the meaning of life, his thoughts of suicide, and how he learnt from a talk with a peasant that man should live for his soul and for God.

His treatment in this novel of the Russian volunteers who went to fight for Servia, was as bold a slap in the face to the Russian jingoes, who were having things all their own way at that time, as Campbell Bannerman's 'methods of barbarism' speech, or Sir E. Clarke's declaration that the reassertion of England's claim to suzerainty in the internal affairs of the Transvaal, was 'a breach of national faith,' was to our jingoes at the time of the Boer war; but it is curious to note the precise position that (speaking through the mouth of Lévin) Tolstoy took up. He did not say that Russia ought not to fight to free the Christian populations of Turkey; he merely said that no individual Russian had any business to volunteer for the Servian or Bulgarian army, or to take any action to urge the Russian Government towards war.

Of Lévin we are told: 'He, like Miháylitch and the peasants, whose feelings are expressed in the legendary story of the invitation sent to the Varyági by the early inhabitants of Russia, said: " Come and be princes and rule over us. *We gladly promise complete submission.* All labour, all humiliations, all sacrifices we take on ourselves, but *we do not judge or decide.*" ' And Lévin goes on to repudiate the idea that the Russian people have 'now renounced this privilege [the privilege, that is, of not taking any part in Government] bought at so costly a price.'

The connection between the roots of Tolstoy's opinions —manifested in these writings of his first fifty years—and his opinions in their ultimate rigid and dogmatic form, as expressed during the last three decades, is in general so close, the dogmas of the later period grew so naturally out

of the sympathies and experiences of the earlier time, that
this point—at which there is a clean line of cleavage (the
difference between obeying Government and disobeying it)
—is worthy of particular note. When finishing *Anna
Karénina* Tolstoy had not yet reached the conclusion that
all Governments employing force are immoral; but his later
teachings are dominated by that view.

Apart from the special points I have referred to, the
general effect and influence of Tolstoy's fiction can hardly
be summed up better than they have been summed up by
W. D. Howells, who says:

'Up to his time fiction had been a part of the pride of
life, and had been governed by the criterions of the world
which it amused. But Tolstoy replaced the artistic conscience by the human conscience. Great as my wonder was
at the truth in his work, my wonder at the love in it was
greater yet. Here, for the first time, I found the most
faithful picture of life set in the light of that human conscience which I had falsely taught myself was to be ignored
in questions of art, as something inadequate and inappro-
priate. In the august presence of the masterpieces, I had
been afraid and ashamed of the highest interests of my
nature as something philistine and provincial. But here
I stood in the presence of a master, who told me not to be
ashamed of them, but to judge his work by them, since he
had himself wrought in honour of them. I found the tests
of conduct which I had used in secret with myself, applied
as the rules of universal justice, condemning and acquitting
in motive and action, and admitting none of those lawyer's
pleas which baffle our own consciousness of right and wrong.
Often in Tolstoy's ethics I feel a hardness, almost an arro-
gance (the word says too much); but in his esthetics I have
never felt this. He has transmuted the atmosphere of
a realm hitherto supposed unmoral into the very air of
heaven. I found nowhere in his work those base and cruel
lies which cheat us into the belief that wrong may sometimes be right through passion, or genius, or heroism.

There was everywhere the grave noble face of the truth that had looked me in the eyes all my life, and that I knew I must confront when I came to die. But there was something more than this, infinitely more. There was that love which is before even the truth, without which there is no truth, and which if there is any last day, must appear the Divine justice. . . .

'As I have already more than once said, his ethics and esthetics are inseparably at one; and that is what gives a vital warmth to all his art. It is never that heartless skill which exists for its own sake, and is content to dazzle with the brilliancy of its triumphs. It seeks always the truth, in the love to which alone the truth unveils itself. If Tolstoy is the greatest imaginative writer who ever lived, it is because, beyond all others, he has written in the spirit of kindness, and not denied his own personal complicity with his art.

'As for the scope of his work, it would not be easy to measure it, for it seems to include all motives and actions, in good and bad, in high and low, and not to leave life untouched at any point as it shows itself in his vast Russian world. Its chief themes are the old themes of art always,— they are love, passion, death, but they are treated with such a sincerity, such a simplicity, that they seem almost new to art, and as effectively his as if they had not been touched before. . . .

'Passion, we have to learn from the great master, who here as everywhere humbles himself to the truth, has in it life and death; but of itself it is something, only as a condition precedent to these; without it neither can be; but it is lost in their importance, and is strictly subordinate to their laws. It has never been more charmingly and reverently studied in its beautiful and noble phases than it is in Tolstoy's fiction; though he has always dealt with it so sincerely, so seriously. As to its obscure and ugly and selfish phases, he is so far above all others who have written of it, that he alone seems truly to have divined it, or portrayed it as

experience knows it.   He never tries to lift it out of nature
in either case, but leaves it more visibly and palpably a part
of the lowest as well as the highest humanity. . . .

'He comes nearer unriddling life for us than any other
writer. He persuades us that it cannot possibly give us any
personal happiness; that there is no room for the selfish joy
of any one except as it displaces the joy of some other, but
that for unselfish joy there is infinite place and occasion.
With the same key he unlocks the mystery of death ; and
he imagines so strenuously that death is neither more nor
less than a transport of self-surrender that he convinces the
reason where there can be no proof. The reader will not
have forgotten how in those last moments of earth which he
has depicted, it is this utter giving up which is made to
appear the first moment of heaven. Nothing in his mastery
is so wonderful as his power upon us in the scenes of the
borderland where his vision seems to pierce the confines of
another world.'

Tolstoy of the later phase, the last three decades, with
which the second volume of this work will deal, differed
from the Tolstoy of the first fifty years; but the later
Tolstoy grew out of the earlier, as the branches of a tree
grow from its roots.

The difference lay chiefly in this : that from about the
year 1878 Tolstoy became sure of himself, succeeded in formulating his outlook on life, and proceeded to examine and
pass judgment on all the main phases of human thought and
activity. His work was sometimes hasty and often harsh; he
painted in black and white, subjects really composed of many
shades of colours ; but what other man has even attempted
so to examine, to portray, and to tell the frank truth about
all the greatest problems of life and death ?

No one really concerned to leave the world better than he
found it—be his line of work what it may—can afford to
ignore what Tolstoy has said on his subject.

No such combination of intellectual and artistic force has

in our times provoked the attention of mankind. No one has so stimulated thought, or so successfully challenged established opinions. Tolstoy has altered the outlook on life of many men in many lands, and has caused some to alter not their ideas merely, but the settled habits and customs of their lives. Only those who neither know nor understand him at all, ever question his sincerity.

Those who have spoken scornfully of him are those who have not taken the trouble to understand him. On the other hand, the small minority who swallow his opinions whole, do so under the hypnotic influence of his force, fervour and genius. To analyse his opinions, and disentangle what in them is true from what is false, is a task no one has yet adequately performed, but for which the time is ripe, and which, bold as the undertaking may be, I mean to attempt.

Tolstoy's marvellous artistic power, his sincerity, and the love that is so strong a feature of his work, have often been dwelt upon; but what really gives him his supreme importance as a literary force is the *union* of all these things : artistic capacity, sincerity and love, with a quite extraordinary power of intellect.

It is not given to any man to solve all the problems of life; but no one has made so bold and interesting an attempt to do so as Tolstoy, or has striven so hard to make his solutions plain to every child of man.

CHIEF AUTHORITIES FOR CHAPTER XII

The literature that has grown up both in Russia and elsewhere round Tolstoy's earlier writings is so voluminous, that I can merely indicate a few of the best known works.

In English we have :

Matthew Arnold's essay : *Count Leo Tolstoi* in *Essays in Criticism, Second Series* : Macmillan and Co., London.

W. D. Howells has written several very readable and excellent essays on Tolstoy. I have unfortunately mislaid my note of them. If any American admirer of W. D. Howells will supply me with a list, I shall be glad to include it in any future edition of this work.

P. Kropotkin's *Ideals and Realities in Russian Literature* gives a very good idea of Tolstoy's general influence and relation to Russian life and literature generally.

In Russian :

Mihaylovsky's articles in his collected works are interesting.

N. Strahof's *Krititcheskiya Statyi o Tourgeneve i Tolstom*, Petersburg, 1895, is excellent.

V. Zelinsky's *Rousskaya Krititcheskaya Literatoura o proizvedeniyakh L. N. Tolstovo* (7 vols.) reprints a large collection of Russian criticisms on Tolstoy's works.

D. S. Merezhkovsky's *Zhizn i tvortchestvo L. N. Tolstovo i Dosto-yevskavo* contains some acute literary criticism, but for all that relates to Tolstoy as a man, it is worse than useless. Merezhkovsky did not know Tolstoy personally when he wrote about him. He relied on the works of Behrs and Anna Seuron, and even that scrappy information he used unfairly. His talk about scents and fine linen, and in general his whole characterisation of Tolstoy, is spiteful, and to those who know the man attacked, it is merely ridiculous.

CHRONOLOGY

As in the text, dates are given old style, except those relating to the Crimean War and to Tolstoy's travels abroad.

1645   Peter Tolstoy born.

1725   Peter Tolstoy made a Count.

1727   Exiled.

1729   Died.

1814   Count Nicholas Tolstoy captured by French.

1822   Marriage of Tolstoy's parents.

1828 (28 Aug. o.s.) **Birth of Leo Tolstoy.**

1830   Death of Leo Tolstoy's mother.

1837   Death of father and grandmother.   Return to Yásnaya Polyána.

1840   Famine Year.

1841   Death of the Countess Osten-Sáken.   Move to Kazán.

1844   **Matriculates at Kazán University.**

1847   Leaves the University.

1848   Passes two examinations at Petersburg University.

1849   Starts Peasant Children's School at Yásnaya.

1851   20 April   **Leaves Yásnaya for Caucasus.**

   „   Aug.   Goes on expedition from Starogládovsk.

   „   Nov.   At Tiflis; writing *Childhood*.

   „   Dec. (end)   **Appointed Junker.**

1852   Jan.   Sádo's friendship.

   „   Feb.   Goes on expedition.

   „   2 July   **Finishes *Childhood*.**

   „   28 Aug.   Receives letter from Nekrásof accepting *Childhood*.

1852	Nov.	*Childhood* appears in *Contemporary*.
„	24 Dec.	*The Raid* finished.
1853	Jan.	Serves against Shámyl.
„	18 Feb.	Nearly killed by grenade.
„	March	*The Raid* appears in *Contemporary*.
„	13 June	Chased by Tartars.
„	July to Oct.	Stays at Pyatigórsk.
„	Oct.	War between Russia and Turkey.
1854	Jan.	**Receives his commission.**
„	2 Feb.	Revisits Yásnaya Polyána.
„	End of Feb.	Starts for Bucharest.
„	March	War : England and France against Russia.
„	„	Tolstoy reaches Bucharest.
„	June (end)	Siege of Silistria abandoned.
„	Aug.	Tolstoy leaves Bucharest for Russia.
„	14 Sept.	Allies land in Crimea.
„	Oct.	*Boyhood* appears in *Contemporary*.
„	17 Oct.	Bombardment of Sevastopol.
„	Nov. (end)	**Tolstoy reaches Sevastopol.**
	Dec.	Stationed at Simferópol.
1855	Jan.	*Memoirs of a Billiard Marker* published.
„	13 April to 27 May	**Serves in Sevastopol, in Fourth Bastion.**
„	June	*Sevastopol in December* published.
„	Aug.	*Sevastopol in May* published.
„	16 Aug.	In Battle of Tchérnaya.
„	Sept.	*The Wood-Felling* published.
„	8 Sept.	Maláhof captured by French. Sevastopol abandoned by Russians.
„	Sept.	Tolstoy returns to Petersburg.
1856	Jan.	*Sevastopol in August* published.
„	Jan. (end)	Death of Demetrius Tolstoy.
„	March	Russia concludes peace with England, France, and Turkey.

1856	March	*The Snow Storm* published.
„	May	*Two Hussars* published.
„	Summer	Engagement with V. V. A.
„	Nov.	Grand Duke Michael displeased about Soldiers' Song.
„	26 Nov.	**Tolstoy leaves the army.**
„	Dec.	*Meeting a Moscow Acquaintance in the Detachment* published.
„	Dec.	*A Squire's Morning* published.
1857	Jan.	*Youth* published.
„	10 Feb. (N.S.)	Leaves Moscow for Paris.
„	April	Visits Switzerland.
„	July	Stays at Lucerne.
„	Aug.	Returns to Yásnaya Polyána.
„	Sept.	*Lucerne* published.
1858	Jan.	Writes *Three Deaths*.
„	March.	Visits Petersburg. Helps to found Moscow Musical Society.
„	Aug.	*Albert* published.
„	Sept.	Signs Resolution of Nobles concerning Emancipation.
„	22 Dec.	Nearly killed by bear.
1859	Jan.	*Three Deaths* published.
„	4 Feb.	Speaks on Art to Society of Lovers of Russian Literature.
„	April	*Family Happiness* published.
„	Winter	**Organises School at Yásnaya.**
1860	15 July	Leaves Petersburg for Berlin.
„	„	Visits Auerbach in Dresden.
„	July and Aug.	At Kissingen for his health.
„	20 Sept.	**Nicholas Tolstoy dies** at Hyères.
„	Winter.	Visits Florence, Rome, Naples, Marseilles.
1861	Jan.	Revisits Paris.
„	Feb.	Visits London.
„	5 May	Re-enters Russia.

1861	26 May	Challenges Tourgénef.
„		Commences work as **Arbiter of the Peace.**
1861-2	Winter	Occupied with his school.
1862	Feb.	*Yásnaya Polyána* magazine appears.
„	May	Discharged from office of Arbiter of the Peace 'on ground of ill-health.'
„	May and June	Takes koumýs cure in Samára Government.
„		**Police raid on Yásnaya Polyána.**
„	17 Sept.	Proposes to Miss S. A. Behrs.
„	23 „	**Marries.**
„	3 Oct.	Minister of Interior disapproves of *Yásnaya Polyána* magazine.
„	15 „	School abandoned.
1863	Jan.	*The Cossacks* published.
„	Feb.	*Polikoúshka* published.
„	28 June	Eldest son, Sergius, born.
1864		*War and Peace* commenced.
„	Sept.	Dislocates arm while hunting.
„	„	Collected edition of Tolstoy's works published.
„	4 Oct.	Birth of daughter, Tatiána.
1865	Jan. and Feb.	**First part of** *War and Peace* **published.**
„	Autumn	Visits battlefield of Borodinó.
1866	May	Second son, Ilyá, born.
„	June	**Defends soldier at court-martial.**
1867	Summer	Treated by Zahárin for indigestion.
1868		Publication of *War and Peace* continued.
1869	20 May	Third son, Leo, born.
„	Nov.	*War and Peace* **completed.**
1869-70		Studies the drama.
1870-1	Winter	Studies Greek.

1871		Works at *ABC* Book.
,,	12 Feb.	Birth of daughter, Mary.
,,	June-July	Koumýs cure in Samára.
1872	Jan.	Re-starts school.
		A Prisoner in the Caucasus published.
,,	Feb.	*God Sees the Truth* published.
,,	13 June	Son, Peter, born.
,,	Sept.	Confined to Yásnaya by Investigating Magistrate.
,,	Nov.	*ABC* **Book published.**
1872-3	Winter	Prepares to write novel of Peter the Great's time.
1873	May	Goes with family to Samára.
,,	17 Aug.	**Samára Famine; Tolstoy's appeal.**
,,	Sept.	Kramskóy paints his portrait.
,,	9 Nov.	Death of son, Peter.
1874	15 Jan.	**Speaks on Learning to Read.**
,,	22 April	Son, Nicholas, born.
,,	20 June	Death of Aunt Tatiána.
,,	Sept.	Publishes article, *On Popular Education*.
1875	20 Feb.	Death of son, Nicholas.
,,		*New ABC* Book published.
,,	Jan.-April	**First Instalment of *Anna Karénina* published.**
,,	Summer	Horse races at Samára.
,,	1 Nov.	Baby daughter, Varvára, born and died.
,,	Dec.	Death of Pelagéya I. Úshkof.
1876	Jan.-April and Dec.	Further instalments of *Anna Karénina*.
,,		Observes Church rites and fasts.
,,	Sept.	Visit to Samára and Orenbourg.
1877	Jan.-April	**Final instalments of *Anna Karénina* published.**
,,		Rupture with Katkóf.

1877	6 Dec.	Son, Andrew, born.
1878	March	Visits Petropávlof Fortress.
,,		Abandons *The Decembrists.*
,,	May	**Reconciliation with Tourgénef.**
,,	7 Aug.	Tourgénef at Yásnaya Polyána.

INDEX

ABC Book, 339, 341, 342, 344-348, 359, 360.
—— Tourgénef's comment on, 347.
Active service, military, 86, 99, 110, 119.
Aim when writing novels, 430.
Aksákof, S. T., 175, 310.
Albert, 52, 166.
Alexander II, Tsar, 180, 287, 379.
Alexándra Fédorovna, Empress, 111.
Alexéyef, V. G., 395, 396.
Alexis, Tolstoy's servant, 32, 111, 284, 285.
—— Tsarévitch, 2, 349.
Algebra, 355.
Ambrose, Father, 384.
Anarchism, peaceful, 58, 139.
Ancestry, 1-7, 14.
Animals, kindness to, 28, 307.
Anna Karénina, 289, 349, 357, 360, 361, 371, 372, 381, 438-445.
—— characters in, 289, 349.
—— impression produced in Russia by, 441.
—— Matthew Arnold's comments on, 438-440.
—— W. D. Howells' comments on, 440, 441, 445-447.
—— Kropótkin's comments on, 441-443.
—— Tourgénef's comments on, 361.
Ant Brotherhood, 18, 19.
Appearance, personal, 7, 26, 64.
Arbiter of the Peace, 211, 226-229, 283.
Arboúzof's *Recollections*, 370.
Arithmetic in *ABC* Book, 341, 359.
Arm dislocated, 302, 303.
Army, enters the, 65, 76.
—— leaves, 152.
—— becomes an officer in, 91.
Arnold, Matthew: comments on *Anna Karénina*, 438-440.
Art, talk with peasant boys about, 257, 258.
—— thoughts on, 186, 275-277, 296, 333, 377, 405.
—— what is it? 260.
Artistic capacity of peasants, 275.
—— element in Literature, speech on the, 185.
Artists, Tolstoy's criticism of, 163, 164.

Astronomy, studies, 341.
Auerbach, B., 194, 212.
Aunt Tatiána. See *Tatiána.*
Austria's pressure on Russia, 97.
Authors, Tolstoy's criticism of the, 162-165.
Autobiographical, 10, 14, 17, 18, 20, 21, 24, 26, 28, 31, 34, 39-50, 53, 54, 59-77, 81-84, 89, 90, 95-104, 106-111, 128, 130, 148, 150, 152, 153-155, 160, 161, 162, 167-173, 175, 177-180, 182, 189, 192, 198, 200, 202, 212, 214, 224, 228, 252, 254, 263, 269, 272, 282-284, 286, 288, 291, 293, 294, 296, 298, 300, 303, 304, 325-327, 333, 337, 359, 365, 383, *and whole of chap.* xi.

BÆDEKER, preacher, 413.
Bárstchina explained, 225.
Baryatínsky, General, 65.
Bashkírs, Tolstoy and the, 335-337.
Bastion, the Fourth, 110, 113, 114, 117.
Bastions, clears Fifth and Sixth, 121. See also *Sevastopol.*
Bear Hunt, The, 342.
Bear-hunt, a, 183-185.
Bee-keeping, 296.
Beethoven, comment on, 276, 377-378.
Behrs family, the, 149, 284, 288, 290.
—— Miss S. A. See *Tolstoy, Countess S. A.*
—— S. A. (*brother-in-law*), 297, 332, 335, 390.
—— —— comments on Tolstoy by, 324, 387, 390, 436.
—— Tánya (Tánitchka; *sister-in-law*), 305.
Belbék, transferred to, 110, 111.
Beliefs, religious, 38-39, 162, chap. xi.
Berlin, in, 193, 194.
Bible, the, 263-267.
Billiards, Chinese, 284.
Birth, Tolstoy's, 9.
Boarding schools condemned, 235.
Bolkónskys, the (*War and Peace*), 434, 435.
Books for the people, 263, 267, 277, 339.
—— that influenced Tolstoy, 31, 44, 45, 160.

Borodinó, visit to battlefield of, 306.
Bótkin, V. P., 161, 168, 174, 316.
—'s comment on *War and Peace*, 315.
—'s criticism of Tolstoy, 223.
Boúlka (dog), 88, 89.
Boutleróf, A. M., Professor, 383.
Boyhood, 31, 91.
—— Tolstoy's criticism of, 160.
Bravery, 64.
Bucharest, in, 95, 96.
Buckle, criticism of, 240.
Buddha, on Life, 407, 409.
Buddhism, study of, 412.
Bulgarian insurrection, 379.
Bull kills keeper, 345.

Captain's Daughter, The, 161, 430.
Cards. See *Gambling*.
Caucasus, in the (see chap. iii.).
—— descriptions of the, 61-63.
—— fighting in the, 61, 87.
Censor, the, 86, 131, 132.
Charity, 216.
Chastity, advocacy of, 13.
Chess, 77, 119, 193, 389.
Chevet's system of Music, 167, 271.
Childhood, 22, 26, 65, 83, 86.
—— Tolstoy's criticism of, 160.
Children, Tolstoy's, 295, 303, 310, 317, 320, 331, 340, 344, 352, 357, 360, 363, 366, 385.
—— education of, 317-320, 366, 385.
—— governesses, 318, 366.
—— punishments of, 318, 319.
—— and the servants, 318.
—— taught music, 366.
—— —— painting, 366.
—— teach in peasant schools, 340.
—— Tolstoy's tact with, 204, 205, 206, 307.
—— toys, 318.
Christian and Greek ideals, 332, 333.
Christianity, study of, 412.
Christ's Hospital, education at, 279.
Church, the Orthodox, 39, 40, 413, 419, 420, 424, 437.
Church ceremonial, 343, 369.
Clarens, at, 168, 170.
Coat of arms, 2.
Collates Artillery Commanders' reports, 121.
Colony, agricultural, in Kansas, 396.
Communion, Tolstoy takes, 290, 421.
Composition, how to teach, 272, 275.
Comte, 396, 397.
Confession, Tolstoy's, 24, 39, 40, 53, 162-165, 167, 202, 203, 282-284, 298, 391, 394. (See also chap. xi.)
Consumptive tendencies, 156, 284.
Contemporary, The, 83, 138, 148, 182, 354.
—— Contributors to, 138, 139, 142.

Contradict, readiness to, 143.
Conversion, 394, 398.
Copperfield, David, 44, 45, 90.
Corporal punishment, 13, 14, 26.
Cossacks, The, 78, 79, 189, 284, 295, 296.
Cossacks, The, Tourgénef's comment on, 296, 393.
Cossacks, 78-80.
Count, origin of Tolstoy's title, 2.
Country life, love of, 308.
Courier to Petersburg, 122.
Court-martial, 310-312.
Crimean War, chap. iv.
—— cause of, 94.

Daily routine, 320.
Dates, Russian, 9.
Death, thoughts on, 342.
—— first experience of, 23, 24.
Death of baby girl, 366.
—— —— baby Nicholas, 360.
—— —— Bótkin, V. P., 316.
—— —— Demetrius Tolstoy, 44, 147.
—— —— Father and Grandmother, 23, 24.
—— —— keeper by bull, 345.
—— —— Nicholas Tolstoy, 197-203.
—— —— Peter, baby, 352.
—— —— Tatiána A. Ergolsky, 358-359. See also *Tatiána*.
—— —— P. I. Ushkof, 369. See also *Úshkof*.
Debts, 48, 49, 53, 55, 71, 72, 284.
Decembrists, The, 145, 299, 386.
Decembrists, the, 14, 386.
Defiance of accepted opinions, 140.
Demetrius Tolstoy. See *Tolstoy, Demetrius*.
Democratic government, advantages of, 144.
Democratic institutions, scorn for, 145.
Dentists, 208.
Diary, 37, 53, 81, 83, 148, 161, 167, 172, 173, 187, 189, 200, 212, 220, 223, 285, 286, 288, 289, 290, 309.
Dickens's influence on Tolstoy, 46.
Diesterweg, educationalist, 213.
Digestive troubles, 293.
Dijon, at, 166.
Dissipation, 52, 92, 97, 127, 140, 161, 162.
Divorce question, the, 441-443.
Doctors, dislike of, 313, 369.
Documents, carelessness with, 51, 65, 85.
Dogs, his, 88.
Dostoyévsky, S. A., 84.
Drama, Tolstoy and the, 297, 326, 327.
Drawing, 310.
—— lessons, 269, 270.
Dresden, in, 194.

Dress, elegance in, 35, 173.
—— simplicity, 309.
Drouzhínin, A. V., 148, 156, 157, 158, 168.
—— criticises Tolstoy's style, 159.
—— criticises *Youth*, 158.
—— letter from, 190.
Duel, a. See *Tourgénef*.
Dumas *père*, as novelist, 208.
—— educational influence, 207.
Dyákof, D. A., 37, 306, 321.

Education, 230-239. See also *School*.
—— at Christ's Hospital, 279.
—— criticism of, 232, 233.
—— definition of, 231.
—— evening lectures, 194.
—— false bases of, 232.
—— speech on, 353.
—— Tolstoy's, 28.
—— —— children's, 317-320, 366, 385.
—— Tolstoy's method of, 278, 353.
—— the right to reject, 235.
—— Zémstvo Committee of, 356.
Educational systems, Tolstoy studies :
—— in England, 194, 210.
—— Kissingen, 195.
—— Marseilles, 206, 207.
—— Saxony, 194.
—— Weimar, 212.
—— system in Germany, criticised, 233.
—— work, Tolstoy on his own, 282, 283.
Emancipation of the serfs, 180-182, 226, 299.
—— Tolstoy's attitude towards, 223-225.
Engagement with V. V. A., 150-155.
Epicureans and life, 408.
Epitaph, an, 382.
Ergolsky, T. A. See *Tatiána, Aunt*.
Estate buying, 300, 337, 359.
—— management, 306, 323, 345.
—— searched, 285-288.
Eucharist, Tolstoy receives the, 290, 419.
Eugene Baumann, 194.
Evangelicals, the, 413.
Examinations, Tolstoy's, 33, 34, 35, 49, 50, 65.
Execution, an, 167, 312.
Executions, the Church and, 424.
Exercise, physical, 84, 128, 173, 308, 367. See also *Gymnastics*.

Fable, an Eastern, 404.
Fame, thoughts on, 129, 183, 401.
Family Happiness, 185.
Famines caused by the Church, 437.
Famine Fund, Samára, 350, 351.
Famines, 30, 304, 350.

Farming, 179, 192, 294, 296, 304.
Fasts, Tolstoy, 419.
Fatherland Journal, The, 152, 354, 355.
Father Sergius, 384.
Faust (Tourgénef's), 156.
Fédka, literary genius of, 272-274.
—— walk with, a, 254-260.
Fet, A. A., 139, 141, 176, 215, 219, 222, 304, 312, 321, 322, 330.
—— letters to, from Tolstoy, 179, 180, 182, 188, 192, 200, 214, 217, 291, 293, 300, 303, 312, 315, 325, 326, 330, 331, 333, 337, 342, 344, 351, 352, 359, 360, 361, 365, 366, 371, 372, 373, 374, 380, 381, 382, 383, 385, 386, 387, 388, 391, 392.
—— —— in rhyme to, 347.
—— Literary Evening in aid of Famine Fund, 314.
—— 's poems, Tolstoy's admiration of, 374.
—— Tolstoy's criticism of, 322, 387, 391.
—— visits Tolstoy, 293-295, 314.
Fet, Peter A., 373.
First Step, The, 209.
'Flock for the shepherd, a,' 234.
Fly, attempts to, 25.
Folk-Songs and Tales, 376-378, 384.
Fort Grózny, at, 86.
Fourth Bastion, in the, 110-117.
Franco-Prussian War, 330, 331.
Freedom of Russian nobles, 55.
French language, the, 176.
—— people, the, 207, 331.
Froebel, Julius, 195.
Future Life, thoughts on, 202, 340.

Gambling, 53, 54, 68, 69, 110, 140, 284.
—— reflections on, 81.
Garnett, Mrs. C., 360, 440.
'Generalship in Literature,' his, 436.
Geneva, in, 168.
Geniality and good humour, 204, 334, 336, 367.
'*Gens comme il faut*,' preference for, 41, 60, 97.
Geography, 33, 269.
Georgia, 61.
Gipsy girl singers, 52, 55, 59, 140, 178.
God, 'There is no,' 24.
—— thoughts on, 73, 189, 190, 371, 416-418.
God sees the Truth, But Waits, 342.
Gógol, 428.
Gortchakóf, Prince M. D., 90, 95, 100, 104, 118.
Gouneba (stallion), 374.
Government approves Tolstoy's schemes, 292, 360.
—— Tolstoy's dislike of, 43, 229, 288, 312, 357.

Grammar in schools, 268.
—— schools, 367.
Grebénsky Cossacks, 78.
Greek and Christian ideals contrasted, 332, 333.
Greek, Tolstoy learns, 331-333.
—— Church. See *Church*.
Grigoróvitch, D. V., 140, 141.
Gymnasiums, Russian, 367.
Gymnastics, 173, 179, 205, 261, 308.

Hádji Mourát, 66.
Handwerksverein, der, 194.
Hapgood, Miss I., 301.
Happiness, plans for future, 74, 75, 76.
—— thoughts on, 79, 80, 83, 447.
Hay saved by personal exertions, 299.
Hegel, criticism of, 239.
Heresy, on, 423.
Hermit, visit to a, 365.
Herodotus, 332, 337.
Herzegovina, 373.
Herzen, Alexander, 143, 208, 209.
Historian, Tolstoy as, 432.
History, criticism of, 36, 268.
—— how to teach, 268, 269.
Home, love of, 323.
Homer, 332.
Homyakóf, A. S., 185.
Honesty, 126, 127.
—— of peasants, 243, 244.
Horse-breeding, 362, 373.
Horse-race at Samára, 364.
House of Commons, 211.
—— sale of, 111.
'Hundred and Ninety-three, The,' trial of, 394, 395, 397.
Hunting, 66, 90, 183-185, 230, 302, 305, 309. See also *Shooting*.
—— accident, 184, 185, 302, 303.
Hussars, Two, 149, 157, 361.
Hyères, at, 197, 203.

Ideals and Realities in Russian Literature (Kropótkin), 441.
Iliad, appreciation of the, 172.
Incarcerated, 35.
Inconsistency, 50.
Infant Schools condemned, 235.
Infected Family, The, 297.
Introduction to a Criticism of Dogmatic Theology. See *Confession*.
Irritability, 140, 141.

Junker becomes a, 65.
——'s life in the Caucasus, a, 79, 80.
Jury, serves on, 330.

Kansas Agricultural Colony, 396.
Kant, 416.
Karalýk, at, 285, 335-337.
Katkóf, M. N., 174, 284.

Kazán, life in, 32-35.
—— University, 32, 33.
Keller, 212.
Kiesewetter (*Resurrection*), 413.
Kinglake, historian of the Crimean War, 133, 134.
King Lear, Drouzhínin and, 157.
Kissingen, at, 195.
Knyaz, meaning of, 3.
Kock, Paul de, 208.
Kólokol, 208.
Koran, 338, 385.
Kornílof, Admiral, 105, 106, 118.
Kotchévka, 335.
Koumýs cure, 284, 306, 333.
Kounák, 69.
Kramskóy paints portrait of Tolstoy, 351, 352.
Kropótkin, P., 397, 441-443.
—— comments on *Anna Karénina*, 434, 436.
—— —— *Sevastopol*, 133.
—— *Ideals and Realities in Russian Literature*, 441.
Kryzhanóvsky, General, 127, 373.

Land, the, 188, 215.
Languages, 129, 331.
—— Oriental, studies, 33.
Lao-Tsze, 358.
Lautiermethode, 353.
Law, studies, 135.
Lelewel, Polish author, 211.
Leóntief, Professor, 332.
Lévin (*Anna Karénina*), 289, 444.
Life in danger, Tolstoy's, 86, 87, 110.
Lisogoúb, D., 397.
Literature as an occupation, 65, 82, 109, 305.
—— 'A General in,' 436.
—— its importance in Russia, 190.
Literacy, Moscow Society of, speech to the, 353, 354.
Lives of the Saints, the, 422.
London, in, 194, 208.
Love affairs, 26, 79, 149-155, 288-290.
Lucerne, 171, 429.
Lucerne, in, 170, 171.
Luther, Martin, 196.
Luxury, dislike of, 309, 317.

Macaulay criticised, 239.
Magazine, Tolstoy's. See *Yásnaya Polyána*.
Maláhof, capture of the, 119-121.
Mariána, 79, 91.
Marie (Másha or Mary) Tolstoy (*sister*). See *Tolstoy*.
—— Tolstoy (*daughter*). See *Tolstoy*.
—— Volkónsky, Princess, (*mother*). See *Tolstoy*.
Marriage, 290.

Marriage question, the, 441-443.
Marryat's novels, 281.
Marseilles, in, 206.
Márya Gerásimovna, 9, 22.
Masquerades, 309, 340.
Master and Man, 91.
Matriculates, 33.
Maude, A., letter to, 301.
Meeting a Moscow Acquaintance, 157.
Memoirs of a Billiard Marker, 91, 157.
Ménshikof, Prince, 2, 3.
—— —— Alexander, 105, 122-124.
Metaphysics, 407.
Michael, Grand Duke, 152.
Middle-classes, Tolstoy's ignorance of, 436, 437.
Middle period of Tolstoy's life, 298.
Mihaylóvsky, N. K., 354, 355, 395.
Military newspaper projected, 108, 109.
Mill, J. S., 396, 397.
Mineral waters, a course of, 81, 313.
Miracles, 417.
Moabit Prison, visit to, 194.
Mohammedanism, studies, 412.
Molokáns, 338, 423.
Moscow Gazette, The, 350.
Moscow Conservatoire, the, 175, 375.
—— Fifty, trial of the, 394.
—— Society of Lovers of Russian Literature, 185.
Mother Vólga (song), 276.
Mouhamed Shah, 350, 362.
Mouravyóf, N. N., 432.
Mowing, 367.
Murder of Countess Tolstoy, 256.
Music, Chevet's method of teaching, 167, 271.
—— his children learn, 366.
—— love of, 51, 52, 175, 306, 320, 374-376.
—— method of teaching, 271.
Musical notation, 271.

Napoleon I, 431.
—— III, 95, 133.
Nature, delight in, 86, 169, 170, 175, 308.
Nekrásof, N. A., 83, 132, 138, 141, 166, 172.
—— comments on *The Wood-felling* and *Sevastopol,* 132, 133.
Neues Leben, Ein (Auerbach), 194.
New ABC Book, 360.
New Religion, would found a, 130.
Newspaper, projected military, 108, 109.
Newspapers, dislike of, 325, 379.
Nicholas, baby, 357.
Nicholas I, 94.
Nicholas Tolstoy. See *Tolstoy.*
Nihilist, The, 297.
'Not Born to be Like Everybody Else,' 81.

Novel writing, 65, 188.
'Numidian cavalry,' the, 369.

Obolénsky, Prince D. D., 310, 323, 345, 384.
Obrók, 224, 225.
Officers, relations with, 63, 82, 127.
Ogaryóf, N. P., 209, 210.
Old style calendar, 9.
Old Testament, the, 263-267.
Olteniítza, in, 96.
On the Eve (Tourgénef), 188.
Óptin's Hermitage, 30, 384.
Orenbourg, at, 362, 373.
Oriental languages, studies, 33.
Originality, 27.
Osten-Saken, Count, 5.
—— Countess A. I. (*aunt*), 29, 30.
Ostróvsky, A. N., 189.
Ouroúsof, Prince L. D., 321, 331.
Ouspénsky, N. V., 253.

Palmerston, Lord, 211.
Panáef, V. I., 84, 138, 161.
—— comments on *Sevastopol in May,* 131.
Paris, in, 166, 167, 207, 208.
Parliament, 211.
Pascal, B., *Pensées,* 383.
Páshenka, 29.
Patriotism, 322.
Peasants' artistic capacity, 275, 378.
Pedagogic tact, 279.
Penmanship, 267, 268.
Pensées, by Pascal, 383.
Peróvsky, Sophie, 397.
Petersburg, in, 48, 50, 138, 139, 151, 173, 386.
Peter, baby, 344, 352.
—— the Great, 2, 348.
—— —— proposed novel of period of, 344, 348.
—— —— study of period of, 344, 348.
—— Tolstoy. See *Tolstoy.*
Petropávlof Fortress, visits, 386.
Petróvsky Fair, 336, 365.
Physical exercises, expertness in, 84, 128, 173, 309, 367.
Piano-playing, 52, 290, 320, 375.
Pilgrims and saints, 9, 22, 29, 394.
Pláksin, Sergéy, 204.
Plays, 297, 327.
Police search at Yásnaya Polyána, 285-288.
Polikoúshka, 211, 295, 296.
—— Tourgénef's comment on, 297.
Polish insurrection (1863), 296.
Portrait by Kramskóy, 351, 352.
Posthumous publications, 66, 384.
Poúshkin, 131, 138, 161, 428.
Prayer, 39, 64, 71, 91, 117, 370, 420.

Prayer, answer to, 68, 72.
Prince, the Russian title, 3.
Printing, questions the utility of, 226.
Prisoner in the Caucasus, A, 86, 341, 342.
—— Tourgénef's comment on, 347.
Prisoners, Turkish, a visit to, 385.
Prisons, visits to : the Moabit, 194.
—— —— —— Petropávlof Fortress, 386.
Progress, thoughts on, 226, 239-245, 283.
Promotion, slow, 85.
Propaganda, social and political, 397.
Proposal by initials, to Miss S. A. Behrs, 289.
—— formal, 290.
Proudhon, visit to, 211.
Public speeches by Tolstoy, 185, 311, 353.
Punishment of his children, 318.
Pyatigórsk, in, 81, 88.

QUESTION-BOXES, 194.

RACES on Samára estate, 364.
Raid, The, 77, 85, 86.
Railways, aversion to, 241-242, 334.
Raven (horse), 27, 28.
Read, Is it worth learning to ? 277.
Readers, Slavonic and Russian, 339, 341, 359, 427.
Reading lessons, 262.
—— practical demonstration of teaching, 354.
Reading Library, The, 148.
Recollections of Count Tolstoy (Behrs), 297, 367.
Reforms in Russia, 144.
—— want of sympathy with, 144, 225, 230.
Religion, on, 130, 338, 343.
—— wishes to found a, 130.
Religious beliefs, 38, 39, 162.
Reports, collates military, 121.
Review, a military, 84.
Revolutionary movement, 394-397.
Riding lesson, first, 27.
Right and Left Hand of Count Tolstoy, The, 395.
Rousseau, J. J., 46, 229.
Rubinstein, Nicholas, 175, 375, 384.
Rudolph, musician, 52, 167.
Rules of conduct, 38, 39, 88.
Russo-Turkish Wars, the, 91, 95, 373. See also *Crimean War*.

SÁDO, 69-73, 87.
St. George's Cross, 76, 77.
Sakya Muni, 407.
Sale of house, 111.
Saltykóf, M. E., (Stchedrín), 174, 354.

Samára, buys estates in, 300, 337, 359.
—— famine in, 350, 351.
—— in, 284, 285, 334, 345, 350, 356, 362, 388.
Samárin, P. F., 346, 356.
Sand, George, hostility to, 142, 320.
School, the Yásno-Polyána, 52, 187, 230, 246-254, 261, 278, 292, 340.
—— —— —— external disorder in, 248.
—— —— —— a fight in, 249.
—— —— —— punishment, 251, 252.
—— —— —— theft, a, 251, 252.
Schools, 230-239, 283.
—— boarding, 234.
—— infant, 235.
—— Tolstoy inspects, 194, 206. See also *Education*.
Schopenhauer, on, 315, 416.
—— on Life, 407, 411, 416.
Schwarzwälder Dorfgeschichten, 195, 212.
Sculptor, Tolstoy as, 310.
Scythians, 337.
Search of estate by police, 285-288.
Self-depreciation, 162, 298.
—— perfecting, 37, 38, 47, 48, 49, 52, 88.
Sensuality, thoughts on, 81.
Sequel, the, 447.
Serfdom, 211, 224, 433.
Serfs, emancipation of the. See *Emancipation*.
—— relations with the, 21, 43, 47, 158, 188, 227.
Sergius Tolstoy (*brother*). See *Tolstoy*.
Servants, relations with, 308, 318, 323.
Sevastopol, 112, 116, 130, 429.
—— the Censor and, 131.
—— comments on, by Kropótkin, 133.
—— —— —— Tourgénef, 133.
—— English edition of, 135, 301.
Sevastopol in August, 119, 157.
Sevastopol in December, 111, 131.
Sevastopol in May, 130, 131.
Sevastopol, map of, 112.
—— Fourth Bastion, in, 110-117.
—— Siege of, 106-109, 112-117.
—— situation in, 105.
—— Star Fort, the, 119.
—— Tolstoy reaches, 104.
—— truce, a, 134.
Shámyl, 61, 66, 86.
Shooting, Tolstoy goes, 84, 85, 90, 304-305, 336.
Shyness, 129, 130.
Si jeunesse savait, 179.
Silistria, recollections of siege, 97-104.
Simplicity, 84.
Sincerity, disbelief in others', 143.
—— his own, 51, 448.
Singer at Lucerne, 171.

Singing lessons, 167, 270, 271.
Slavophilism, 160, 161.
Sleep, respect for, 325.
Smoke, comments on, 313.
Snow Storm, The, 91, 157.
Socialism, 395-397.
Social tact, 129.
Society, organisation of, 434.
Socrates on Life, 407-409.
Sokólniki, at, 59.
Soldier, pleads for life of, 311.
—— popular sympathy for, 312.
Soldiers' Song, 122-126, 152.
Solomon, 407, 409, 411.
South Kensington, at, 194.
Spiritualism, 82.
Sportsman, Tolstoy, the, 66, 84, 85, 90, 183-185, 230, 302, 304-305, 306-309, 336.
Sports, organises, 364.
Spring, influence of, 175.
Squire's Morning, A, 47, 158.
—— Tourgénef's comment on, 158.
Staff-officers, disapproval of, 118.
Stallion (Gouneba), 374.
Star Fort, the, 119.
Starogládovsk, in, 61, 64, 76, 78.
Stáry Urt, 68.
State service, 43.
Stchedrín, 174, 354.
Stendhal, 93.
Stolýpin, 108, 285.
Story-teller, an itinerant, 384.
Stráhof, N. N., 321, 326, 344, 383, 384.
Strength, great physical, 367, 369, 403.
Strenuousness, 323.
Style, Drouzhínin criticises Tolstoy's, 159.
Suicide, thoughts of, 402, 406, 410, 418.
—— in *Anna Karénina*, 349.
Syómka and Fédka, literary genius of, 272, 274.
—— —— walk with, 254-260.

'Take care of that young man,' 111.
Tartar warfare, 77.
Tatiána, Aunt, 13, 17, 29, 31, 52, 59, 154, 176-179, 295, 358, 359.
—— —— letters to, 59, 61, 65, 66, 73, 76, 82, 84, 95, 96, 98, 109, 152, 153, 168, 195, 198, 212, 285.
—— —— peasants' opinion of, 358.
Tchaykóvsky, N., 396, 397.
Tchérnaya, battle of the, 119.
Tchitchérin, B. N., 174.
Teach, What must I? 163, 235-238.
—— How must I? 238-239, 263-271.
Telegraph, peasants and the, 176.
—— Tolstoy's criticism of, 240-242.
Temeshóf, Doúnetchka, 20, 21.

'Temple of Science,' the, 36.
Tennyson, 135.
'Tests' himself, 151, 154.
Theodore Ivánitch (Rössel), 12, 17, 18.
Thought reading, 289, 290.
Three Deaths, 174, 186, 357.
Three Hermits, The, 384.
Titles of nobility, Russian, 3.
Todleben, 105, 118.
Tolstoy, Alexandra A. (*aunt*), 174, 175, 196, 286, 351.
—— —— letter to, 175.
—— Alexis, 4.
—— Andrew (*son*), 385.
—— Dmítry (*cousin*), 4.
—— Demetrius (Dmítry or Mítenka ; *brother*), 20, 28, 41, 42, 43, 148.
—— —— relations with serfs, 43.
—— Elias (*grandfather*), 3, 4, 5.
—— Ilyá, 64.
—— —— (*son*), 310.
—— Leo (*son*), 317.
—— Marie (*mother*), 5, 9.
—— Mary (*daughter*), 331.
—— —— (Marie or Másha ; *sister*), 9, 75, 82, 83, 84, 153, 173, 177, 285, 288, 289, 304.
—— Nicholas, I (*father*), 4, 5, 6, 21, 23.
—— —— (Nikólenka ; *brother*), 18, 42, 55, 60, 61, 191-193, 196-203.
—— —— letter to, 98.
—— —— (*son*), 357, 360.
—— Peter, 1, 2, 3.
—— —— (*son*), 344, 352.
—— S. A. (*wife*), 149, 289-296, 302-303, 317, 340, 344, 348, 368, 385.
—— —— letters from, to S. A. Behrs, 348, 356.
—— Sergius (Sergéy or Seryózha ; *brother*), 19, 20, 28, 41, 42, 196, 305.
—— —— letters to, 48, 89, 90, 106, 110, 148, 150, 152, 198.
—— —— L. (*son*), 295, 303, 340, 366, 389.
—— Tatiána L. (*daughter*), 303, 320, 340, 366.
—— family and servants, the, 21, 22, 318.
—— name, the, 1, 9.
—— spelling of, 9.
Tourgénef, 84, 133, 139-141, 149, 166, 168, 189, 190, 193, 214-223, 303, 338, 339, 357, 388, 389-393, 428.
—— challenged by Tolstoy, 166, 217.
—— challenges Tolstoy, 219.
—— comments on *ABC* Book, 347.
—— —— *Anna Karénina*, 361.
—— —— *Cossacks, The*, 296, 393.
—— —— *Polikoúshka*, 297.
—— —— *Sevastopol*, 133.

Tourgénef, comments on *Squire's Morning, A*, 158.
—— —— *War and Peace*, 314.
—— letters to Fet, 190, 220, 221, 296, 338, 339, 357.
—— —— in verse, 187.
—— ——Tolstoy, 155, 156, 217, 218, 388.
—— on Tolstoy, 338, 339, 392, 393.
—— reconciliation with Tolstoy, 388-391.
——'s Faust, 156.
——'s *On the Eve*, Tolstoy's criticism of, 188.
——'s *Smoke*, Tolstoy's criticism of, 313.
—— Tolstoy's quarrel with, 216-223.
—— translations with Mme. Viardot. See *Viardot*.
'Towards the People' Movement, the, 394.
Training College for Teachers, a, 347, 355, 356.
Translations, 301, 440.
Traveller in the Well, The, 404.
Tree-planting, 313.
'Trials of the Pen,' 300, 303.
Trollope, A., 320.
Troubetskóy, Princess Catherine (*grandmother*), 6.
'Tsar-Liberator,' the, 225.
Tsar, prayers for the, 420.
Tschaikóvsky, P. I., 375-377.
—— letter to, 376.
Turkey, war with, 379.
Turkish prisoners in Tóula, 385.
Turks, ferocity of, 103.
Twenty-three Tales, 342, 384.
Two Hussars, 157, 361.

UFANIZING. See *Farming*.
Universities, dislike of, 36, 235.
University degree, failure to take, 37, 51.
'—— in bark shoes,' a, 347, 355, 356.
—— studies at Kazán, 32-37.
—— —— at Petersburg, 48, 50.
Unmethodical habits, 51, 65, 85.
Úshkof, P. I. (*aunt*), 31, 369.
—— V. I., 4, 31.

VANITY, thoughts on, 81.
Varvára Engelhardt, 6, 7.
Viardot, Madame, 357, 361.
Vólga, journey down the, 285, 334.

Volga, Mother (song), 276.
Volkónsky, Prince Nicholas (*grandfather*), 6, 7.
—— —— S. G., 386.
—— Princess (*mother's cousin*), 174.
—— —— Marie (*mother*), 5.
Voltaire, influence of, 47.
V. V. A., love affair with, 150-155.

WALKING, love of, 204, 308, 309.
—— tour, 168-170.
War and Peace, 303, 304, 309, 314, 317, 395, 430.
—— characters in, 304, 435, 436.
—— preparations for, 300.
—— Tolstoy's comment on, 303.
—— Bótkin's comment on, 315.
—— Tourgénef's comment on, 314, 315.
War, active service in, 86, 99, 110, 119.
—— the Church and, 424.
—— horror of, 78, 137.
—— thoughts on, 133, 135, 136, 432.
Wealth, 243, 244.
Weimar, in, 211, 212.
What is Art? 260, 342, 378, 430.
What Men Live By, 384.
Wife. See *Tolstoy, S. A.*
Wine, on, 137.
'Wishes to be great,' 183.
Women, relations with, 40, 44, 52.
Wood-Felling, The, 77, 130, 131, 132.
Wood, Mrs. Henry, 320.
Works, first collected edition of, 300.
—— list of, 427.
—— published before *War and Peace*, list of, 301.
Writer, Tolstoy the, 441, 445-447.
Writers, criticism of the, 162-165.
Writing lessons, 268.

Yásnaya Polyána, magazine, 231, 242, 246, 291, 292.
Yásnaya Polyána, house and estate, 16, 111, 309.
Yásno-Polyána School, Chap. VIII. See also *School*.
Youth, 130, 156, 158, 160.
—— criticised by Drouzhínin, 158, 159
—— —— by Tolstoy, 160.

ZAHÁRIN, Professor, 313.
Zémstvo, elected to the, 251.

Printed by T. and A. CONSTABLE, Printers to His Majesty
at the Edinburgh University Press

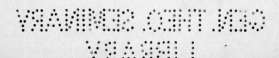